ROS

THE INFINITE IDEAS
CLASSIC WINE LIBRARY

Editorial board: Sarah Jane Evans MW and Richard Mayson

There is something uniquely satisfying about a good wine book, preferably read with a glass of the said wine in hand. The Infinite Ideas Classic Wine Library is a series of wine books written by authors who are both knowledgeable and passionate about their subject. Each title in The Infinite Ideas Classic Wine Library covers a wine region, country or type and together the books are designed to form a comprehensive guide to the world of wine as well as an enjoyable read, appealing to wine professionals, wine lovers, tourists, armchair travellers and wine trade students alike.

The series:
Port and the Douro, Richard Mayson
Cognac: The story of the world's greatest brandy, Nicholas Faith
Sherry, Julian Jeffs
Madeira: The islands and their wines, Richard Mayson
The wines of Austria, Stephen Brook
Biodynamic wine, Monty Waldin
The story of champagne, Nicholas Faith
The wines of Faugères, Rosemary George MW
Côte d'Or: The wines and winemakers of the heart of Burgundy, Raymond Blake
The wines of Canada, Rod Phillips
Rosé: Understanding the pink wine revolution, Elizabeth Gabay MW
Amarone and the fine wines of Verona, Michael Garner

ROSÉ

UNDERSTANDING THE PINK WINE REVOLUTION

ELIZABETH GABAY MW

infiniteideas

Copyright © Elizabeth Gabay, 2018

The right of Elizabeth Gabay to be identified as the author of this book has been asserted in accordance with the Copyright, Designs and Patents Act 1988.

First published in 2018 by
Infinite Ideas Limited
www.infideas.com

All rights reserved. Except for the quotation of small passages for the purposes of criticism or review, no part of this publication may be reproduced, stored in a retrieval system or transmitted in any form or by any means, electronic, mechanical, photocopying, recording, scanning or otherwise, except under the terms of the Copyright, Designs and Patents Act 1988 or under the terms of a licence issued by the Copyright Licensing Agency Ltd, 90 Tottenham Court Road, London W1T 4LP, UK, without the permission in writing of the publisher. Requests to the publisher should be emailed to the Permissions Department, permissions@infideas.com.

A CIP catalogue record for this book is available from the British Library

ISBN 978–1–908984–13–5

Brand and product names are trademarks or registered trademarks of their respective owners.

All web addresses were checked and correct at time of going to press.

Front cover image Bernd Schmidt/Alamy Stock Photo. Back cover image of Château Barbeyrolles © Hervé Fabre. Colour plate photos page 8 courtesy of Centre du Rosé.

Typeset by Digitrans Media, India

Printed in Britain by 4edge Limited

CONTENTS

Introduction: the ugly duckling	1
1. The history of rosé wine	5
2. Viticulture and winemaking	11
3. Historic rosé regions	31
4. The rosés of Provence	65
5. Classic French regional rosés	89
6. North American rosé	105
7. The southern hemisphere	129
8. Pink sparkling wine	159
9. Spanish and Portuguese rosé	175
10. Italian rosé	197
11. Rosés from Northern and Central European Varieties	215
12. French-influenced Mediterranean rosé	231
13. The Balkans, the Adriatic and the eastern Mediterranean	257
14. The business of rosé	279
Conclusion: the swan emerges	311
Appendix: Rosé wine terminology in other languages	313

Bibliography	315
Acknowledgements	317
Index	321

INTRODUCTION: THE UGLY DUCKLING

In 1975 Pamela Vandyke Price wrote that 'Pink wines are not among the great classics'. Rosé has made great strides since then, so that today, I would have to disagree.

Rosé wine has benefited over the last twenty-five years from a boom in quality and production volume. Rosés are often considered simple, fresh and undemanding, appealing to young, first-time drinkers otherwise intimidated by the complex world of reds and whites.

While this notion has been great for sales, it has not helped rosé's image. After a wine is promoted as 'simple, fresh and undemanding' for twenty-five years, the idea takes hold. When combined with successful marketing, illustrating the beauties of a pink wine, often by the sea or pool, with a leisurely lifestyle of glamour and fun – the role of rosé might appear immutable.

But luckily, winemakers are creative. Now that the skills for producing good rosé have been widely mastered, an ever-increasing number are doing something a little different. If oak, amphorae, *battonage*, maceration and grape varieties are used differently, how might rosé change? Often the new styles produced are so different to the rosé wines most people know, that they have been difficult to sell or fail to receive acknowledgment. Darker rosés can lose marks in competitions and be commercially unsuccessful because their colour is unfashionable. Complex rosés suffer as they are too demanding.

Economics and marketing are both of great importance in the world of rosé. While often a winemaker continues to produce wines in his commercial style – to pay the bills – he may also sell a few cases of the special rosé to those who appreciate it. These 'unicorn' rosés remain largely unknown, unreported and unrecognized, and are often difficult to find. A treasure trail through connections, friends of friends, journalists and local wine bloggers has helped me discover many that remain hidden to most consumers.

As I looked into the range of rosés available, I realized that I first needed to answer the question 'What is a rosé?' This sounds simple, but every rule has its exceptions.

Rosés are pink? Well, yes, but some rosés are so pale they are almost white with just the faintest tinge of creamy blush. Other rosés are so dark, they are almost red. Some countries even have names for different colours of rosé, to indicate different styles. Rosé is a catch-all name.

Rosés are made like a white wine? Yes, but … . Unlike red wines, rosés are not fermented on the skins, although some *start* fermentation on the skins and are then bled off. But they are not white wines, and they have more in common with amber (or orange) wines if they have extended skin maceration.

Researching this book has been a voyage of discovery, with many rosés exciting me as much as good red and white wines. Far from feeling I fully explored rosé, I realize there are many more rosés: styles previously unknown; rosés known only to locals; rosés exclusively for export; rosés newly created. Sometimes I had to press producers to show me wines that are not usually available.

As rosé is increasingly recognized as a serious wine, its potential quality is leading to a growth in niche wines. Some producers are returning to local traditions and varieties, others are exploring and creating new styles. Looking at rosé in more detail is vital in enabling consumers to be aware of the variety of serious and beautiful styles available and to enable them to look beyond its 'ugly duckling' past. I look forward to the day when more rosés achieve that 'wow' factor now given only to great reds and whites, to when restaurant wine lists for reds and whites are rivalled by their selection of rosés.

As Ruth Ellen Church wrote, long ago in 1966, 'If you think pink, why not adventure a bit, for every wine growing country produces pink wines.' Of course, with thousands of rosé wines produced all over the world it has been impossible to taste all. I have tried to highlight the amazing variety and potential for quality, and the inventiveness of winemakers. With the limited space in this book, it has been impossible even to include every rosé I have tasted.

For me, rosé is moving forward and becoming more exciting. I hope this book not only reflects my growing enthusiasm, but also draws the reader in to seek and discover more rosés.

This book is an acknowledgment of the energy and creativity of winemakers who are experimenting with and pushing the boundaries of rosé-making.

1
THE HISTORY OF ROSÉ WINE

In the oldest written reference to winemaking, the book of Genesis records that 'Noah, a man of the soil, proceeded to plant a vineyard'. Geographically this fits in with the oldest physical remains of winemaking currently known, which are located in Georgia, north of Mount Ararat, with evidence of winemaking in large clay jars (similar to modern *kveri*), dating back to 6000 BC. His wine must have been potent stuff, as the next sentence refers to Noah's drunkenness. Since later descriptions of Mesopotamian wine do not refer to pressing the wine to extract colour and tannins, we can guess that Noah was probably fermenting the juice with the stalks, skin and pips.

Greek wine was dark, strong and drunk diluted with water to reduce the alcohol. The Romans were more sophisticated in their wine production, and appreciated different varieties and terroirs. Their complex system of pressing allowed for anything from lightly pressed to heavily extracted wines. Additional flavours, smoking, as well as diluting with water, created a wide range of styles.

In medieval Europe, the Church, especially the monasteries, kept winemaking alive. Many vineyards can trace their origins back to monastic lands. During this time, the traditions outlining which lands were best for viticulture, which for agriculture and which for grazing, were established, laying the groundwork for modern appellations. 'Wines possess different natures and virtues according to the country's diversity of climates and terroirs,' noted Nicolas-Abraham de la Framboisière, in 1669.

Wine was often made from field blends. The late-sixteenth century agriculturalist, Olivier de Serres recommended planting five or six varieties in the vineyards to offset the risk of crop failure or disease. These field blends did not just affect the colour. As grapes ripen differently, the harvest would have included both fully-ripe and under-ripe berries. The first would contribute fruit and sweetness, the latter, freshness and acidity.

The light red of *clairet* was undoubtedly influenced by using both dark and light-skinned grapes. This style of wine was found in many regions and was variously described as '*gros clairet*', '*clairet nouveau*' and just '*clairet*'.

A range of colours was admired. La Framboisière, in 1669, played a significant role in the identification of wines by colour and origin in his book *Les Oeuvres*. He recognized three types of wine by colour. White wine, *clairet* (which was described as *paillet* or *rougelot*), and red wine (which was *vermeil* – vermillion – or black). La Framboisière notes that, 'Clairet wine is in the middle of the two others. Which is why it excels over the others.' De Serres describes *clairet*'s colours as *rubis orientalis* (the red of the setting sun), *oeil de perdrix* (the pale pink of the eye of a dying partridge) and hyacinth pink, tending to orange.

Clairet that was too pale or lacked sufficient fruit and body, often in cooler regions, was topped up with red wine. These paler wines were called 'grey wine', because the colour was neither white nor red. The addition of red wine also contributed extra fruitiness. In 1755, the agronomist Sieur Liger advised that these wines were best drunk young and fresh.

Pouring weak, pale wines over the dregs of the red wine resulted in pink wines with a light flavour and strength. They were called *breuvage* or *piquette* and were reserved for the workers. In fact, their low quality and alcohol meant that they were not even taxed.

In 1851 Cyrus Redding observed the methods of vinification used to obtain the different colours. In Cahors, 'The rose-coloured wines are made with the weakest white wines upon the murk of the black wines, which are never pressed. They gain colour and strength by this operation, but are not in great esteem.' He goes on to describe the wines of Gannat, in the Allier department in central France, where they made, 'A vin gris, a grey or rather brown wine, … by leaving the must to ferment for forty-eight hours. A rose-coloured wine is also manufactured by racking it after three or four days' fermentation in the vat. This last wine is excellent, of a very agreeable taste, but, what is singular, has not yet become an article of commerce.'

Ironically, the improvements in red winemaking marked the decline in the reputation of the paler red wines, now seen as failed 'proper wine'. By 1800, Chaptal had studied which soils, exposures and extraction produced the best red wines and concluded that unripe, acidic berries, included in a bad season, destroyed the wine with their harsh malic acid. Throughout the nineteenth century, red wines were increasingly made in a deeper and more concentrated style, often by bleeding off some of the juice. These red wines, with their ageing potential, power and structure were highly regarded. The bled-off juice was used to make a pale red wine for local consumption.

At the beginning of the twentieth century, pale red rosé made up approximately 10 per cent of French wine production. The wine's pale colour was obtained by a brief maceration, technically *vin de 24 heures* or *vin d'une nuit*. A wine halfway between pink and red, called *vin de café* was, according to Julian Jeffs (1971) 'a comparative newcomer and dates only from the 1920s. It was grown principally around Montpellier and its purpose, as its rather odd name suggests, was to produce a light style of wine that was, and is popular in some of the French cafés.'

In America, the dark pink wines of Tavel and Californian Grenache-based off-dry rosés were enjoying success. When American soldiers arrived in Europe during the Second World War, they represented a ready market for wines similar to those they knew at home. Enterprising producers Lancers and Mateus in Portugal, and Five Roses from southern Italy, made large volumes of rosé for these troops, and after the war exported their product to America.

In the 1950s, rosé was briefly fashionable in Europe and America, but continued to be regarded as a simple wine compared to red and white. *Clairet* was reinvented in 1950, Rosé d' Anjou and pink Champagne both became fashionable and the first pink Pinot Grigio was bottled in the 1950s.

By 1971, Julian Jeffs in *The Wines of Europe* was highly critical of many rosés on sale: 'Very cheap beverage pink wines are undoubtedly blended in France by wholesale merchants using a mixture of red and white wines. And one has heard terrifying references to cochineal.'

Pamela Vandyke-Price in *The Taste of Wine* (1975) noted that pink wine was:

made to give pleasure in a light-hearted, undemanding way ... No one, I think, has ever sat discussing a pink wine for more than a few minutes except to establish whether it is pleasant as a wine in its own right or as a shadow of something else that might be white or red. Pink wines can merely be shadows of the red or white wines into which they could have been made ... A well-made pink wine should have a certain balance, and the discriminating drinker will also try to gain something from the smell and the flavour of the wine ... If you have previously deduced what a particular local wine may be like, you will know what to expect from a pink wine from the same area.'

In 1978, Jerry Mead noted a 'snob attitude' towards rosé, which was not considered worthy of serious connoisseur discussion; it was simply sweet and pretty. Eight years later, in 1986, at a tasting dedicated to rosé, Maureen Ashley MW noted in *Decanter*, 'It was both brave and forward thinking of Food and Wine from France to show the Trade and Press a wide range of rosé wines, and only rosé wines, from all over France'. It may have been a turning point in the reputation of modern rosé, as she concluded:

We all know that rosé isn't a serious wine, don't we? Or, to be more precise, that 'serious' wine drinkers don't drink rosé. But why? Surely we haven't let the image of one brand prejudice us against any other pink (or light orange) wine. Surely we don't naively believe that because it looks pretty it can only taste 'pretty'. Surely we don't operate on the basis that pink implies an ability to decide between red and white. Yet most of the time we just don't drink rosé (or don't admit it if we do).

The most important result of the tasting, according to Ashley, was that it proved 'that there *are* rosé wines which are *real* wines, not just things that look pretty for neophyte drinkers.'

In 1988 *The Grocer* ran a piece entitled 'Rosé: a victim of consumer ignorance'. In an interview, Janice Wilson, marketing manager at *Food and Wine from France*, said they were working on rosé's 'image problem'. With rosé regarded as simply an easy option drink, few bothered to spend time learning more. Many believed that rosé is made by blending red and white wines. Rosés tended 'to sell in the low to mid-price range [and] developed a cheap image.' Marketing played on the image, not the quality. The retail trade was encouraged to use its imagination, using rosé's colour to make a dramatic statement. 'Rosé is a very attractive wine and if it is highlighted, prompts a good consumer response. We've already seen this happen with pink sparkling wines and Champagne. With a bit of effort, there's no reason why rosé should not be successful.'

The aim was to create a solid foundation for rosé sales, then explain regional and style variations. 'Loire rosés are more delicate while those from Provence have a much stronger character. There's a lovely variety, but we can't hit the customer with too much information for the moment.'

During the 1990s rosés started to regain their reputation, with the creation of lighter, more delicate rosés and, during the latter half of the decade, the creation of the *Centre de Recherche et d'Expérimentation sur le Vin Rosé* which, for the first time, focused research into varieties, terroir and vinification, to improve the style. The year 2007 appears to have been a turning point throughout the world, with a massive increase in production and consumption. It also marked the increase in marketing focusing on pale pink 'Provence-style' rosé and a lifestyle image of beaches, pools, glamour and millennial-girl pink fun.

This has created a Jekyll and Hyde scenario with, on the one hand, quality improving, and serious rosé (ranging from aperitif to more complex 'gastronomic' styles) emerging and on the other, the market being swamped with commercially successful pale pink, easy drinking rosé, leading to the style being frequently dismissed. It is the former style I will be concentrating on in this book.

2
VITICULTURE AND WINEMAKING

A recurring theme in my research into rosé, was that rosé appears to be more market-led than producer-led. Producers despair that consumers so often want only pale pink, delicate, fresh rosé, drunk ice-cold in hot summers; they struggle to convince the customer that the range and variety of rosé styles is as exciting as for red and white wines. Textbook descriptions of how rosé is made are confined to a classic procedure for creating this style.

It is easy to blame modern marketing for this lack of awareness of regional and historic styles, but this simplistic view of rosé wines has been around for a while. Maynard Amerine (1967) noted, in a sweeping manner that (American) rosé wines 'should be light, fruity, quick-maturing.' In 1985, Philip Jackisch in *Modern Winemaking*, defined rosés as wines made with minimal skin contact of a few hours, often just from free-run juice, depending on the variety and ripeness.

Today, reviews in magazines and papers dwell on the fresh and fruity style of rosé during the summer, enticing consumers with suggestions of barbecues, a Mediterranean diet, hot weather, beaches and swimming pools.

My original intention was to give an outline of making rosé, highlighting the range of rosé styles in terms of technique alone, leading to an understanding of how the techniques used can help to identify the many variations. Rosés are, however, changing. For some the changes are subtle, for others radical. There can be heated discussions over techniques; which are right and which wrong when making a good rosé. Traditional, modern, even experimental styles, are discussed. The renaissance of old traditions and varieties, combined with new innovations, is rapidly changing the spectrum of rosé styles. Many key advances of the past 30 years have radically changed, and improved, the quality of rosé winemaking.

So, instead of *clarifying* the 'What?', 'How?' and 'Why?', in researching this chapter I have opened a can of worms – differences of opinion between winemakers, consumers and the wine trade over style. Some say rosé should be nothing more than a fresh, fruity, uncomplicated wine, while others believe rosé can stretch the imagination and bring far higher complexity and quality.

IN THE FIELD

The foundation for good wine is in the field. Rosé is no exception. This is where the strongest new trends are emerging, as producers identify the impact on rosé styles of varieties and terroirs, and is referred to more closely in the review of regional styles.

Site location

This can be divided into two categories: winemakers who have switched from red to rosé or make rosé bled off their red wines, and those who are planting from scratch for rosé.

In regions where vines for red wines had been planted in cooler areas, on higher altitude sites or on cooler soils, which never quite succeeded for red wine, the move to use these vineyards for rosé has been for the good. Recent comments on the rise in the share of rosé in Bandol to 70 per cent, caused concern amongst lovers of Bandol reds. Producer Eric de Saint Victor, of Pibarnon, was not alarmed. He pointed out that expanding vineyards to make more red wine had required planting in cooler plots, resulting in lighter, weaker reds. By turning these over to higher-yielding rosé, rosé is made only at the expense of poor-quality reds.

Winemakers planting for rosé can consider higher-altitude and north-facing plots in warmer areas, and match vine varieties to soils. Many Mediterranean rosés come from vineyards planted at 600 metres or higher. Limestone soils give fresher acidity, while volcanic and schist soils provide a range of mineral characters. Sandy soils result in wines of paler colour, especially for Grenache.

Winemakers in Tavel have long used their different terroirs to create structure and complexity. Elsewhere, the impact of terroir on rosé is beginning to be appreciated. Vineyards such as the **Cave Cooperative Saint Roch Les Vignes** (www.vignerons-saint-tropez.com) in Cuers, in the region of Côtes de Provence Pierrefeu, and **Chevalier Torpez** (www.vignobles-saint-tropez.com) in Saint-Tropez, have recently been fermenting Grenache by parcel, to identify the different characteristics of the soils. The introduction in Provence of *denominations de terroir* has also highlighted the impact of soils on styles of rosé.

Choice of variety

As with sites, varieties used reflect whether the rosé is made by transferring from red winemaking or the variety is chosen specifically for rosé. In regions where rosé is important, such as Provence, the varieties used are generally those best suited to rosé production. There is little choice of variety when producers, responding to market demand, must use vines already planted for red wine production. Appellation rules in Europe restrict the choice to traditionally planted varieties. Producers may play safe, keeping their options open by using varieties suitable also for red wine. As usual, they must consider adaptability to climate and terroir.

Late-ripening varieties, such as Mourvèdre, need heat to open-up and provide fruit in a rosé. Paler-skinned varieties usually allow more fruit extraction without jeopardizing a lighter colour, although the range of vinification techniques available does not preclude use of darker varieties. Current research for the next generation of varieties to be planted is concentrating on disease-resistant clones and varieties adaptable to heat and drought.

Age of vines

Young vines are often used for fresh, fruity rosé wines in red-wine producing areas. Appellations like Bandol prohibit the use of vines of less than ten years old in reds. Often an increase in rosé production can be tied to investment in new plantings. Winemakers looking to make more complex rosés can use older vines for extra weight and complexity.

Yields

In contrast to the lower yields regarded as ideal for the greater concentration needed for red wine, higher yields are traditionally preferred for rosés to produce light and delicate wines,. This has led some to treat rosé as a cash crop. High yields, up to 50 per cent higher than for red wine, are not unusual, but these high yields also diminish the intensity of fruit and terroir flavours.

To make wine through direct pressure in a fresh and fruity style, a high leaf-to-fruit ratio is required, since this achieves a greater concentration of richness and polyphenols, adding to aromatic potential. When planning to make rosé using maceration, phenolic ripeness of the grapes is essential to avoid astringent, green flavours.

Date of harvest

Early harvesting, between ten and twenty days earlier than for reds, creates balance of fruit and acidity, a crucial element for good rosé. Harvest a fraction too soon, to keep freshness, and the wine can be bland and lacking fruit. Harvest too late, and the wine can have fruit but lack zest, and sometimes have a bitter phenolic finish. However, if planning some maceration in the winemaking, the grapes have to be riper, to avoid extracting hard, green flavours. Correct harvest dates, blending of grapes from different harvest dates, and the use of different sites and varieties, combine to create balance. There are variations according to varieties and regions. When rosés are made using *saignée* as part of red winemaking, all grapes, implicitly, are harvested at the same time.

Depending on the style, vintage, the thickness of the grape skins, and the amount of juice, the length of time to macerate the grapes can vary from around 0 to 96 hours before bleeding the juice off the skins. However, there is no fixed amount of time and the colour of the juice must be checked every two hours.

Method of harvesting

In warmer regions, night-time harvesting helps to preserve freshness. This is typically done by machine but, recently, manual harvesting with the help of a head torch has been introduced in Provence. Machine or manual harvesting is an ongoing matter for discussion.

Machine harvesting, introduced in the 1960s, is faster, so grapes are brought in at the moment of optimal ripeness, in the cool of the night, to a cool cellar. Machine harvesting is cheaper but can damage the grapes, especially with older machines. With state-of-the-art technology, the grapes harvested can be selected, sorted and destemmed quickly, before the fruit even enters the cellar.

Manual harvesting is slower, but more precise, and brings in the grapes intact, allowing for whole-bunch pressing. The downside is finding sufficient labour, at a moment's notice, to bring in all the grapes quickly. Régine Sumeire has manually harvested her rosé grapes, since the late 1980s, to ensure whole-bunch pressing, for greater acidity and freshness.

IN THE CELLAR

Pressing

As soon as the grapes come into the cellar, they are processed. There are three ways to obtain the juice.

The free-run juice, obtained through the weight of the grapes, is run-off and fermented immediately.

Whole bunch clusters can be pressed, which Sumeire describes as being equivalent to squeezing grapes lightly in your hand, compared to pressing destemmed grapes, which is like using a liquidizer and sieve.

Or the grapes can be destemmed and crushed, freeing up the pulp, the skin, the seeds and the juices, which are collectively referred to as the 'must' before pressing.

The objective for rosé wines that are pressed directly is fast release of quality juice to obtain the best aromas without extracting colour. Companies such as Laffort strongly recommended the use of enzymes during the filling of the press. Some winemakers find this method extracts the colour too rapidly, along with undesirable aromas such as vegetal notes and skin tannins, and so eschew the use of enzymes.

Pectinase blends are available which can increase free-run juice yields, shorten press cycles and reduce phenolic extraction during pressing. Reductive handling has become an important part of rosé winemaking. Reducing the grapes' contact with oxygen produces a rosé (or white) with more freshness and varietal character. Poor handling of oxygen can lead to a browner colour and oxidation. The big question is how to protect the juice and make the wine in a reductive environment.

Because of the rapid degradation of grape antioxidants in free-run juices, especially in varieties like Grenache, reductive measures are needed during crushing and pressing. Inert gases such as carbon dioxide and nitrogen are used. Since the 1960s, experimental presses have been developed to obtain non-oxidized juice under a cover of carbon dioxide. During the 1990s, the application of inert gases during harvest (mainly carbon dioxide from dry ice), combined with prefermentation maceration, allowed non-oxidized free-run juice to be obtained. The wines produced were fruity and remained stable for longer, allowing for longer ageing.

The move to pneumatic presses during the 1990s changed the direction of rosé winemaking significantly. Making rosé wine 'like white wine', by pressing the grapes gently, resulted in lighter wines with less skin contact. This transformed Provence rosés dramatically, leading to much paler, more delicate rosés and a move away from the darker, more structural styles achieved with longer maceration.

Bucher Vaslin, a manufacturer of winemaking equipment, developed a press called Inertys®, which presses under a controlled atmosphere, guaranteeing that 100 per cent of the pressed juice is extracted without oxidation. The gas used is recycled by means of a flexible reservoir, and can thus serve several times, reducing operating costs.

Fermentation without maceration

After the juice is pressed, it is allowed to settle, usually in tank, before being taken off the lees and fermented straight away. To work with 'clean' juice with no lees at all, enzymes can be added to help precipitate the lees faster.

When the juice is taken off after settling, it leaves a layer of lees (*bourbes*) mixed with some juice. This remaining juice is extracted, using a lees filter. The *bourbes* are put in a separate tank and kept cold for flavour extraction, and may be added back in small quantities if extra flavour is needed.

Sam Harrop MW notes that most producers he encounters who have the cooling facility, cool prefermentation juice to around 5°C to settle before racking and inoculation.

Maceration

Alternatively, the must may or may not be followed by a period of prefermentative maceration, when the juice can be left in contact with the gross lees, to extract as many flavour precursors as possible from the lees before fermentation begins. If this occurs at a temperature below 20°C, microbial action tends to be retarded, and greater aromas and flavours extracted.

The amount of maceration will depend on the variety (colours can range from deep and intense to very pale pink), ripeness of the grapes, the temperature and the desired style of wine. Careful surveillance during maceration is required to prevent too much colour extraction or polyphenols. Enzymes can be added to speed up the extraction of fruit and flavours, without too much colour.

The length of maceration is up to the grower and can be anything from zero hours to four or five days in tank, after the addition of inert nitrogen or carbon dioxide. Extended maceration in Tavel and for *clairet* in Bordeaux is from 6 to 72 hours. In Provence, from zero (except the amount of time it is in the press) to 10 hours is typical.

Experiments in Bordeaux on Merlot macerated at two different temperatures showed that within 35 hours at 20°C the maximum colour saturation for *clairet* (ICM[1] colour intensity of 2.5) had been achieved, whereas maceration could continue for 48 hours at 13°C before maximum colour was achieved.

The shorter, hotter maceration also results in shorter length, less fruit, reduced intensity and lower acidity. In contrast, Cabernet Franc and Cabernet Sauvignon can be macerated at warmer temperatures, around 20°C to speed up the extraction of colour and fruit flavours. At 24°C, the colour extraction is intense for rosé, reaching a limit for colour after macerating for between 16 and 20 hours, for Bordeaux *clairet*. At these warmer temperatures, there is a noted increase in fruit, floral notes, intensity, balance and length. If macerated at a lower temperature for longer, more vegetal notes appear, along with a certain hardness.

The riper the fruit, the quicker the juice darkens. Experience and precision is required to judge when to stop the maceration. During fermentation, age and filtration, the wine will lose colour, losing between 20 and 80 per cent by the time the wine is finished. The colour obtained

---

[1] ICM = Intensité Colorante Modifiée. It is the average optic density measured with wavelengths at 420 nm, 520 nm and 620 nm.

during maceration and the level of colour loss depends on the amount of anthocyanins present and the quantity of sulphur dioxide used. The longer the maceration, the more anthocyanins will be released, protecting the colour from the sulphur dioxide, which reduces colour intensity. The Chambre d'Agriculture de la Gironde has carried out considerable research into maceration and has established that a (probable) final colour can be calculated by measuring the amount of anthocyanins. At higher levels of anthocyanins there is the danger of tannin extraction, which continues until the juice is completely bled off the skins.

It is important that maceration occurs under anaerobic conditions. This limits oxidation of important volatile thiols, and protects anthocyanins from oxidative discolouration. Adding pectolytic enzymes during maceration not only improves flavour development, but also increases colour stability. Both features are important to the shelf-life of the resulting rosé wine.

Short maceration limits anthocyanin uptake, giving only the fashionable, slightly pinkish colouration. However, because few tannins are extracted, rosés tend to show poor colour stability, with much of the colour being derived from unstabilized free anthocyanins, or their self-association or co-pigment complexes. Despite their relatively low anthocyanin content, they still act as important antioxidants. Unless the grapes were comparatively immature (before full colouration), the anthocyanin content of the press-run juice is often too high for use in rosé. Anthocyanin contents for rosé wines are generally in the range of 20–50mg/litre. Addition of sulphur dioxide will initially bleach the anthocyanin pigments; it also stabilizes them from oxidation to brown polyphenols.

After maceration, the must is pressed to separate the solid part, the pomace (skin, seeds), from the juice, and the juice is bled off the skins (*saignée*). When applicable, the remaining concentrated must is used to produce red wine. The technique is primarily used in years, or with cultivars, where colour extraction may be less than desired for producing red wines.

Bleeding

This is one of the most controversial, least understood, elements of rosé winemaking. Most people speak of *saignée* in derogatory terms, linking it to rosé as a 'by-product' of red winemaking. As Julian Jeffs wrote in *The*

Wines of Europe (1971), 'the finest vins rosés are excellent wines in their own right; and they are not particularly cheap. The best of these wines are not the afterthoughts of the great red wine districts, but rather the products of areas which specialize in them, such as Tavel or Anjou.'

However, some producers make excellent rosé as part of their red wine making. Mathilde Poggi of Il Fraghe in Bardolino makes an excellent *chiaretto* with her red wine. As she explained, it is ecological as no part is wasted. In weaker vintages for reds, many winemakers do bleed off juice to concentrate the wine, and the juice may be thrown away (see page 117 for one US winemaker's solution). Sometimes a portion of juice bled off a red wine is useful for blending into rosé wine to give extra weight and flavour.

For rosé wines made after brief maceration where the juice is bled off the must, the remaining must still has plenty of fruit, tannins and colour. Amerine wrote in 1967, 'Since some sugar and red pigment remain in the pomace, it may be added to fresh must and used to make ordinary red wine.'

In a novel solution to grape waste in the juice industry, studies have looked at adding dehydrated red grape skins to white wine to produce a rosé. Apparently, the results have attributes equivalent to those of more traditionally produced rosé wines. Introduction of this technique would, however, likely be hotly contested within the EU.

With partial *saignée*, juice is bled off for rosé, leaving the remaining juice on the must to continue fermenting to make red wine. If the making of a *saignée* rosé is connected to making red wine, the grapes may be considerably riper than for the other methods, with lower acidity and greater weight.

Complete *saignée* is used in some traditional rosés such as Tavel (*méthode Taveloise*), Rosé de Riceys and *clairets/claretes/chiarettos*. In these cases, *all* the juice is bled off after maceration and then fermented.

Whole grape fermentation (carbonic maceration)

Whole-bunch fermentation, when entire clusters of grapes (including stems) are fermented before being crushed, is distinct from whole grape fermentation, also known as carbonic fermentation. Historically, most wines underwent some partial carbonic fermentation, with the amount dependent on the shape and size of the vessel storing the grapes prior to crushing. If grapes are stored in a closed container, grapes above will crush those on the bottom, releasing grape juice, which ferments. Carbonic maceration is often done with added yeast. Ambient yeasts will interact with the sugars in the grape juice to start conventional ethanol fermentation. Carbon dioxide is released as a by-product and, being denser than oxygen, will push out the oxygen through any permeable surface (such as slight gaps between barrel staves) creating a mostly anaerobic environment for the uncrushed grape clusters to go through carbonic maceration. The deeper the vessel, the greater the proportion of grapes that could be exposed to an anaerobic environment caused by the release of carbon dioxide from the crushed grapes on the bottom. Carbonic maceration can either suppress or enhance varietal character (Bénard et al. 1971). Rosés made using this method include rosé de Riceys and Tierra de Leone.

Fermentation

If pigment extraction is insufficient, the grapes are crushed and fermentation may be conducted briefly in contact with the seeds and skins. Once sufficient colour has been obtained, the fermenting must is pressed to separate the juice from the pomace. The duration and temperature depends on the winemaker's preferences and how maceration affects the varietal aroma.

Otherwise, fermentation of the juice is conducted without skin contact. If the juice is high in pH, it may be acidified on pressing. Alternatively, the wine may be cooled and sulphited to prevent deacidification by malolactic fermentation.

Rosé with its phenolic content has a more reductive make-up than white wine. As such, winemakers do not use excessive sulphites throughout the winemaking process and aim to minimize the amount of sulphides produced during fermentation by having a sensible nutrient regime. As Harrop describes it, 'Yeasts are like humans. Without the right number of people on a job, then either the job is not completed or it is done really badly. Like humans, if yeasts don't get enough food they don't perform. In addition, if they get the wrong food, they produce rather unattractive aromas such as hydrogen sulphide (rotten egg), that complexes into more earthy, vegetal sulphides. These characters smother fruit and can and often do dominate to the extent where the wine is deemed disagreeable/faulty, by the mindful consumer.'

If using white grapes, full or partial fermentation on skins can result in copper-pink coloured wines such as *ramato* and orange wine. *Ramato* is the Italian word for a rosé that is copper-coloured – not necessarily from extended skin contact. A false rosé is a red wine, fermented on the skins but using such a light pigmented variety, such as Poulsard in the Jura and Grignolino in Italy, that the colour resembles a dark pink rosé. In taste they are more tannic.

Temperature control

As use of gentler presses became more prevalent, technology improved for controlling temperature. Rosé fermented in a cooler environment, like white wine, encourages fresher, fruitier aromatics. Victor de Pez of Château d'Aqueira in Tavel remembers that when he started making wine in the mid-1970s, all was fermented in wood. 'As soon as the first tank was cooled to 20°C, they would move onto the next tank and the first started to warm up again … winemaking was non-stop running between the fermenting barrels trying to cool them down.' Sumeire remembers how in the early 1980s the tanks were cooled down by running a constant flow of cold water over them. This water needed to be clean, and if there were not enough, they would heave a large block of ice to the top of the tank and blow a fan past to cool down the air. Another method described by Sumeire, to keep the fermenting wine cool, was to use the *poussette* (pushchair) method, where cold must was slowly added to the tank, with each new batch, hopefully, lowering the ambient temperature.

Cool fermentation, at 14°C, will emphasize the primary fruit characters. Esters are also an important part of the aromatic profile. Fermenting at lower temperatures, for example, 12°C, will increase ester production, with aromas like bananas and pineapple.

Old underground cellars, like those of Cigales and Ribiera del Duero in north-western Spain and around Bourgeuil in the Loire, have been used for centuries to maintain an even temperature. New cellars are often built into hills, to simplify cooling.

Yeast

Yeast is a hot topic amongst many rosé wine makers, important in defining the rosé style. Winemakers choose a yeast according to their varieties and terroir, but also according to the style of wine they want. The winemaker looking to create his or her personal style, needs to select an appropriate yeast and to ensure a suitable addition rate. The yeast needs be rehydrated under ideal conditions and with sufficient sterols to achieve a healthy fermentation, resulting in a wine with more purity and freshness, and free from faults. This is rarely the case with spontaneous fermentation with ambient yeasts.

Using ambient yeasts (natural ferment) has considerable risks. For some winemakers, the negatives include stuck ferment, sulphides, volatile acidity, less fruit and more minerality. There is less certainty, less control and less expression of the site, with *more* expression of a struggling yeast! All of this is true. However, throughout the book I have included rosés made using ambient yeasts for several reasons.

Most rosés made have a 'pure, fresh and pristine style', which Harrop notes is what most customers want. Selected yeast inoculation and management of healthy fermentation provides this consistency. Though customers may be happy with more diversity in red and white wines, they are more conservative with rosé. For this reason, I think the use of ambient yeasts, amongst other different winemaking techniques is important. They challenge ideas and perceptions of what rosé can produce.

Some popular commercial yeast strains, such as GRE, Rhone 4600, D254 and, more recently, Clos, are yeasts selected from 'nature'. Genetically modified yeasts are only permitted in North America and Moldova. Lalvin ICV GRE™, selected in Cornas in 1992, reduces any potential vegetal character found in varieties like Merlot, Cabernet Sauvignon, Grenache and Syrah. In rosés with more balanced maturity, it emphasizes the red fruit. IOC Fresh Rosé highlights the aromatic intensity of floral, citrus and spicy notes in rosé wines, and creates complex, rounded rosés; particularly for varietal expression of grape varieties such as Syrah and Cabernet Sauvignon. Viniferm Diana enhances full-bodied varietal typicity and releases the volatile thiols (beta-lyase activity) that are key components of the aroma of rosé wines found in Merlot, Cabernet Sauvignon and Mourvèdre, adding notes of blackcurrant. Lalvin Clos® was selected in Priorat, Spain and has been tried on Carignan, Grenache, Syrah, Zinfandel and Tempranillo with excellent results for aromatic complexity, structure and mouthfeel.

Rosés designed for early purchase, from the early spring following harvest, to be finished by the end of summer, favour yeasts which show attractive fruit character early on their development. Yeasts can accentuate the strawberry fruit character, the grapefruit style, exotic fruit or rich buttery notes. Jo Ahearne MW is not keen on the grapefruit character, which lacks the essential red fruit, and notes that it is popular in Provence, but in few other regions. The R2 yeasts can produce more of the boxwood characters seen in the thiol 4MMP (4-methyl-4-mercaptopentan-2-one). There are more neutral yeasts as well.

Thiol is a buzzword today when describing the aromas, and can include those such as pineapple, grapefruit, passion fruit, citrus, coffee, star anise and even cannabis. Harrop commented that certain yeasts, such as IOC Revelation Thiols, are very efficient at producing thiols such as 3MH (passion fruit, guava, grapefruit, citrus), while Ahearne noted that the discussion around thiols in general is full of dissent, with wildly varying trends in different regions around the world.

As the market has changed, with rosés promoted as good over the following autumn and winter, even for longer-term ageing, further studies into yeasts have taken place. Results suggest that rosés which are most attractive when young, and which often do best in early reviews and competitions, may not age the best. Wines which appeared as fresh and fruity in youth, can take on more vegetal character with age. Indigenous yeasts provide another dimension and can be used to lower the level of alcohol.

Harrop notes that 'One of the technical issues I am seeing, especially with screwcap use in rosé, is the production of savoury "complexed" sulphides, post bottling. If the nitrogen level is too low and/or excessive ... inorganic nitrogen is used as a supplement during ferment, then the yeast will produce sulphides that can then bind under reductive conditions.'

Sugar

Although many rosés emulate the Provence style of light, dry, pale pink wine, most rosés with consumer appeal have some residual sugar. Four to eight g/l (depending on the amount of acidity) can make a wine attractively fruity and give appealing softness and charm. Such rosés are a significant part of global production, in the *rosés tendre* of the Loire, Zinfandel blush in America, and the sweeter rosés of South Africa and Australia.

How dry is dry, when considering the Provence style? While 4g/l residual sugar is the maximum amount permitted for dry Provence rosé, quality rosés rarely retain any sugar and are fermented dry. Rosés with even a few grams of sugar will need to have arrested fermentation through chilling, filtration and sulphur dioxide.

Alcohol

As most rosés are made to be light and fresh, they generally have lower alcohol. Vandyke Price (1975) wrote, 'Pink wines are not necessarily light in alcohol as is sometimes supposed, and the alcoholic strength cannot be determined by tasting.' A drive in New Zealand for lower alcohol wines has resulted in some interesting variety blends (see pp. 143–4).

Ageing on lees and malolactic fermentation

Lees contact, and use of inactive yeast for a time, post-ferment, can help keep dissolved oxygen levels down and protect the wine from oxidation. The fermented lees and inactive yeast products also release polysaccharides that add a certain texture and viscosity to the wine, and help balance out the tannins and acid, with less need for residual sugar. Ageing on the lees, with regular stirring (*battonage*) is used for fuller bodied wines. Zoltán Heimann in Szekszárd, Hungary, is experimenting with ageing his rosé in barrel, on Viognier lees, and bottling unfiltered.

Traditionally, malolactic fermentation is stopped in rosé, to make the crisp fruit style for young drinking. A slow end to fermentation, where it might take ten days to finish the last fifteen or so grams of sugar, increases the risk of effects of lactic acid bacteria. Diacetyl from malolactic fermentation can greatly impair a fruity rosé's quality. It also seems to accelerate the wine's ageing, developing a dirty butterscotch or rancid-cream quality when the esters, thiols and other fermentation aromas start to fade.

Increasingly, malolactic fermentation is being considered for more complex rosés. Rosé des Riceys and some Tavels use this. Wines which have gone through malolactic fermentation are more stable and require less sulphur dioxide at bottling.

Ageing under a film of yeast (flor) also produces interesting results. The most famous rosé produced this way is the Tibouren of Clos Cibonne in Provence. Other producers using or experimenting with this method include Domaine des Hautes Collines (Provence), Bryan Martin of Ravensworth (Australia) and Randall Grahm (California).

Wood

The key is to have a rosé with the weight, complexity and ageing potential to deal with the oak. This is often achieved by using older vines, lower yields and vinification methods resulting in more complex wines. It becomes apparent with tastings of rosés vinified and/or aged in oak, that there is no single oaked-rosé style. Winemaking is important, but there is plenty of variation and experimentation, with old or young barrels, type of wood, size, fermentation, lees stirring or just ageing. The use of old neutral barrels, *foudres*, or new neutral oak barrels such as Stockinger, for vinification can result in the oak being barely visible. Using fruit with naturally good weight and extract, a broader mouthfeel and rounder texture is achieved without diminishing the fresh fruit, acidity and elegance of the wines. Experiments on ageing rosé underwater are also being trialled (see p.144).

Fining and filtration

Polyvinylpolypyrolidone (PVPP), is a synthetic polymer effective in absorbing and precipitating polyphenols, which can be used to remove colour. This can result in paler rosés, and is effective when used with decolourizing carbon. Some appellation regulations specify that carbon filtration cannot be used. Jonathan Hesford of Domaine Treloar commented on carbon filtration: 'One of the problems is that I can taste the use of carbon, added to reduce colour, in many Languedoc rosés.' Curious, I asked what a rosé treated this way tasted like. 'Hard to describe,' he admitted. 'A bit like licking charcoal drawing sticks. It makes the wine taste flat and hard.'

Blending red and white wine

Proposals within the European Union in 2009 to allow mixing red and white wines to make rosé, led to heated debate. Many regions protested that mixing red and white table wine would lead to an inferior product, which, being easier to create as a pink wine, and therefore cheaper, would put other winemakers, with highly developed traditions and skills, out of business. The exception to the rule is champagne, where this is specifically allowed and followed. Blending red and white wines is permitted outside of the EU.

THE IMPORTANCE OF COLOUR

Colour is a key factor for the consumer, with colours ranging through bluish pink, dark pink-red, orange, tawny pink, bright pink to a clear pink. The range of tones for a rosé, vin gris or clairet has been admired, in a way that red or white wines rarely are. 'They should have a bright pink to light red color without excessive orange or purple shading', wrote Amerine in 1967. Vandyke Price in 1975 noted that the prettiness of the wines was played on to entice tasters. 'One of the most charming tastings I have attended was of a wide selection of pink wines, with a vase at each tasting station containing the rose that in colour came closest to that of the wine. Pink wines range from dark, vivid pink a bare shade away from red, through orange and tawny pink to light, bright pink to a clear pinkish-pearl and a faint almost bluish-pink.'

Not all colours were equally appreciated. During the 1960s Amerine conducted surveys which indicated that the most successful colours were bright pinks and pale red. Orange or purple notes were not appreciated. He observed that Petite Sirah produced orange notes (which were not liked), while Carignan produced a more attractive pink. Syrah and Mourvèdre give deeper blue-pink hues. Grenache, prone to oxidation, produced an orange-pink if not carefully made.

The name 'blush' was first used by Mill Creek Vineyards in Healdsburg in California, registered by Bill Kreck in 1981. By 1986, Maureen Ashley commented at a tasting of French rosés that 'novelties around the tasting had to include the new buzz word blush. The wine was a Vin de Pays du Jardin de la France called "Beaujour" and had just a touch of colour "just like a maiden's blush" ... The wine itself didn't have a lot to offer except its novel colour.'

In 1975 Vandyke-Price connected the colour with the style: 'Pink wines from southern regions tend to be darker in hue than those from the north, possessing more fruitiness; pink wines from northern vineyards seem to have less flavour though with freshness, crispness and bouquet predominating. Pink wines from large wineries will also demonstrate the style of the establishment as well as that of the region.' These 'rules' are still repeated, even though no longer accurate. Within twenty-five years, following Sumeire's introduction of the gentle press for rosé, the opposite was true, with Provençal rosés aiming for the palest pink.

Colour descriptions for rosés became more complex during the 1980s, moving on from simply pale or deeply coloured, with descriptors for Provençal rosés including 'onion skin' and 'salmon'. By the beginning of the twenty-first century, these 'savoury' descriptors were regarded as detracting by some, so the Centre de Recherche et d'Expérimentation sur le Vin Rosé (CREVR) in Provence, introduced fruit comparisons such as peach, mango, redcurrant and melon. The amount of colour in the juice and the rate of extraction from the skins depend on the variety of grape, the region and season, the time of picking, the physical condition of the grapes, the temperature of the must, and other factors. The favourite colour in 2016–17 in Provence is 'coral'. In the Loire, *négociants* demand a pale colour even if it impacts on the quality and taste of the wine.

In 1983 Professor Peynaud studied the importance of colour. 'One of the most revealing experiments on the influence of color is the one outlined by Pierre André. The color of the rosé wines here covers a broad spectrum from pale orange to bright cherry-red. Winetasters tend to make an instinctive association between color and character: "a more deeply colored wine = a more full-bodied wine" and "a paler wine = a lighter, more supple wine."'

A group of professional and non-professional tasters were given a series of six rosé wines of different colours. They were first asked to rank, in order of preference the wines based only on colour appeal. In the second round their judgement was determined by colour and taste. In the final round, the wines were tasted blindfolded and were judged on taste alone. When they could see the colour of the wines, tasting these hardly changed the order of their preferences. When they could not see the colour, the order changed significantly. Peynaud's conclusion was that this shows 'the importance of sight in tasting, and demonstrates that colour plays a significant part in the appeal of wines of moderate quality. So long as they look attractive the consumer will be less critical about their flavour, provided they have no obvious defects.'

Another interesting observation, maybe particularly significant in the marketing of rosé wines, is that, overall, the non-professional tasters were more influenced by the colour. Perhaps most people have a greater visual than taste vocabulary. The professional tasters were far more cautious about placing too much emphasis on the colour.

Gilles Masson at CREVR researched the colours of rosé wines, and tracked the subtle variations. He found that, as the colour of rosé is so important, producers and the wine trade needed an easy way to refer to precise colours. After initial trials of printed colour charts, transparent liquids were felt to be easier for matching colour. After considerable research on features like colour stability, coloured gels were found most durable and a kit of nine reference colours, seen as typical of rosé wine, was introduced, packaged in wine glasses (the *nuancier*). For this work, the Académie Amorim awarded him its Grand Prix in 2006. He monitors the colour of wines available, and has seen a steady increase in paler rosés produced around the world since 2007. In 2013, just over half the world's rosés were in the darker range of tones.

Masson believes that the attractive colours of rosé are an important part of its success story, their beauty enticing the consumer. However, he does not favour the view that pale is better than dark. He hopes that consumers will learn to appreciate that a paler colour indicates more white fruits such as peach and melon, that rosés with a slightly more pronounced pink will have more red fruits, that darker pinks have more black fruits, so that consumers can make an informed decision when buying. Colour does *not* indicate quality, but style.

LIGHT STRIKE

With clear bottles preferred for rosé to show off the colour, light strike is a problem. The idea that light can damage wine is not new, informing as it does the standard advice that cellars should be kept dark. The speed with which light strike occurs, however, is only now becoming appreciated. Light can damage wine irreversibly in as little as one hour. Therefore, it is in shops, bars and restaurants, not cellars, where this is most likely to occur. Both sunlight and light from fluorescent bulbs include the wavelengths responsible. Some of the damaging wavelengths are produced by LED and incandescent (traditional filament) lighting, resulting in a reduced, but still potentially damaging, effect. Shops could do much to reduce the risk of their lighting damaging the wine.

Light strike occurs when a wine is exposed to blue and ultraviolet light, causing the transformation of amino acids into particularly stinky compounds such as dimethyl disulphide (DMDS for short). One of the main chemical ingredients is 3-methyl-2-butene-1-thiol, created by riboflavin reacting with the amino acids to create sulphur compounds.

Imbibe magazine investigated this in 2015. Christine Parkinson from Hakkasan felt that light strike 'is the great ignored wine fault. If only the trade paid as much attention to the effect of light as they did to other faults.' 'Fruit flavours become first tainted, then completely occluded by characters of overcooked cabbage, damp cardboard, and sewage,' said Geoff Taylor at food and drink research centre Campden BRI. 'Diminished aroma and flavour are the most common symptoms but off-flavours can also emerge. These can include cabbage, wet wool and onion, and can also take the form of oxidative or reductive characters, with subdued, muted, earthy, dirty and pond water notes emerging.'

Bottle colour has a huge influence on how much light reaches the wine itself; the current fashion for clear glass is not helpful. Unfashionable dark amber glass blocks 90 per cent or more of harmful light. Green glass blocks upwards of 50 per cent, depending on hue, darkness and thickness. Clear glass can block as little as 10 per cent of light strike wavelengths but, despite this, is becoming ever more popular.

Clear glass's increased popularity is directly related to the increase in sales of rosé, often enjoyed as much for its colour as for its taste. Producers say that it would be difficult to sell their rosé if the colour were not seen. Mateus Rosé recorded a 10 per cent leap in sales in the first six months of changing to clear glass. Alex Hunt MW wrote on Jancis Robinson's Purple Pages that clear glass bottles bring no benefit to the wines, their sole benefit being cosmetic, while their only effect on quality is to jeopardize it. Rosé risks tasting murky if left in clear glass, but always looks murky if bottled in mid-green. The thinner glass of lightweight bottles diminishes their light-blocking properties.

Light strike occurs once a wine is in bottle, but can affect all susceptible bottles equally, as its presence is down to how those bottles are stored. Days sitting on a brightly lit supermarket shelf take their toll, but if the wine remains in its case until the last minute before being opened, surely it should be fine? Not necessarily. It may have been exposed to harmful light before being boxed at the winery. Unless precautions were taken, there is a chance the wine may have sat about in a processing facility, bathed in fluorescent light.

Sparkling wine is particularly prone to light strike, as the bubbles amplify the off-aromas, so rosé fizz is arguably the most at-risk category. Fortunately, it is more often found in coloured glass than its still counterparts. Brad Greatrix of Nyetimber commented that 'it's a bugbear of mine. I think bottling in clear glass is recklessness. Education is also a big part of light strike, too few recognize it, even though it's much more prevalent than TCA [cork taint] in clear glass. Dark glass is a useful first step because it's so easy for wine to be light-exposed during the supply chain.'

Gilles Masson noted that winemakers are aware of the problem, and the CREVR is working on how winemakers can take action to minimize the effect of light strike:

- By minimizing lees ageing, because yeast autolysis can increase methionine and riboflavin levels, but this influences the wine style.
- Yeast selection can reduce riboflavin concentration. Riboflavin is mainly produced by yeast during alcoholic fermentation so a low-riboflavin producing yeast could be used, provided that it is satisfactory in other respects.
- Some fining agents can remove riboflavin, though also removing both desirable and undesirable wine components. Some commercial fining agents are promoted for reducing riboflavin levels.

3
HISTORIC ROSÉ REGIONS

Two world wars, global recession, depopulation of rural areas, ease of travel and changes in taste during the twentieth century contributed to massive developments in the evolution of wine styles. A few regions managed to retain part of their historic wine heritage. At a basic level, these historic rosés divide into two styles, darker *clairets* and paler *vins gris*. The *rosés tendres* of the Loire appear to have developed from the *clairet* styles, and sparkling champagne from *vin gris*. Appellation authorities are often strict over the colour, and have been known to refuse wines outside these limits.

CLAIRET-STYLE ROSÉS

These are darker rosés, the production of which involves longer skin contact through maceration and some form of bleeding off (*saignée*) from the skins, either as part of red winemaking or independent of red wine.

This clear, pale red wine, *clairet,* was the default option for most wine until the eighteenth century. A medieval drinking song mentions *clairet*, implying high alcohol which made the singer dizzy, in comparison to the wines of Anjou and Arbois which were lighter.

Quand je bois du vin clairet	When I drink *clairet* wine
Ami tout tourne tourne tourne	Friend everything turns turns turns
Aussi désormais je bois Anjou ou Arbois	So now I drink Anjou or Arbois

These wines developed a bad reputation, as by-products of red wine, and were seen as failed, weak red wines. By-product has become a derogatory term, often closely associated with *saignée*, suggesting rosés too high in tannins, with moderate acidity and darker colours. However, in many cases modern winemaking techniques have been able to use the by-product method to create rosés with greater fruit, weight and structure, often producing a style preferred by red-wine drinkers.

Clairet, Bordeaux

Henry II's marriage to Eleanor of Aquitaine, in 1152, gave the *clairets* of Bordeaux a ready market in England, where they were appreciated for their vivacity and freshness.

By the end of the seventeenth century, after Aquitaine returned to French ownership, the Dutch became the main importers of Bordeaux wines, bringing improvements to winemaking techniques. Longer fermentation and reduced risks of oxidation and spoilage created 'black' (or darkly coloured) red wines with ageing potential. The market responded, and throughout the eighteenth and nineteenth centuries asked for ever darker, more tannic red wines. Wines were macerated for longer and longer stretches, resting longer in tank on the lees, producing stronger wines.

Clairet remained a term for lighter coloured reds or dark rosés throughout France. Redding wrote in 1851:

> *There is no pure wine in France like that which is designated claret in England. This wine is a mixture of Bourseaux [sic] with Benicarlo, or with some full wine in France. Clairet wines in France signify those which are red or rose-coloured. Thus rose-coloured mousseaux wine is called clairet or rosé; there is no such original term as claret in France for wine; it is an English corruption of clairet.*

Clairet became less popular as the great red wines of Bordeaux became popular. Bizarrely, the name 'claret' continued to be used in Britain for red wines from the region, even dark red wines.

Clairet was becoming increasingly rare and had almost died out in Bordeaux. With the brief boom in rosé after the Second World War, *clairet* experienced a revival. In 1950, the famous oenologist Emile Peynaud 'reinvented' the Bordeaux *clairet*, at the **Cave de Quinsac** (www.cave-de-quinsac.com), which resulted in the launch of the appellation 'Bordeaux Clairet' and the town Quinsac becoming known as the *clairet* capital. Originally made with maceration lasting up to four days, today the Quinsac cooperative's *clairet* – which has the words of the medieval drinking song on its label – is in a slightly fresher style with the grapes (90 per cent Merlot and 10 per cent Cabernet Sauvignon) macerated for between 6 and 48 hours, making a dark pink wine with a touch of tannin, fresh acidity and supple black fruit, reminding me of some of the 'luncheon clarets' I used to sell in the 1980s.

In the 1970s **Château Thieuley** (www.thieuley.com) started producing a *clairet*, which Joanna Simon described in 1988 as 'buttery, blackcurranty'. Two generations later, Marie and Sylvie Courselle still produce Thieuley *clairet* (and a rosé). Sylvie Courselle describes *clairet* as being generally young, light and fruity with floral notes, fresh acidity and a hint of tannin, halfway between a light red and a dark rosé.

Some Bordeaux producers who make both a *clairet* and a rosé say the difference between the wines begins in the vineyard, with the best Bordeaux rosé coming from deep clay soils, while *clairet* does best on clay over gravel, which produces wines with elegance. Courselle agrees. She selects different parcels for her *clairet*, not necessarily by soil, but by the parcels where the grapes grow larger and juicier, showing greater freshness, so there may be variation from year to year. The grapes are harvested earlier than for red wines, but sometimes a few days after the rosé harvest.

Length of maceration and temperatures are discussed in detail on pages 17–18. In traditional red wine regions such as Bordeaux it is, in theory, easy to switch from red to rosé production or, if using the *saignée* method, to make rosé alongside red wines as part of making a more concentrated red. In 2008, 99 per cent of rosés and *clairets* in Bordeaux were made as a by-product of red wines. When making rosé as a by-product of red wine, care has to be taken to avoid the *clairet* being over-ripe and over-alcoholic, and to retain the essential freshness.

In Bordeaux, any of the permitted red varieties may also be used for rosé: Cabernet Sauvignon, Cabernet Franc, Côt (Malbec), Carménère and Petit Verdot. Each brings its own character. Cabernet Sauvignon brings acidity and aromatic potential, particularly strawberry and blackcurrant fruit while Merlot brings smoothness and a fuller body. *Clairets* can be a blend of two or more grapes or consist largely of one variety, with another used in a supporting role. Vintage variation will affect percentages of varieties in the blend as well the possibility of full, partial or no malolactic fermentation, resulting in the style ranging from crisp and fruity to round and smoother. Thieuley's *clairet* has 60 per cent Merlot and 40 per cent Cabernet Sauvignon with more leafy acidity and wild berry fruit than found in a red wine, and a gentle tannic structure.

Clairet has an image problem against the paler pink styles now being made. Its darker colour, fresh, fruity style and tannic edge make it less fashionable. Gavin Quinney at Château Bauduc admitted that in all the time he has lived in Bordeaux, he has never been offered a *clairet* to drink.

Tavel

Tavel, despite its small production, has been the most famous rosé for almost two hundred years. Even with the growth in Provence rosé, Tavel still holds on to its pre-eminent reputation. Its vineyards lie on the sun-baked undulating hills, on the west bank of the southern Rhône around the small town of Tavel. The town shows evidence of once greater prosperity, with large, old buildings made of the local white stone. Today it is more of a backwater, but close enough to the city of Avignon, on the eastern shore of the Rhone, to be a dormitory village.

Vines were originally cultivated in the area by the Greeks, and later grown by the Romans. Tavel was located on a major communication route between the *oppidum* in Roquemaure and Nîmes, and lies near the major trading route of the Rhône. King Philip IV, le Bel, supposedly travelled through Tavel on a tour of the kingdom, where he was offered a glass. He emptied this without getting off his horse, and afterwards proclaimed Tavel the only good wine in the world. His dispute with the papacy led to Avignon becoming a papal seat during the fourteenth century, when Pope Innocent VI kept Tavel from the Prieuré de Montézargues in his private cellar. The wines continued to find success. The Sun King, Louis XIV (1643–1715), is supposed to have been fond of the wine (and many others around the kingdom) which helped maintain its reputation.

Until the early nineteenth century, the vineyards of Tavel were concentrated on the sandy alluvial soils to the south of the village. These were easier to cultivate than the forested limestone soils to the north or the rocky hills to the east. In the early 1800s, the forests were turned over to agriculture, including some vines. These sandy and limestone soils produced very fresh, light wines.

In *The American Farmer* (1826) Tavel was described as having a 'Bright rose colour, flavour and aroma, delicate'. In 1834, a poetic 'epistle' on Tavel by William Stewart Rose says '... liquid ruby, Tavel; / The juice of paler grape which loves the gravel, / Or that which runs in purer stream, which gushed / From clusters richer, riper, and uncrushed.' George Hodder Tinsley reminisced about drinking Tavel in the 1860s when, 'In ordering his dinner his great fancy was for *quelque chose appétissante*, as he called the lighter form of entrées, and a bottle of Tavel'.

The wine list at the restaurant Les Trois Provençaux in the nineteeth century, includes Tavel amongst the red wines of Burgundy. In 1872 the wines were described as 'First Class: Red wines, not vatted. Tavel: Very dry, very light-coloured wine; improves much by age ... Lirac: Very dry wine, more firm than Tavel, of a lively rose-colour.' Modern producers say that the light colour is because the original vine-growing area of Tavel was on the sandy soils south of the village, a terroir which typically results in lighter wines.

The fortunes of Tavel declined when, in the 1860s, the railway bypassed the town. Worse followed. In 1870, the owner of Château Clary in the neighbouring village of Roquemaure made the unusual decision to replant his vineyards with American vines. Unbeknown to him, these were infected with the phylloxera bug, which spread rapidly round the region, making Tavel one of the first hit areas in France. By 1873, 'the rose colour wines of the Côtes du Rhône, such as the dry and insiduous Tavel, the firm and generous Lirac, and the robust Roquemaure, with the luscious Chusclan and St Geniés, and pleasant sparkling Laudau, the majority made [by] default, [had been] more or less overrun by the *Phylloxera vastarix*.' The reference to 'rose colour' does not mean this was a rosé wine but more a dark rose petal pink and the 'default' may refer to the grapes not fully ripening, leading to wines of a weaker colour. Many vineyards were abandoned and not replanted for some years, as viticulturists struggled to keep up with demand, supplying vineyards with vines grafted on to American rootstocks.

To survive, winemakers discovered they had to group together. In 1902, Tavel vineyard owners and winemakers formed a union, the *Syndicat des Propriétaires Viticulteurs de Tavel*. To promote their wines, members participated in national and international fairs, including those in Lyon, Marseille, Strasbourg and Liège. The sandy soils were the first to be replanted, followed by the stoney limestone plateau by the early years of the twentieth century.

The First World War decimated agricultural communities across Europe, as manpower was diminished and rural areas depopulated. Demand for wine from the nearby urban centres along the Rhône rescued Tavel. The current estate of Château d'Aqueria was founded in 1919 and Domaine Mejan-Taulier (now Florence Mejan) in 1920. Upon the suggestion of Baron Pierre Le Roy de Boiseaumarié, in 1927, the Chairman of the *Syndicat*, Aimé Roudil, and forty winemakers of Tavel, petitioned the Gard courts to officially define the production area.

In *Les Grands Vins de France* (1931) the wines of Tavel were recorded as being an amazing dark pink colour, similar to the great wines of the Côtes du Rhône. The vineyards were described as lying in the recently defined region, in a warm and sheltered amphitheatre amongst the hills on chalk and limestone soils, surrounded by forests of evergreen oaks and aromatic *garrigue*. It was acknowledged that the definition of vineyard territory was essential to prevent wines of a lower quality from being produced. With only 2,500 hectolitres actually produced annually, much that was claimed as Tavel was from further afield. Variable quality did exist, so the right estates needed to be selected. Tavel wines were cultivated by numerous small producers, primarily from Grenache, blended with Clairette, Cinsault, Carignan and Bourboulenc. Amongst the best was Château d'Aquéiria, a 20-hectare estate owned by M. Jean Olivier. Other top producers included M. Héraud, M. Roudil, M. Fraissinet and Château Montézargues.

Particularly interesting is the detailed description of the wines. Tavel rosés had a 'quick' maceration of twelve to twenty-four hours in order to achieve the required colour, a little darker than the final desired colour. The wines then rested in *barrique* for at least one year, often two. They were regarded as having good ageing potential, lasting up to forty years! However, they lost their pink colour with ageing and became the colour of yellow quartz. At three to five years of age, they still had all their Tavel qualities, '*capiteux et corsés*' (heady and full-bodied), with high alcohol of 13–15% abv. At this age, the colour was a beautiful golden pink, ruby with hints of topaz, not dissimilar to the wines of Arbois.

Aromas of wild strawberries and iris developed with age. The wines were described as very dry, soft and delicate. They were best drunk cooled rather than at room temperature, and were an excellent accompaniment to bouillabaise and oysters.

When the first wine appellations were created in 1936, Tavel was amongst them, which preserved their traditional *clairet* style of rosé winemaking (neighbouring Lirac rosé is not made the same way). The early definition written up in the appellation differs slightly from the 1931 description, which noted that the light red wine style found on the sandy soils was the essential character of the wines. Gael Petit, chairman of the Tavel union in 2017, is a lawyer and amateur historian who has researched the archives looking for descriptions and references to Tavel. He noted that while Tavel has evolved, the appellation regulations have slowed down the evolution of the style.

In 1938 the cooperative was opened, with its rooftop slogan proclaiming '*Tavel, 1er rosé de France*' (Tavel, first rosé of France). After the Second World War, Tavel was able to take advantage of its appellation status. New domaines were created, such as Domaine Lafond 'Roc Epine'. In 1948 d'Aqueira started to export to America, through Kobrand, a working relationship which has continued for nearly seventy years.

Ernest Hemingway claimed he could not have lunch without a bottle of Tavel, and frequently mentioned it being served with meals. '"What I want to be when I am old is a wise old man who won't bore," he said, then paused while the waiter set a plate of asparagus and an artichoke before him and poured the Tavel,' wrote Lillian Ross in her interview with Hemingway in the *New Yorker* in May 1950. In a letter to Hemingway, his friend A. E. Hotchner wrote in 1955, 'The turtle steaks preserved beautifully and were consumed with cold Tavel and nothing repeat nothing, can go up against that. What makes Tavel so much better than any other rosé? Just the soil or is there some other secret like a special bee, indigenous to the area, who shits on each grape.' In *The Garden of Eden*, Hemingway calls Tavel the 'wine of Love'. In 1960 he wrote of his journey in Valdepeñas in Spain, where he describes the wine as the 'poor man's Tavel but it does not need to be chilled [unlike Tavel].' The Valdepeñas is a 'wine with no pretensions. It tastes roughly smooth and clean … it grew and was pressed to be drunk at all temperatures and it travels in a wineskin.'

The popularity of Tavel, and indeed of rosé, during the 1950s encouraged producers to think of expanding production. In the mid-1960s the chalk and limestone hills were once again cleared of forest and prepared for growing vines.

In 1965 Allen Sichel wrote that, 'Unlike the general run of rosé wines, both Tavel and Lirac are made from a mixture of red and white grapes, fermented together. The poorness of the soil on which the vines grow assures the finesse of flavour … they age well in bottle, particularly Tavel.' Before the 1970s, Tavel was fermented in *foudres*, which gave colour, but without temperature control the wines had more of a red wine style.

In 1977, Maynard Amerine appeared to be the first to voice criticism over the quality of Tavel wines. He mentioned that the colour of these long oak-aged wines was 'out of kilter' with that of other pink wines being made. He noted that Tavel, which was 'well known in France and occasionally exported to the United States,' had winemaking issues, as did Provence, with the high degree of sulphur required to stop the Grenache-based wine from oxidizing and turning brown. Higher alcohol levels were also a problem. The more expensive rosés were still well regarded (*Black Enterprise Magazine* 1982): 'While France produces many fine rosés, most of the better ones are rather expensive … for picnic drinking. If price is no object, Château d'Aqueria Tavel Rosé, Domaines Ott Bandol Cuvée Marine [Château Romassan] and Château de Selle Coeur de Grain [Domaines Ott, Côtes de Provence] are excellent choices.' Nevertheless, the American market was changing, and Victor de Pez, of Château d'Aquéria, noted that the trade to the United States started declining, especially after 1984, as Zinfandel blush became popular.

In a forerunner to some of today's trends for rosés aged in oak, made to age, or go with food, Tavel was described as able to age well compared to other rosés. In 1986, Maureen Ashley MW commented that 'The 1985 Château d'Acquéria from Le Chemin des Vignes, while warm and ripe on the nose was still young and raw on the palate and will need some time to show its colours.' '*Tavel* is the only Grand Cru of rosé, yielding a spicy, solid, aromatic wine that can stand up to food', wrote André Gayot in *Gault et Millau* (1996).

As in Provence, the 1990s saw improvements in quality, with the introduction of technology, tanks and temperature control. As the pale

Provence rosé has grown more successful, some producers have attempted to compete with it, with earlier harvesting and shorter maceration. De Pez, says there is currently a big discussion amongst producers in Tavel on whether they should become more like Provence rosé or should keep their uniqueness. De Pez supports the traditional style, which he feels can be marketed all year, not just in summer, and noted that since quality started to improve, from 2012, Tavel has begun to regain its popularity.

Tavel wines have moved on from being the 'solid' wines of 1996 to being generally fresh and fruity, with a structure which appeals to red-wine drinkers. Ripe red fruit (sour Griotte cherries, black cherries, strawberries and raspberries), sometimes with notes of bitter almond (d'Aqueira has notes of cherry and almond), often with a mineral or spice core, is typical. The wines have a hint of silky tannic structure, and long, fresh acidity, with a vibrancy of wild hedgerow fruit. Some have a touch of perfumed, floral character, especially those from vines from the sandy soils. Depending on the length and temperature of maceration, the wines can have quite a chewy structural character.

The weight and intensity varies between domaines, terroirs and vintages. Wines made from a blend of the three soils will differ depending on varieties and maceration. Some wines are made from a single terroir, such as **Mordorée**'s (www.domaine-mordoree.com) Reine de Bois, which uses the white varieties Clairette and Bourboulenc for freshness and acidity and red Cinsault for delicacy, to balance the ripe Grenache and Syrah and give a classic quality Tavel with restrained sour cherry, raspberry and strawberry red fruit and freshness, a firm, mineral structure and a hint of tannin.

Some take advantage of the greater ripeness and structure of recent years and are making wood-aged *cuvées*.

In the field

The climate is Mediterranean but not maritime, with the northerly mistral the prevailing wind. The cold cevenol wind blows from the Massif Centrale at the end of September, which shuts the grapes down but generally guarantees a dry harvest. The range of grape varieties is also typically Mediterranean.

The main varieties are Grenache (red, white, grey), Cinsault, Bourboulenc, Clairette (pink and white) and Picpoul (black, white, grey).

Together, they have to make up the major part of the blend, but in reality, Grenache is the main variety. Mourvèdre and Syrah were added in 1969 to replace Carignan and Calitor, which cannot be more than 10 per cent. Grenache provides fruit, sweetness and volume, Cinsault finesse, Syrah colour, Clairette fruit and Mourvèdre stability of colour (and structure). A small amount of Carignan can bring freshness, as can the addition of white varieties.

The geology varies significantly throughout the appellation. Blending from these different sites is important, although some wines are made from single sites.

The original area in the south is comprised of flat sandy rocky fields, chalky with little gravel, which are easy to cultivate and good for ripening. Although poor for water retention, with sufficient depth of soil, the vines do better in drought years. The grapes from this area give finesse and elegance, due to the large diurnal temperature variation, which helps restrain the sugar in Grenache. Grapes from the sand and *terres blanches* sites give good balance for alcohol and acidity.

To the north of the village is an alluvial area formed by the Rhône, whose deposits cover the lower and middle terraces of the Lirac and Tavel AOCs. These deposits are rarely very deep and overlay limestone bedrock. The large *galets* (river-rolled rocks), as in Châteauneuf-du-Pape, act as storage heaters, ensuring great ripeness. However, since 2003 there has been a noticeable increase in hot summers, and now this extra ripening is not so important. This terroir gives very structured, complex red wines, so care must be taken in using wines from this part for rosé. On *galets* the vines suffer in drought, but the extra ripeness contributes to greater weight and structure. Richard Maby of **Domaine Maby**'s (www.domainemaby.fr) single vineyard Prima Donna, planted on the *galets* with old vine Grenache and Cinsault, illustrates the distinctive character of this terroir. The natural extra ripeness of the terroir is balanced by fractionally longer maceration for greater structure. The wine has opulent, ripe raspberry, blackberry and black cherry and hints of silky tannins. Maby has also tried an oak-aged version with grapes from this terroir.

To the west of the village, lie the Terre Blanches, notable for marl limestone deposits. *Lauze* (flagstone), found in the valleys, is very stony with hard limestone. The quality of cultivation depends on the depth of the hard subsoil. Here, low-yielding vines produce deep, aromatic wines. Grapes from the *lauze* have finesse, elegance and fruit.

Global warming has affected the wines of the region, with 2003 marking a divide. In the 1930s, the highest alcohol levels were around 12.5% abv. While relatively high alcohol fits the Tavel style, contributing to roundness, too much can lead to imbalance and goes against the current trend of lighter alcohol rosés. Before 2003, harvest was in early October for maximum ripeness, with some chaptalization in one in every three years. Since 2003, chaptalization has not been required and the harvest occurs mid-September; harvesting any later causing the wines to exceed 15% abv.

Since the 1980s, malolactic fermentation has been stopped by most producers, although Demoulin of **Trinquevedel** (www.chateau-trinquevedel.fr), whose vines are on sandy soils, believes these soils can give sufficient freshness to allow malolactic fermentation. Biodynamic producer Eric Pfifferling of Domaine de l'Anglore also does malolactic fermentation.

In the cellar

Balancing acidity, lower alcohol, ripeness and structure is vital for rosés such as Tavel. If producers want the extended maceration for the fruit and structure *and* need the fresh acidity, greater work is required in the vineyards, making sure the soil is well turned over and removing leaves to reduce overproduction of sugar. The skins and pips must be fully ripe to avoid bitter greenness, which could be extracted during the extended maceration. Maceration time can range from six to seventy-two hours. Typically it is between ten and thirty-six hours. The time depends on the winemaker's choice of colour and style. Trinquevedel's wines, from sandy soils, with twelve- to twenty-four-hour maceration are on the lighter side of traditional Tavel, with paler colour and more floral and strawberry fruit than traditionally. Producers who choose to make a paler Tavel, macerating for just six hours, can pick earlier for greater acidity, but this is atypical of Tavel.

After the maceration, the juice is bled off (*saignée*). Sometimes, as is the case with Trinquevedel's Autrement *cuvée*, some of the must is kept with the skins longer, then blended into the lighter must.

The term *méthode Taveloise,* is preferred to describe the method for making Tavel, including the maceration, but largely referring to the bleeding off of the juice in its entirety, avoiding the term *saignée* which suggests that the juice is bled off to concentrate red wine. Robert Parker in *The Wines of the Rhone Valley* (1987 and 1997) was confused when he said that Tavel could be made in one of two ways.

> *Most Tavel is produced not from blending white and red together as many people imagine, but from tacking up the freshly picked whole grapes in stainless steel tanks, letting their weight do a light crushing, and then permitting the juice to sit on the skins for one or two days, just long enough to give Tavel its vibrant salmon colour. All this must be done carefully at cool temperatures to prevent oxidation of the aromatic intensity and freshness of Tavel's bouquet. The second method, commonly employed elsewhere in the world, but not used with great enthusiasm in Tavel, is what the French call* saignée. *That is the process of bleeding off the top of the vat when the wine's colour has sufficient pink to be rosé. In the latter method, the balance of this wine mass continues to macerate with the skins, resulting in a red wine.*

Despite Tavel's reputed ability for ageing well, the wine has suffered from the reputation of lighter, less concentrated rosés, which age less well. Evidently the wine matures, evolving from more explosive fruit to greater spice (cinnamon, nutmeg and cloves), intense dried fruits (sour cherries, black cherries and cranberries) and savoury notes (dried orange peel and some rich, gamey notes). The extra maceration in the wines of Tavel contributes to the ageing capacity of these wines.

Rosé des Riceys

The three Riceys villages of the Aube in southern Champagne lie only a few kilometres north of the viticultural region of Burgundy. They were backed by competing bishops, respectively those of Dijon (Riceys-Haut), Troyes (Riceys-Bas) and Auxerre (Riceys Haute-Rive). Each has a church, even though they are barely a kilometre from each other. The best south-facing slopes (*côtes*) of the Riceys, such as the Côte de Tronchois, were owned by the nearby Abbey of Molesme, for – in this northern location – the warmest slopes were highly appreciated. In hotter years a pale red could be achieved, in cooler years nothing more than a shimmering *vin gris*.

Since at least the eighteenth century, the wines of les Riceys have been known further afield. Local legend says that stonemasons from the region brought their local wines to Paris while working on the palace at Versailles; the image though of the Sun King chatting to the builders and trying their wine seems a little far-fetched! It is more likely that one of the abbots from the Abbey of Molesme may have introduced the wine to a grander audience.

In a survey of the Aube region in 1852, thirty-nine red and white grape varieties are listed as grown. Pinot Noir was the most appreciated, but other varieties were noted for their pink, rather than red juice, such as Sevigé, Pineau Buret or Gris, and the Poivrier also known as Épicier or Muscat Rouge. The varieties were planted on different soils and blended together, depending on their success in any given vintage. After phylloxera, the vineyards were replanted with Pinot Noir.

Before 1911, local producers could only use their grapes to make Rosé des Riceys or still white Coteaux Champenois, or sell them to the big champagne houses in the north of the region. After the 1911 riots of the Révolte des Vignerons de l'Aube, the regulations were reconsidered, leading to full legal integration into the champagne rules in 1927. The appellation for Rosé des Riceys was granted in 1947, and amended in 1971 to specify that Rosé des Riceys could be made only from Pinot Noir, from vines at least twelve years old. The rules aim to keep the winemaking traditional. Oliver Horiot commented: 'With Rosé des Riceys we are continuing an artisan tradition that could easily have died out, because turning the grapes into Champagne is financially enticing, and easier to find a market once in bottle'.

The Riceys region has a total vineyard surface of 866 hectares, of which 300 could theoretically be vinified as Rosé des Riceys, but only 30 hectares are. The vines tend to grow on steep, south-facing slopes of clay, chalk and Kimmeridgian marl, rising up to 100 metres. The soils apparently give a *lardé* (savoury-smoky) character to the wines. Diurnal temperature variations between cool nights and hot days create the aromatics. These vineyards are selected for Rosé des Riceys because the Pinot Noir grapes must reach a natural ripeness to produce 170g/l potential sugar. To reach 12% abv when the natural sugar is lower, the producers chaptalize. If the vintage produces more natural sugar in the grapes, producers must seek a derogation from the appellation bodies.

There were high sugar levels in 2003, with high acidity years such as 2009 considered a better vintage.

Maximum annual production can reach 80,000 bottles, although the three biggest producers barely make 10,000 bottles each. However, Rosé des Riceys is not made every year, only when the fruit is sufficiently ripe. It must be made at least once every five years, or, according to INAO rules, the appellation dies out.

In the 1970s, when producers increasingly sold grapes for higher prices to the bigger champagne houses, the appellation was in danger of doing just that. Between 1970 and 2001 the yield fluctuated. There is a quota for all grapes harvested including Rosé des Riceys, coteaux champenois and champagne. The quota changes every year; in 2009, it was 9,700 kilogrammes per hectare. Quantities change depending on vintage and quota. A particularity of the champagne rules is the possibility to set wine aside in case of low yields in the following years. This *réserve individuelle* is blocked and cannot be bottled and sold.

Both machine- and hand-harvested grapes are permitted, as long as whole bunches are harvested. The grapes are usually whole-bunch pressed and fermented using semi-carbonic maceration. Alternatively, they are left with the skins for several days in a prefermentation cold soak. This helps to increase the fruit (often emphasizing more black than red fruit notes) and aromatic intensity, extract the colour and soften the astringency. Additional crushed grapes can be added to the tank full of whole clusters for maceration. The proportion of these additional grapes varies by producer, from 10 per cent (**Olivier Horiot** – www.horiot.fr) to as much as 40 per cent (**Horiot Père & Fils**). Some producers, such as Olivier Horiot perform some pumping over and do not close the top of the tank. This process gives a distinct flavour to the wine, often described as similar to liquorice.

The grapes and juice are closely monitored for taste, but maceration generally lasts for between two and seven days (48–168 hours), probably the longest time for any rosé. Other considerations for the length of maceration include the percentage of the berries crushed before maceration, the winemaker's style and the terroir of each vineyard. The maceration is stopped before the wine becomes a red wine. It is this fine timing which makes the wine difficult to make. The tannic extraction makes this a rosé which can take long ageing.

The juice is next bled off the must and fermented, either in stainless steel or in large, old, open wooden vats at a slightly higher temperature. At Olivier Horiot the temperature in these wooden vats is between 18 and 25°C. During fermentation, the juice is separated from the grapes. The yeasts used for Rosé des Riceys are usually purchased laboratory yeasts, different from those for typical champagne, and suited to still, coloured wines.

All producers also carry out malolactic fermentation. The June following harvest, all the producers taste the wine to agree on whether the wine can be bottled as Rosé des Riceys, then on 1 July the wine can be released in dark green or amber bottles, embossed with a special logo. However, many do not release for a further three to five years.

Instead of bottling immediately, Horiot racks the wine into old Burgundian casks in the cellar, for ageing for one year; this is followed by six months in cement. Morel ages in oak casks for 6 to 18 months.

Rosé des Riceys is like a *premier cru* in Burgundy, showing well at 5–8 years old. The Olivier Horiot 2010, tasted in 2017, had amazing vibrancy and vitality. Like a Black Forest gâteau, there were aromas of black chocolate and black cherries, leading to good, fresh length and great elegance on the palate, whilst the cherries were more Griotte with hints of wild raspberry and redcurrant edged with a fine silky tannin core.

The 2012–13 vintage is now being released, and continue to age well. At a vertical tasting held by Eric Pfanner in 2012, reported in the *New York Times*, wines from 1982 and 1989 from three producers, Guy de Forez (Francis Wenner), Morel Père & Fils (Pascal Morel) and Jacques Defrance, showed how well they survived. 'The wines had long ago lost any sharp edges. They were lightly oxidized, yet they had retained much of their youthful fruit. The range of flavours was broad, from wild strawberries to almonds to liquorice.'

Cigales, Spain

From Roman origins, the number of vineyards in Cigales increased significantly during the Middle Ages under the influence of the monasteries. *Clairet* wines were produced throughout northern Spain, and wines from Cigales, then called *aloque*, are recorded as being sold to Valladolid and other cities as well as the Spanish Court. The writers Cervantes (1547–1616), Lope de Vega (1562–1635) and Calderón (1600–81) all mentioned the wine of Cigales. The area had close connections with royalty. Mary of Austria, Queen of Hungary, died in Cigales in 1558, and her great-niece Anna, the fourth wife of Philip II and Queen of Spain, was born there in 1549. Many vineyards around today, such as the Bodega Remigio de Salas Jalón (1737) and Hiriart (1750), started producing centuries ago.

Cigales received its DO in 1991. It covers 2,700 hectares of gentle undulating hills at altitudes of 700–800 metres overlooking the river Pisuerga, which flows into the Duero, downstream (west) from Ribera del Duero. Its limestone soils, over clay and marl, are relatively dry and stony, with a continental climate of baking hot summers and ice-cold winters. Cellars, often shared by small winemakers (*bodegueros*), were built underground, 10 to 15 metres below the surface, where a cool, constant temperature would be maintained. Those at Hiriart were excavated in 1750 and maintain a temperature of 15°C with 75 per cent humidity. The cellars are ventilated by short chimneys called *luceras*.

Half of Cigales produced is *clairet* or *rosado*, with 46 per cent red and 4 per cent white. There has been an increasing amount of red wine since the 1990s, as this commands a higher price and is easier to sell.

Rosado Cigales *nuevo* are *jóvenes* which must be labelled with the vintage year. *Rosado* Cigales may not be sold until after 31 December of the year following the vintage. Both must be made from a minimum of 60 per cent Tinto del País (Tempranillo) and at least 20 per cent white varieties.

The red varieties, besides Tinto del País, are Garnache Tinta (black), Garnacha Roja (gris), Merlot and Cabernet Sauvignon. The white varieties are Verdejo, Albillo and Sauvignon Blanc. Tempranillo is good for rosés for its aromatic potential, colour, richness in extraction and contribution of violet colour to the wines. Garnacha brings to the wine freshness, alcoholic degree, fruit and softness. Verdejo is vinified with the rest of the varieties, to obtain rosés and nose aromatics, whilst Albillo gives aromatics and sugar. For Cigales *rosado*, the vines are traditionally at least forty years old, giving greater complexity than rosés made with young vines (which produce fruitier styles).

The *rosados* come in a variety of pinks, with pale red seen as bringing in more money. Investment in the cellars, including temperature control, has resulted in good *rosado*.

Bodegas Hiriart (www.bodegahiriart.es) make three styles of *rosado*. Lágrima is fresh, fruity and modern; Elite, from grapes selected from the best vineyards, has more weight and structure and Sobre Lías Aromatico is fermented in French oak barrels with battonage lees stirring.

Originally, winemakers used a traditional beam press and fermented in ceramic and wood tanks. These were replaced by mechanical, and later hydraulic, presses and cement tanks in the nineteenth and twentieth centuries. The story goes that many technological improvements were brought back from France by wool merchants who also made wine, although vinification is kept as traditional as possible by most winemakers.

With its traditional dark pink colour, Ruth Sierra de la Gala, winemaker at **Bodegas Sinforiano** (sinforianobodegas.com), says that modern Cigales *rosados* are cleaner, fruitier, fresher and more elegant than ever, and better adapted to current tastes. Nowadays, she claims, the wine is made 'within the traditional style while thinking of what the customer wants.' A light sparkle is typically maintained from fermentation, to provide 'freshness with volume on the palate and an easy-drinking style.'

Schiller, siller, Fuxli

Schillern means 'to shimmer' in German and refers to the shimmering quality of the pale pink, grey, cream colour of this wine, first mentioned in the sixteenth century. *Schiller* is found in Central Europe from Germany, Austria and Hungary down to Serbia.

Although the modern pink wines of Alsace are rosés, in their *cahier des charges* (specification) they are also called *Schiller* or *clairet*.

Schiller, Germany

In 1794 the French invaded and occupied the Ahr region, where the owners of vineyards were not only subjected to higher taxes but also faced competition from inexpensive and more powerful French wines. As a result, Ahr winegrowers rapidly developed a trade in their lighter red wines with Belgium. These wines became known as *ahrbleichart*. According to the 1845 *Guide to Bonn and its Environs,* 'Wallportzheim, at the entrance of the narrower valley of the upper Ahr, produces the best *Ahrbleichart*. (*Bleichart* is a German word equivalent to the English Claret) an excellent dark red fruity wine.'

Schillerwein or *Schiller*, is a mixture of white and red grapes which are harvested, crushed and fermented together. It is produced in small quantities in Baden-Wurttemberg and can include any locally grown variety at the level of quality wine from a specific area (QbA). Below QbA in Württemberg and Saxony, it can be called *Rotling*.

Schiller, Switzerland

The *Schiller* wine of Graubünden in Switzerland is produced in small quantities. It is a rose-coloured wine produced from a mixture of red and white grapes, which are harvested from the same parcel, pressed and fermented together. In Graubünden, the proportion of red grapes must equal that of the white ones. Varieties such as Pinot Noir, Pinot Blanc and Chardonnay are commonly used. A Garanoir and Müller-Thurgau blend is another example.

It can also be found in St Gallen (near Austria), and the Valais, where 85 per cent white Fendant and 15 per cent Pinot Noir are vinified together.

Schilcher from West Styria (Weststeiermark), Austria

Schilcher is a dark pink wine produced solely in the southern Austrian region of West Styria, near the border with Slovenia. West Styria is alpine with very steep vineyards, some at 600 metres. *Schilcher* production dominates the region and is legally protected. It can only be made from Blauer Wildbacher, an old variety said to date back to Celtic times, supposedly related to Blaufränkisch. It is late ripening, with high, crisp acidity, fresh, light red fruits and relatively low alcohol, around, 11.5–12% abv. Some examples can be quite lean with sour, wild berry fruit. Johannes and Luise **Jöbstl** (www.joebstl.eu) make a single-parcel *schilcher*, Ried Krass, which is confidently harvested a little later to obtain generous rosehip, raspberry and strawberry fruit with floral overtones. The high acidity helps the wine age well. **Domaine Kilger** (www.domaines-kilger.com), owned by Christian Reiterer from Styria, and Hans Kilger from Munich, also manages extra ripeness from their grapes on steeply-sloped, warm vineyards at 400 metres altitude. The grapes are harvested at an advanced stage of ripeness, giving their wines extra raspberry fruit with floral perfume and weight.

Although not traditional *schilcher*, Kilger's sparkling brut, with eight months on the lees, has perfumed, blue flower fruit, good weight and long acidity.

In 2017 *schilcher* was granted DAC (Districtus Austriae Controllatus) Schilcherland appellation status.

Siller, Hungary

This was traditionally produced in areas formerly settled by German-speaking Swabians in the southern wine regions of Villány, Szekszárd and Hajós-Baja. The *siller* style bridges rosé and light red wine and often has a refreshing, slightly dry, tannic finish. While rosé has become increasingly popular, *siller* remains a good style to accompany food. Unlike the German and Swiss *Schillers* made with red and white grapes, Hungarian *siller* (pronounced the same as *Schiller*) is made like *clairet* from black varieties with longer maceration and traditionally fermented in large wooden barrels. Drunk too cold it can seem lean. Served at room temperature it opens up in the glass to became a luscious, fresh wine.

Fuxli (fox-coloured) is the brand name, created in 2011, for the *siller* wine in the Szekszárd region. Only small quantities are produced, due to perceived commercial weakness compared to paler rosé. Traditionally, *siller* has gentle, silky tannins with red fruit, soft minerality and high acidity.

Kadarka is a traditional variety for *siller* because of its uneven ripening. Without green harvesting, the harvest can result in bunches of mixed ripeness and a lighter wine. Today, many winemakers throw away the unevenly ripened bunches, but traditional producers like Villány producer Zoltán **Polgár** (polgarpince.hu) uses them to make *siller* with 18–20 hours maceration.

Pastor (pastor.hu/en) and **Tüske** (www.tuskepince.hu), both in Szekszárd, use traditional fermentation methods. Pastor blends Kadarka and Kékfrankos, picked early, followed by maceration for 48 hours. Natural yeast is used, with a slow start to fermentation in tanks, and then just as the fermentation starts, the juice is bled off and the wine is fermented over two weeks at a controlled temperature of 15–18°C.

Tüske blends Kékfrankos, Merlot and Kadarka. Grapes are harvested when fully ripe. Kékfrankos and Merlot (70 per cent of the blend) are fermented on the skins for four to five days and then bled off before continuing fermentation. The finished, bright cherry-red wine is then blended with a small amount of Kadarka wine. The resulting wine is redolent of raspberries, strawberries and cherries, with lively, fresh acidity, ripe, fresh fruit, and a hint of dry tannins on the finish.

More modern *sillers* macerate for slightly shorter times for a lighter style. **Vesztergombi** (www.vesztergombi.hu) and **Schieber** (www.schieberpinceszet.hu) in Szekszárd with 100 per cent Kadarka.

Malatinsky (www.malatinszky.hu) in Villány and **Heimann** (www.heimann.hu) of Szekszárd blend Kadarka, the more structured Kékfrankos and light-coloured, softer Portugieser. **Heumann** (heumannwines.com), in Villány, blends young vine Kadarka (70 per cent) with 30 per cent Syrah. To extract both structure and fruit the Kadarka is fermented at a warm 25°C, while the Syrah has longer maceration before blending.

Šiler, Serbia

German settlers who moved southwards to Banat in North Serbia during the days of the Austro-Hungarian Empire brought the tradition of *šiler* (*Schiller*) wine, a light wine for everyday consumption, not intended for commercial use. Black and white grapes were mixed together, although the predominant red varieties are Skadarka (Kadarka) and Portugieser, made with a short maceration. *Šiler*, in North Serbia, is considered a separate category and in local wine competitions is distinguished from rosé wines.

Cabernet d'Anjou and Rosé d'Anjou

These *rosés tendres* (sweet rosés) appear to be amongst the most modern of the historic rosé styles. They come from hills between the Loire and the River Layon, a largely agricultural area with fruit, grain, flowers, livestock and vines. Numerous old wind- and watermills scatter the landscape, with substantial stone manor houses and small châteaux, proof that this region, between the great port of Nantes to the west and the grand châteaux to the east, was once affluent.

Early medieval evidence refers to the *clairet* or red wines of Anjou. By the seventeenth century Dutch wine merchants encouraged the production of sweet white wines. By the late nineteenth century, rosés accounted for the largest percentage of production, making up 45 per cent of the wines made, followed by sweet whites at 30 per cent and reds at 25 per cent. By the late 1980s rosés had risen to nearly 55 per cent of wine produced in the Anjou district.

The subsoil is mainly slate, sandstone and carboniferous schists as well as volcanic rock, with a maritime climate of mild winters, hot summers, plenty of sunshine and small variations in temperature. Some schist is good for acidity to balance the sugar. Too much can donate excessive structure. Visiting Anjou in June, the air is perfumed with the scent of roses growing in gardens and hedgerows, reminiscent of the forest of thorns and roses which grew up around the castle of Sleeping Beauty, inspired by the Château d'Ussé, a little further east.

Before phylloxera, many varieties were used, but with the replanting at the end of the nineteenth century, the selection diminished to Cabernet Franc, Cabernet Sauvignon, Côt, Pineau d'Aunis, Gamay Noir, Grolleau Noir (aka Groslot) and Grolleau Gris. Grolleau has become the main variety in Rosé d'Anjou, and is allowed only in rosé, not red.

The similarity in name and style means that many consumers confuse these two rosés. Rosé d'Anjou is the more commercial, and described by Jancis Robinson as being 'often grimly sweet' and compared to a Californian Zinfandel blush. Cabernet d'Anjou, which has higher amounts of residual sugar, with no limit to sweetness, is regarded as the finer wine.

Rosé d'Anjou

During the nineteenth century, the wines of Anjou were shipped to Paris, and gained renown as the wines of the bars, cafés and nightclubs. The *négociants* dictated wine styles and the quantity required, with sugar covering any unripeness. They pushed for the appellation Rosé d'Anjou, which was granted in 1957. It can be made with Cabernet Franc, Cabernet Sauvignon, Côt, Pineau d'Aunis, Gamay Noir, Grolleau Noir and Grolleau Gris. As there are so many potential combinations of varieties, there is no consistent style. This made it easier for producers but did not encourage quality. The finished wine must have a minimum of 7g/l residual sugar and a minimum of 9% abv.

Rosé d'Anjou remained popular, especially in cafés and restaurants. In 1959, Ian Fleming's *Goldfinger* has James Bond going to the Hôtel de la Gare and drinking an iced pint of Rosé d'Anjou with a large *sole meunière*.

Many modern domaines were started during the 1960s and 70s boom time, but after their hour of glory in the 1970s, interest turned from Loire rosés, and quality declined, followed by a reduction in production. Its success was part of its downfall; Rosé d'Anjou was known as a cheap, generic wine in the local market, mostly sold in north-west France. In 1989 Joanna Simon wrote in *The Sunday Times* that 'Personally, I do not much like Rosé d'Anjou (medium sweet and usually made from

Groslot) … but they are popular, especially with people who have spent their holidays in the Loire.'

With the decline in Rosé d'Anjou, Grolleau started to fall out of favour: plantings have dropped to around 2,000 hectares (2016), around 15 per cent of Loire vine plantings, mostly in the middle Loire region, but it remains the third most cultivated red grape variety in the Loire after Cabernet Franc and Gamay. Five clones of the Grolleau vine can be used.

As Grolleau is high-yielding, yields must be controlled, although pruning (for maximum exposure to sun) allows for higher yields than for red wines. The grapes ripen reliably and relatively early for the cool climate. They are typically thin-skinned with few phenolic compounds, with a range of colour intensity depending on the clone.

In a move away from simpler rosés made with young vines and high yields, **Domaine de Flines** (vinsmottron.com) – 100 per cent Grolleau – and Domaine de Clesserons – 75–80 per cent Grolleau, 20–25 per cent Pineau d'Aunis – use older vines with lower yields, to make Rosés d'Anjou which are less perfumed, but place more emphasis on the soft, ripe, fresh strawberries, cherries and raspberries, with barely-there mineral structure, and well-balanced sweetness and acidity.

The inclusion of lighter (or white) grapes in a rosé blend is used in many regions to allow for extended maceration without the deeper colour. Jean Louis Lhumeau of **Domaine des Hautes Ouches** (vinsjean-louislhumeau.com), combines 50 per cent Grolleau Noire with 50 per cent Grolleau Gris to produce a light pink rosé with maximum flavour from very ripe grapes, harvested later than most winemakers. His Rosé d'Anjou 2016 has intense dried apricots and peach fruit, given added richness from 20g/l residual sugar, balanced with long fresh acidity.

Despite the cheaper commercial reputation of these wines, Rosé d'Anjou made with Grolleau certainly impresses, as a tasting of a few older vintages demonstrated.

A 1989 Rosé d'Anjou from a private cellar had turned a tawny orange colour and had aromas of flowers, herbs and potpourri. On the palate, a long mineral acidity carried the ripe floral and summer fruit. The 1996 from the same cellar, was a dark orange. Aromas were of blue flowers and rose water, while on the palate, leafy acidity, salty apricots with sweet apricot jam and intense dried apricots were noted.

> **Domaine de la Petite Roche**
> 49310 Trémont, France
> Tel.: 02 41 59 43 03
> www.domainepetiteroche.com
>
> When blending Grolleau with the other varieties, winemaker Antoine Poupard commented that it was important to get the most from each of them through different techniques, whether by direct pressure, skin contact or *saignée*. To achieve the required must sugar level, the grapes need to be harvested at full phenolic ripeness, but with sufficient acidity to balance the sugar and give the essential fruit-sugar and fruit-acid balance. Vintage variation can also contribute to overly high acidity, especially with Grolleau. A minimum sugar level at vintage is essential, but acidity is even more crucial. Poupard will harvest before the acidity starts to fall, even if the sugar is not as high as he wants. Prioritizing acidity over sugar changes the style vintage to vintage, but the balance must be right.
>
> The date of harvest and maturity of the variety affects the length of time for maceration. Harvested too early, Grolleau can take on peppery notes with longer than five to six hours skin contact. Poupard carries out cold maceration (8-10°C) for his Grolleau for 12-24 hours, which helps to soften the acidity, and contributes a feeling of roundness to the wine. Evidence of the fine balance achieved and weight from extraction can be seen in Poupard's Rosé d'Anjou (80 per cent Grolleau, 20 per cent Gamay), which has intense floral notes (violets) and exuberant cherry and raspberry fruits. With around 20g/l residual sugar, the sweetness is cut by mandarin acidity. The arrested fermentation leaves the wine with a delicate 10.5% abv.

Cabernet d'Anjou

The first Loire rosé made entirely from Cabernet grapes appeared in 1905. It was popularized on French radio by the long-running comedy drama of *La famille Duraton* (1935–55). M. Duraton enjoyed cooking and particularly liked Cabernet d'Anjou. The appellations for Cabernet d'Anjou and Saumur, made only with Cabernets Franc and Sauvignon, were created in 1957. Cabernet d'Anjou is the best-selling rosé in France after Provence rosé, with a less seasonal market than drier rosés

To ensure sufficient residual sugar levels, the must levels should have a minimum sugar content of 170g/l. The finished wine for Cabernet d'Anjou must have 10g/l or more residual sugar (with no upper limit), with 10.5% abv. These high sugar levels are understandable when you see these vineyards sloping down to the river Layon and touching the vineyards of Bonnezeaux. The winemakers who make these sweet rosés also produce unctuous Chenin Blancs.

Some producers discussed the impact on ageability of the trend towards paler rosés with reduced maceration. Etienne Jadeau at **Domaine de la Gauterie** (www.vignoble-de-la-gauterie.fr) remembered that before the current fashion for very pale rosés, the grapes were macerated to give a more *clairet*-style wine and were generally sweeter. Today, grapes are harvested around fifteen days earlier for fresher fruit, shorter maceration and cool fermentation. Increasingly Cabernet d'Anjou is becoming fresher, drier and paler.

Wines may be made from either Cabernet Franc or Cabernet Sauvignon, as a single variety, or as a blend in any proportion. This evidently influences the style of wine over and above terroir and vinification. The wines mentioned below have between 20 and 30g/l residual sugar.

Some Cabernets d'Anjou have a peach Melba character of ripe peaches, redcurrants and a hint of creamy vanilla. **Domaine des Fontaines'** (www.domainedesfontaines.com) wine made predominantly from Cabernet Franc, with 30g/l residual sugar, has a touch of bitter chocolate on the finish; **Domaine de la Clartiere**'s (www.domainedelaclartiere.com) has fresh melon mid-palate, and that of La Petite Roche, as with their Rosé d'Anjou, has perfumed aromas of flowers, rose petals and peaches with added bergamot and exotic and tropical fruit.

Other Cabernets d'Anjou are more evidently Cabernet in character. The wine from **Domaine de la Gauterie** (www.vignoble-de-la-gauterie.fr) – 100 per cent Cabernet Franc – has fresh, leafy acidity, with red berry fruit and summer pudding redcurrant freshness. That of Domaine de Flines (with 24 hours cold maceration) has floral, leafy notes with raspberry and cherry fruit and greater weight. **Domaine des Deux Arcs** (www.domainedesdeuxarcs.com) produces a wine that has strawberries, raspberries and rhubarb, and long, fresh mineral acidity. Chateau de Boissy's has red cherries and strawberries with a hint of bitter chocolate.

Olivier Lecomte at **Château Passavent** (passavant.net/en/) used to macerate for one night to make a *rosé de garde*, but the rosé was regarded as too dark by consumers. A perfectionist, he is working to balance commercial demands with quality. Finding that a lighter colour reduced the intensity of the wine, he has returned to a slightly darker colour with a greater concentration of strawberry and redcurrant fruit (although the use of ambient yeast reduces the overt fruit character). Mineral structure and hints of dry tannins on the end balance the rich sweetness.

At the other extreme of the peach Melba style, and still with the same balance of sugar and acidity, is Jean Louis Lhumeau's rare 100 per cent Cabernet Sauvignon (the Cabernet Franc is kept for his red wine). Typical of his house style, he harvests quite late so that this sweet rosé has more of a red wine character, with dark red berries and strawberries, mineral core, very delicate, dry tannin on the finish and beautifully balanced sugar and acidity.

Over and above these expressions of fruit and balanced sugar and acidity, technological developments have improved quality. Lucie Chassevent, an engineer at the Ecole Supérieure d'Agricultures (ESA) in Angers, has been working on the interaction between terroir, pre-fermentation maceration and yeast, the amount of direct pressure for Cabernet Sauvignon, Cabernet Franc and Côt, and how these varieties need balanced structure with fruit and spice aromas.

The amount of residual sugar in these wines means extra care is required. Clean, healthy grapes are essential. There are also challenges when it comes to stopping the fermentation and leaving the required amount of residual sugar. Stopping the fermentation reveals the skill of the winemaker, as clumsy treatment can ruin the wine. The addition of too much sulphur has been a major cause for the decline in popularity of this wine. Two main methods are used:

Mutage traditionnel involves chilling the wine to 3°C, filtration and some sulphur dioxide. Heavy handling can destroy the wine so high levels of sulphur dioxide are usually needed. Chilling the wine for an extended period of up to three weeks before filtration enables reduced use of sulphur dioxide without the danger of destroying the wine.

Mutage alternative involves new technology, also aimed at reducing sulphur use. After chilling, cross-flow filtration, centrifuge or flash pasteurization are used. In these cases, much lower levels of sulphur dioxide are needed. Further chilling for several weeks is recommended.

Although Cabernets d'Anjou are produced to be drunk when young, tasting older vintages showed that some wines, especially those with slightly longer skin contact, have an excellent ability to age and take on more complex character. The combination of sugar and acidity provides a sound base for ageing, but as with Provence rosés, the change from primary fruit character to more mature, complex ones initially causes confusion.

Tasting the 1959 Château Passavent Cabernet d'Anjou showed how beautifully they can age. In the past, only good vintages, such as this one, were bottled. Although comparable to the sweet wines of Côteaux du Layon, they will never have botrytis as they are harvested earlier. Until recently, the grapes had slightly longer maceration which not only gave a deeper colour, but also greater structure, allowing them to age for longer. This wine, a tawny orange, had aromas of dried figs and apricots. On the palate the same dried fruit was apparent, with honey, and white peach acidity to give freshness, all infused with a delicate floral perfume.

VINS GRIS

'The difference between a *vin gris* and a *vin rosé* is that the former will have been made as if it were a white wine, so that only a very slight colouration from the must or from the skins might be expected, whereas in the latter the colouration is deliberate and results from the fermentation of the must in contact with the skins, the degree of colour being in proportion to the time of contact,' wrote Julian Jeffs in 1971 in his book *The Wines of Europe*.

Vin gris is usually paler than most rosé, an off-white wine tinged with pink. In taste, it can be difficult to tell apart from white. The principal difference between *vin gris* and rosé is in the vinification. *Vins gris* are obtained by direct pressure. The red grapes are pressed after being destalked to obtain a light-coloured juice. The juice is quickly removed from contact with the skin which means that all the fruit, aroma and colour is from the juice alone. It is then fermented in stainless steel tanks, and almost never aged in wood.

Two styles of *vin gris* exist. Wines from more northerly climates have the freshness and acidity of a northerly white wine. Those from hotter regions have more roundness and fruit, in a Provence rosé style. The rosés of Provence have moved from being *clairet*-style rosés to *vins gris*. A *gris de gris* is a *vin gris* made from pale skinned gris grapes (see Chapter 12).

Vin gris of the north

Pink champagne

In the past, rosé champagne was more commonly known as *taché* or 'stained'. In the court of Louis XIV most vineyards in Champagne were planted with black grapes, so if made the normal way, the grapes were shaken *en route* to the press, resulting in rosé champagne rather than the white champagne the court wanted. It was essentially a sign of poor workmanship. The first champagne house to sell rosé was Ruinart, which has records proving it sold this as early as 1764. Veuve Clicquot was the first house to export a rosé champagne, to Switzerland in 1775. In 1851, Cyrus Redding in *A History and Description of Modern Wines* says:

> *The grey Champagne wine is obtained by treading the grapes for a quarter of an hour before they are submitted to the press. A rose-coloured wine is obtained by continuing this process a longer period; but in the arrondissement of Rheims, the rose-coloured wines are only wines of the second quality, lightly tinged with a small quantity of very strong red wine, or with a few drops of a liquor made at Fismes, from elderberries. It is needless to say, that both the taste and quality of the wine are injured by this mixture. Indeed, no one who knows what the wines are at all, would drink rose-coloured Champagne if he could obtain the other kinds.*
>
> *In Haut Marne, a rose-coloured wine is made, called tocanne in the country. The must is racked after being twenty-four hours in the vat. White wine is also made there with the red grape, which is pressed without treading, and the murk thrown into the vat. The Pineau plant is used. The wine made at Montsaugeon will keep many years in bottle. The price of the best kind is thirty-five francs the hectolitre.*

All champagne used to have a pinkish hue, because the colour from the skins of the black grapes that go into champagne leeched into the white juice during pressing. With improvements in crushing technology, the colour grew paler. Late in the nineteenth century, technology had made such strides that a wine made from red grapes could be entirely colourless. This coincided with the belief that proper champagne should be light, in both colour and body.

Sparkling pink wines became popular during the 1920s and into the 1930s, amongst young women who considered themselves bold and daring. 'Pink champagne' was all the rage at Charleston and Black Bottom dance parties. During Prohibition, these were probably made with sweetened bootlegged liquor made fizzy with carbon dioxide. A popular drink, 'Cold Duck' was made from sparkling white wine to which a touch of red burgundy was added, with a touch of sugar to create an off-dry, pink sparkling wine. Sadly, this seems to have been a drink made from mediocre, unripe wines with sugar to cover any faults. The name 'Cold Duck' seems to have originated in Bavaria, where it was called *kalte ende* (cold end), a drink devised to use up the leftovers of sparkling wine. *Ende* became *ente*, meaning duck.

In response, champagne producers slowly started to look at making pink champagne again. The first attempts were not very good, made largely by adding cheap Pinot Noir to standard champagnes to give them their pink-orange colour.

Mme Bollinger did not help pink champagne's cause when, in the 1940s, she declared, in no uncertain terms, that 'champagne is white.' But pink champagne become associated with romance and glamour. Pommery produced a pink champagne for the coronation of Elizabeth II in 1953, on which occasion her sister, Princess Margaret, took quite a fancy to it. Subsequently, she was photographed in Parisian *boîtes* (clubs) with other members of the chic international set, a cigarette in one hand, a flute of pink champagne in the other. Feeling the pressure of a rarefied demand, the champagne houses responded. Pol Roger started making rosé in 1955. Laurent-Perrier were pioneers, with their saignée rosé from the 1964 vintage and launched in 1968 in a distinctive squat bottle. It remains a market leader.

Anecdotal tradition recounts that pink champagne was the artist Salvador Dali's favourite champagne and its surreal reputation continued with the reference in 1976 to 'pink champagne on ice' in 'Hotel California' by The Eagles.

From the 1960s, rosé champagne was firmly part of the repertoire, but quality still needed working on. Jeffs (1971) wrote, 'For some unfathomable reason it has a reputation for outstanding excellence. It certainly looks pretty in the glass. But that is all. It remains a mystery why anyone should be prepared to pay extra for a taint of vulgarity.' He described the vinification of pink champagne, saying it could 'be made in either of two ways: by adding a little of the local red wine, usually Bouzy, or by leaving the skins for a short time in contact with the must. Not a little is accidentally made that way.' Pink champagne styles are discussed in Chapter 8 (pp 159–163).

Côtes de Toul, Lorraine

The vineyards which make Côtes de Toul wine today are the remnants of a once-flourishing wine industry that covered large swathes of both Alsace and Lorraine. The area was not only known for its Riesling; it also produced a significant quantity of base wines for use in the sparkling wines of Champagne.

The dukes of Lorraine and the bishops of Toul owned vineyards, and there are still parcels called La Vigne l'Évêque and Au Chapitre. In 1650 the dukes of Lorraine wrote out rules which remained in effect until the Revolution. The former employees of the bishopric became private domaine owners.

The region reached its peak in 1865 when 6,000 hectares were recorded as planted in Toulois, and 47,000 in Lorraine. In 1882, following years of inefficient vineyard management, industrialization and rural exodus, phylloxera hit the region, leaving its viticultural heritage struggling. The First World War caused depopulation as well as physical destruction from battles. The final blow came in 1919, with the introduction of a law restricting the use of the name 'champagne' to wines made from grapes grown in the Champagne region, preventing the champagne houses using grapes from Toul. Without the once-reliable market, there was little incentive to replant what was left of the region's vineyards.

The wine of the region would have disappeared, had not some thirty wine producers worked hard to keep it going. After the Côtes de Toul VDQS was created in 1951, plantings started to slowly expand in size. In 1998 appellation status was granted, and plantings are now around 100 hectares. Of just over twenty producers, a dozen make their own wine; half of production goes to a cooperative or a *négociant*. Though the appellation allows *vin gris*, red and white wines, *vin gris* makes up 75 per cent of production. Must sugar at harvest has to reach a minimum of 153 g/l. The wine is pressed as for white wine, with slow, gentle, pressure for 6–8 hours. Côtes de Toul *vin gris* is predominantly Gamay, with Pinot Noir. Neither can exceed 85 per cent of the blend; Pinot Noir must make up at least 10 per cent. Secondary varieties Auxerrois, Aubin Blanc and Meunier together cannot exceed 15 per cent of the wine.

The appellation is small, only 20 kilometres in length, on south and east facing slopes. The hills along the Moselle shelter the region from westerly winds. Most of the vineyards are in the south, unsurprisingly considering these are amongst the most northerly vineyards in France. The wine typically develops intense fruity and floral flavours.

Oeil de perdrix de Neuchâtel, Switzerland

The *oeil de perdrix* (or *perdrix blanche*) style is believed to have originated in the Middle Ages in the Champagne region of France, not far from the Côtes de Toul. From the Middle Ages, the Champenois competed with the Burgundians for the favour of the royal court and the lucrative Paris market. As red wine was particularly popular, the more northerly Champagne region had difficulties competing with the fuller-bodied reds of Burgundy. The Champenois began experimenting with creating a fuller-bodied white wine from red wine grapes, that they alone could market. Despite their best efforts, they lacked the technical expertise to make a truly 'white' wine from red grapes (*blanc de noir*), instead producing slightly pale-coloured wines, which became known as *oeil de perdrix* (eye of the partridge).

Somehow, the making of pale pink-white wine from black grapes, along with the name, made its way from Champagne, presumably through Burgundy, to Switzerland and the Canton of Neuchâtel, once part of medieval Burgundy. With the modernization of viticulture and separation of grapes, the term *oeil de perdrix* disappeared in France but remained in Neuchâtel. As with other off-white-pink wines of this period, they may have also been made from a field blend of black and white grapes.

Dr Guyot found the oldest surviving evidence of *oeil de perdrix* in Neuchâtel with a label from 1861 from Domaine Louis Bovet, a wine maker from Areuse.

Contemporary accounts describe how the vineyards were placed to capture sun on slopes facing south, east and west, beside Lake Neuchâtel. Vineyards planted in the 1850s separated the red and white varieties; white vines were planted where the soil was deep with clay (presumably cooler) and red varieties on the shallower gravel and sandy soils (warmer).

Today, the vines are trained low down near the ground, with a bed of straw on the soil. Specific varieties were chosen to suit the region, such as the white varieties Chasselas or Fendant Gris or Vert, and the red Pineau or Plant de Bourgogne. Easterly exposure and sheltered sunny slopes with gentle breezes result in good maturity, finesse and roundness. Wines are described as light and dry, with a tendency to fizz in the spring. The German cantons were the biggest buyers of the red wine, while Vaud prefered whites. After the Second World War, *oeil de perdrix* became better known, and the market expanded around Switzerland. However, this success led to *oeil de perdrix* wines also being made in the Geneva, Vaud and Valais cantons around Lake Geneva. When the appellation system was created, the Canton of Neuchâtel claimed sole use of the *oeil de perdrix* appellation, but this was refused; now all producers can use the name.

According to Joelle Nebbe-Mornod, of Alpine Wines, the *oeil de perdrix* from Neuchâtel are more extracted, serious and concentrated; they are a little less dry in the Valais and lightest in Geneva. Benoit de **Montmollin** (www.domainedemontmollin.ch) describes his wines of Neuchâtel as being round and elegant, those from Domaine de Chauvigny (Bevaix) as drier and those from Gorgier as having more intense minerality.

De Montmollin and Louis-Philippe Burgat at **Domaine Chambleau** (www.chambleau.ch) make their wines largely from Pinot Noir. They are part direct pressed with short skin contact from earlier harvested grapes, and part bled off the red wine, especially from parcels with higher yielding, less ripe fruit. The cooperative **Caves de Béroche** (www.caves-beroche.ch) makes three *oeil* cuvées. Their classic cuvée is La Béroche, their premium wine, Domaine de Coccinelles. Coccinelles is made from grapes from the best parcels and includes some Pinot Gris, especially in years when the Pinot Noir is too acid, to give roundness. Jean-Pierre Küntzer of the biodynamic **Domaine Saint-Sébaste** (www.kuntzer.

ch) makes his *oeil* from specially selected parcels, using a traditional vinification with a 24-hours maceration. His wines are considered more concentrated and require a year or two of ageing. **Antoine Bovard's** (www.domaine-antoine-bovard.ch) in Lavaux, exclusively uses juice bled off his red wines. The ripe fruit makes for opulent redcurrant and strawberry fruit.

Vin gris of southern France

Sable des Camargue, formerly Sables du Golfe du Lion

This wine is made in three departments: Gard, Hérault and the Bouches du Rhône, under IGP Sable de Camargue. This covers 100 kilometres of the coastal region, between beaches, coastal lagoons, salty marshes, forests and *garrigues*. The area between Saintes-Maries de la Mer and Aigues Mortes produces the most wine, largely with Grenache, on land reclaimed from the Rhone delta in the nineteenth century, when ditches and pumps were constructed.

The principal enterprise has always been salt production but vines were also grown. The earliest records of les Sables vineyards were royal letters patent in the fourteenth century, and of vine on the Isle de Stel, the early fifteenth century. Since medieval times the canals (*roubines*) and drainage channels have allowed the area to be cultivated. The Compagnie des Salins du Midi planted vines in the 1880s, unusually on their own rootstocks, as the sandy soil protected them from phylloxera. Following the Second World War, the vineyards and canals were reconstructed. The company **Listel** (www.listel.com; named after Isle de Stel), was founded in 1955, to create a *vin gris* rosé brand. The indication 'Vin des Sables', covering almost 3,000 hectares, was officially created in 1961 changing to Vin de pays des Sables du Golfe du Lion in 1973, and becoming IGP Sable de Camargue in 2011. In 1986 Maureen Ashley MW said that Listel's rosés 'tend to be in the white wine style rather than the red, if you know what I mean. Superb winemaking was ever present, most noticeably in the Domaine de Jarras 1985.'

The land is made up of sands and minerals brought in by the sea winds. Between the salt marshes and the plain of the Camargue, the beaches, 'petite Camargue', lagoons, reeds, sand dunes and pine forests, lie the vines of the Sable de Camargue. The climate is maritime Mediterranean. In winter, the sand is susceptible to wind erosion, with sand dunes forming amongst the vines. To stabilize the sand, hedges made of stakes are placed in the sand, which is then planted with grass during the winter, to protect the area from heavy winds.

The smallest properties are no more than a few rows of vines owned by families. Grenache Noir and Gris are principal varieties, and on the sandy soils give paler wines, as seen in Tavel. Direct press with minimal skin contact and a cool fermentation of 14–18°C result in very pale, fresh wines.

Vin gris in the Languedoc

The village of Bessan lies on the Hérault river, near the city of Béziers, just off the major east–west Roman road *via Domitia*. Its port, on the river Orb, was used to ship wines and other spirits. Bessan was known for producing bulk and sweet wines. Rosés were first recorded as being made here in the nineteenth century as Terret de Bessan. The Terret variety produces white, pink and black grapes due to field mutation, resulting in naturally lighter wines – the darker the grapes, the more highly valued. Bessan rosés were also made with Aramon, possibly bled off the local red wines and therefore more like a *clairet*.

The cooperative was created in 1938 with 350 members; from the beginning, it concentrated on the production of rosé wine. Today, the cooperative has 115 members, cultivating 400 hectares under IGP Bessan. Their rosé no longer includes Terret or Aramon, but must include Cinsault (70 per cent), Carignan, Syrah and Grenache.

The traditions of the rosé de Bessan are upheld through the Confrérie du Rosé et de la Croustade de Bessan association. According to tradition, the rosé wine was discovered by a local Madame Jacomel de Cauvigny in the early years of the twentieth century, when she had the idea of making the wine just from the juice: a forerunner of the direct press, free-run juice pale rosés of today. The wine is served with a local cake, the *croustade*, made with puff pastry, apples, raisins and nuts, at an annual festival.

Cabrières, west of Montpellier, around 30 kilometres north of Bessan, also has an historical reputation for its pink wine. The archives of Montpellier hold a reference from 1357 to the *vin vermeil* of Cabrières which was probably more of a *clairet*, as *vermeil* (vermilion) implies a deeper colour than a light rosé. It was still made into the twentieth century: Rosemary George MW noted seeing a bottle of *vin vermeil* from 1950. The Cave Coopérative des Vignerons de l'Estabel, founded in 1937, produced nothing but Cinsault-based rosé until around 1950. George, during her interview with the president of the cooperative, M. Trinquier, noted that he remembered rosé being sent in barrel to England in the early 1950s, although they started bottling in 1948. Today the rosés of Cabrières are still allowed a higher proportion of Cinsault (minimum 45 per cent) than is usual in the Coteaux Languedoc.

4
THE ROSÉS OF PROVENCE

After centuries of light red and pink wines, the current fashion for rosé wine has taken the world somewhat by surprise. The rosés of Provence have been at the forefront of this so-called rosé revolution, and are regarded as the market leader.

Surprisingly, despite this popularity, often little is known known of Provence's rosés, other than their pale pink colour, ripe fruit and dry finish. Philippe Guillantin, of **Château Margüi** (www.chateaumargui.com), is concerned that making rosé as a technological wine that can be produced anywhere will leave Provence struggling to copy its own style. If the only definition of Provence rosé is that it is a pale pink, dry wine with hints of fruit and minerality, it could fall victim to imitation 'Provence-style' wines from around the world.

HISTORY

Provence, the first province of the Roman Empire, has had a long history of winemaking as part of the local polyculture. Farms with vineyards, olive groves, grain, fruit, vegetables and livestock existed throughout the region. Access was never easy, due to the ranges of mountains and hills between the Alps and the Rhône. Its best-known wines were, until the mid-twentieth century, from vineyards near the coast and major rivers. With the difficulties of transport, it was noted that white wine, often lightly sparkling, travelled badly, but that red was sturdier. Some reds were exported to America through the port of Toulon.

Red and white wines were made and, like elsewhere, a range of colours in between. The colour depended on the proportions of red and white

66 ROSÉ

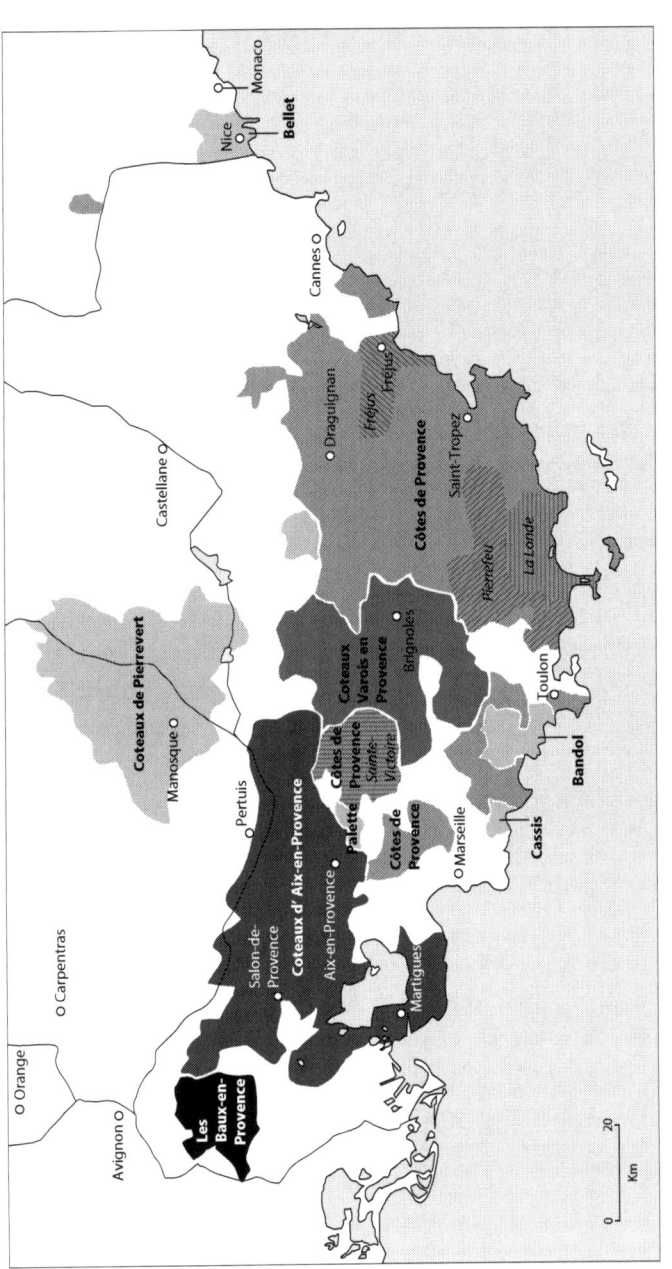

The rosés of Provence

grapes: 'the proportion which should be kept between the quantity of these kinds is different, according to the design which everyone has of keeping their wines,' wrote Philip Miller in *The Gardener's Dictionary* (1768). 'Those that desire to have a wine of deeper red, should make more than half the quantity of all the rest.' In a dictionary of Provence (1835), the noted local wine of Trets (Sainte-Victoire) was a *vin clairet* and in the 1860s, the Marseille town hall served red, white and sweet muscat wine, but not the local *clairet*, which was 'neither red, nor white, but between the two.'

The best areas for wine were where the weather was gentle, the soil fertile and the vineyards surrounded by forests, olive groves and fruit orchards, moderated by maritime breezes. To shield the grapes from the hot sun, the vines were sheltered by olive and fruit trees, or were trellised high with grapes hanging under the leaves, keeping them fresh and juicy. In hot areas, the grapes were often dried and raisined. The local sweet *vin cuit* (local wine, cooked and reduced until sweet) was sometimes added to strengthen the red wine. The different soils throughout the region were identified as early as 1781 by M. Muraire,[2] along with the qualities they gave to the wines. The regions identified then correspond to the current *dénominations de terroir*, other than areas which are now built up.

The most praised wines in the eighteenth and nineteenth centuries by the first tourists to the region, doing the Grand Tour, were the sweet Muscats of Saint Laurent du Var, made from grapes dried on the vine. In 1820 M. Lardier talks of sweet wines – which may have been pink – such as those made with two-thirds Muscat and one-third Mourvèdre in Cassis. M. Courvechel[3] talks of sweet wines made with Tibouren, popular with desserts from Antibes to Marseille. In 1835, James Busby (regarded as the founder of Australian viticulture) recorded conversations with Ferand Negrel (a local producer) about the quality of the local sweet wine made with dried Muscat, Panse and Arignan grapes. Negrel mentioned the high-yielding black variety Bouteillant which was used for making red wine, but had weak colour. The best red variety, Brunfourcat, was lower-yielding (and is still to be found in the appellation of Palette at Château Crémade).

---

2 Author of *Mémoire sur les espèces de raisins de Provence qui sont les plus propres à faire les vins de la qualité la meilleure.*
3 *Traité des Fruits, tant indigènes qu'exotiques et dictionnaire carpologique* (1839).

From the nineteenth century, with the advances in making bigger, more powerful reds, full-bodied wines became increasingly popular, and the light-red wines were less frequently made. After phylloxera hit the region in the 1880s, the opportunity was taken to replant different varieties. Despite the former popularity of the sweet wines, Muscat was less popular compared to the higher-yielding vines such as Alicante and Carignan.

In the 1880s, the Calais–Méditerrannée express train started bringing wealthy holidaymakers south. A group of property owners with vineyards in the Var decided to group together, in 1895, to pool their efforts to improve the image and quality of their wine. In 1923, the train was renamed *le Train Bleu*, a name used in English advertisements, exhorting British holidaymakers to: 'Summer on the French Riviera by the Blue Train', bringing in even more tourists.

The tourism boom was short-lived. From 1929, the Great Depression reduced the number of wealthy British and American travellers to the Riviera. In 1936, the new Popular Front government in France introduced the paid two-week vacation for French workers. Second-class and third-class sleeping cars were added to the train to carry middle and working-class French people on holiday to the South of France. After the private railway companies in France were nationalized, in 1938, *le Train Bleu* was run by the new French national railway company SNCF as an ordinary night express train.

Despite the economic downturn, progress was being made in the vineyards. In 1933, a group of young winemakers, including Baron Henri Rasque de Laval, owner of **Château Sainte Roseline** (www.sainte-roseline.com), and Marcel Ott of Château de Selle, formed the Syndicat des propriétaires vignerons du Var to support one another and promote their wines. Ott, an agricultural engineer, had come from Strasbourg to Provence in 1896. In 1912 he bought Château de Selle, in 1936 **Clos Mireille** (www.domaines-ott.com) and by 1938 was exporting rosé to the US. In 1936 Gabriel Farnet, a local producer from Domaine de Châteauneuf in Vidauban, bought **Château Minuty** (www.minuty.com).

After the Second World War, glamourous holidays on the Côte d'Azur were re-established and the Cannes Film Festival, delayed from 1939, started in 1946. This link to tourism is vital in the development of Provence wines. Without even being exported, these wines reached a wide audience, as tourists from around Europe and America visited the region. The wines became associated with summer holidays, and the dark pink wines, looking particularly pretty in the summer sunlight, helped return glamour to Provence.

In 1947 experts at Institut National de l'Origine et de la Qualité (INAO) selected twenty-three domaines in central Provence as part of a study to evaluate the terroir, and the quality of each domaine. In 1951, Côtes de Provence was granted the status of VDQS (Vin Delimité de Qualité Superieure). Surveys were carried out and maps drawn up of the terroirs and winemaking traditions. During this period, estates increasingly moved from polyculture to viticulture. In 1955, the twenty-three domaines which had been studied from 1947 were designated *crus classés*. Almost all belonged to wealthy landowners with châteaux.

In the same year (1955) as the domaines declared *crus classés* – of which four were on the Saint-Tropez peninsula (Château Minuty, Domaine de la Croix, Château Saint-Maur, Domaine du Noyer) – *And God Created Woman,* directed by Roger Vadim and starring Brigitte Bardot, was filmed in Saint-Tropez. They ate at a café on Pamplonne Beach, which was renamed Club 55, marking the arrival of the jet set in the region. This was a pivotal event contributing to the rosé fashion during the 1950s.

In 1956 the VDQS appellations Coteaux des Baux de Provence and Coteaux d'Aix were officially recognized. Between 1956 and 1962 the return of French colonists, *pieds noirs,* from Algeria, Morocco and Tunisia, many of whom had been winemakers, gave a new impetus in the creation of wine estates. Georges Brunet, who arrived from Algeria in 1958, restored Château la Lagune in the Haut-Médoc, before moving to Provence, creating Château Vignelaure in 1962. He brought cuttings of Cabernet Sauvignon which he successfully planted and blended with Syrah. As a result, Cabernet has been a typical part of the make-up of the wines of Coteaux d'Aix.

MODERN TIMES

The early 1970s saw a leap forward as the wines of Provence became recognized by a wider market. In 1977, the appellation Côtes de Provence was created, under the aegis of Fernand Brun of Château la Brigue, then president of the Syndicat. This marked the start of growing expertise in winemaking. The first Montpellier-trained winemaker in Provence, Emmanuel Gaujal, arrived at **Château Montaud** (www.vignoblesravel.com), owned by the *pied noir* family Ravel, in the 1970s. Gaujal then moved on to Vignelaure, where he employed a young Eloi Durrbach from the newly created Domaine Trevallon, and Philippe Bru. Bru stayed on at Vignelaure, and Durrbach returned to his family domaine, taking with him Cabernet cuttings. Gaujal went on to be responsible for creating many Provence wines.

The quantity of Provence appellation wine increased when, in 1985, Coteaux d'Aix was granted full appellation status. In May 1986, the French marketing office SOPEXA held a tasting of French rosés, with 'unsurprisingly, plenty of examples from Provence.' Maureen Ashley MW reviewed the tasting for *Decanter*. Among the wines she singled out from Provence, regional character was evident. The Marquis de Saporta Cuvée Spéciale 1985 (Coteaux d'Aix) had 'an addition of about 10 per cent Cabernet Sauvignon to the standard Grenache/Cinsault/Carignan blend – a proportion that is likely to increase in future years. It was light and delicate with a touch of tannin and with bags of aroma.' Ashley noted that the rosé from Château Minuty, Saint-Tropez was a 'warmer, stronger wine but with a good flavour and balance' and that from Saint-Roch-les-Vignes in Cuers-Pierrefeu was 'dry, slightly earthy, powerfully flavoured and with good balanced acidity.' In 1989 Joanna Simon commented that the Loire, Bordeaux and Bergerac had better-value rosés, but many would want the 'characteristic scent and soft herbal fruit flavour of a Provence', as typified by Carte Noir of Les Maîtres Vignerons de Saint-Tropez. These stronger, herbal characteristics, with notes of the Provence *garrigue*, were typical of Provence rosés of this time.

Tourism was boosted further in the late 1980s with the publication of Peter Mayle's book *A Year in Provence* and the films *Jean de Florette* and *Manon des Sources*. Tourists arrived in increasing numbers, no longer just for holidays on the coast, but also in the *arrière pays* (hinterland). Rosé again became associated with a desired lifestyle. Sales from the cellar door became important to many local vineyards, with some relying on the flow of tourists renting villas, then buying their wines in local restaurants. However, as Joanna Simon noted in 1989, after taking wine home '… bringing the taste home is often fraught with disappointment. On the one hand, the wine never *tastes* quite the same, because even ex-holidaymakers equipped with a barbecue smouldering with *herbes de Provence* cannot quite manage to recreate the magic of the Mediterranean.' Simon went on to complain about the quality of Provence rosés sold in the UK, as 'the wine is often *not* quite the same because many Provençal rosés sold in the UK are already old and stale. It is a vicious circle; people overcome their prejudices against pink when they are abroad, only to have them reaffirmed back home.'

Changes were happening. In 1985, Régine Sumeire, of **Château La Tour de l'Éveque** (www.toureveque.com) and **Château Barbeyrolles** (www.barbeyrolles.com), both Côtes de Provence, visited her friend Jean-Bernard Delmas at Château Haut-Brion in Pessac, near Bordeaux. In the cellar, she saw he was using an old hydraulic Coq press, which Delmas said he had been using for pressing whole-bunch white grapes very successfully, and suggested she try the same. That harvest, Sumeire decided to test the press on the first grapes harvested, some Grenache. The results were as much a surprise to Sumeire as anyone else. The juice came out fresher, with great acidity and with less of the heavier herby character. It was also, incidentally, paler. Her first commercial bottling in 1987 of a pale rosé, took some time to be accepted.

In 1990, the Farnet-Matton family at Château Minuty, next door to Sumeire's Château de Barbeyrolle in Gassin, decided to expand their business. Their big achievement then was working with temperature control from the moment the grapes were harvested and throughout the cellar. Grenache oxidizes easily and Grenache-based rosés were often an orange colour. Temperature control had remained a difficulty. Running cool, clean water over the tanks was good, if there was sufficient water. Blocks of ice and fans were an extra back-up. The Farnet-Mattons installed cooling heat-exchange coils round the tanks allowing for cool fermentation that produced fresh, fruitier styles of rosé that were lower in sulphites.

Sumeire's first vintages in the early 1990s caused a ripple of interest. I remember producers talking about this new, more delicate style, aptly named *pétale de rose* (rose petal). Consumers reacted well, so other producers quickly started to follow, often mixing gentle press and *saignée* wine together. This was largely due to the economics, as direct-pressed rosé took grapes away that could otherwise be used for red, while *saignée* left a large quantity of bled juice that could be used in reds but not in rosés. At this time, Sumeire made 20 per cent white wine, 40 per cent red and 40 per cent rosé. By 2017, she was producing almost 90 per cent rosé, in reaction to buyers' demand.

This quality revolution with Sumeire's lighter and more elegant rosé style quickly gained support. François Millo, who joined as director of the Conseil Interprofessionnel des Vins de Provence (CIVP, the Provence Wine Board) in 1992, started to market the rosé wines with vigour. Millo recognized that changing consumer tastes represented a big growth opportunity for Provence rosé, building on a combination of less formal entertaining, lighter Mediterranean cuisine and an affluent younger market.

Producers felt the need to create better wines, in particular rosé, and by 1995 formed an association to support innovation and research into the making of rosé. Through this, Claude Bonnet (local producer and president of the Syndicat from 1980–98) pushed for more concrete action, and in 1999 it moved into headquarters in Vidauban. Bonnet became the first president of the Centre de Recherche et d'Expérimentation sur le Vin Rosé (CREVR). Its first objectives were to research vinification and teach producers about advances in winemaking. Back in 1987, my first memories of going around cellars were of cement tanks with no temperature control, and the smell of sulphur. The introduction of gentler presses and cooling systems was a good start. Now, thirty years on, many wineries are equipped with the Inertys system for their presses, and cellars and fermentation tanks have carefully regulated computer-controlled temperature.

At first, only local producers contacted the CREVR. Research was focused on the terroir, viticulture and vinification techniques. Slowly, producers from other regions and countries started to contact the centre, and knowledge of rosé wine techniques increased. As the quality of Provence rosé has improved, so producers and consumers around the world have come to identify the Provence-style as being the epitome of rosé style. Gilles Masson, director of the centre, is not happy about this and wants to encourage global variety; to aim for all rosé wine in a single style would be self-destructive, and could eventually kill the market.

THE PROVENCE STYLE

With all the talk about 'Provence-style' rosé, let us examine just what that means.

'Provence rosés are pale'

This is partly due to the varieties used. Grenache, Cinsault and Tibouren are all relatively light-pigmented varieties. The Provence appellations also allow white varieties to make up as much as 20 per cent of the blend. Vinification using direct press and free-run juice results in very pale colour. These wines could also, technically, be labelled *vin gris* or *blanc de noir*.

Not *all* Provence rosés, however, are very pale. Mourvèdre, Syrah and Cabernet Sauvignon can give slightly more colour. Longer skin contact and a small percentage of *saignée* can contribute colour.

'Provence rosés are dry'

The maximum amount of residual sugar for rosé is 4g/l. This caused some controversy when it was raised a few years ago from 3g/l residual sugar, and is actually quite a significant point.

Provence rarely has a problem with ripeness of fruit. The 2014 vintage was a difficult year for ripeness. The art in making rosé is to have enough fruit without losing acidity. Sometimes, if the acidity is enough, the fruit can be a little lacking, and leaving up to 4g/l of sugar can make a considerable difference to the perceived fruitiness. Top rosés are generally fermented completely dry.

Patrick Schmitt MW, editor of *The Drinks Business* noted when reviewing the 2017 Rosé Masters that 'there is much quality variation in Provençal rosé, with some wines showing a leanness, and sometimes even a hard herbaceousness – and only the best had mastered the balance of fruit sweetness and citrus freshness, as well as that gently viscous mid-palate, cut short with that all important bone-dry bright finish.' Those that achieved the balance had 'a mix of just-ripe red fruits, a touch of peachy, oily palate weight and a refreshing finish.'

In many other regions, there are winemakers who aim for the dry 'Provence-style', but have 4g/l residual sugar or even higher to balance any unripe acidity.

Provence rosés have 'searingly high acidity'!

Much to my surprise, I have been told that this is one of the qualities of Provence rosé. On the contrary, I would state that they do not.

Considering Provence's hot summers, and with the varieties used, no Provence wine is 'searingly' high in acidity. Dry, mineral (especially on schist soils), or saline (in coastal vineyards) notes, or occasional austerity, could potentially be mistaken for high acidity, but generally, acidity is balanced.

BIG NAMES, HOLLYWOOD AND *NÉGOCIANTS*

In the early 2000s, Sacha Lichine from Bordeaux decided to invest in Provence, buying **Château d'Esclans** (esclans.com), and to make a premium rosé there. Premium rosés did exist, but were sold at modest prices, in style similar to other rosés, with maybe some extra weight and complexity. In 2006 Lichine challenged existing preconceptions that rosé had to be a light, fresh apéritif wine. He marketed his Garrus wine as the most expensive rosé in the world, bringing in Bordeaux winemaker Patrick Léon, and using winemaking techniques more akin to those of white Bordeaux with temperature-controlled barrels.

Garrus had a big impact and made some rosé producers and consumers think differently: maybe rosé did not only have to be light, fresh and relatively inexpensive. Priced at around €80 (US$95) a bottle, the wine was initially bought by the Cote d'Azur yachting crowd, where price and exclusivity made it a major attraction. Today, Garrus is often included on wine lists of upmarket restaurants, as the most well-known example of serious rosé. Lichine showed that by making rosé with the same attention to detail as a great white wine, not only could he command a high price, but serious wine lovers could also appreciate rosé wine. Capitalizing on the success of Garrus and the resulting image of the Château, Lichine has introduced a range of *négociant* wines which, especially in the US, has had phenomenal success, achieving sales of around 4 million bottles of Whispering Angel alone.

Brad Pitt and Angelina Jolie further confirmed the glamour of Provence by renting the wine estate **Château Miraval** (miraval-provence.com) in 2008, to stay there during the Cannes Film Festival. By 2012 they had bought the estate and taken on its winemaking with the help of the Perrin family of Beaucastel. Their 2013 vintage was marketed with considerable success, with the rosé sold *en primeur*, before it was released. The 'Brangelina' effect on the rosés of Provence was considerable, giving the wine film-star status. To satisfy demand, Miraval has had to buy in grapes and is now, in effect a *négociant* wine. The Hollywood connection has continued with, in 2017, George Lucas adding Château Margüi, across the road from Château Miraval, to his Skywalker portfolio.

The rise of the large volume *négociant* wines has been an economic success story and raised the profile of the wines of the region with a classic 'Provence-style' rosé: pale, dry, with ripe fruit and moderate acidity. These *négociants*, either owners of small domaines or with no domaine at all, buy in grapes or wine, either direct from vineyards or via cooperatives, then make it up or blend it according to their own house style. This enables them to produce large quantities. Properties owned by larger businesses, property developers, bankers, film stars, négociants and cooperatives, are often the only ones with the financial ability to heavily invest in technology and staff.

The success of these bulk producers in producing high quality and consistent rosé, ensures a wide reach in the export market and they act as brand-Provence ambassadors. Ott and Minuty have long established success behind them, while the famous d'Esclans, and newcomers Stephen and Jeany Cronk of **Mirabeau Wine** (www.mirabeauwine.com), have shown how they can play social media for their own ends in marketing their wine. Accessing rosé from around the region allows them to use a range of styles and varieties. The art is to have a good blender who can pull the wines together to create attractive, commercial styles.

In many cases, it is these successful, larger operations, which have the money to invest. The major cooperatives employ soil engineers, chemists and winemakers to contribute to the research and development of winemaking.

Based on their marketing successes, smaller individual producers have been able to leverage themselves into the export market. After all, Whispering Angel, Ott, Minuty and the Brangelina Miraval are Provence rosés too.

A SENSE OF TERROIR

At the opposite end of the scale, there are winemakers working to create Provence rosés with a sense of terroir. This is a contentious issue, as for many rosé producers around the world, rosé is a style created by the winemaker, not a wine made to reflect its variety and place. Many Provence producers may be frustrated that they have competition from other regions making 'Provence-style' rosé, but until producers accept that their rosé can reflect their unique origins, this will continue to be a challenge.

Provence is not a single, homogenous region. It has two major geological formations.

- To the north and west, the mountains are gleaming white limestone. This includes the wine regions of Les Baux, Coteaux d'Aix, Côtes de Provence Sainte-Victoire, Palette, Bandol and Cassis.
- The central southern coastline, from Saint-Tropez to Toulon, around the Maures and Tanneron has crystalline rock masses. This includes the wine regions of Côtes de Provence, Côtes de Provence Pierrefeu, Côtes de Provence la Londe and Coteaux Varois.

A third, minor region in terms of quantity of wine produced lies further east from Saint-Tropez and includes the area around Fréjus. Here, the crystalline rock mass is broken up by the red rocks of Roquebrune and the volcanic soils of the Estérel Massif. This includes the wine regions of Côtes de Provence Fréjus.

Provence has seven appellations, all of which include rosé. These can be divided chronologically into three groups:

1. The original appellations of Cassis (1936), Bandol (1941), Bellet (1941) and Palette (1948).
2. Newer appellations of Côtes de Provence (1977), Coteaux d'Aix-en-Provence (1985), Coteaux Varois en Provence (1993), Les Baux-en-Provence (1995).
3. The *dénominations de terroir* or regional zones of Côtes de Provence: Sainte-Victoire (2005), Fréjus (2005), La Londe (2008) and Pierrefeu (2013). Shortly to be joined by Notre Dame des Anges.

The largest of the four original appellations is the coastal appellation of Bandol, which lies on limestone and clay hills. Although best known for its red wines, 70 per cent of its production is now rosé, boosted by high production from the local cooperatives and Château Romassan, part of the group of Ott domaines, which almost exclusively produces rosé. Despite some journalists crying out in horror at this high percentage and fears that red Bandol is decreasing, it is worth pointing out that Mourvèdre is not an easy-ripener, and sites which produce less-ripe fruit are better off as good rosé wine than weak red. Technically the rosés are made from Grenache Noir, Cinsault and Mourvèdre (60 per cent of the total) with a medley of other varieties, but two distinct styles of rosé are emerging in Bandol: those with a high percentage of Grenache, designed for drinking young and fresh, and those with a higher percentage of Mourvèdre, with greater ageing potential. See pages 82–3 for more on Mourvèdre in rosé.

The remaining three appellations are small:

- Coastal Cassis is tiny, with only 200 hectares, of which 30 per cent is rosé. Maritime winds, north facing slopes, limestone and, where possible, altitude contribute to their acidity, freshness, and a frequent hint of saline minerality.
- Palette is even smaller, with only 46 hectares, located just to the east of the city of Aix. The three principal producers are **Château Simone** (chateau-simone.fr), **Château Crémade** (www.chateaucremade.fr) and **Henri Bonnaud** (www.chateau-henri-bonnaud.fr). Their rosés have to be aged eight months before release. Simone and Crémade make delightfully complex rosés which age beautifully.

Bellet, another small (50 hectare) appellation, nestled on the hills behind Nice, is the odd appellation out in the region as, until 1860, it was part of the kingdom of Savoy and has more in common with the wines of Liguria. Currently there are ten domaines with vineyards scattered amongst encroaching urban development. Vineyards are located at around 300 metres altitude, on terraces facing varying directions and cooled by maritime breezes from the south and alpine breezes from the north. A third of the wine is rosé, made largely from the variety Braquet, unique to the appellation. It can have a very floral character with fragrant roses and strawberries (**Château de Crémat** – www.chateau-cremat.fr), wild roses and orange peel (**Clos Saint-Vincent** – www.clos-st-vincent.fr)

and slightly more restrained red fruit (**Château de Bellet's** Baron G – www.chateaudebellet.com).

The main appellation of the region, and maybe one of the best known, apart from Bandol, is Côtes de Provence, with 20,000 hectares – equivalent to 130 million bottles, 90 per cent of which are rosé. It is difficult to define this region due to its size and scope, reaching out to vineyards such as Clos Saint Joseph in the foothills of the Alps, north of Nice, to the vineyards of the Iles de Porquerolles, off the coast of Hyères. Vineyards lie on the coast and on mountain slopes, on a range of soils. There are 420 domaines, 39 cooperatives and 100 *négociants*. For this reason, regional zones have been identified in recent years (see pages 80–82).

Coteaux d'Aix-en-Provence is the second largest region and is equally diverse. The region's borders are the River Durance in the north, the River Rhône in the west, Mont Sainte-Victoire to the east and the Mediterranean in the south. Running east–west across the region, parallel to the sea, is a range of hills. The soils include alluvium, washed down by the Durance and Arc rivers, clay, chalk and sand.

The rosés tend to be a touch darker pink if Cabernet Sauvignon is in the blend, with a fraction more structure and weight, than those of Côtes de Provence. A greater percentage of Syrah and Cabernet Sauvignon is used in these rosés, with Grenache and Cinsault. Syrah tends to become jammy in hot vintages, so picking earlier to make rosé wine probably suits it, contributing to the lovely ripe red fruit character evident in many of the Coteaux d'Aix rosés. The Cabernet Sauvignon, especially in the higher altitude vineyards, contributes to the more structural style of the wines.

Coteaux d'Aix-en-Provence has four distinct zones.

- *Terroir Mediterranéen*: The most southerly, low lying (0–100 metres) area located around the large saline lake Étang de Berre, near the coast. The hottest part of the region is tempered by maritime winds. The most mineral, salty and austere wines can be found here.
- *Terroir du Mistral*: The north-westerly region, located between the lower banks of the Durance and Rhône, rising up to the foothills of Les Alpilles (200 metres). The mistral wind dominates, resulting in dry conditions, preventing rot and moderating the heat. The harvest is a few

weeks behind the coastal vineyards. Château Bas creates a fine rosé with ageing potential

- *Terroir des Coteaux*: Vineyards located on the foothills (*coteaux*) of the Eguilles mountains and the Trévaresse hills, which rise from 100 to 300 metres. North- or south-facing aspects add further complexity. The harvest is a little after the Terroir du Mistral zone.

- *Terroir des Haut Plateaux*: The coolest region, a plateau lying between 200 and 450 metres. The area is colder and more continental, with cooler mountain winds from Mont Sainte-Victoire. Springs are late and autumns fresh. The harvest is the latest in the region. **Châteaux Vignelaure** (www.vignelaure.com), **Revelette** (revelette.fr) and **Pigoudet** (www.pigoudet.com) produce fine wine in this region.

Closely affiliated and sometimes overlapping is the appellation of Les Baux-de-Provence. Originally given its appellation status in 1985 as Appellation Coteaux d'Aix – Les Baux, it was given independent status in 1995. The vineyards are largely divided between the north and the south of the Alpilles mountain. Those to the south tend to have bigger, riper fruit, while wines produced in the north are more austere and Rhône-like. Eighty per cent of production is red and rosé, of which most is red. The rosés of Les Baux are composed of a minimum 60 per cent Cinsault, Grenache and Syrah with a similar requirement as the AOC red wine that no two grapes varieties comprise more than 90 per cent of the blend.

Coteaux Varois en Provence, is an enclave within Côtes de Provence, but identified by vineyards at an average altitude over 350 metres, with some parcels around 500 metres, amongst the highest in Provence. Harvest dates can vary between two to three weeks between the north (sheltered behind the Besillon mountain) and south (touching the valley of Pierrefeu) of the region. The soils are largely limestone, and clay and limestone mixes, but there are also vineyards with gravel and flint soils. The combination of limestone and altitude gives the rosés of Coteaux Varois en Provence good fresh acidity and vibrant fruit. Producers such as **Château Duvier** (www.ferienbeim-winzer.com) in the north and **Domaine du Deffends** (www.deffends.com) in the south show the range of styles.

DENOMINATIONS DE TERROIR OF CÔTES DE PROVENCE

The four *denominations de terroir* are interesting for several reasons. They have been identified by their location and terroir as having the potential to create distinct styles. In addition, stricter rules ensure the unique typicity of each *denomination*, with lower yields and specific varieties. Not everyone is in favour of these micro-zones, fearing they will further confuse the customer.

The Sainte-Victoire denomination, granted in 2005, lies just on the east of the Côtes de Provence appellation. The region has a Mediterranean climate with some continental characteristics – hot dry summers and cold winters. To the south, coastal hills provide shelter from the cooling maritime breezes. The Mont Sainte-Victoire ridge reduces the intensity of the cold, northerly mistral winds, although strong gusts still occur. The white limestone rock of the mountain is said to reflect the sun's light and heat. The poor and shallow soils, formed by limestone and gravel clay sandstone, are well drained and the limestone results in good acidity. The highest vineyards on the lower slopes of Mont Sainte-Victoire benefit from the extra coolness of altitude, the reflected light of the limestone and the high limestone content in the soil, to produce very fine wines. Amongst the highest vineyards are **Domaine de Saint Ser** (www.saint-ser.com) at around 420 metres and **Domaine des Masques** (www.domainedesmasques.com), which achieves altitudes of up to 500 metres. Many domaines in the region have vineyard parcels on these slopes for their premium Sainte-Victoire wines. Above these, the terrain is increasingly rocky, difficult to plant and cultivate, which discourages planting vineyards any higher. The rosé wines, which make up 94 per cent of production, have a juicy, fresh fruit and good acid character. **Château Gassier** (www.chateau-gassier.com) and **Château Ferry Lacombe** (www.ferrylacombe.com) are concentrating on producing premium rosés as their flagship wines. **Mas de Cadenet** (www.masdecadenet.fr) owned by the Négrel family also make fine rosés. Excellent producers such as **Domaine Richeaume** (domaine-richeaume.com) are here but not in the Côtes de Provence appellation.

At the easternmost edge of the Côtes de Provence appellation, the Fréjus denomination, granted in 2005, comprises foothills running from west to east and along the Argens river, flowing south to Fréjus. The effects of the Mediterranean here create a special climate for the Fréjus sector, with maritime breezes moderating the heat.

This region uniquely requires a minimum amount of Tibouren, which contributes to a distinctive elegance. The Fréjus sector has complex soils including some volcanic elements from the Esterel, and vividly red rocky soils.

Only eight domaines currently use the Fréjus denomination, largely because many producers choose not to use the irregularly-ripening and low-yielding Tibouren. **Château du Rouët** (www.chateau-du-rouet.com) and **Château Paquette** (www.chateaupaquette.fr) are two of the leading domaines supporting the Fréjus denomination; Rouët's Fréjus rosé has stony mineral notes with hints of bitter orange spice, ripe peach and floral fruit, finishing with long acidity. Typical of this region, the rosés are quite lean in youth and opening out to show richer fruit with a year's age.

The Garrus wine of Château d'Esclans comes from what is generally regarded as the best terroir in this zone, with vineyards at higher altitude allowing it to benefit from the cooling maritime winds. The vineyard itself is planted with eighty-year-old Grenache vines.

The vineyards of the La Londe denomination are located along the coast south-west of the Maures mountain range, home to outcroppings of extremely weathered shale. The proximity of the sea provides this area with its own microclimate. Winter and summer are temperate. Yearly rainfall is extremely low, sun exposure is high and ventilation from sea breezes is nearly constant and brisk. There are multiple types of soil, varying in the amount of shale and quartzite. **Château Léoube** (chateauleoube.com) and **Château Malherbe** (www.chateau-malherbe.com), with vineyards almost touching the sea, have the bone dry, mineral freshness, balanced by delicate fruit, typical of this region.

I attended an interesting tasting to contrast the rosés of Côtes de Provence Pierrefeu's **Hermitage Saint Martin** (www.hermitage-st-martin.com), and **Château Sainte Marguerite** (www.chateausaintemarguerite.com) of Côtes de Provence La Londe, both of which are owned by the Fayard family and use the same winemaker and winemaking techniques. Both wines are made with 70 per cent Grenache. Sainte Marguerite's Symphonie has 20 per cent Cinsault and 10 per cent

Rolle which gives an extra peach fruit character. Hermitage St Martin in Pierrefeu stopped using Rolle (Vermentino) in their IKON rosé, because they felt it was giving an extra hardness to the rosé when planted on the chalky soil, and the rosé has more delicate red fruit. The Fayards chose not to use Syrah, which would contribute too much red fruit. Pierrefeu, they noted, has more rain, lies further inland and has a chalky soil. The rosé was fresh and mineral. La Londe has a schist soil and is on the coast leading to a rosé that was more austere, with a saline minerality.

The Pierrefeu region is bordered to the southeast by the slopes of the Massif des Maures mountains, and to the northwest by the limestone uplands of the Var. Though the vineyards never reach the sea, the region's climate still benefits from the effects of the Mediterranean, though further inland is hotter. Vineyards are planted at up to 400 metres altitude. Soils are largely red clay, schist and gravel. **Château la Gordonne**'s (www.vrankenpommery.com/en/marque/chateau-la-gordonne) La Chapelle, made from Grenache and Syrah, has the typical mineral, stony dryness of the appellation, combined with the ripe-fruit intensity of this warmer region.

THE FOUR CLASSIC GRAPE VARIETIES OF PROVENCE ROSÉ

Because Provence appellation rosé is always a blend – it must always have at least 10 per cent of a secondary grape – varietal typicity has proved of less interest than that of terroir. The main varieties, Mourvèdre, Tibouren, Grenache and Cinsault are supremely adapted to the climate. Mourvèdre (dark fruits, structural) and Tibouren (fine acidity and floral character) excel in the hot coastal vineyards, while the high sugars of Grenache allow it to be harvested early for acidity and still contribute ripe, red fruits. Cinsault is pretty, floral, pale, and the icing on the cake. Achieving the ripeness without higher levels of sugar is a key indicator of quality.

Mourvèdre

Mourvèdre berries are moderate in size and medium-dark in colour, with very thick skins. These thick skins are important because with its extremely late ripening, Mourvèdre is often still on the vines at the time of the first rains of autumn, and is in its element in the hottest, sunniest regions, with its 'roots in the sea and its branches in the sun' in Bandol, along the coast. Its thick skins protect it from the swelling and splitting to which thinner-skinned grapes (such as Grenache) are susceptible.

Mourvèdre rosé falls into three rough categories.

1. From areas where Mourvèdre does not ripen quite enough (further inland in Provence), which – while providing solid structure – leads to a lack of fruit and charm.
2. From hotter regions (along the coast in Provence) but made in a classic rosé style – fresh, attractive fruit, but with a fraction more weight.
3. A more traditional Bandol-style, made in a reductive way, often by fermenting in oak.

The big question for many producers is what style of rosé they want to produce. To make a rosé for early and quick consumption, from February to October, it is best to avoid Mourvèdre, as its wines need time to open-up.

In Bandol, the style of rosé depends strongly on which market it is destined for, Grenache-based for younger drinking, Mourvèdre-based for rosés which age.

Grenache

One of the principal varieties in Provence rosé; Grenache probably has been the most studied in the making of Provence rosé. High in sugar, even if harvested ten days early to retain acidity, it will still have ripe fruit. Its pale skin means that it rarely produces a rosé with much depth.

However, as noted on page 71, the strong tendency of Grenache to oxidize used to be a major problem. From the 1990s, gentle pressing and temperature control helped overcome this problem. The colour can vary from very pale red-pink through to pink with orange lights, influenced by terroir, ripeness and vinification.

Analysing the influence of the terroir on Grenache is producing interesting results. But for rosé this is still quite new. After years of being regarded merely as a technical wine, made in the cellar, these terroir wines are an essential element of the *denominations de terroir*. Grenache beautifully reflects its terroir, ranging from the more austere mineral style to almost exuberant wild raspberry fruit such as that from the biodynamic **Château Gasqui** (www.chateau-gasqui.fr).

Cinsault

While Grenache has the capability to make great red wines (look no further than Châteauneuf-du-Pape), as well as attractive rosés, in Provence, Cinsault is almost exclusively used for rosé. Its tolerance to drought and heat allows it to retain its naturally light colour and its pretty floral and soft red fruit character contribute a delicate elegance to the blend.

Tibouren

Tibouren is regarded by many in Provence as *the* traditional variety for making rosé, unique to the area. Tibouren is a pale-skinned grape suited to making rosé, as it allows for fuller fruity character to be developed without extracting lots of colour. Early ripening, it does best in sunnier sites, usually the hotter coastal regions with damper maritime winds. Plantings have never been extensive, as it is regarded as slightly temperamental, susceptible to *coulure* (poor fruit-set after flowering), and irregular yields. Most Tibouren is from old vines, but since 2001 the CERVR has researched clonal selection, and a higher yielding clone 57 has been introduced, so plantings now stand at around 450 hectares. DNA analysis suggests a close connection with the equally rare Rossese, used for red wine in Dolceacqua, western Liguria, Italy.

Some critics say that Tibouren contributes an earthy, *garrigue* character to the wine, one often associated with slightly rustic winemaking. The aromas of *garrigue* are more than just dried herbs, and describe the way the aromatic oils of lavender, thyme and rosemary become more intense in the summer sun. From my tastings of rosés with a high percentage of Tibouren, fresh, red fruit with white floral notes and, possibly due to the irregular ripening, fine, long, fresh acidity, is typical. **Clos Cibonne** (www.clos-cibonne.com) has the added complexity of savoury notes behind the wild raspberry fruit, from ageing in large old *foudres* under a light layer of flor yeast, while **Château du Galoupet's** (www.galoupet.com) Tibour has very rich, ripe fruit with creamy acidity.

OAK

The use of oak is hotly debated in Provence; some love it, while others hate it. Styles range from the more overtly oaked wines with weight and structure, such as Château d'Esclans' Garrus, Château Gassier's 946, the oaked rosé of Château Pigoudet (with some saignée for greater balance with the oak), or the Légende wines of **Estandon Vignerons** (estandon.fr) to more delicately oaked styles, such as the Mourvèdre-based rosés Oak from **Château de Brigue** (www.chateaudebrigue.com) or Nuances from **Château du Pibarnon** (www.pibarnon.com) which is also partly aged in amphora.

OLD ROSÉS, *ROSÉS DE GARDE*

The most common descriptive words for rosé include fresh, fruity, lively and floral. All are adjectives which allude to the wine when young. The vibrant, pink colour of these young wines is a positive attribute. White and red wines by contrast have a vocabulary of descriptors to praise their maturity, such as honeyed, nutty, creamy, cedar or dried fruits. Rosé wines do change and take on secondary notes with age but, as with white wines, as long as they maintain their fresh acidity, these more mature notes give added complexity. Words such as nuts, dried orange peel, spice and red fruits appear in tasting notes for older rosés. Régine Sumeire has noticed that her buyers are increasingly asking to taste older vintages to see how the rosé evolves. However, a good sommelier is required to be able to explain how and why an older rose has a different taste profile.

Many wine merchants complain that come the spring and the start of the rosé season, customers demand the new vintage, ignoring older vintages. But frequently, Provence rosés show no signs of fading away for at least three years, with many showing attractive mature fruit character and richness after a year or two in bottle. Brian DiMarco of Barterhouse Wines in New York expressed frustration that customers will ignore rosés showing age and complexity in favour of young, and often still 'closed' wines. This is a challenge Provence producers are now addressing seriously by looking at varieties, ripeness at harvest, different yeasts, use of *saignée* off red wines (for some tannins), oak, lees ageing and malolactic fermentation to create wines with greater weight, complexity and ability to age.

As long as the wines continue to show fresh vibrant acidity, to support more complex and mature fruit, they are attractive wines, but the vocabulary for assessing these wines is slightly different. The wines move on from being light, fresh and mineral with red fruits or peach notes. Cooler vintages, such as the 2014, which had been quite lean in youth, show with age, softer acidity and more complexity, with fruit flavours coming to the fore. Hotter vintages age more erratically. The pink colour seems to last for at least four years before taking on more golden colours, and the fruit starts to move from fresh to dried fruit. After six years of ageing, the ability to age, or not, becomes far more evident with a greater divergence of styles. This could also be due to the fact that six years ago, fewer producers were considering making a rosé which could age. Examples of rosés made to age show potential. The 2008 Nectar, from **Grand Cros** (www.grandcros.com), made with longer maceration and some oak ageing, was still youthful even with nine years of age, with ripe, creamy fruit, fresh acidity and well-integrated oak. Cuvée du Temple 2003, **Château Bas** (www.chateaubas.com), Coteaux d'Aix, made by Philippe Pouchin, who has been working on making *rosés de garde* using ambient yeast and oak ageing, still had youthful ripe strawberry and Griotte fruit as well as more mature intense strawberry confit, honeyed orange and fresh mineral acidity. Mourvèdre-based rosés from Bandol are well known for their ageing ability.

With age, rosés can develop in different ways. Some take on rich, bitter orange; marmalade and dried apricot notes generally start to emerge. Some develop rich peach and cream character while others develop rich red fruit notes. Floral details, either perfumed or potpourri, develop. The reasons for the variations appear to be vintage driven, with vertical tastings of some wines displaying all three styles.

The oldest example of Côtes de Provence rosé I have tasted (the very last bottle of its vintage in the cellar) was the 1992 Grand Cros – twenty-five years old! A pale tawny colour, with aromas of brown sugar with savoury hints, its fruit character had long since evolved into bitter orange, black chocolate and salty acidity. Despite an oxidative character, the acidity was still very long and fresh. The umami character of the wine, while not rosé was delicious and would have complemented strong cheeses, such as gouda with cumin or mature goat's cheese.

CONCLUSION – DIVERSITY AND EVOLUTION

A good Provence-style rosé will have ripe fruit without being overtly fruity and fresh but not high acidity; the wines are dry, often with a mineral or saline structure. But styles are changing. Ten years ago, the aim was to make a rosé which was simply fresh and vibrant, often with crisp, red fruit and zesty grapefruit notes. Today, diversity is the key. There is space for many variations: fresh aperitif style, a weightier, creamy wine that is oaked and aged, or simply a more intense rosé which reflects more closely its terroir.

Understanding what the terroir of Provence contributes, continuing to work on the quality of the wine and experimenting to raise the level – producing rosés which age, or adopting different techniques, for example – is the way ahead.

More important are the producers who are taking their wine one step further and experimenting and exploring different ideas to make more serious and more complex rosés. By being the market leader, the onus is now on the region to lead the way in advancing the rosé style, while at the same time encouraging a diversity of styles around the world.

As Louis Fabre of **Château l'Aumerade** (www.aumerade.com) said at the recent fortieth anniversary celebrations of Côtes de Provence, the young generation has grown up with the wealth and success of Provence rosé. They cannot remember the poverty when it was a backwater appellation. It is up to this generation to take Provence forward, but *how* is still to be decided.

5
CLASSIC FRENCH REGIONAL ROSÉS

Whilst not regarded as major rosé producing areas, Bordeaux, the Loire, Alsace, Burgundy and Beaujolais produce an interesting range, made primarily from Merlot, Cabernet Sauvignon, Cabernet Franc, Pinot Noir and Gamay. These modern classics, often made by producers well-known for their red and white wines, illustrate the continuing evolution of rosé wine.

BORDEAUX

The Bordeaux region has a fresh climate, with a cool, oceanic influence, and interesting terroirs, making it suitable for creating fresh and delicate pinks from blends of Merlot, Cabernet Sauvignon and Cabernet Franc.

In 1975, the English wine writer Pamela Vandyke Price wrote that, 'It would be [uneconomic and] impractical if, in the Médoc region of Bordeaux, where red wines predominate, a producer attempted to make a pink wine, although in certain bad years, wines of impeccable estates are deep pink rather than red; they are, however, *not* sold as "vin rosé".' Attractive style rosés were found elsewhere in the south-west region. Joanna Simon (1989) was enthusiastic about the fruity rosés of the south-west, mentioning 'the glorious 1987 Château la Jaubertie Bergerac Rosé, an exuberantly fruity blend of merlot and cabernet sauvignon' and 'an appealingly juicy cabernet sauvignon, Côtes de Gascogne 1988 Domaine de Lafitte.'

Esme Johnstone at **Château de Sours** (www.chateaudesours.com) made a small quantity of rosé which achieved near cult status during

90 ROSÉ

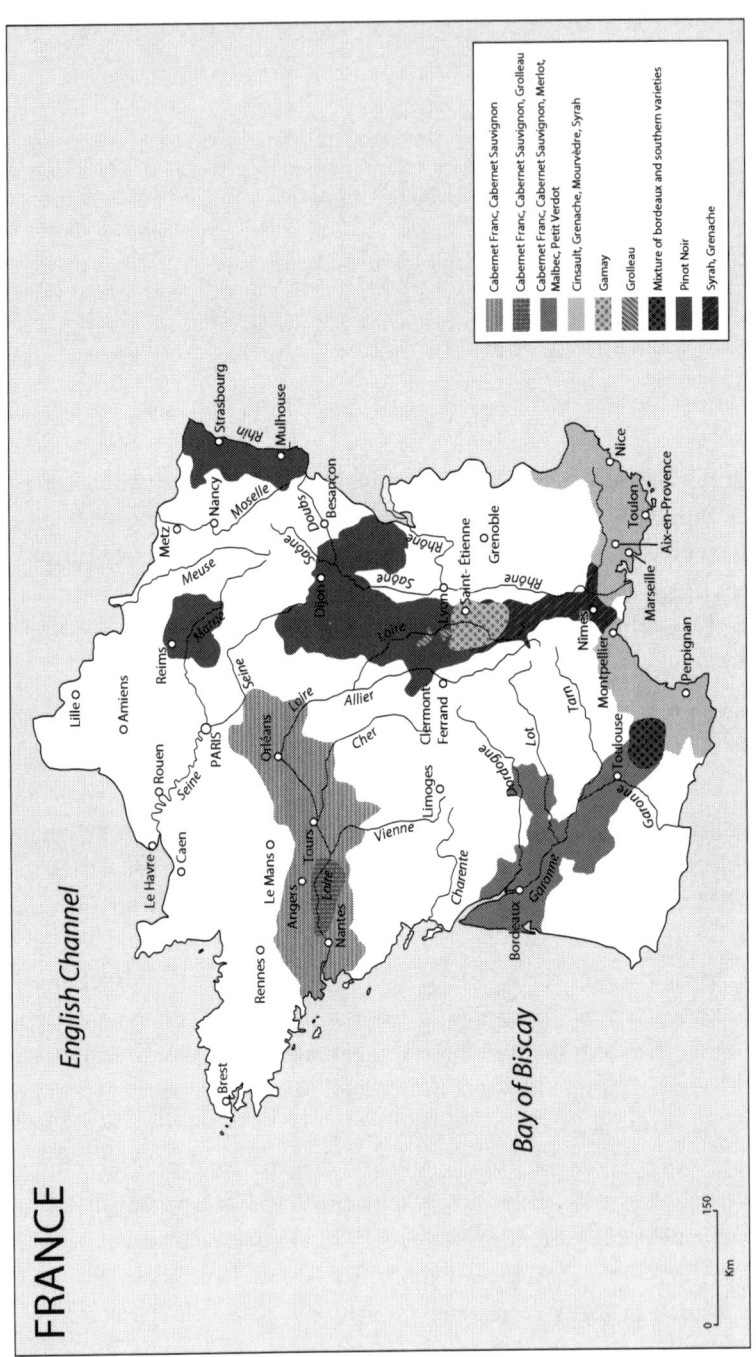

A simplified guideline to the varietal styles of French rosé.

the 1990s and revitalized the move towards modern Bordeaux rosé production. Auberon Waugh described it in *The Spectator*, in 1992.

> *A massive attack, a gigantic explosion of every fruit known to man, it in fact comes from the merlot grape, bled off within minutes of the must touching the skins and fermented very cold, very slowly. This wine is completely unlike any other I have tasted. Blind-tasted, it might be identified as some sort of sauvignon blanc on super-boost. I have been told that one in a hundred people finds it utterly disgusting, but I have yet to meet such a one. Everybody I have given it to has raved about it. The 1990 was the first rosé I had recommended for six years. The 1991 has a slightly paler, less bilious colour but is, if anything, even better. It is, quite simply, a marvellous wine, possibly the best rosé in the world.*

In 1991 Régine Sumeire also launched her pale Pétale de Rose rosé in Provence, influenced by conversations with Bordeaux winemakers regarding their white wine production.

In Bordeaux, there appears to have been a surge in replanting vines around 2000. An increase in rosé production could be attributed to producers using young vines, not yet ready for red-wine production, for rosé. Château de Sours, until 2010, made their rosé with young vines after a large amount of replanting. As these vines have aged, they are of greater interest for red-wine production, which makes greater economic sense, as quality red wines achieve a higher price. It remains to be seen whether rosé will be made from other young vines being planted, or from vineyards specifically dedicated to their production. Successful sales make it unlikely they will reduce production.

In 2006, Sacha Lichine, with Bordeaux winemaker Patrick Leon, launched Garrus in Provence. This was billed as the most expensive rosé in the world, not as a marketing gimmick, but because it was made like a serious white wine, fermented and aged in barrel. Did this rosé trigger some winemakers to reconsider the potential of serious rosé? In 2006 Richard Bampfield MW held an informal tasting with Jean Christophe Mau of Château Brown, and some English journalists on a *pinasse* (flat-bottomed boat) on the Bay of Arcachon, where the potential of dry rosé came up in conversation. D'Esclan was not yet a big phenomenon, and no record seems to have been kept of the tasting, but Richard remembers that rosés from Domaine Ott and Bandol's Domaine de Pibarnon were included. The event was repeated in 2007, and in 2008 when Gavin Quinney of Château Bauduc joined them.

The event proved an important sounding board. Until the 2007 vintage, Quinney had done maceration overnight before bleeding off the juice. Following the tasting, he decided his rosé was too strong, so from the 2008 vintage made a lighter, more delicate style with direct press. This was more successful, becoming the house rosé at Rick Stein's fish restaurant in Padstow, south-west England.

When, in 2010, the Bordeaux Wine Board (CIVB) was reviewing its marketing strategy and the role of Bordeaux in the international market, the members saw that *clairet*, with its darker colour, was becoming a niche product, while the paler pink, dry rosés were more internationally recognized and were reaching out to a younger, dynamic market. Promoting these more modern rosés was perceived as a means of attracting a new, younger audience to the wines of Bordeaux. As Allen Sichel of the CIVB said, 'in attracting consumers to the category, one feature stands out as particularly important, the colour. It needs to be pale. The pale colour is quite universal, all consumer research agrees.' Provence rosés are seen as the epitome of fashion, and are commonly served at the Atlantic beach restaurants where many Bordelais take their holidays.

Pale rosé production has grown to five times that of *clairet*. In 2011 624 hectares were given to *clairet*, compared to 3,422 for rosé. From 2011 to 2014 Bordeaux rosé sales grew 36 per cent. Despite these figures, production remains small, with *clairet* and rosé together making up 4 per cent of the region's production in 2016.

However, it is not the extreme paleness of colour which is important. For Quinney, the shade of pink is more important, its prettiness. Bordeaux rosés have a blue tinge, with no hints of orange-salmon. This character of Bordeaux rosés comes from the terroir, varieties and their acidity. The most obvious difference between *clairet* and rosé, according to the appellation regulations, is the colour, with *clairet* being significantly darker, verging on pale red. The intensity of colour (ICM) is measured to decide the type. *Clairet*, with its longer maceration, has to measure 0.9 to 2.5 ICM with aromas of ripe fruits, good weight with some structure, and can be defined as a light red. Bordeaux rosé has to measure 0.4 to 1.2 ICM with aromas of floral notes and fresh fruit and a light, fresh palate.

This highlights an issue for all regions with both *clairet*-style and pale rosé style: how to make them different? The aim is not to have increasingly weaker versions of the red wine, but to create two different wines.

Starting in the vineyard, rosé producers will assess several plots. This can change from year to year, but generally, the cooler, fresher parcels are favoured for rosé. According to Patrick Carteyron, of **Château Penin** (www.chateaupenin.com) in Génissac, grapes used for rosé thrive in deep clay, where the plant is not stressed and the soil produces the best aromas. Quinney keeps a careful eye on his parcels. After flowering, he selects those which have rosé potential and will not de-leaf, as he aims for big, juicy berries, not the fully ripe, concentrated fruit for red wines. However, not until *veraison,* when the grapes start to turn red, is the final decision made over which parcel will go to the rosé vat.

For rosé, harvest can be between ten days to three weeks before that for red wine, with that for *clairet* somewhere between rosé and red. This illustrates the caution over rosé or *clairet* wines made as by-products of the red wines. Merlot, which makes up two-thirds of the region's plantings, can easily come in a whole degree of alcohol higher than the Cabernets, and if harvested too ripe can unbalance the rosé and make it too alcoholic. Merlot is therefore best harvested at least ten days before phenolic maturity with 11 per cent potential alcohol, and past the vegetal notes of unripe fruit.

The next big decision is whether to opt for direct press with minimal skin contact or longer maceration. If the grapes are harvested early for freshness, care has to be taken that they are not under ripe, as this results in a green character coming out in maceration. However, the riper the fruit, the quicker the juice darkens during maceration. Depending on the variety, the length of time and temperature of maceration will vary. Merlot is better at a lower temperature, around 15°C, to slow down extraction of colour and optimal fruit character. Higher temperatures give a heavier wine with less balanced freshness, unsuitable for a rosé. Twenty-four hours is generally the maximum time for maceration. The longer the maceration, especially with higher percentages of Merlot, the more fruit driven the flavours, a good example being Le Rosé de Malartic from **Château Malartic Lagravière** (www.malartic-lagraviere.com), made by Michel Rolland, which has 65 per cent Merlot with longer maceration.

Some recommend a very brief maceration before pressing, as they believe that using only direct press will result in wines which are too pale and only faintly aromatic. **Château de Fontenille**'s (en.chateau-fontenille.com) Belle Rosée is a blend of 70 per cent Cabernet Franc, 10 per cent Cabernet Sauvignon and 20 per cent Merlot which is pressed with no maceration. André Lurton's **Château Bonnet** and **Château Tour de Bonnet** (eng.andrelurton.com) both made with an equal blend of Merlot and Cabernet Sauvignon, use a gentle direct press and macerate for 12–24 hours.

Styles appear to have changed, with some early rosés made from 100 per cent Cabernet Sauvignon. Fréderic le Clerc at **Château de la Tour de By** (boutique.la-tour-de-by.com) made his first rosé in 2005, in tiny quantities just for family and private clients, from 100 per cent Cabernet Sauvignon, using the *saignée* method and low temperature fermentation. Their first commercial rosé, aimed at the UK and Dutch markets, appeared in 2008 and for this they reduced the Cabernet Sauvignon to 70 per cent of the blend, with the remaining 30 per cent being Merlot. **Château Thieuley**'s (thieuley.com/en) first rosé, also 100 per cent Cabernet Sauvignon to begin with, with 10–12 hours maceration, has also evolved. In 2016 the blend was 40 per cent Merlot, 30 per cent Cabernet Sauvignon and 30 per cent Cabernet Franc, with 8–12 hours maceration.

Château Brown
5, allée John Lewis Brown 33850 Léognan
05 56 87 08 10
www.chateau-brown.com/en/
Director Jean-Christophe Mau came away from Bampfield's tastings inspired to go down a different path, and decided to make an oaked rosé, although it was not until 2012 that he launched his first vintage. Like Lichine, his aim was to demonstrate the potential of Bordeaux rosé as a quality wine. It was made with 60 per cent Cabernet Sauvignon and 40 per cent Merlot, selected from identified plots of deep gravel soils, with an average vine age of twenty-two years. Manual harvesting in small boxes takes place between freshness and peak ripeness. After harvesting, grapes are destemmed and whole bunch pressed, with four hours maceration. Cold settling, fermentation in tank and ageing for four months with *battonage* in lightly toasted French oak barrels aims to produce a smooth, round mouthfeel, rather than imparting oak character, allowing the fresh and vibrant Cabernet fruit to shine.

Some *grand cru classé* châteaux make rosés under the appellation of Bordeaux Rosé. Rarer than standard rosé wines and more expensive, they are popular in Asia, notably Japan. The signature rosés made by the *grand cru classés* are only made in certain vintages when the red wines need concentrating. Often vinified in stainless steel, they then go into barrel with *battonage*.

When Martin Krejewski took over Château de Sours from Esme Johnstone in 2004, after being a minority shareholder, he inherited a strong existing customer base. After his purchase, he immediately set about capitalizing on the success of the rosé, by doubling production with the addition of new parcels of grapes, and introducing a more modern look and feel with a screw-cap rather than cork closure. Among his many successes were adding old vine, barrel-fermented red, white and rosé wines, called La Source, to the normal Château de Sours range. Having

---

Château Auguste
www.dancingmermaidsrose.com

Tom Sullivan, an American billionaire (founder of Lumber Liquidators) has ambitious plans for Château Auguste (30 hectares, Bordeaux Supérieur), which he bought in 2016. Located in Entre-deux-Mers, it currently produces mainly red Bordeaux Supérieur (around 200,000 bottles a year). Sullivan plans to change this, to produce mainly pale Provence-style rosés. He explained: 'We were looking for a quality rosé vineyard in Provence, but during a blind tasting that included four rosés from Provence, four rosés from Bordeaux and two other rosés ... our first two choices were both light pink Bordeaux wines.' The rosé is called Dancing Mermaids and comes in a unique curvaceous bottle. Hubert de Boüard is providing advice on the viticulture and vinification for the rosé.

Sullivan already owned three other estates: Châteaux Gaby, Fronsac; Moya, Castillon Côtes de Bordeaux and du Parc, Saint-Emilion Grand Cru. Gaby's winemaker, Damien Landouar, who has been at the property since 1999 will remain in place to become technical director of the four estates. Sullivan plans to shake up US wine distribution by using his own distribution channel for sales in America, the Miami-based company, Wine Traders International (with Steven Howard, previously at Zonin Prosecco, as director of US sales). His objective is to offer a quality Bordeaux wine at the most competitive price possible.

now left Château de Sours, he makes, with his winemaker daughter, a rosé, l'Exuberance, at **Clos Cantenac** (www.closcantenac.com).

Pale rosé is not the only new style in Bordeaux; sparkling wine production is also growing at top speed – an eight-fold increase over recent years according to the CIVB. Only a handful of wineries are capable of making sparkling wine, but their production is expanding. Château de Sours sparkling rosé is not an AOC Crémant, as the local regulations suggest, but simply a vin de France sparkling rosé, made according to the 'traditional method' of a secondary fermentation in bottle, and left on the lees for three years before release. The 80,000 bottles produced have created a whole new category of wine for the estate.

THE LOIRE

Further up the west coast of France, the Loire finishes its 1,021 kilometre journey, from the Cévennes in the Ardeche, to the sea at St Nazaire. The Loire viticultural area covers almost 400 kilometre in length of vineyards and offers a large diversity of rosé styles from west (coast) to east (central) vineyards. The western regions have a similar, although slightly cooler, climate to the region of Bordeaux, becoming increasingly continental eastwards. Because of the range of varieties used, Loire rosés can range from very pale *vins gris* to dark pink-red Cabernets.

The Loire was well represented in the 1986 SOPEXA French rosé tasting. The best wines, according to Maureen Ashley's *Decanter* review showed a 'pretty, delicate, light, flowery nose and a dry, clean, attractive palate with excellent acidity that freshened the taste without stinging the mouth.' This reference to the stinging acidity may be why so many Loire rosés back then were better with a touch of residual sugar. Joanna Simon (1989) was less keen on a Rosé de Loire, 'dry and usually partly Cabernet Franc', but preferred the 'Cabernet Franc blended with the black-curranty Cabernet Sauvignon, as in, for example, the crisp, aromatic 1988 Haut Poitou Cabernet Rosé, Cave de Haut Poitou.'

Some dry rosés found along the Loire came from producers making rosé as a by-product of their more valuable red wines. The juice comes from two principal sources: from vines too young for red wines or from *saignée* from concentrating the red wine. Others are making 'niche' rosés, which are gaining ground to the detriment of red wine.

Some are made with a blend of Loire varieties, such as Hubert et Olivier Sinson's rosé in the AOP Valencay, made with a blend of Gamay, Pinot Noir, Côt and Pineau d'Aunis to produce a dry, fruity rosé, with delicate tannins and mouth-watering acidity or Château de Boissy's Rosé de Loire, made with Grolleau, Cabernet Franc and Gamay, with a lovely minerality from the schist soil, long, fresh acidity and opulent strawberry fruit.

Biodynamic producer Château de Passavent's Penser Nature is an IGP Loire *vin gris* made with Grolleau Gris. This could have been a Rosé d'Anjou, but has 40g/l residual sugar, instead of the maximum 20g/l. This wine is quite a surprise, with firm minerality and high acidity from the schist soils. The 2015 vintage was full of honey and dried Hunza apricots with aromatic muscat notes. The Grolleau Gris variety had fallen out of fashion over the past twenty years and been steadily dug up, but now its aromatic fruit and good acidity is being appreciated again. As Jean Louis Lhumeau notes, the pale colour of this variety allows them to extract more flavour and texture without extracting colour. His Rosé de Loire is half Grolleau Gris and half Grolleau Noir, and shows intense perfume, spice and peaches.

Domaine des Sablonnettes
L'Espérance, 49750 Rablay-sur-Layon
Tél.: 02 41 78 40 49

Owners Christine and Joel Ménard originally made a dark Cabernet rosé which was regarded officially as too dark to be labelled a rosé, so they called it 'Ceci n'est pas un rosé' (This is not a rosé). Their current rosé 'Passerillé', is much paler. The grapes are harvested late, in mid-October, when they are *passerillés*, (with concentrated sugar and less juice). The wine is made from a blend of juice obtained through direct press and juice from a gentle maceration.

Coteaux du Vendomois

Situated on the rolling hills to the north of Vouvray, Coteaux du Vendomois received its appellation in 2011, using Pineau d'Aunis grapes, for both light red, tannic wines and *vins gris*. The variety has a long local history, by legend introduced by Geoffroy Martel in 1030. According to tradition, the d'Aunis part of the grape's name comes from the Prieuré d'Aunis, a monastery in the Saumur region of the Loire valley, where it is thought the monks first 'discovered' and planted the variety. DNA suggests it is related to ancient vines in Anjou or Saintonge. Over-fertilization and cropping led to a decline in its quality and reputation. However, with good viticulture and vinification it can produce intense, fruity wines with notes of spice, bitter almond and saffron.

Patrice Colin at Coteaux du Vendomois makes two *vins gris*: Vin Gris Jeunes Vignes and Le Gris Bodin, from Pineau d'Aunis planted in 1920 by his grandfather, Georges Colin and which gives particularly intense fruit. Benoît Braziler, president of the Syndicat des Coteaux du Vendomois, makes a sparkling pink at **Domaine Brazilier** (www.coteaux-vendomois.com), aged on the lees for twelve months.

Reuilly

Reuilly, just to the west of Sancerre, received the Gris de Reuilly AOP in 1961. It is the only place in the Loire that allows a 100 per cent Pinot Gris rosé.

Denis Jamain (www.denis-jamain.com) at Domaine de Reuilly makes two Pinot Gris rosés: Les Fossiles and Les Chatillons. The vineyards have been biodynamic since 2015 and are harvested manually. Vines grow on sandy-gravel soil, which encourages a fresh fruity style. Jamain uses direct press with minimal skin contact to produce pale, shell-pink wines. The wine is creamy, with ripe apricot and white peach fruit, a touch of spice and balanced acidity. **Gerard Cordier** (vins-quincy-reuilly.com/gerard-cordier) also manually harvests his Pinot Gris, to make a very pale, dry rosé, with a delicate, rosehip bouquet and tangy, redcurrant acidity.

Sancerre

Sancerre lies in the eastern part of the Loire valley with almost all the appellation lying on the left bank of the Loire, opposite Pouilly-Fumé. Though primarily associated with Sauvignon Blanc, it also grows some Pinot Noir, accounting for around 20 per cent of the region's production, and making mostly light red wines and some rosé.

The region was historically linked to the Duchy of Burgundy, which may have played a role in the introduction of Pinot Noir to the area.

Sancerre's position as an administrative centre ensured healthy local markets for its wines, light reds (*clairets*) made with Pinot Noir and Gamay. The wines were exported to Flanders and England. In the late nineteenth century phylloxera devastated the area, wiping out most vines. While some Pinot Noir vines were retained, most of the Gamay was lost. The vineyards were replanted with Sauvignon Blanc, partly because it grafted better onto the American rootstocks.

The steeply sloping chalk hills, part of the same geology as Champagne, Chablis and the South Downs of England, provide the grapes with enough direct sunlight and warmth to fully ripen, while allowing cold air to flow off the slope, and pool into the valleys below. Each valley has its own microclimate and terroir. Sancerre was one of the first appellations awarded, in 1936.

The rosés are defined in the appellation regulations as being delicate and fruity, with a pale pink to darker salmon colour and a maximum of 4g/l residual sugar, with no carbon filtration to remove colour. Although they may be sold from 1 December following the vintage, Sancerre rosé is better with some age, especially if made by a reputable Sancerre white wine producer.

Domaine Pierre Martin's Chauvignol Sancerre has typical Pinot cherry-fruit aromas. On the palate, it has fresh, cherry fruit, silky structure, long acidity, and hint of dry tannin on the finish. The 2016 was not yet in bottle in May 2017. Le Rabault 2015, from **Domaine Joseph Mellot** (www.josephmellot.com), has ripe, perfumed, almost floral fruit aromas followed by ripe cherries and redcurrants with a mineral, savoury core, a hint of orange peel and long chewy acidity. **Domaine Picard**'s (www.domaine-picard.com) 2015 has deceptively soft, creamy red cherries, balanced by crisp acidity. The length goes on and on, suggesting that the breadth and richness of fruit hides the high acidity.

Saint Pourçain

Although Saint Pourçain is physically closer to the Loire Valley, the Gamay variety and sandy granite soils make its style of rosé closer in character to that of Beaujolais. *Vin gris* rosé is also made. There are no direct rules on vinification, and some allow full or partial malolactic fermentation. Until at least 2008, producers were more likely to use *saignée* in weaker vintages, when the red wine needed concentrating.

Rosé production hovers between 16 and 21 per cent of the total. The rosés are dry in style (under 4g/l sugar). In 2008 the **Cave de l'Union des Vignerons de Saint Pourçain** (www.vignerons-saintpourcain.com) vignerons produced a small quantity of Pinot Noir rosé with 8g/l residual sugar, which was exported to the UK under the La Grille label.

ALSACE

Alsace, better known for its white wines, also makes a growing number of quality red wines, which thirty years ago achieved only *clairet*-style lightness, and a few pale rosés (also referred to in the *cahier de charges* as *clairet*, or by the German word *Schillerwein*). At a French rosé tasting in 1986, only one Alsace domaine, Laugel, showed rosé. The 1983 wines shown by Laugel were, according to Ashley in her *Decanter* review, 'a weighty Pichet d'Alsace and a very firm Pinot Noir with high acidity which aroused varied comments on its unusual bouquet.'

With global warming, red-wine production in Alsace has increased in importance. A *grand cru* status is being discussed and most producers would prefer to direct their Pinot Noir grapes to red wine, rather than rosé. Even if production of rosé in Alsace increases, it will always remain marginal compared to the still white and *crémant* wines. Only 10 per cent of plantings are Pinot Noir, of which 38 per cent is used for *crémant*.

Alsace rosé can only be labelled AOC Alsace or Vin d'Alsace. The must weight must be a minimum of 160g/l sugar. The finished wine must have a maximum of 4g/l sugar and 13 per cent abv. Carbon filtration cannot be used to make the wine paler.

Alsace rosé is made in small quantities, so is not distributed widely. With the tradition in Alsace of quality wines reflecting certain sites, some producers would like to move on from producing a generic Pinot Noir rosé from Alsace, to having a Traenheim rosé or an Ammerschwihr rosé, for example. Pinot Noir gains power from the clay and finesse and texture from the limestone. Good rosés can show typical Pinot Noir characters of floral and spice aromas and ripe, red fruit.

Many producers do now make a small quantity of rosé. **Wolfberger** (www.wolfberger.com), one of the largest producers in Alsace, started producing the occasional rosé, called Petite Folie, in the early 2000s. In 2011, they decided to go with the current fashion and make a small amount every year. Hauller in Dambach-la-Ville produces a small quantity, to broaden the range on offer to clients from April to September. Neither has made any great marketing push, and the rosé remains simply a refreshing summer option.

SAVOIE, BUGEY AND CERDON

Rosés are widely made, mostly aimed for drinking in the summer, and can be decent and refreshing, from Gamay, Pinot Noir, Mondeuse or a blend. Mondeuse gives rosé fragrance and an extra kick. According to Wink Lorch who has explored the wines of the region in depth, Mondeuse Gris is an obscure variation of the Rouge that has been revived experimentally by Philippe Grisard. For Bugey, a minimum of 50 per cent of Gamay and Pinot Noir, alone or together, must be used. Mondeuse Noire, Pinot Gris and Poulsard are allowed as accessory grapes. Pale skinned Poulsard makes a false rosé.

BURGUNDY

Vineyards have been present throughout Burgundy since early medieval times, often as part of the great monastic lands. In 1395, Philip the Bold decided to improve the quality of wines and prohibited the cultivation of the Gamay grape on his land in favour of Pinot Noir. The Abbey of Bèze, the Bishop of Autun, the Dukes of Bourgogne, and many others, have owned vines in Marsannay, and the wines were apparently appreciated at the royal court of Louis XIV and Louis XVI.

Marsannay is the northernmost wine village in the Côte de Nuits in Burgundy and the source of the majority of Burgundy's rosé wine. Vineyards now compete with the encroaching urban sprawl of Dijon. In 2008, 230 hectares of vineyard were used for Marsannay wine, of which 15 per cent was for white and rosé.

Formerly known only for its rosé wine, Marsannay received its appellation in 1987 for all three wine colours. It is the only village-level appellation which may produce rosé wines. The name of the appellation may be followed by the name of the *climat*. Marsannay producers are permitted to use Pinot Noir and Pinot Gris as principal varieties, and Chardonnay and Pinot Blanc as secondary varieties (up to 15 per cent) for rosé, but no Gamay, which largely disappeared in the 1960s. Grapes must be harvested at minimum 180g/l sugar in must. Final maximum residual sugar is 3g/l. The rosés are described in the appellation as being *tendres* (soft) and fruity with notes of peach and red fruits, with a lively acidity. These rosés are not *clairet* in style, but relatively pale in colour, with varying amounts of skin contact, depending on the producer.

The vines extend from north to south along the best parts of the hill-slope and the valley, at heights from 255 to 390 metres above sea-level. Exposures range east to south. In the valley, the soil has more clay, and vines are more exposed; the cooler microclimate leads to lighter, more acidic wines. On more sheltered hills with gravel soils, the wines are riper.

The rosé sells for less than the red and white. In 1997, Clive Coates MW in his book on Burgundy, wrote 'Much of the rosé can be ripe and fruity, tending towards a more commercial, confected style resulting in Marsannay rosé not being considered as a serious wine.' Today, the more exciting producers have created more complex wines, which balance fruit and acidity with great elegance and show ability to age well.

Fleur de Pinot from Domaine Sylvain Pataille in Marsannay is aged for 18 months in old 500 litre barrels. The oak is evident in youth, but does not dominate the fruit, and serves to provide depth, concentration, structure and potential to age. **Domaine Bruno Clair** (www.bruno-clair.com) uses 100 per cent Pinot Noir, with *saigneé* after 48 hours maceration, for a wine that has intense Pinot cherry fruit.

In 2016 John Tilson of undergroundwine.com tasted the aged-in-bottle Marsannay rosés of Domaine Joseph Roty, from the 2009, 2010, 2011 and 2013 and vintages. Obviously, there were vintage variations, but it is interesting to see the taste evolution of this wine in the summary of his tasting notes. The youngest, a deep, reddish-pink, was perfumed with hints of rose petals and strawberries with delicate citrus acidity. The 2011 was already showing slight golden-orange colour notes and had floral aromas with spice and berry on the palate and fresh, crisp acidity. At six years old, the 2010 was showing a distinctive pink and gold colour. The floral aromas were still in evidence, with raspberry and spice fruit, and ongoing crisp acidity that showed no signs of fading away. The oldest wine, from 2009, was more reddish gold. The distinctive floral aromas were still there, but this wine, judging by colour, and the mulberry and exotic spice was possibly made with longer skin contact, giving a richer taste. The acidity was still crisp and lively.

BEAUJOLAIS AND REGION

In Burgundy's southern neighbour some vineyards fall between two appellations, resulting in a few non-appellation Pinot Noir and Gamay rosés. Coteaux Bourguignons and Coteaux du Lyonnais, both IGP, make Gamay rosés. The Beaujolais appellation produces more than 13,500 hectolitres of rosé each year, whereas Beaujolais Villages rosé, produces roughly 4,000.

Beaujolais dry rosé is made principally from Gamay, although up to 10 per cent Gamay de Bouze Noire and Gamay de Chardonnay Noire can be included. Although rare, production is currently on the rise. Gamay traditionally makes fruity, light reds, so is ideally suited to producing rosés that are light pink in colour. Sugar in the must at harvest has to be 161g/l or over in Beaujolais AOP and 170g/l for Beaujolais Villages.

Beaujolais rosés have a charming, opulent fruit character with peaches, sour cherries, redcurrants, strawberries and wild strawberries giving them the same charm as fresh red Beaujolais. Some of them have a broader creamy acidity, some are more vibrant and citrussy but all have a fine mineral core. Differences between the styles in weight and intensity are due largely to different lengths of maceration and malolactic fermentation. Cool fermentation in tank produces vibrant rosés.

Grapes are manually harvested, often with parcel selection from old vines, to give a stronger sense of terroir. Some vineyards use single site selection, such as **Domaine Piron**'s (www.domaines-piron.fr), single site Le Clos du Vieux Bourg at Courcelles, which has a mixed granite, clay and limestone soil planted with old vines. Other weightier wines include Piron's classic 2016, with powerful, wild strawberry character, cherry and blackberry fruit, mineral structure and mouth-watering acidity. **Pierre-Marie Chermette** (www.chermette.fr) Les Griottes 2016 is intense and succulent, with sour cherry fruit, and long, mineral, mouth-watering acidity. Notre Rosé Maison 2016 from **Domaine Bernard Jomain** (www.bernardjomainvigneron.com) has weightier red wine fruit.

Fresh, fruity styles include those from **Domaine Longère** (www.domaine-longere.com), whose Beaujolais Villages has creamy peach acidity, redcurrants, sour cherries and a mineral core, and Terroir de Bully 2016, **Louis Tête** (www.tete-beaujolais.com), with strawberry, redcurrants, sour cherries and long, mineral freshness.

Mischief and Mayhem's (www.mischiefandmayhem.com) 2016, Coteaux Bourguignons is pale in colour with intense, peach fruit with hints of redcurrants, fresh citrus acidity and a long mineral core. Louis Tête Coteaux du Lyonnais 2016 is similarly creamy-peach flavoured, with intense, peach fruit and long, mineral, mouth-watering acidity.

Beaujolais nouveau rosé 2016

Beaujolais nouveau rosé is developing a market presence in France, Japan and Britain. In 2015 Marks and Spencer introduced a Beaujolais nouveau rosé. Their winemakers Sue Daniels and Thierry Coulon worked with local vignerons to produce a refreshing, mouth-watering example, with no oak, that was full of flavour with no hard edges.

6
NORTH AMERICAN ROSÉ

Much of the modern marketing hype for rosé is being generated in America. Pink festivals, rosé shortages in the Hamptons, and a general passion for rosé wine, have led to the biggest export market for Provence rosé. But the American taste for rosé is nothing new, although it has been somewhat obscured by the often derided Zinfandel blush. Instead, the revival of rosé worldwide is intricately caught up with the history of North American rosé.

Starring wines are made today in California, Washington and Oregon and in a scattering of other states, showing an exciting creativity and imagination, but to find them outside their region of origin, let alone in Europe, has been almost impossible. Suffice it to say, there are small quantities of great rosé being made, 'unicorn' wines, known only to a few wine insiders. 'It's one of the great reasons to visit during the late spring and early summer as most of these wines are only sold at the winery,' commented Stuart Spencer, Program Manager of Lodi Winegrape Commission.

Whether quantities will increase sufficiently to reach a wider market is difficult to judge, but many producers feel their rosés are so different to the high-volume ones generally sold and consumed, that the wider market will not appreciate them. The few I have tried have been glorious, complex and interesting.

The history of rosé in North America is closely tied with Tavel, southern Italy, Prohibition and the Second World War.

THE BEGINNINGS OF NORTH AMERICAN ROSÉ: 1857–1940

Grenache was probably introduced to California in 1857, and by 1859 was one of the varieties recommended for planting in California for making dry, light-red wines. The Grenache-based wines of Tavel were appreciated from early on. Other rosé styles were also made. By 1874, Hyatt's Handbook described wines, with apparently some sweetness, made from grapes such as Pink Malaga ('pink or light wine color; juicy and sweet') and Portugal ('slightly pink in color.')

Making white wines from black varieties was a practice that developed early on. In 1887, the Olivina Winery in Livermore made a 'white' Grenache, while Dunfillan Vineyards in Sonoma sold a white Pinot Noir called Oeil de Perdrix. In 1905, Paul Masson began marketing the first Californian *blanc de noirs* sparkling made from Pinot Noir, also called Oeil de Perdrix. A little later, the Cribaris,[4] who had come from Calabria in 1904, established vineyards around Fresno where they made a very light red (false rosé) from the north Italian, pale-skinned Grignolino.

Prohibition

During Prohibition (1920–33), prolific-growing grapes such as Grenache were planted and sold as fruit or for fruit juice which – by accident – may have started to ferment on the way home. Grenache continued to be used for sweet, strong, fortified, port-style wines to make the sacramental wine that slipped through a loop in the Prohibition laws.

Pink wines remained popular in America, without the reputation of being leftover red wines. Beaulieu released a rosé just after Repeal (in 1933), Cribari's New Orleans Special rosé was launched in the late thirties and, also at that time, Marcel Ott from Provence began to export his Provence rosé to America.

Many styles were made, reflecting the origins of the winemakers, as well as responding to the different markets across America. Grenache plantings grew steadily in the 1930s and 1940s, mostly in California's Central Valley. Grenache's high sugar content and naturally pale colour produced commercially successful off-dry, pale-red jug wines and port

---

4 Now owned by Gallo.

blends. The majority of pink wines were, however, made by blending red and white wines.

THE SECOND WORLD WAR TO 1973

As the American GIs knew and liked these wine styles, when the US Army arrived in Europe during the Second World War, wine producers made off-dry rosés to supply the off-duty GIs. Mateus and Lancers, in Portugal (see p.188), and Five Roses (see p.211), in southern Italy, were the most successful. After the war, these wines found a ready market in North America and were exported in large quantities.

Frank Schoonmaker, winemaker at Almaden during the 1940s, was interviewed for an oral history programme. He remembered that the biggest problem was getting 'the large masses of the public' to try what they called 'sour' wines, that is dry table wines. Schoonmaker recommended 'a dry rosé similar to that of the Rhône Valley, the Tavel rosé which was made from the Grenache grape (of which there was an abundance … in California), so, we came out with Almadén Grenache Rosé … It was probably the most successful single wine product in the country.' Although it had only low residual sugar, it was made to be very fruity and not too acidic, which made it appear sweeter than it was. Launched in 1945, it was intended for drinking while still young and fresh.

The same year Robert Mayock launched his Los Amigos rosé. Throughout the 1940s, the quantity of Grenache planted continued to grow, reaching over 3,200 hectares (8,000 acres) in California. In 1948, Louis and Angelo Cassa founded the Cassa Brothers Winery in the Santa Clara Valley and successfully produced a Grenache rosé called, rather unimaginatively, Rosé Grape Wine. These rosés, aimed at novice drinkers, ranged from off-dry to sweet. In 1956, Garrett & Co. added a sweet pink wine to their red and white Virginia Dare range, made at their California winery. Advertised as 'America's first after-dinner wine' it appealed to a young, aspirational market, newly married and wanting to entertain friends in a modern way, at home.

Ruth Ellen Church, in the *Chicago Tribune*, March 1966, remarked on the many different styles and that 'almost everybody had a different favorite. Some liked the sweet rosé wines; some insisted upon dry ones.'

In 1970, Maynard Amerine, the pioneering viticultural researcher, had suggested that a wider range of rosé styles should be made, including an even drier style, to appeal to more experienced drinkers. Sugar levels alone could not define a quality rosé and work was done to improve the wine on many levels. In 1962 *Life* magazine published a round-up of the best wines of California in which a few rosés were included: 'Almadén Grenache rosé, Buena Vista Rose [sic] Brook, Charles Krug Vin Rosé, Mayacamas Cabernet rosé and Zinfandel rosé'.

Grenache plantings increased slowly to 4,000 hectares (10,000 acres) by 1960, but most was destined for then-trendy red wine. As red wine's popularity grew, so did plantings of red varieties. Grenache peaked at 8,000 hectares (20,000 acres) in 1974. Then the fashion swung to white wine. Growers were left with acres of red varieties – and several options for what to do next. They could dig up their red varieties and replant with white, losing production for four years; they could graft white varieties onto red vines; or they could make white wines from black grapes.

WHITE ZINFANDEL AND THE ARRIVAL OF 'BLUSH'

According to the story told by Bob Trinchero of Sutter Home Winery, his original white Zinfandel in 1973 was 'accidental'. In the 1970s Sutter Home was a producer of premium Zinfandel red wine in the Napa Valley. To increase concentration of these, they used the *saignée* technique to bleed off some of the grape juice before fermentation, and fermented the excess juice as a dry wine, in the way that most Provence rosés were made at the time. That the resulting wine was a white, tinged with pink, suggests the juice was bled off within an hour or two.

Two years later, in 1975, in another twist of fate, the white Zinfandel experienced 'stuck fermentation', a problem that occurs when the yeast dies before consuming all the sugar. Trinchero set his problem juice aside. Some weeks later he tasted it, and preferred this accidental result, which was a sweet, pink wine. This is the style that became popular as white Zinfandel, even though it was pink. Cabernet blanc or white Cabernet were also made, but white Zinfandel remained the most successful wine.

Using names referencing European *oeil de perdix* wines, gave these wines a sense of heritage. **Sebastiani Vineyards** (www.sebastiani.com) in Sonoma, produced a white Pinot Noir in 1975, called Eye of the Swan because its pink colour was 'the same as the eye of the black Australian swan'. By stopping fermentation to keep the sweetness, these wines were generally lower in alcohol, around 10% abv. Almaden followed suit with a sparkling Eye of the Partridge wine, which was included in the *Chicago Tribune* of 6 December 1976 review of wines for the upcoming festive season:

> *Eye of the Partridge: The newest drink of the season sparkles, but it's not champagne. It's* oeil de perdrix, *or Eye of the Partridge, being introduced for the first time by an American vintner, Almaden. 'Actually, it's a rosé wine,' said Max Zimmerman, who has offered a European* oeil de perdrix *imported by Sichel for some years at his Loop liquor store. The American version is made from a combination of Pinot grapes which give it its characteristic bronze tint and will sell at about the same price as the company's* Blanc de Blancs *Champagne. Zimmerman says the European version is not quite as dry as a brut champagne, which Almaden compares its product to. The wine goes back to Louis IX of France, who served a version when his son came of age. It is still prized in Switzerland for 'encouraging liveliness and wit in those who drink it.' … Why the unusual name? Look a partridge in the eye sometime.*

The rise in popularity of white Zinfandel and other pink wines in California in the 1980s, led to the need for a name other than 'rosé', which was associated with the old-fashioned wines from Mateus and Lancer. A new name was required to support the marketing story of a pink wine made from black grapes, particularly if a varietal was indicated on the label.

Bill Kreck, whose winery made the first wine called 'blush' told me how the name came about:

> *In the early 1970s, noting another local winery, Sebastiani, had produced a 'white' wine from Pinot Noir grapes, and named it Eye of the Partridge, we produced our first* Blanc de Noirs *from the*

harvest of 1976 using Cabernet Sauvignon grapes. We produced only a few hundred gallons at that time. Although we were hoping for a wine of little color, fall rains just prior to harvest softened the Cabernet Sauvignon skins and resulted in more of a rosé than a blanc de noirs style.

Following harvest, we were interviewed by a wine writer relatively new to the Los Angeles market, but in his short tenure had acquired a respectable following. We hosted Jerry Mead at our home and presented a number of our new wines for his consideration. The last we showed him was the blanc de noirs. At the time, the wine was unnamed. Noting the darker color than the Sebastiani counterpart, Jerry suggested the word 'Blush' instead of the standard 'Rose of Cabernet'. At first, we were not too excited about the word. We talked to our northern California sales team and they were even less excited than we were, and, in fact, suggested they would be reluctant to sell the wine thus named. Jerry, on the other hand, was both excited about the wine itself and the name and promised to give it great attention in his columns. We made the decision to split the inventory and name that destined for northern California Rose of Cabernet Sauvignon and that to be shipped to southern California Cabernet Blush. Jerry, true to his word, mentioned the wine a number of times and So Cal sales outpaced Nor Cal sales by at least four to one. Before the end of that vintage, we were soaking off Rose labels and relabeling them Blush.

Kreck describes how he trademarked the name 'blush':

In 1978, we were working with a Trademark and Patent attorney for the registration of our winery name, Mill Creek Vineyards, and in that conversation the word 'blush' came up. He suggested we trademark that word as well. So in 1978, the word 'blush' was applied for and eventually approved by the US Patent office [in 1981].

Sales of Mill Creek's blush wine were successful, even though they made up just a small proportion of Mill Creek's production.

Production of blush expanded quickly and by the early 1980s, we were producing close to 3,000 cases annually. It was first, and foremost, a wonderful wine. Using premium Sonoma County Cabernet Sauvignon grapes, it was flavorful and distinct. With just a hint of residual sugar, chilled, it was superb and refreshing on any warm California afternoon.

Ultimately Mill Creek chose not to fight other users of the name 'blush'. As Kreck wrote, 'So it came to pass that blush transitioned from a trademarked word, to a term to describe a general category of wines.'

Blush-style wines became increasingly popular during the 1980s. By 1988, a survey of Californian wine showed that 28 per cent of wine produced was defined as 'blush'. But by the end of the decade, the market for quality rosés and *blancs de noirs* fell. Kreck went on to say:

Just as various grape varietals have their days in the sun, as Pinot Noir from Russian River Valley does now, wines, for whatever reason, fall out of favor and so did roses and blanc de noirs *by the end of the 1980s. By the end of the decade, we saw it harder to sell blush and, given the value of the Cabernet Sauvignon grapes from which it was made, decided to terminate the program and divert that fruit into our Estate Cabernet Sauvignon wine.*

Until the late 1990s blush was the popular term for pink domestic wine, which gobbled up 22 per cent of all wine consumed in the US.

The success of 'white Zin' gave pink wine a bad name in terms of quality. A marketing challenge then arose. What is the difference between wines which are pink, rosé or blush – or even in some cases – white? Some identify blush as being paler and sweeter – the writer Julian Jeffs noted that 'American rosés were generally sweeter' than European rosés. He also highlighted the marketing challenge presented by not indicating the level of sweetness on the label, especially when colour cannot be used as a guide.

According to Stuart Spencer, Program Manager of Lodi Winegrape Commission:

Lodi produces over 40 per cent of California's Zinfandel, making it a significant part of the region's production. In recent years, however, the 'White Zinfandel' category has declined due to demographic and market preferences and market competition from other simple sweet wine. The appeal of the sweeter style can be seen in the fact that in the US many of the fast-growing red blends are also upwards of 2 per cent sugar [20g/l]. At the same time, in recent years dry roses have taken off. Almost all Lodi wineries are making their version of a dry rose, from all sorts of grapes, and utilizing many different techniques from native yeast, to barrel fermentation.

On the international scene, exports of Californian blush have seen huge growth in recent years. The biggest market for Californian producers outside the US is the UK, with wines like Blossom Hill. At the same time, blush is falling out of favour locally, especially among American Millennials.

THE RHONE RANGERS AND THE RISING INFLUENCE OF PROVENCE ROSÉ

Grenache plantings declined in the 1990s to 4,500 hectares (11,000 acres). Some 90 hectares (220 acres) remained in the coastal counties, where Grenache often commanded equal or higher prices than Zinfandel. The Rhone Rangers (www.rhonerangers.org), a group of winemakers including Randall Grahm of **Bonny Doon** (www.bonnydoonvineyard.com), in Santa Cruz, grouped together together in the 1980s to use and promote southern French varieties. Amongst the other early members, making a range of serious rosés, were Joseph Phelps of **Joseph Phelps Winery** (www.josephphelps.com) in Napa, with their vin de Mistral Grenache rosé in the 1990s, John MacCready of **Sierra Vista Winery** (www.sierravistawinery.com) in the Sierra Foothills (Grenache rosé), Fred Cline of **Cline Cellars Winery** (clinecellars.com), Sonoma, who now make an old vine Mourvèdre blanc de noir rosé, Steve Edmunds of **Edmunds St. John** (www.edmundsstjohn.com) with a Gamay rosé and Bob Lindquist of **Qupé Wine Cellars** (www.qupe.com) who has made a Pinot Noir rosé since 1982. In 1996, despite plantings decreasing, Grenache was still the fourth most planted red variety in California. With the Rhone Rangers enthusiasm, Syrah and Mourvèdre plantings increased.

> **Sine Qua Non**
> PO Box 1048, Oak View, CA 93022
> Tel.: 805 649 8901
> www.sinequanon.com
> Here, they have been making high quality (and expensive) rosés since 1995 with a different name and label for each vintage. It is made with either Grenache or Syrah, and in one vintage as a Rhone blend. Only twenty-five cases (300 bottles) of the first vintage, Queen of Hearts, made with Grenache, were produced. In 2014 one bottle from this vintage was sold at auction for a record-breaking $37,200. The 2001 vintage Pagan Poetry (made with Syrah) also regularly commands high prices.

Frank Prial wrote in 1997 that 'few American winemakers are interested in rosé, but the handful who are have produced some charming wines. The mistral doesn't blow through the Napa Valley, but Joseph Phelps, one of the first wineries in the valley to produce Rhone-style wines, offers Vin du Mistral Grenache Rosé, a lineal descendant of that Almaden jug wine of long ago'. Nick K. Dokoozlian, of E & J Gallo, notes that, 'In 2002 Grenache was used primarily for the production of varietal rosé and blush wines in the San Joaquim Valley.' Grahm made a rosé, Vin Gris de Cigare in 2002, with 34 per cent Grenache, 25 per cent Cinsault, 19 per cent Mourvèdre, 12 per cent Counoise, 8 per cent Syrah and 2 per cent Viognier. While this is a Provence blend, to make such a rosé in California was unusual.

From 2008, as French rosé imports introduced American consumers to a dry, crisp style, the market increasingly accepted a style very different to blush. By 2014, American winemakers of premium rosé were increasingly trying to replicate the French style instead. Successful Provence rosés in the US are considerably fruitier than many sold in France.

In 2014, sales of sweet blush wines in America fell compared to the previous year; white Zinfandel was down 10.5 per cent while dry rosé wines increased in volume by 5.1 per cent during the same period. Nonetheless, crisp and slightly sweet white Zinfandel wines still account for the majority of blush wine consumption in the United States.

Michaela Rodeno, who retired as CEO of St. Supery in 2009, told me:

For many years (most of my 44 years in the wine biz, albeit in Napa Valley), American rosé was deliberately made sweet to suit the American palate. Marketers and vintners believed that Americans talk dry and drink sweet. Whether they drink sweet because that was what was on offer, or because they genuinely preferred sweet, is not clear to me. This is certainly changing at the high end of the market, where dry rosé has been successful for the past few years ... A good friend tried for years to get me to make a dry rosé but I had to tell him, regretfully, that it wouldn't sell. A man ahead of his time, and a fan of Provence. Even so, today the idea persists that rosé is sweet, so that winemakers/marketers have to make very clear that their wine is dry. (In like manner, when white Zinfandel, the archetypal 'blush' wine, was selling by the millions of cases, people who wanted traditional dry red Zinfandel, a much smaller presence in the market, had to be explicit or they'd be served a glass of sweet, pinkish plonk.) So, yes, dry rosé is hot today, but the old shibboleth about rosé as sweet wine still exists too. As one descends the price scale, that belief grows stronger. For the most part, today dry varietal rosés are coming from the high end of the wine market, and are priced accordingly.

Other producers began following Grahm's Provence blend. Varieties such as Grenache Noir, Grenache Gris, Mourvèdre, Counoise, Syrah, Petite Sirah, Carignan and Cinsault were used to make wines in the classic way, with varying degrees of minimal skin contact, cold fermentation and malolactic fermentation blocked to preserve acidity. These wines are as close as one can get to a Provence style with Californian fruit and different terroirs.

Stuart Spencer of Lodi sees a difference from Provence wines: 'Despite the use of Provence varieties, these wines have their own distinctive style. The rosés made in the classic way of direct press, minimal skin contact and cool fermentation in tank are the closest in style. But technique alone does not make the same style and Californian fruit has a more overt, cool climate character.' These innovators have sufficiently carved out a category with the trade and the consumers are responding: 'We are now starting to see the "thundering herd" follow suit. This is where the large wine companies, see an opportunity to make money, and develop their version of a dry rosé, and try to use their distribution leverage to push into retail and on-premise[s]. We will see how successful this is in the coming years.'

Others, often in very small quantities, are making exciting variations, using old vines, varying degrees of skin contact, whole-cluster pressing (sometimes extended for several days), some use of oak, lees stirring and malolactic fermentation. Examples include:

- Ode to Lulu Old Vine Rosé, **Bedrock Wine Co.** (www.bedrockwineco.com), Sonoma Valley. Named in honour of Lulu Peynaud, of Bandol's Domaine Tempier, this uses a blend of early-picked 50 per cent old vine Mourvèdre, 30 per cent old-vine Carignan and 20 per cent Grenache (including Gris) from vines planted between 1888 and 1922. Winemaker Morgan Twain-Peterson MW alters the percentages each year, to achieve the weight and complexity desired. The grapes are whole-cluster pressed and aged in stainless steel with no malolactic fermentation.
- William Allen, a *garagiste*, uses only Rhône varietals. One of his wines from the historic Mendocino County Gibson Ranch vineyard, is **Two Shepherds** (twoshepherds.com) Grenache Gris Rosé, from 100-year-old vines, harvested fully ripe and with extended maceration for seven days, prior to a long slow fermentation in French oak with indigenous yeasts and malolactic fermentation. It is aged in tank on the lees. The resulting wine is light in colour, with savoury notes from the extended skin contact, and fresh citrus notes with creamy peach fruit, giving a fuller flavour and character. Complex and textured, it is, sadly, of limited quantity.

A cluster of vineyards in Mendocino are making Carignan rosés. Poor Ranch makes ninety-five cases of a 100 per cent Carignan wine, fermented in barrel; and bottled unfined and unfiltered. Two Shepherds makes a 100 per cent Carignan rosé, fermented in barrel then aged in tank to make a vibrant, fresh, fruity style. Only one barrel is made, or 25 cases. There is also Clambake Single Vineyard Carignan rosé (900 cases) and Lioco Indica Carignan rose (2,350 cases).

OTHER ROSÉS

Other, non-blush style rosés are made which do not follow the Provence style, but typically are dry. The range and variety of these makes it almost impossible to define a Californian style. Italian-style rosés are made using varieties such as Sangiovese, Nebbiolo and Grignolino. Other producers favour Bordeaux and Cabernet varieties, while still others use the Portuguese varieties Touriga Nacional, Tinta Roriz, Tinta Cão, and Tinta Amarella. Pinot Noir remains among the most popular with both winemakers and consumers, and is often grown where sparkling wine is made.

In other words, California's rosés are extremely diverse, an observation which has been only briefly touched upon here. Less obvious though, but very much the trend, is that many of these rosés do not hit the grocery shelves, but often are available only in small quantities, to be sold at the winery or through the many wine clubs. Many of these dry rosés are new and available only in the tasting room, but are increasingly entering national distribution.

TO *SAIGNÉE* OR NOT TO *SAIGNÉE*?

By no means pertinent only to California, this question can be asked anywhere traditionally making red wine. As Michaela Rodeno comments:

> *Red wine makers vying for critical acclaim are taking advantage of the new market interest in dry rosés to monetize* saignées *intended to improve density of their red wines by bottling this otherwise wasted by-product as dry rosé. Cash flow wine instead of discards – the bank loves this. It also explains why there are so many different red varietals showing up now as dry rosés [including Nebbiolo], and why one perceives tannin in many of them – the grapes were picked to make red wine, not rosé. Sommeliers are onto this, and will grill salespeople about the winemaking method used to create a rosé on offer (the right answer is not* saignée*). If it's an intentional rosé picked early for low alcohol/high acidity and exhibiting a natural (not bright pink or nearly red) rosé colour, that works for*

restaurants with a high-end wine clientele, or patrons familiar with Provençal rosés.

This must also apply to several unusual red varieties used for rosés. Her favourites? 'Pinot Noir and Sangiovese make the best dry rosés, especially if purpose made.'

Jeff Morgan, author of *Rosé, A Guide to the World's Most Versatile Wine* (2005) disagrees. He recalls the wet summer he spent working in a winery on Long Island, New York in the mid-1990s:

Our Merlot grapes didn't ripen well. So, we 'bled' the early, pink juice from the fresh-crushed Merlot in hopes of concentrating what would eventually become red Merlot wine. We put the pink juice in a few old barrels and forgot about them until harvest was over. What emerged from those barrels was a gorgeous rosé reminiscent of what I had enjoyed during my years in France. Some 10 years later, I had moved to the Napa Valley. A lot of my winemaker friends were also 'bleeding' their red grapes at harvest. But they were throwing the pink juice down the drain. At the time, very few California winemakers were focused on rosé, and the market for it in the U.S. was weak. My colleague, Daniel Moore, and I started 'harvesting' pink, unfermented 'bleed' from various wineries. We fermented the wine the way I had inadvertently done it back on Long Island to create our rosé brand, SoloRosa. Consumer response was positive, and we grew from one barrel in 2000 to some 200 barrels by 2007!

Jeff and Daniel founded an organization aimed at promoting rosé – taking credit for jump-starting the rosé renaissance – but eventually fell victim to the success of this campaign, losing market share to other producers eager to benefit from the trend. SoloRosa's last rosé was made in 2008.

Making rosé as a by-product of red wine is a controversial path to take. It can be derided as merely a way of using leftovers, or it can be praised for being an ecological and economic use of grape juice. In the hands of a good winemaker *saignée* rosé can be gorgeous.

> **Tablas Creek**
> 9339 Adelaida Road, Paso Robles CA 93446
> Tel.: 805 237 1231
> tablascreek.com
>
> Dianthus is made with a blend of 49 per cent Mourvèdre, 37 per cent Grenache and 14 per cent Counoise. The vines were from cuttings from the Famille Perrin's Château Beaucastel, in Châteauneuf-du-Pape, planted at Tablas Creek in 1994. The first vintage was in 1999, for a red wine. Barbara Haas (wife of the owner Robert Haas) wanted a rosé wine, so decided to use the juice bled off the red wine rather than throw it away. They discovered that, while this did not make a pale, dry rosé, it did produce a luscious darker rosé. Harvested together and cofermented on the skins in tank for 48 hours, the juice is then bled off and fermented dry, away from the skins, giving a bright pink wine with ripe, red strawberry and raspberry fruit, fresh cranberry acidity and a touch of tannin on the finish.
>
> Jason Haas told me that Tablas Creek has not exported much rosé over the years, largely because they sell everything locally, to customers who regard the rosé as a serious wine. They have 'increased production over the last five years from around 1,000 cases in 2011 to around 4,000 cases in 2016 and it still has not been enough to keep up with demand. We're aiming to make 6,000 cases this year, but still expect it all to sell out in the US.' Haas feels that with the current fashion for rosé, it is an easier category for both retail and restaurants where the style does not need to be explained (if the rose is a straightforward 'classic' style). He went on to say, 'I don't think most people who order rosé, know or care much about what the grapes are that go into it ... and the wines in most of these restaurant list sections reflect that. There is no separate "Pinot rosé" section from "Rhône-style rosé" or "Cab Franc rosé". It is just one category – rosé.' However, he feels this may be changing, with a number of places beginning to have 'multiple rosés in different styles offered by the glass and by the bottle. It wasn't long ago that there was only one rosé on most BTG [by the glass] lists. That's definitely changed.'

In my conversations with winemakers concerning a single Californian rosé style, it is evident that over and above regional styles and varietal influence, rosés fall into four different categories:

1. Off-dry blush (which can range from light to dark).
2. *Saignée* rosés bled off red wines, which can have a firm tannin structure.
3. Intentional rosé, which can be in a darker, fruitier Italian or Spanish style.
4. Increasingly, a light, dry Provence style or a more complex style.

All styles are made with different price points and markets.

Kathleen Inman of **Inman Family Wines** (www.inmanfamilywines.com), a UC Davis trained winemaker, commented that 'the appetite for rosés has grown in the thirteen years since I first started making a direct to press, intentional rosé. At the time there were a few American *saignée* rosés, and of course white Zinfandel, but producers didn't think consumers would pay the prices that intentional rosés demand because of the cost of growing quality fruit and the opportunity cost of not producing red wines, which command higher price points.' Nevertheless, her Endless Crush Rosé retails at $35 and the 880 cases of 12 sell out within three weeks of release.

Inman agrees that despite the growing popularity of rosé, with many producers jumping on the 'pink wine bandwagon' since 2004, 'the wines are unlikely to reach export markets because of the limited quantities produced and the high costs.' The majority of quality Californian rosés are sold by producers direct to consumers. It is the only way to make a profit when using expensive grapes. If you have to give 50 per cent of the value to an importer or a wholesaler, it doesn't make financial sense.

THE PACIFIC NORTH-WEST

Most north-west wineries do not make much rosé. Some is limited by allocation; local restaurants and individuals may perhaps be allowed to buy just one case. According to Nicholas Paris MW, these are made in the Sancerre or Marsannay rosé style, as they use Pinot Noir, but have greater body, richness and fruit. In Oregon and the Williamette Valley, most rosés are made from Pinot Noir, the variety which put the state on the world winemaking map when it was first planted there 50 years ago. I was told that it was not unusual for producers to harvest at maximum ripeness to obtain full fruit character at the expense of fresh acidity, and then to acidify later to obtain a vibrant, cool-climate freshness.

Oregon

Kris Fade, co-proprietor of Analemma Wines in Oregon's Columbia Gorge AVA, commented that Oregon wines are generally made by small producers, who place importance on quality over quantity. Rosés are made by design, from field to bottle, rather than, as she put it, as a (*saignée*) 'by-product'. **Firesteed** (www.firesteed.com) Pinot Noir rosé was first made in 2008, with a small percentage of Fade's overall production. He aimed at a serious wine from the start, and is not worried if the wine is not in a Provence style. He feels the US market is moving to more serious rosé styles and away from the sweeter blush wines. Despite aiming at a serious wine, the wine is not made to age. The selling season is April to the end of summer, and Thanksgiving, with no sales over the winter.

Williamette Valley

The fresh fruit character typical of the wines of this region, are well demonstrated in the Pinot Noir Rosé from **Elk Cove Vineyards** (elkcove.com), with classic sweet raspberry, strawberry and cherry fruit, and fresh acidity. Some producers are creating more complex styles. Jason Lett at **Eyrie Vineyards** (www.eyrievineyards.com), made his first oak-fermented Pinot Noir rosé in 2011, using old barrels and indigenous yeasts that work well in barrel, followed by malolactic fermentation. This combination of fermentation techniques shows the typical cherry fruit of Pinot Noir but in a less fruit-driven style. The oak and yeasts contribute to more complex, savoury and umami notes and a weighty structure. The Huntington Hill Rosé of Pinot Gris from **Anne Amie Vineyards** (anneamie.com), is also barrel fermented, resulting in a rich, luscious raspberry fruit with savoury notes and orange zest on the finish. Kim Kramer at **Kramer Vineyards** (www.kramervineyards.com) makes two serious rosés. A Pinot Noir with extended skin contact of around three days and a Pinot Gris with around nine days' skin contact.

The Chehalem Mountains region is known for rich, elegant and complex wines including benchmark Pinot Noir. A couple of producers make Pinot Gris pink wines, inspired by the traditional *ramati* of northeast Italy and Slovenia.

> **Sokol Blosser**
> 5000 Sokol Blosser Lane, Dayton, OR 97114
> Tel.: 503 864 2282
> sokolblosser.com
> At Sokol Blosser, rosé production has really escalated since 2007. Their Pinot Noir fruit comes from a specific block of high yielding clones planted in sedimentary rock. In 2012 the next generation started taking over winemaking and began putting whole berries in the press for five hours, to produce a dry, crisp, red fruit which was light and elegant, with long acidity. The fruit was early-harvested to preserve acidity (removing the need to acidify). They are now doing trials on ambient yeasts selected from vineyard and cultivated.

Washington

Washington rosés are typically composed of the same Bordeaux or Rhône wine grapes that go into the state's powerful, age-worthy reds, with a handful using Italian grapes such as Nebbiolo and Sangiovese. Two different examples include Vino from **K Vintners** (www.charlessmithwines.com) in the Columbia Valley, which is made with Sangiovese harvested at higher altitude at full ripeness. The winemaker, Charles Smith, uses direct press for a juicy peach and red fruit rosé with fresh acidity. The other example, **Gilbert Cellars** (www.gilbertcellars.com) Rosé, Wahluke Slope, uses 78 per cent Mourvèdre and 22 per cent Grenache. The resulting wine has raspberry, peach, and pink grapefruit flavours with herbal and mineral notes, and long, fresh acidity.

VIRGINIA

Wine has been produced in Virginia since the days of the early colonists, in the seventeenth century. Its hot, humid summers can be challenging for viticulture; only within the last twenty years has the industry developed beyond novelty status. *Vitis vinifera* varieties represent 75 per cent of total production, French hybrid varieties nearly 20 per cent, and American varietals about 5 per cent of the total. As of 2012, some of the top varietals used in rosés were Cabernet Franc, Merlot, Barbera, Cabernet Sauvignon, Chambourcin, Mourvèdre, Nebbiolo, Norton and Petit Verdot.

The rebirth was led in part by the investment of the Zonin family of Italy in a new vineyard in **Barboursville** (www.bbvwine.com) in 1976. Their rosé is made with a blend of French and Italian varieties. Since the 1980s, many wineries and vineyards have been created, with over 230 wineries operating in Virginia by 2012. Almost all are small and family owned, with only the largest having developed distribution networks. As a result, most wineries rely on wine tourism and direct sales. Virginia dry rosés are often more European in style than West Coast rosés.

TEXAS

Grape growers and winemakers are increasingly setting aside plantings to make rosé, which used to be (and sometimes still is) a mere by-product in the production of red wine. 'We have the perfect climate and weather for rosé,' commented Doug Lewis of Johnson City's **Lewis Wines** (www.lewiswines.com) in a panel discussion at the Texas Wine Revolution festival in 2016. Texas, 'especially the Hill Country and the High Plains, has a competitive advantage in making a good rosé.' Local sales of rosé wine have doubled in recent years, encouraging producers to make more. Varieties such as Cinsault, Grenache, Sangiovese and Mourvèdre are the key grapes.

LONG ISLAND

Long Island is one of the few wine-growing regions surrounded by salt water. The resultant ocean breeze provides a natural, balanced acidity to the grapes, for dry, fresh, elegant wines. Early-ripening Bordeaux varieties such as Cabernet Sauvignon, Cabernet Franc, Merlot, Petit Verdot and Malbec grow well here, in loamy and sandy soils, much of which used to be potato farms.

Wölffer Estate
139 Sagg Road, PO Box 9002, Sagaponack, NY 11962
Tel.: (631) 537 5106
www.wolffer.com

This winery in the heart of the Hamptons was founded in 1988, and makes rosés with five to six different grape varieties (see p.157 for their Argentine rosé). Two-thirds of their production today is rosé. In 1992 just 82 cases were made, but now some 43,000 cases are produced. Three ranges are made. Summer in a Bottle is 57 per cent Merlot, 20 per cent Cabernet Franc, 12 per cent Chardonnay, and 11 per cent Gewürztraminer, for floral notes. Estate Rosé uses 49 per cent Merlot, 9 per cent Cabernet Sauvignon, 8 per cent Cabernet Franc, 30 per cent Chardonnay and 4 per cent Riesling, and in the cellar minimal skin contact and cold fermentation are employed. The Grandioso Rosé is made from 32 per cent Merlot, 21 per cent Cabernet Franc, 41 per cent Chardonnay, 5 per cent Gewürztraminer and 1 per cent Riesling. Free-run juice from all varieties is fermented together in French oak and kept on the lees, with *battonage* but no malolactic fermentation. A high percentage of white varieties, in the last two, contributes to a pale colour and freshness.

Croteaux Vineyards
1450 South Harbor Road, Southold, New York 11971
Tel.: (631) 765 6099
www.croteaux.com

Founded in 2003, this winery produces exclusively rosé wine. Co-owner Michael Croteaux explains that 'with rosé, you make it and sell it all in the same year. It was the only wine that made sense for us, the farm, and our lifestyle. We were always serious beach people, not serious wine people.'

Shinn Estate Vineyards
2000 Oregon Rd, Mattituck, NY
Tel.: (631) 804 0367
shinnestatevineyards.com

Midwesterners Barbara Shinn and David Page settled in New York in the early 1990s and built their vineyard a few years later. Their rosé, Rose Hill, is a simple, fresh Merlot.

Channing Daughters Winery
1927 Scuttlehole Road, P.O. Box 2202, Bridgehampton NY 11932
Tel.: (631) 537 7224
www.channingdaughters.com

A third of the 16,000 cases made are rosé. Winemaker–partner James Christopher Tracy's rosés are Italian-influenced. Rosé production began in

2005 and now seven different wines are made. Rosato di Syrah (368 cases); Rosati di Sculpture Garden Vineyard, a Merlot-based field blend with Blaufrankisch and Teroldego, processed and fermented together (298 cases in 2016); Rosato di Refosco (335 cases); Rosato di Merlot (1208 cases); Rosato di Franconia (398 cases); Rosato di Cabernet Sauvignon, using grapes from some of the oldest vines planted (in 1975) on Long Island (518 cases) and Rosato du Cabernet Franc (1,228 cases). They also make a Pinot Gris *ramato*.

Sparkling rosés

These are made by some producers in Long Island. **Sparkling Pointe** (www.sparklingpointe.com) in Southold, North Fork was founded in 2002. As the name implies, all wine at this vineyard is sparkling. Cuvée Carnaval Rosé is made by the *méthode traditionelle*, and described by the winery as 'a lovely apéritif for summer entertaining'. **Lieb Cellars** (liebcellars.com), Mattituck, North Fork was founded in 1992, since when, they say, 'Every vintage of our Bridge Lane Rosé has been made in the dry style'. The sparkling pink wine is from 80 per cent Pinot Noir and 20 per cent Chardonnay, with 420 cases produced.

Eric Asimov, the wine columnist of the *New York Times*, has written a number of excellent reviews of rosés from around the world, so I asked him how, in his opinion, American rosés compared and how he would sum up the style. With such wide diversity he felt that it was 'impossible to generalize about American rosé,' not because of the differences in terroir but because in his experience 'it has been a "made" wine rather than a wine of place, exhibiting the inclinations of the producer rather than any terroir characteristics.' Making a rosé to fit the demands of the international market is a trend happening in many places around the world. 'American rosés are made from all sorts of grapes that are grown in all sorts of places. Producers dictate the styles, and while I say I have had many excellent, refreshing rosés, I've probably had even more that were too heavy, too fruity and too alcoholic. But at least there is diversity.' He did note though that he had sampled 'many excellent American rosés, dry, savory, even minerally' and that for him these were the rosés of most interest. The biggest problem for the rest of the world is obtaining a bottle of some of these more interesting rosés.

CANADA

From the 1970s, rosés were made with lots of residual sugar to keep pace with the white Zinfandel trend, with dry rosé production unfashionable until the late 1990s. As Canadian wine writer Treve Ring says, 'producers are now embracing dry, finessed and grown up rosés. Colours range from near clear to deep pink, … with good acidity.' Though the fashion now is for dry wines, white Zinfandels still make up about 10 per cent of the Liquor Control Board of Ontario's (LCBO) pink sales.

Reviewing the year 2016–17, the LCBO reported that among Vintners Quality Association (VQA) Ontario appellation wines, rosés were the only growth area, stating: 'Growth was driven by VQA rosé, which was the fastest-growing subset at 38.6 percent and generated an increase of more than $1 million.'

There are two main areas of production in Canada: Ontario in the east, on the northern shores of the Great Lakes, and British Colombia in the west, particularly the Okanagan Valley.

Ontario

Ontario and Niagara have a continental climate of hot summers and freezing winters moderated by nearness to the lakes. Their rosés include blends of Cabernet Franc, Gamay and Pinot Noir; Cabernet Franc, Merlot and Cabernet Sauvignon; Chardonnay and Merlot, and single varieties such as Pinot Gris, Cabernet Franc and Pinot Noir (although this variety achieves better commercial value as a red wine). The rosés typically show crisp, mouth-watering acidity with fresh, cool-climate fruit of rhubarb, redcurrants, raspberries and wild strawberries.

Malivoire Wine Company

4260 King Street East, Beamsville, Ontario L0R 1B0
Tel.: (866) 644 2244
malivoire.com

Headed by Martin Malivoire, a Hollywood special effects director, this winery business in Niagara Peninsula has grown since his purchase in 1995, and now produces more than 24,000 cases of wine a year. The Ladybug Rosé (a blend of Cabernet Franc, Pinot Noir and Gamay) is the top selling rosé across Ontario in the LCBO, and a brilliant local success story.

Southbrook Vineyards

581 Niagara Stone Road, Niagara-on-the-Lake, Ontario L0S 1J0

Tel.: (905) 641 2548

www.southbrook.com

Here, Ann Sperling makes an interesting rosé of 50 per cent Cabernet Sauvignon and 50 per cent Cabernet Franc with a natural ferment in barrel (no malolactic fermentation). The resulting wine is a serious, dry style with excellent acidity which will open out with age and take on more complex character.

> **Icewine**
>
> Ontario produces 80 per cent of the world's icewine, including pink icewine (labelled as red wine), made from Cabernet Sauvignon (which contributes black fruit notes) and Cabernet Franc (rhubarb notes). Vintage variation regarding the extent of the freeze and the balance between sugar and alcohol contributes significant difference to the richness and intensity. Some vintages, like the 2013 saw a double freeze (freeze, thaw, freeze), resulting in good quality fruit that was harvested between November and February.

Pillitteri Estates Winery

1696 Niagara Stone Road, Niagara-on-the-Lake, Ontario L0S 1J0

Tel.: (905) 468 3147

www.pillitteri.com

The Reserve Cabernet Sauvignon icewine is basket pressed to deal with the small concentrated berries. Pressure of 350 bars yields 12–20 per cent of the grapes, resulting in a concentrated fruit wine. Because of the high degree of sugar, the juice is fermentated for four to six weeks, resulting in moderate alcohol levels (11.5% abv), 220g/l residual sugar and 8.8g/l acidity. The beautiful dark pink wine has pronounced aromas of roses and cherries and is smooth, creamy and rich, with rich black cherry fruit.

Lake View Cellars

1067 Niagara Stone Rd, Niagara-on-the-Lake, Ontario L0S 1J0

Tel.: (905) 685 5673

www.lakeviewwineco.com

Cabernet Franc icewine from Lake View Cellar is a pale, tawny pink with fresh strawberry and rhubarb fruit.

British Columbia

British Columbia, on the west coast, is a warmer region, with a moderating maritime influence. Centred around the north–south Okanagan Valley, the province produces rosés from classic varieties such as Pinot Noir, Cabernet Franc and, to a lesser degree, Gamay and Zweigelt, with a smattering of southern-French varieties in warmer pockets. Playing with the range of temperatures and altitudes helps to add complexity to the fruit and acidity. Some producers are trying exciting new techniques, beyond minimal skin contact and cold fermentation, making off-dry to dry rosés, many with high alcohol, suggesting that they have potentially been bled off red wines harvested at later maturity. Nevertheless, all have crisp acidity and are fruit driven – exhibiting varying degrees of success, but all with potential.

Pinot Noir styles are made with many techniques: using specific clones, whole cluster pressing, short to long skin contact, *saignée* from young vines, wild ferment, full malolactic fermentation and barrel ageing, to give a range of fresh, vibrant, fruit rosés with differing levels of complexity. Those from the southern reaches of the Okanagan valley show more opulence, with dark cherry fruit, while wines from the cooler northern slopes have more minerality and rhubarb notes.

Cabernet Franc rosés use a slightly less varied range of techniques including whole cluster ferment, lightly crushed or foot trodden, short to long skin contact, wild ferment, tank and barrel. Rhubarb, Griotte cherry and wild strawberry flavours can be found. Some rosés also retain some residual sugar yielding wines with more strawberry and cream and jammy fruit notes.

In warmer regions of the Okanagan Valley, some are making rosé with Mediterranean varieties. **Stag's Hollow** Rosé (stagshollowwinery.com) is dry and powerful, similar to Tavel in its structure, using 70 per cent Syrah and 30 per cent Grenache. **Red Rooster**'s (www.redroosterwinery.com) Reserve Rosé is a blend of Syrah, Malbec, Mourvèdre, Grenache and Petit Verdot, made by cold soaking on the skins for three days before fermentation in tank, for a big style rosé that is far crisper, and more redolent of cool climate fruit than normally associated with these varieties.

Sparkling Canadian wines

Bella Cavada
4320 Gulch Road, Naramata, British Columbia, V0H 1N1
Tel.: (778) 996 1829
bellawines.ca

Bella Cavada in the Okanagan Valley makes a range of sparkling wines from Gamay grown on different parcels and with different techniques. The differences are fascinating and show the potential complexity for sparkling rosé. Their basic sparkler comes from the Naramata Bench and is fresh and fruity (12g/l residual sugar). The other three come from the volcanic soils of Westbank South. The traditional method Westbank wine (half destemmed and half whole cluster) has crisp cranberry and rhubarb freshness, wild strawberries and hints of complex orange-peel notes. The Westbank *methode ancestrale* is made in six barrels, filled and placed under the cherry trees at Bella's Naramata site to wait for a full wild ferment – only 30 cases are made – it is more concentrated and intense. Westbank Reserve (also only 30 cases) is made in the 'traditional method' and spends three years on the lees. It has delicate strawberry and cherry notes with much firmer mineral and saline structure and a toasty lees character.

Peller Estates
290 John Street East, Niagara-on-the-Lake, Ontario L0S 1J0
Tel.: (905) 468 4678
www.peller.com

Located on the Niagara Peninsula, they make a distinctly Canadian sparkling rosé called Ice Cuvée. The base wine is made from Pinot Noir and Chardonnay. To this is added red Gamay wine for colour and Vidal icewine for sweetness. The resulting pink wine has beautiful aromatic, floral perfume with fresh, red fruit and acidity and 21g/l residual sugar.

Other Canadian pink sparkling wines include Pinot Noir, Pinot–Chardonnay, Pinot–Gamay and Gamay, made in the traditional method. They tend to have good red fruit character supporting their pink colour. Some have a touch of residual sugar to balance the naturally high acidity.

7

THE SOUTHERN HEMISPHERE

The focus of this chapter is southern hemisphere wine regions, whose rosés emerge in the northern hemisphere market as fresh young wines at the end of the northern summer season. This timing was important a decade ago, but is less so now as rosés are proving to age better.

AUSTRALIA

In 1824, at the age of twenty-three, Scotsman James Busby emigrated with his family to New South Wales. He was already interested in wine, and returned to Europe in 1831 to explore winemaking. We have already seen him in Provence, discussing local varieties. He published his findings in 1833 and sent hundreds of cuttings back to Australia, many of which survived and were planted in the Sydney botanic gardens. As with California, Grenache was one of the earliest varieties to be planted, with the first Grenache vineyard possibly planted in 1838 in the McLaren Vale. During the first half of the twentieth century, the fashion was for big, rich, often fortified, reds. Big red wines continued to be popular, but in recent years, a move to cooler climate wines and lighter, more elegant styles has become fashionable and, interestingly enough, there is also a growing interest in rosé.

When Andrea Pritzker MW (wine buyer for Qantas epiQure, the retail online wine business of the Qantas frequent flyer program) first arrived in Australia in 2003, 'rosé was rare and derided by most consumers. A lot of rosé was deep fuchsia pink, or fire-engine raspberry, made in a medium-sweet style and often sold in retail for under AU$10 (US$8). It was difficult to find a good quality rosé on a wine list.' Rosé was perceived as a lesser wine, often sweet 'lolly water', that few respected winemakers would work with. Tasting notes included descriptors such as confectionary, strawberry, raspberry, cherries, luscious, soft, well-rounded, full-flavoured, succulent and, above all, easy drinking.

As winemakers began harvesting earlier to achieve better acidity, the wines changed. Australian wine writer Huon Hooke noted that they were 'often made from Cabernet Sauvignon, which was harvested early to achieve low alcohols, and therefore had green tannins which further compounded the poor drinkability.' This he feels was partially due to a confused idea of the style they should be creating. 'Australian winemakers, possibly led more by show judges than consumers, used to think rosé should be deep purple in colour, with strident acidity cutting through shrill fruit and relatively high sweetness,' reflecting some of the big, bold red and white wines being made in the 1980s and 90s. The Alicante Bouschet rosé by Rockford was described by Felix Riley (a French rosé importer) as 'one of the grand-daddies of rosé in Australia'. Its dark cherry colour and sweet fruit, as well as limited availability, gained it cult status. However, its modern relevance is diminishing as Provence-style rosé takes over.

Recently, winemakers have been making rosé differently, in a more balanced style, with the fruit, acidity and residual sugar components in greater harmony with each other. Key initial producers in the early years were Barossa's **Turkey Flat** (www.turkeyflat.com.au) and **Charles Melton** (www.charlesmeltonwines.com.au), as well as pioneers like the dry, light Pinot Noir rosé from Yarra Valley's **Dominique Portet** (dominiqueportet.com).

Pritzker observed that producers were starting to make rosé 'as an experiment (winemakers like to drink it), but mostly sold it as a cellar-door only wine,' possibly because 'buyers in the dominant supermarket-owned chains were not that interested in rosé and/or the volumes being produced were not commercially viable to range nationally.' A similar situation can be seen worldwide. By 2013 James Halliday commented that 'the number of rosés on the market continues to grow, seemingly unabated and unstoppable.' Pritzker noted that it was around 2010–13 that 'rosé finally started to get more traction.'

The value of rosé has continued to be a problem in dissuading some producers from making higher quality wine. Some complain that even when the quality of fruit and winemaking is as good as their red and white wines, buyers demand lower prices (a problem not unique to Australia).

Fran Austin of **Delamere Vineyards** in Tasmania (www.delamerevineyards.au) told me how she laughed the first time her friend John Hurlston told her of the price Chateau d'Esclan's Garrus was selling for (€80). However, she was intrigued by the idea of making such a high quality (and expensive) rosé, and after some experimenting, she and husband Shane Holloway, in memory of Hurlston who had died, released Hurlo Pinot Noir rosé 2015. With only 60 cases made, and at AUS $80 a bottle (the most expensive in Australia), it attracted attention. Fermented in barrel previously used for their Chardonnay, the wine was a success. According to Max Allen, writing in *The Australian* the wine had, 'enticing floral, gentle berry and woody spice aromas and a rich, creamy, deeply satisfying flavour and texture on the tongue.'

In October 2016, Wine Australia declared that rosé was Australia's fastest-growing category. AC Nielsen figures show the value of sales of still rosé wine grew by 26 per cent and jumped 44 per cent for sparkling rosé in the 12 months ending June 2016. Nevertheless, dominant retailers have far fewer rosés than one would expect from a nation with a warm, sunny climate.

When Pritzker started at Qantas as a buyer in January 2016, the list of 650 wines included three still rosés and two sparkling. A year later, Pritzker had listed over twenty rosés, and plans to add more. Qantas is evidently not the only buyer, as producers admit they are having problems keeping up with demand. From rosé being almost an afterthought, producers are now working on a dedicated production requiring a lot more grapes, with many doubling or tripling output and still selling out.

At the German trade fair Prowein in 2017 Kay Brothers' marketing manager, Steve Todd, explained that the fastest-growing rosé market is in Sydney. As in the rest of the world, its historical customer base was women, but men are increasingly interested, especially those who do not like white wine. Compared with some of the reds and whites available, rosé is seen as easy-drinking and affordable. He predicts that in ten years, rosé consumption will equal that of white, and regional and varietal styles will develop and become more defined.

This sudden growth in interest in rosé appears to have come from several directions. Pritzker attributes this to imports introducing new styles, and journalists reaching out to a wider market when talking about rosé. The increase in imported rosés (often from Provence) appearing on Australian wine lists introduced consumers to a drier, paler style of wine. Hooke also believes that drinkers, having graduated from sweeter imports such as Mateus Rosé, to drier styles, contributed to the surge in popularity in the past decade. 'In the last 15 to 20 years, the consumption and appreciation of imported wine, from every corner of the globe into Australia has exploded. The lights were turned on, and rosé was one of the styles to benefit from that awakening ... recently our winemakers have looked towards southern France for their ideal. I give Steve and Leanne Webber of De Bortoli's Yarra Valley winery much of the credit for waking Australia up to the wonderful drinkability of this kind of rosé, from Provence, the southern Rhone and Languedoc.'

Pritzker feels that sometimes the 'status of imported rosé is very high (even if the quality isn't always there). This has been largely due to the impact of seeing trendy Provençal rosé on top restaurant lists, ... with wider variety of choice (not just one or two "token selections").' She also notes the 'major players ... bringing in their own rosés direct and heavily marketing them ... thus driving sales to the imported sector.' With Australians tending to perceive foreign rosés as sophisticated, 'many Australians are choosing to buy imported rosé, perhaps not quite realizing that the quality of domestic rosé on offer in Australia is fantastic,' says Pritzker. Reviews from wine journalists such as Max Allen, Huon Hooke and James Halliday, to name but a few, indicate that Australian rosés are becoming drier and more food-friendly.

Australian rosés fall into three main groups, although these can overlap:

- Australian style,
- Provence style,
- serious international style.

A fourth group, aromatic rosés, is small but worth noting.

James Halliday noted the wide range of styles in his *Australian Wine Companion* (2012), 'There are no rules: they can be bone-dry, slightly sweet, or very sweet. They can be, and are, made from almost any red variety, red blends or red and white blends. They may be a convenient way of concentrating the red wine left after the rosé is run off from the fermenter shortly after the grapes are crushed, or made from the ground up using grapes and techniques specifically chosen for the purpose. The vast majority fall in the former camp.'

Jacob's Creek (www.jacobscreek.com), owned by Pernod Ricard, makes a range of rosés in the current styles available commercially. Their 2016 Shiraz (Syrah) rosé is a typical benchmark Australian rosé, with sugar balanced by vibrant acidity and sour cherry fruit, with dark pink hues. The newest wine in the range, is the Petit Rosé, made in the 'French style' and marketed as a Provence style rosé. Already a big seller in 2016 in Australia, this Pinot Noir–Grenache–Mourvèdre blend with grapes sourced from numerous places in South Eastern Australia, is not attempting to be a serious wine reflecting a sense of place, but to be a commercially successful drier rosé.

Australian style

The most noticeable consequence of using red wine by-products was the use of very ripe fruit with longer skin contact creating a darker *clairet* style wine with tannins. Leaving in residual sugar served to accentuate the fruit and balance the tannins and, by arresting the fermentation to keep some sugar, served to prevent overly high alcohol levels.

A progression from old by-product rosés, made with the Cabernet (Sauvignon and Franc), Shiraz and Grenache varieties, with some residual sugar. These are often made with ripe, red grapes, cold-soaking to extract fruit and colour with fewer tannins and less skin contact for bright, jewel-like colours. These wines often fall mid-way between rosé and red. They are full and fruity in character, many with a higher level of residual sugar, often around 9g/l, but balanced with acidity, and lower in alcohol – around 11% abv. They are refreshing and flavoursome.

Descriptors are similar to early Australian rosés, but the quality is improving with more bold and dynamic fruit, well-balanced with a subtle, tannic finish. They are best drunk when fresh, youthful and vibrant. Charles Melton Rosé of Virginia is typical of this style.

This style allows for greater varietal character to show through, and some producers are making some interesting wines from varieties which would have otherwise been lost in big red blends, such as Spanish or Italian varieties.

Rosé Saignée from **Gilbert Family Wines** (www.gilbertfamilywines.com.au) in Orange, New South Wales (87 per cent Sangiovese, 10 per cent Shiraz and 3 per cent Barbera), uses grapes from vines planted at high altitude (830–60 metres) to give fresh acidity. In an Australia meets Puglia wine, Vino Rosato from **di Lusso** (dilusso.com.au), Mudgee, New South Wales, is made from 95 per cent Aleatico with a touch (5 per cent) of the acidic northern variety Lagrein. The fruit is emphasized by 9g/l residual sugar. A few rosés use Tempranillo, but usually as part of a blend. In 2016 **Gemtree** (gemtreewines.com), in McLaren Vale, South Australia, used Tempranillo because of the short supply of Grenache and Shiraz (which are reserved for reds), to make a dry, austere rosé.

Playing on the reputation of Rockford's original Alicante rosé, the 1919 Series Alicante Rosé from **Taminick Cellars** (www.taminickcellars.com.au) in north-east Victoria, is made from 100-year-old Alicante Bouschet vines. Alicante's near-black juice means this is always a darker pink wine. Cold soak pre-maceration takes place before gentle, whole-bunch pressing, followed by fermentation in a mix of tank and new French oak barrels, using a mix of ambient and selected yeast. Another historic rosé is **Marco Cirillo**'s (cirilloestatewines.com.au) *rosato* from possibly the oldest Grenache in the world.

Syrah/Shiraz is a popular variety. A fruity style Shiraz rosé can sometimes have peach notes and extra opulence, from up to 8 or 9g/l residual sugar. 'Turkish delight' frequently crops up as a tasting note amongst critics, as well as 'wild-berry fruit-bombs.' Longer maceration gives a deeper colour and structure for a typically Australian-style rosé. Well-made Shiraz rosés have international appeal. **Chapman Grove**'s (www.chapmangrove.com.au) Shiraz rosé 2016 (Western Australia), with its dark, vibrant, salmon-pink colour, luscious strawberry and cream fruit and hints of vanilla, has sufficient complexity of fruit character, weight and fresh acidity, to win a gold at the International Rosé Championship in Poland.

When a producer labels the wine as Syrah it is an indication that it is more likely to be in the serious international style. Early harvesting and cold fermentation gives these Syrah rosés extra crispness and some classic herb and pepper notes, accentuated by a touch of oak. **Mad Fish**'s (www.madfishwines.com.au) Syrah rosé 2016 (Western Australia) was, the winemaker felt, too dry. This assessment might demonstrate more about what Australians expect from wine than it does about the wine itself: it had classic red berry and fresh cherry fruit, light, fresh, zippy acidity and a faint, dry tannic finish.

Rosés made with Bordeaux blend varieties, and Malbec, originally from south-west France, are popular. Many are by-products of red wine, making them cost effective. With grapes harvested later, the wines show typical varietal fruit, 6–9g/l residual sugar, fresh, leafy acidity and soft, tannic structure. Cabernet rosés, especially from cooler climates, or earlier harvesting, have an extra leafy freshness to balance the full, fruity styles.

These can be found throughout Australia. Some of the names given to wines in this style indicate the fun approach to rosé. **Bloodwood Wines** (www.bloodwood.biz) claim that their Malbec rosé Big Men in Tights 'is *the* wine for wrestlers; (and bikers and their grandmothers) … in fact it's for anybody who is genuinely serious about not being too serious about wine.'

Both fruity and more complex Pinot rosés are made which bridge the Australian–Provence styles. Kym Milne MW at **Bird in Hand** (www.birdinhand.com.au), Adelaide Hills, makes a pale pink one, with juicy, vibrant cherry fruit, overt Pinot character and good acidity. A slightly more complex, fruity version comes from **St Maur Wines** (www.stmaurwines.com.au), Southern Highlands. From volcanic soil in north-facing vineyards at 700 metres altitude, the wine has vibrant acidity and is dry, and full of Australian cherry, raspberry and strawberry fruit.

Not all Australian-style rosés are successful. As Bloodwood Wines say on their website, 'Although [rosés are] often good quality drinks, they can often show more extraction, tannin, alcohol and residual sweetness than is necessary in what is essentially a fine, light and refreshing style of wine.'

Provence style

This is a term sometimes used on labels and websites or in publicity. In general, this means the rosé is paler in colour, less fruity and fractionally drier. However, this has also resulted in some wines with no fruit, creating rather weak and neutral wines. Unfortunately, paleness is often perceived by consumers as a sign of higher quality. Dryness is also associated with a European style when the wine can be described as 'traditional, dry, European-style rosé.' Since 2014, the trend has been to make paler, drier 'Provence-style' rosés, moving away from the sweet, fruit-bomb styles. Not all Australian Provence-style rosés are successful. By harvesting earlier with minimal skin contact to achieve lighter colour, restraint and acidity, many miss the mark, resulting in weak and light wines that achieve the 'pale and dry', but lack the distinctive saline/schist minerality, balanced with ripe fruit, of Provence.

Schwarz (www.schwarzwineco.com.au) of Barossa Valley makes a Mataro (Mourvèdre)–Grenache blend, which is pale and bone dry. 'It's one wine which gives my Provence rosés a run for the money,' says French wine importer Felix Riley.

Cranberry, with its acid-fruit character, is a frequently used descriptor for Grenache-based Provence-style rosés. **Spinifex** (www.spinifexwines.com.au) Rosé 2015, Barossa Valley, South Australia, is a Provence-style rosé in terms of colour and make-up with Grenache, Cinsault, Mataro (Mourvèdre) and Ugni Blanc, with ripe, fresh cranberry fruit and hints of spice. Winemaker Peter Schell worked for a couple of vintages in Provence.

It's no surprise that Not Your Grandma's Rosé from **Chaffey Brothers** (www.chaffeybroswine.com.au), is not a traditional Australian style. It is made with a Provence blend of 62 per cent Grenache, 30 per cent Mourvèdre with the remaining 8 per cent a blend of Riesling, Gewürztraminer and Weißer Herold) to give a hint of aromatics.

Hooke attributes the rise in popularity of Australian rosés to the move to these drier, lighter styles. 'The problem before was, we didn't have those wines here and little rosé was imported.' Now, with an increase in imports and more wines being made in a drier style, their appeal is growing.

Modern Australian/serious international style

These wines are generally dry, but not necessarily so. They come from winemakers with a proven track record for making premium wines.

By Farr
101 Kelly Lane, Bannockburn, VIC 3331
Tel.: (61) 3 5281 1733
www.byfarr.com.au

The winery is owned by Gary Farr (winemaker at Bannockburn) and his son Nick. In a hot and dry region, with moderating maritime winds with cool nights, they make two Pinot rosés. Rosé By Farr is the more complex, with natural barrel-fermentation at cool temperatures, followed by full malolactic fermentation. The wine is then aged in used barrels for ten months.

Pike & Joyce
730 Mawson Rd, Lenswood, SA 5240
Tel.: (08) 8 389 8102
www.pikeandjoyce.com.au

Here, they have been making their *saignée* Pinot Noir rosé since 2006. This is fermented in 228 litre old French oak barrels, using ambient yeast. The natural acidity from vines grown over 500 metres is retained with no malolactic fermentation. The wine is aged on the lees in barrels for two to three months. According to winemaker Neil Pike, the wine has 'complexity, slight richness and roundness coming from the barrel ferment and the slightly "funky" notes that come from the warm ferment and the underlying strawberry, cherry fruit that ultimately drive the wine. Its complexity and low residual sugar makes it a terrific food wine.' The wine was originally called The Bleedings but after negative comments from the trade, was changed to Les Saignées.

'International' style Syrah rosés are also seeing success, especially a handful of biodynamic producers such as **Ngeringa** (www.ngeringa.com) Rosé from the Adelaide Hills and **Castagna** (castagna.com.au/vineyard) Allegro, a barrel-aged rosé made in Beechworth, Victoria.

Sangiovese often shows weight and structure more in keeping with Mourvèdre rosé. Friends and Lovers from **Down the Rabbit Hole** (downtherabbitholewines.com.au) is an almost biodynamic 100 per cent Sangiovese rosé with lovely complexity and good structure that is savoury with a slight yeastiness. It goes beyond straightforward fruit and acid and the weight and savoury notes carry the usual wild-berry fruit far further than usual. Sue Trott of **Five Geese** (www.fivegeese.com.au)

makes a delicious firm, structured and savoury Nero d'Avola rosé called La Volpe.

Nebbiolo is proving a successful variety for rosé in Australia, where the extra ripeness brings out strawberry, cherry and peach fruit, but in less opulent style than a traditional Australian-style rosé. The natural tannins make it ideal for a pale, bone-dry wine. Bryan Martin at **Ravensworth** (www.ravensworthwines.com.au) in Murrumbateman, was introduced to Clos Cibonne from Provence, where the Tibouren is made under flor, by the Israeli winemaker Guy Eshel. Martin is now trialling ageing Nebbiolo (and Pinots Gris and Noir) under flor in barrel for the first time with his 2017 vintage, to see if he can create more savoury characters. The wine will be left untouched for at least a year.

> **Logan Wines**
>
> 1320 Castlereagh Highway, Apple Tree Flat, Mudgee, NSW 2850
> Tel.: (61) 2 6373 1333
> loganwines.com.au
>
> The vineyards are situated at 950 metres altitude which contributes to the freshness and acidity of the wines. The Hannah Rosé is a blend of 35 per cent Meunier, 30 per cent Shiraz, 20 per cent Cabernet Franc and 15 per cent Pinot Gris. Over and above the unusual blend is complex vinification, which is increasingly seen for serious rosés. The Pinot Gris is oxidatively handled and crushed to a small fermentation vessel, where it undergoes alcoholic and and malolactic fermentation on skins for 14 days, without the use of sulphur or inert gas. The rest goes through cool, short maceration to extract fruit but not tannin, and fermentation in a combination of stainless steel tank and French and Hungarian oak barrels with malolactic fermentation.

Emma Raidis of **Raidis Estate** (www.raidis.com.au) leaves her Pinot Gris on the skins for four days, creating a weighty wine with creamy texture and peach and savoury fruit. Her first vintage of Cheeky Goat in 2010 was hard to sell because of the pink tinge, but now the fashion for rosé sells the wine.

With significant climatic variation within each region, it is difficult to group the wines and styles by geographic origin. Felix Riley feels that 'it's less about regionality and more about style, with the general conundrum of drinkers asking "is this sweet or dry", which for the casual buyer lacking guidance can still be a random punt in making a choice. If anything, many Barossa and McLaren Vale producers are seeking to shake off the impression that their region only makes sweet styles.'

Producers are exploring which sites are best for rosé, with higher altitude for extra coolness and freshness appearing popular. Whilst most vineyards can add new plantings dedicated to rosé, almost all recent increases in rosé production come from diverting existing fruit from reds to rosé.

Aromatic rosés

With the Australian consumer's soft spot for fruity rosés, these aromatic styles still have their place in the market.

Pink Moscatos such **Innocent Bystander** (www.innocentbystander.com.au) Moscato from Swan Hill in Victoria are often exuberant and fruity. According to Wine-Searcher, in the year to June 2017, while the top nine Moscatos searched for were Italian, Innocent Bystander's pink Moscato came in at number ten. It is the top-ranked pink Moscato in the world in terms of searches. Sales of carbonated Moscato (white and pink) have soared in America and Australia. Phil Sexton sold the Innocent Bystander brand to Brown Brothers in 2016 on the back of its Moscato success. **Audrey Wilkinson**'s (audreywilkinson.com.au) Winemaker's Selection Moscato, Hunter Valley, has arrested fermentation halfway through resulting in a fresh, aromatic, fruity rosé with just 6% abv.

White wine tinged with red to make a rosé has appeared in a few places (Australia, New Zealand and California), which is disconcerting. Tasting a white wine (Sauvignon Blanc, Chardonnay or Riesling) with a pink colour confuses the taster's brain. So I was less than enthusiastic when Phil Reedman contacted me about his Gewurztraminer rosé. He had a block of 1980s Gewurztraminer in the Riverlands, but as this variety is unfashionable, he could not sell its wine. So he added 1.5 per cent Shiraz – enough to make it pink, but not enough to add flavour. The combination works amazingly well. The exotic aromatics of tea roses and spice mentally match the pink colour and show the power colour exerts on the opinion of the taster. The wine is currently sold through two different outlets under two different labels: 'Rosé' without varietal qualification on one and the mellifluous 'Savagnin Rose Aromatique', on the other. Savagnin Rose is an authorized synonym for Gewürztraminer, according to Wine Australia.

Many rosés are also made with Italian varieties, even including Italian–American *vitis labrusca* varieties. **Baratto Wines** (www.barattowines.com) makes a 'limited release' Fragolina rosé, explaining that 'the intoxicating perfume of ripening Fragola grapes brings back fond memories of a long-ago childhood where every Italian toolshed had one of these grape vines growing over it. Our Fragolina is … a sweet delight of ripe strawberry aromas and flavours', with low alcohol (8% abv). To my mind, Fragola grapes always have the faintest foxy whiff, which to others is described as spicy (see also Austrian *uhudler* p.222).

Interesting sparkling rosés, not just champagne-style, are also available. **Krinklewood**'s (www.krinklewood.com) Wild Pink is a blend of Verdelho, Gewürztraminer and Shiraz, which is lightly sweet, fragrant and frizzante. Wicked Secrets from **Stonefish** (stonefishinternational.com.au) in the Hunter Valley, is a sparkling-pink Moscato aimed at a female audience. According to the Stonefish website, 'The two wines in the Wicked Secrets wine range are sweet and refreshing, with vibrant fruity palates.'

Marketing Australian rosé

Rosé is still, on the whole, not seen as a high-quality wine, but as part of the fun-loving lifestyle. This image of rosé on the beach, for the barbecue and as part of summer living has pervaded much of the marketing and descriptions of Australian rosé. Back in 2006, Clint Hillary, sommelier at the Gazebo Wine Garden in Elizabeth Bay, noted in *The Sun-Herald*, that a younger crowd was increasingly drinking rosé. Beach culture is evident in Australian rosé promotions, such as on Instagram, which focuses on a chilled glass of rosé on the beach, in a café or by the sea. Lifestyle is emphasized over quality, indeed importer 84Vin's marketing slogan is 'Rosé isn't just a drink … it's a lifestyle!' and that of Rosé Imports is 'Follow the rosé way of life here'. Sales of Jacobs Creek Petit Rosé have promoted it as ideal for hot weather, drunk very cold, and even served as a frosé (frozen rosé). The lighter styles of rosé wine are increasingly appreciated as an accompaniment to summer dining. Dry, Provence-style rosés are recommended as the perfect accompaniment to a wide range of salads, grilled seafood and shellfish, while darker, Australian-style rosés are a popular alternative to red wines, during the hot summers.

'Australia is catching up with the rest of the world in matching rosé with food ... Rosé has undergone a complete image transformation over the past decade, emerging as a favourite for summer refreshment, and for matching with a wide range of cuisines. It's hip and happening,' wrote Australian food and wine journalist Winsor Dobbin on the Nine Kitchen food blog in February 2017. Andrea Pritzker is also 'very excited about the future of Australian rosé ... it's a style that Australians are finally realizing is really made for this climate [it] pairs well with the kind of food Australians like to eat.'

As winemaker Phil Reedman MW commented, 'I see Australia continuing to develop its rosé culture. The fashion for pale coloured wines will be exploited, while long-standing producers such as Charles Melton, Rockford [and] Turkey Flat will continue with their styles which reflect variety and place. Inventive winemakers will develop new styles using the alternative varieties which are coming on stream. So, while colour will vary with fashion, diversity of style will increase.'

NEW ZEALAND

Rosés have been around for a few years in New Zealand although the approach of producers has been tentative. Esk Valley Estates' first rosé was produced in 1991. In 2003 only 905 cases of rosé were exported. A glimpse of how these early rosés tasted can be seen in an anecdote from Dave Clouston, the **Two Rivers** (www.tworivers.co.nz) owner-winemaker, on Cuisinewine.co.nz in 2013. In 2005, he went to make wine in Aléria in Corsica, where he 'explained to the locals the common New Zealand method of rosé production. They were scandalised at the dark red Kiwi version. They showed me that rosé fruit needs to be picked early, to be treated like white wine. Everything there is geared to achieving that pale salmon colour, vibrancy and purity.' By 2011, rosé exports had increased to 69,111 cases. The 2012 guide to the wines of New Zealand gives a snapshot of the burgeoning New Zealand rosé market. An explosion in the number of rosés produced was noticeable, as was an increase in quality, and by 2012 it was evident that Pinot Noir and Merlot were the grape varieties most commonly used in New Zealand rosés. Regional variations have continued to develop, with further styles emerging, generally reflecting the varieties used for red wine production. For many vineyards though, rosé remains an 'add-on' with no details of varieties; a simple, fresh quaffer, not a serious wine.

Dom Maxwell, winemaker at **Greystone** (www.greystonewines.co.nz) in North Canterbury makes an interesting point on the evolution of New Zealand rosés. Consumers were so used to the overt fruit characters of local wines 'with Sauvignon Blanc paving the way and being such a dominant force' that consumers looked for overtly fruity rosés too: 'To begin with, it was the more is better mindset for many wineries and even consumers, if they weren't getting high perceived levels of flavour then they were being mizzled out of their hard-earned money.' The change came, he feels, as consumers began to appreciate the 'more subtle nuances due partly to increasing vine age and partly due to the rise of Pinot Noir as a variety here… Pinot Noir has character and interest without having to be dark in colour or extracted.'

Waiheke Island through to Hawke's Bay

Rosés from the middle and upper North Island, Hawkes Bay, Gisborne and Auckland, tend to be Merlot based, fuller bodied and drier. Historically Waiheke Island was known for its Bordeaux-style red blends then, about ten years ago, its growers branched out into award-wining Syrahs. Dry, darker Syrah rosés are beginning to emerge, such as those made at **Jurassic Ridge** (www.jurassicridge.co.nz), Waiheke, where, through whole-bunch pressing and long cold fermentation, they create a dark pink wine, full of raspberries, cherries and spicy black pepper.

Many, however, are still Merlot dominant, fresh, very fruity wines, sometimes with a touch of residual sugar to emphasize the fruit. **Cable Bay**'s (cablebay.nz) 100 per cent Merlot is dry with fresh strawberry, juicy plum and pink grapefruit flavours. **Poderi Crisci**'s (www.podericrisci.co.nz) rosé (predominantly Merlot) is dry, with fresh summer fruits and mineral structure. **Tantalus Estate**'s (www.tantalus.co.nz) Merlot-dominant rosé has fruity, red fruit with fresh acidity and flinty minerality.

Hawkes Bay to Waipara

A Bordeaux-style rosé is more common, with an emphasis on Merlot and Malbec and including some Cabernet Franc. Styles range from the soft, round, juicy style of the **Villa Maria** (www.villamaria.co.nz) Private Bin, to

Kim Crawford's (www.kimcrawfordwines.com) Hawke's Bay Pansy! with full-bodied, ripe, red, fruity sweetness, leafy acidity and a dry finish, and **Esk Valley**'s (www.eskvalley.co.nz) rosé, which includes some Cabernet and Malbec for complexity and structure.

Waipara

From here southwards, rosés start to become more Pinot Noir–dominant with three main styles emerging: dry and quite rich, the mass-market, sweeter, fruity styles and, more recently, the delicate, pale and dry, savoury, Provence-inspired styles. There are also some intriguing experiments.

At **Waipara Springs** (www.waiparasprings.co.nz) they bleed the juice off their Pinot Noir red for a crisp, fruity, slightly darker rosé with 8g/l residual sugar. Waipara Hills and The Winemaker's Wife also make fruity Pinot rosés with a touch of sweetness. Rosés with greater weight include those made at **Mount Brown,** (www.mountbrown.co.nz), where they macerate their Pinot Noir for 24 hours to create a rich, strawberry and cream style, and **Terrace Edge**'s (terraceedge.co.nz) dry Syrah rosé, made with slightly longer skin contact.

Nelson and Marlborough

South Island and Waipara rosés, usually made from Pinot Noir, are typically fresh, fruity and crisp. Brent Marris, at **The Ned**'s (thened.co.nz) Pinot Noir rosé has rich red fruit with hints of tangerine, redcurrants and nuts, lovely complexity and the fresh balance of extremely long, clean acidity. Some producers are trying to temper the fruitiness by incorporating varieties like Cabernet Franc, Malbec or Syrah: **Fromm Winery** (frommwinery.co.nz) does a weighty and dry Pinot Noir–Malbec–Syrah blend.

Dave Clouston's first rosé under the Two Rivers label appeared in 2013, a tribute to his vintages and lessons learned on Corsica, called L'Ile de Beauté. It is made from Pinot Noir, with ripe, red-berry fruit and leafy, mineral acidity. It is vibrant but not overtly fruity, 'a good example of "less is more"' says Ben Glover, Group winemaker for Accolade New Zealand.

In 2016 **John Forrest** (www.forrest.co.nz) first made Doctors' Rosé, using Pinot Noir with the addition of the aromatic and lower alcohol white variety Arneis, resulting in a pretty rosé with only 9.5% abv. The grapes were picked a little early, put in the press and cold soaked together. Following a big push by the government for lower alcohol wines, winemakers have been looking for ways to reduce sugar through innovations such as canopy manipulation, plucking the higher part of the canopy to slow down sugar accumulation but retain normal hanging time, different yeasts and ferment treatments in the winery.

Another way to make a fresh vibrant rosé is to use white grapes. Producers, such as **Mud House** (www.mudhouse.co.nz), make a Sauvignon Blanc Rosé with a small amount of Pinot Noir red. I admit to still being slightly confused by this style, with Sauvignon Blanc's floral aromas and fresh, tropical fruit mixed with Pinot Noir's berry and spices.

Sparkling rosés are also made, including **Cloudy Bay**'s (www.cloudybay.co.nz) pale pink Pelorus Rosé NV. Vinified in the traditional method, from 80 per cent Pinot Noir, it is fruity on the nose with minerality and sweet spice.

North Canterbury

Stephen Wong MW, New Zealand-based wine consultant, describes this region as, 'A hotbed of experimentation with both the traditional Pinot Noir rosés there as well as unusual examples.'

Greystone Wines
Tel.: 03 314 6100
www.greystonewines.co.nz

Winemaker Dom Maxwell decided to trial a different method for ageing their rosé. They wanted the lighter colour, which was easily achieved when using Pinot Noir grapes, but also wanted complexity and a subtle tannin grip. They experimented with handpicked Pinot Noir, wild fermented in old, French, oak *barriques*. Half the barrels were then lowered under water (freshwater inside the large winery tanks) and weighed down, to ensure they stayed underwater. Some ullage (space in the barrel, normally caused by evaporation) allowed for expansion and the bungs were tightly screwed down to keep water out. They wanted to see the effect of ageing under pressure and specifically allowing the wine to go through natural malolactic fermentation while underwater. The barrels were left underwater for varying lengths of time, between one and four months. The results seemed to show that the wine absorbed some tannin, presumably from the vigorous agitation as the wine goes through malolactic fermentation without a means for gas escape, and that the wine retained its freshness.

Black Estate

614 Omihi Road, Waipara Valley, New Zealand
Tel.: 3 314 6085
blackestate.co.nz

Home Rosé is a cofermented blend of ungrafted Pinot Noir with young-vine Cabernet Franc, Chenin Blanc and Chardonnay, after skin maceration ranging from one to twenty-eight days, depending on variety, combining rosé and orange wine techniques and giving extra complexity with dark cherry and peach fruit, notes of orange peel and spice, and a touch of dry tannin.

Mount Beautiful

11 Hall St, Cheviot 7310, New Zealand
Tel.: 3 319 8155
mtbeautiful.co.nz

The rosé is a blend from eight Pinot Noir vineyard blocks at high altitude, of different clones from young vines. Thirty per cent of this wine had minimal skin contact; the remaining 70 per cent was crushed and left to macerate for 24 hours. Eighty per cent was tank fermented and 20 per cent barrel fermented, bringing more texture and a creamy mouthfeel to the wine. The result is a complex, serious rosé with 14% abv.

Central Otago

This is almost exclusively Pinot Noir rosé country, although **Brennan Wines** (www.brennanwines.com) makes one from Tempranillo.

Aurum Wines

140 State Highway 6, Cromwell, Central Otago 9384, New Zealand
Tel.: 3 445 3620
aurumwines.co.nz

Winemaker Lucie Lawrence makes an atypical rosé from Pinot Gris. 'The idea was to make the most of the Pinot Gris skins and create a wine with more aromatic quality and a creamy mouthfeel even though the wine is dry.' Lawrence was inspired by the rosés of southern France with their 'delicate colours, mouth-watering and perfect with food.' She feels that the increasing number of rosés on offer, with their range of styles, is encouraging the consumer to become more discerning.

Felton Road
319 Felton Road, Bannockburn, R.D. 2, Central Otago 9384, New Zealand
Tel.: 3 445 0885
www.feltonroad.com

The Vin Gris is made from Pinot Noir, and is only produced in certain vintages. Whole-bunch pressing of young-vine Pinot Noir results in the very pale, copper colour of a *vin gris*. Fermentation in stainless steel tanks with ambient yeast, followed by ageing on the lees adds to the weight, richness and complexity of wild strawberry fruit with hints of fennel.

Unique dessert-wine style rosés are also made, such as Tickled Pink by **Wooing Tree** (wooingtree.co.nz), Cromwell, thought to be a first in New Zealand. Only 80 half-bottle cases were made in its first year (2017), from three rows of grapes left for a month after the usual harvest. Strawberry flavours come through strongly in the low-alcohol, high-sugar wine. The next bottling will be dependent on vintage conditions.

SOUTH AFRICA

Cathy van Zyl MW, of *Platter's South African Wine Guide*, recalls that the first rosé she remembers seeing 'on a shelf and on restaurant wine lists was Lanzerac Rosé, packaged in its iconic skittle-shaped bottle. That would have been around 1980.'

Back in the 1980s, South African rosés were typically a blend of white and red varieties, with little vinous character, and most of their 'charm' came from a few grams of residual sugar. Very few serious wine farms or estates made rosé – it was left to the big brand owners and cooperatives. During the 1990s, as South African winemakers became more accustomed to the *saignée* technique, several started fermenting and bottling the juice drawn off their red varieties, in a bid to concentrate the final wine. These wines were generally called 'blanc de noir' to differentiate them from the white–red blends, and they were usually a little more structured and a little drier.

In 1997, *Platter's Guide* listed only eight dry rosés, twenty-one that were off-dry or semi-sweet and forty-six *blancs de noirs*. Ten years later in 2007, the figures were somewhat reversed with 98 dry rosés, 95 off-dry or semi-sweet and 38 *blancs de noirs*. Despite the advent of *blanc de noirs*, rosé wine suffered a lacklustre reputation until the late 2000s, with too many considering it a semi-sweet, bland, 'ladies' wine. A 2007 report into premium rosé production by Anchor Yeasts, written up by Karien Lourens in *Wineland Magazine*, discussed what it saw as a recent 'upsurge in interest in rosé in all parts of the world'. It noted that, 'Having previously suffered the connotation of being a sweet housewife wine that is only sold in supermarkets, it now features, *inter alia*, on the wine lists of top Manhattan restaurants.' Yet the majority of South African consumers still believed rosé was an inexpensive, sweet, pink wine. So the big question became *how* the value and quality of rosé wine might be raised. Anchor Yeasts, in conjunction with various winemakers, carried out research in 2006 to investigate and propose guidelines for quality rosé.

It was noted that Pinotage (a South African cross of Pinot Noir and Cinsault) might produce rosés better than it did red wines (and would be unique to South Africa); that there was a market surplus of red wines, and rosé would offer a suitable alternative using the same varieties; that there were 'a fair amount of virus infected red vineyards that struggle to achieve the required sugar for premium red production. These vineyards may be used for the production of good quality low alcohol rosé, rather than attempt the impossible, namely the production of good quality red wine.'

Anchor Yeast asked twenty producers of rosé and *blanc de noirs* to discuss their winemaking. They identified three categories of wines:

- Single cultivar or blend of more than one cultivar, dry. The fastest growing market, especially with regard to exports. This category sold at the highest price points under the producer's premium label. They were made using direct press or *saignée*, never by blending red and white wines. *Saignée* rosés (by-products of red wine making) were described as having higher alcohol and a fuller style, while the pressed rosés were light and fruity.
- Single cultivar off-dry or semi-sweet. Second best, with good sales, on the domestic market especially, but not nearly as good as the single cultivar dry rosé abroad.
- Blended semi-sweet and sweet. These did not do well, with the exception of one or two brands that were doing well on the domestic market. Sweet

wines have recently become very popular in South Africa, to the point that in 2016, Distell stated that its 'easy-drinking' sweet rosé 4th Street 'is now the biggest wine brand in South Africa' (see also Chapter 14).

From this preliminary study, it was evident that there was a growing market in South Africa and abroad for single cultivar, dry rosé with a premium label. Of the varieties used, the most popular were Pinotage, Cabernet Sauvignon and Shiraz. Leading producers of top quality rosés said the quality of the vineyard was as important as the variety. Up to 15 per cent of another variety can be added without stating so on the label, and it was noted that 15 per cent Cabernet Franc provides structure and acidity in a Pinotage rosé, while 10 per cent Muscat de Frontignan may be added for additional aroma (Delheim makes a Pinotage rosé with 5 per cent Muscat de Frontignan). Good acidity and lower alcohol was found to enhance the light, fruity, crisp, and at times mineral, style.

While much of the discussion regarding winemaking techniques may seem obvious now, back in 2007 many of these ideas were completely new. The variety vinified determined the duration of the skin contact. In general, longer skin contact took place when the grape sugar was lower. For Cabernet Sauvignon, Cabernet Franc or Pinotage, skin contact was usually very short, to avoid too many phenolic compounds. Varieties such as Gamay Noir and Pinot Noir had longer skin contact. Gary and Kathy Jordan of **Jordan Wine Estate** (www.jordanwines.com) launched their pink Chameleon in 2007, the year following Anchor Yeast's research. They specifically planted Merlot for a fruity style, and picked earlier for higher acidity level, freshness and drinkability.

Some of the producers interviewed were convinced that rosé had a promising future and were already producing increasing volumes of high quality dry, single cultivar rosé for the US market. **Mulderbosch**'s (www.mulderbosch.com) Cabernet Sauvignon rosé was big in the States for at least a decade following the Anchor Yeast research, before being sold in South Africa. Producers with good domestic sales are those with strong brands and aggressive marketing campaigns.

As rosé's popularity grew abroad, its reputation also began to change in South Africa, and between 2007 and 2014 rosé wine sales trebled. Rosé production was becoming serious, yielding increasingly drier and more structured wines, with some barrel-aged, sourced from old or single vineyards or even barrel fermented.

The 2018 edition of *Platter's Guide* shows a dramatically changed rosé market. There are 314 dry rosé wines – the off-dry rosés have decreased to 74 and the *blancs de noirs* almost held steady with 43.

Fiona McDonald, former editor of *Wine Magazine* (South Africa), believes this is because rosé winemaking is one area where winemakers can experiment with styles and varieties. South Africa's grape plantings have changed over the years, with more and more 'unusual' grapes being cultivated. While producers wait for vines to establish to be used for red wine, they can experiment with rosé. **Waterford's** (www.waterfordestate.co.za), winemaker Mark le Roux makes the Stellenbosch estate's popular Rose-Mary from Shiraz, Tempranillo, Merlot, Sangiovese and Malbec grapes for that very reason. Some rosés advertise the grapes' region of origin as opposed to stating a generic style. Year of the Rooster Rosé from **The Drift** (thedrift.co.za), Bruce Jack's family farm near Napier, a non-traditional grape growing area, is a Touriga Franca dry pink.

Many of the rosés have a dry, fruity minerality. Different varieties present distinctly different rosés. Cabernet Sauvignon and Shiraz boast more natural tannin than Pinotage and Sangiovese rosés, which show lovely cherry, berry zippiness. Katharien Syrah Rosé 2016 from **Kleinood Tamberskloof** (www.kleinood.com) in Stellenbosch was first made in 2007, with fifty bottles for Katharien de Villiers fiftieth birthday. The first vintage was 'dreadful and far too sweet', admitted Katharien's son, Spicer de Villiers. Each year the wine has improved, with techniques inspired by the northern Rhône. Vineyards are in the shadow of the mountains, giving cool mornings and evenings. Manual harvesting and barrel fermentation has yielded a rosé with potential to age for two to three years, with white spice, hints of orange peel, ripe strawberry fruit, good weight and structure, and a tannic finish. **Rustenberg** (www.rustenberg.co.za), commissioned by UK supermarket Marks and Spencer to make a rosé completely different from those of Provence, created a dark, fruity rosé from Petite Verdot.

McDonald feels Pinotage is one of those grapes which lends itself to the production of 'pleasant pinks … full of raspberry, strawberry, youngberry and blueberry flavours and when that is kept young and fresh, with a light backing of acidity.' Cathy van Zyl's favourites include **Antebellum**'s (www.antebellum.co.za) Saffronne Pinotage rosé, significantly made using older vines which would otherwise have been used for red wine. This is slightly darker than commercial pale wines, fermented dry, according to van Zyl, with 'baked strawberry flan, elegant flavours of red cherry leading into a crisp mineral dry finish.' She also likes **Lukas van Loggerenberg**'s (vanloggerenbergwines.co.za), Break a Leg Blanc de Noir 2016, from 100 per cent Cinsault, which has 'delicate, complex aromas. A serious, finely textured wine, its cranberry fruit gives light, tart freshness.'

> **Waterkloof**
> Sir Lowry's Pass Road, Somerset West, 7129
> Tel.: (021) 858 1292
> www.waterkloofwines.co.za
> The Cape Coral Mourvèdre Rosé is barrel fermented. Winemaker Nadia Barnard explains that 'Mourvèdre can be a little reductive and fermenting in old French wood fermenters, which are too old to give any oak character, but are great to give a slow oxygen ingress during the fermentation works well with Mourvèdre.' Tasted at six months old, the oak was barely evident, other than in providing a firm structure behind vibrant blackcurrant fruit.

While I was writing this chapter Natasha Hughes MW and Madeline Stenwreth MW returned from a trip to South Africa, and urged me to include Mike Craven's Pinot Gris rosé in this chapter. Initially, in 2014, Craven made a barrel-worth 'just for fun as we thought the vast majority of people wouldn't get it'. In 2017, he produced 5,000 bottles. The wine is made with a mix of whole bunch and destemmed pressed grapes in open-top fermenters; grapes are fermented on the skins with light pumping over. The wine is briefly aged in old barrels. The process is reminiscent of Rosé des Riceys. Hughes' description sums up the wine: 'It's definitely left field. Deeply coloured, a kind of deep pink with an orange tinge. Really rich aromatics, orange zest, strawberries and apricots, tinged with spice and a floral, rose petal note. There's some tannic grip to it, quite raspy in fact, but it's also bright and lively, with a decent finish. I don't think I've ever tasted anything quite like it before.

It's not really a crowd pleaser, though, I think it's too off beat for that. It's a serious wine for members of the natural wine brigade, adventurous drinkers and those seeking life's little curiosities.'

Serious pink sparkling wines are made using the *méthode traditionelle*, called *cap classique* in South Africa. They have been around for longer than serious dry rosé wines. **Graham Becks**' (www.grahambeckwines.co.za) Brut Rosé vintage, from the Robertson vineyard is whole-bunch pressed with a coferment of Pinot Noir (80 per cent) and Chardonnay (20 per cent). The wine spends 36 months on the lees. It has pronounced strawberry fruit with rich cream and yeasty complexity.

SOUTH AMERICA

An influence from south-west France and Spain seems to have led to the creation of two parallel styles of paler, lighter pink; one sweeter, in a more American style, and a darker *clairet* style.

Uruguay

After Argentina, Chile and Brazil, Uruguay is the fourth-largest producer of wine in South America, with a relatively small vineyard area of 6,750 hectares in 2016, down from 8,000 hectares in 2012. Nevertheless, Uruguay is emerging as an exciting wine region with plenty of new money being invested in developing vineyards and existing producers getting the recognition they deserve. Figures in 2015 show that rosé accounts for just over half of all wine sales in Uruguay, although less than 3 per cent of exports and just under 5 per cent of imports are rosé. So, although production is relatively small, Uruguay can be regarded as a major rosé producer and consumer, though largely uninvolved in international trade.

Uruguayan wines have two levels of classification: *vino de calidad preferente* (VCP), for quality wine made from *vitis vinifera* varieties, and *vino común* (VC), a table wine category. VC wine is often sold in demijohns and cartons; much of it is rosé.

In 2003 production was 33 per cent red, 30 per cent *clarete* (clairet), 25 per cent rosé and 12 per cent white. The *clarete* style was only produced at the level of *Vino Común*, often using Criolla and País, generally with some sweetness achieved by the incorporation of Muscat Hamburg in the blend.

There is a steady increase in the amount of quality wine being produced at the expense of large volumes of lesser quality wine, spread throughout the country. Most of the family enterprises with brand names, well-recognized by consumers of mid- and high-income levels, are improving sales through quality, new varietals, competitive pricing and redesigned labels. The number of wineries declined from over 240 in 2012, to 193 in 2015. The equation for wine producers seems to be complex, as large wineries with an annual output over 500,000 litres have suffered the most. Wineries producing less than 100,000 litres/year have actually increased in number during the same period, and production has fallen.

Rosé wine in Uruguay is a very traditional elaboration: the first ones came from the Muscat family of grapes that were introduced in the eighteenth century from the Canary Islands. By the end of the nineteenth century, rosé wines were being produced from Tannat and other red grapes. Today, Uruguayan rosés are made from plenty of varieties, into many styles, predominantly semi-sweet and sweet for table wines, and dry for fine wines.

The climate and soils are very different from those of its neighbours in Chile and Argentina. The wine-producing areas are on the 34th parallel South, the same as Santiago, Mendoza, Stellenbosch and the Barossa Valley. Uruguay is largely flat with, in the main winemaking areas, a mix of alluvial clays, silts and sand with some gravel, overlying a limestone bedrock. The highest point is only 514 metres above sea level. In general Uruguay produces a more European, Old World style of wine with less jammy fruit, less alcohol, more acidity and structured tannins.

Most vineyards and wineries are in the hills north of the capital Montevideo, in the departments of Canelones, Montevideo, Colonia, Maldonado, and San José. Canelones, situated around the capital and next to the Rio de la Plata (the world's widest river) is the main wine-growing region, with two-thirds of wine production. The highest area gently rises to 100 metres. Soils are clay or a clay and limestone mix, both of which retain water well during dry periods, so vineyards do not need irrigation. Although it can be dry, the vines are rarely water-stressed.

Uruguay's flat landscape and its proximity to the Atlantic Ocean, with chilly Antarctic currents (it is the only Latin American country completely outside the tropics), along with sometimes fierce winds that blow inland from the sea, give the southern coastal region a cool, temperate maritime climate, comparable to Bordeaux, or Margaret River in Australia.

Viticulture represents 14 per cent of agricultural production. with some 250 small-scale, family-owned wineries, producing approximately ten million cases annually. Many Uruguayan *bodegas* are owned and operated as family businesses, some dating back generations. Low yields are favoured, harvesting is done by hand, and wines reflect both the terroir and the individual winemaker.

Among the *vinifera* grapes, Tannat is the most common (36 per cent of plantings by area). Other common varieties are Merlot (10 per cent), Chardonnay (7 per cent), Cabernet Sauvignon (6 per cent), Sauvignon blanc (6 per cent), Cabernet Franc (4 per cent), Criolla, País, and some Muscat Hamburg.

The range of rosés I tried were neither fruit bombs, nor delicate in style, but perhaps reflected the importance of rosé in the national wine culture. Yes, *saignée* was used as a 'by-product' of red wine, but for me these wines worked, reflecting the quality of fruit and acidity, and an understanding of the product. The wines below were all serious, showing complexity, the ability to age and to go with food. Generous, ripe fruit, good acidity and sometimes well integrated use of oak, showed the potential of quality rosé wine in Uruguay.

Bodega Garzón
Calle 9, 20401 Garzón, Maldonado Department
Tel.: 4224 1759
bodegagarzon.com/en

A family with over 200 years of winemaking expertise in Uruguay, their traditional Rosé Saignée 2016 (100 per cent Tannat) is made with their best grapes from Las Violetas-Canelones, used to produce their red wines. The juice is bled off after 16 hours of cold maceration and fermenting in tank at 16°C. This dark pink wine displays gorgeous strawberry and cream fruit with broad honeyed character, fresh redcurrant acidity, firm, mineral structure and dry tannins on the finish. At 14% abv, this is not a delicate rosé, but a good gastronomic style and a rosé with ageing potential.

Bodega Familia Deicas

Route 5 Km 34.200, Camino Cirefice, Progreso, Canelones
en.familiadeicas.com

The Deicas family, originally from Valtellina in northern Italy, arrived in Uruguay a hundred years ago. This wine is made in a traditonal style, bleeding off the juice from their red wine from the five top parcels and fermenting it in barrel for three months to create their Atlántico Sur 2017 Tannat Rosé Reserve. The new oak is very evident on the nose and palate, which on a more delicate rosé would have been overwhelming, but this is beautifully balanced by vibrant cherry and raspberry fruit, strawberries and cream and long mouth-watering acidity (13.5% abv).

Bodega Marichal

R 64 km 48,5, Etchevarría, Canelones
Tel.: 4332 1949
www.marichalwines.com

In the 1910s, Don Isabelino Marichal, whose family originally came from the Canary Islands, settled in the area of Etchevarría. He founded the vineyard and planted Tannat, and by 1938 they had created a small winery with underground cellars. Today it is run by the third and fourth generations. Their Reserve Collection Blanc de Noir (60 per cent Pinot Noir, 40 per cent Chardonnay) is fermented and aged for four months in French and American barrels giving a burnt copper colour. On the nose it has a soft oak character (the American oak being more obvious), with butterscotch, nuts and orange peel. Perfumed and mellow, with creamy redcurrants, hints of tangerine peel and long acidity, it is complex and unusual.

Pizzorno Family Estates

Route 32 Km 23 (Crossroad with Route 68), Canelón Chico, Canelones
Tel.: 2368 9601
www.pizzornowines.com

This small family winery, founded a hundred years ago by settlers from Italy, makes a sparkling rosé, Brut Nature Pinot Noir, a golden-pink coloured wine, with red cherry fruit. Quite weighty and structural, rather than delicate and pretty, it has long, fresh acidity and is good with food.

Above: Aubun vines planted on their own roots near Les Baux-de-Provence are flooded for forty days every winter to kill phylloxera bugs.

Below: Vineyards on the volcanic rocky soils of the windswept Atlantic islands of the Azores are protected by dry stone walls.

Above: Turnau Vineyard, 120km south of the Baltic Sea, lies in the north-west corner of Poland. The vineyard, planted in 2009, has a climate moderated by maritime influences. A crisp, fruity, off-dry rosé is made with Rondo and Regent.

Below: Jo Ahearne's pressing of the Darnekuša variety grown in the island vineyards of Hvar, Croatia.

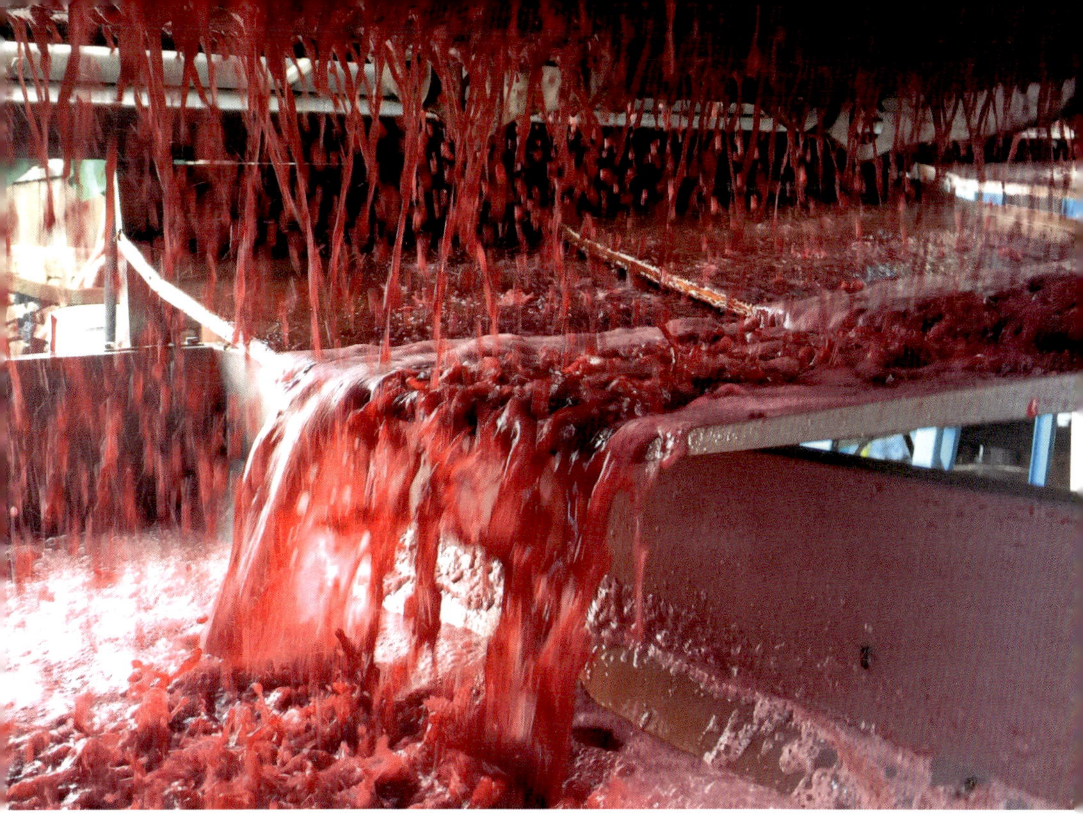

Above: Domaine Kramer in Washington State make a Pinot Noir rosé from grapes planted at 238 metres. Harvested on 5 October 2017, they were destemmed and cold soaked with daily pumping over until they had arrived at the right colour extraction. The grapes were pressed on 8 October (seen here), settled and racked into tanks for cool fermentation.

Below: Prieto Picudo variety in Tierra de León, Spain, made in the traditional *madreo* method – a combination of direct pressed juice, juice with extended maceration and unpressed grapes.

Above: Chateau d'Esclans Grenache juice. Left free run juice with almost no colour, middle first press, right final press with darkest colour.

Below: Eyrie Vineyards in Oregon make their Pinot Noir rosé using ambient yeast and fermenting in wooden casks.

Above: Stelios Kechris selecting the resin which will be placed in the barrel during fermentation to make the Kechri retsina. The source and size of resin will vary from vintage to vintage.

Below: Domaine Pibarnon in Bandol makes a high percentage Mourvèdre rosé with greater complexity for longer ageing using neutral Stockinger barrels and *jarres de grès* (amphora).

Above: Domaine des Hautes Collines ages its rosés for three months outside in these glass bonbons. Protected by the thin layer of flor, they also experience some oxidation.

Below: Judging rosé at the Decanter World Wine Awards, where the rosés are shown region by region.

Above: At Dalton Winery in Israel tasting five different batches of rosé. From the left, Pinot Gris, Grenache Noir, Shiraz, Shiraz and a field blend of Barbera, Zinfandel and Shiraz. They will be blended into two different styles of rosé wine at the winery in the Upper Galilee, Israel. This is taken from a late stage of the fermentation for Guy Eshel's primary blending session.

Below: The art of the *négociant* is blending different varieties from around the region to create a classic Provence rosé. See here the blending at Mirabeau.

Above: Gilles Masson at the Centre de Recherche et d'Experiméntation sur le Vin Rosé has created a reference guide for the colours for rosé. Here a range of colours is displayed in bottles with their fruit-influenced names.

Below: Masson's 'Nuancier' colour chart shows the large range of rosé colours found in Provence.

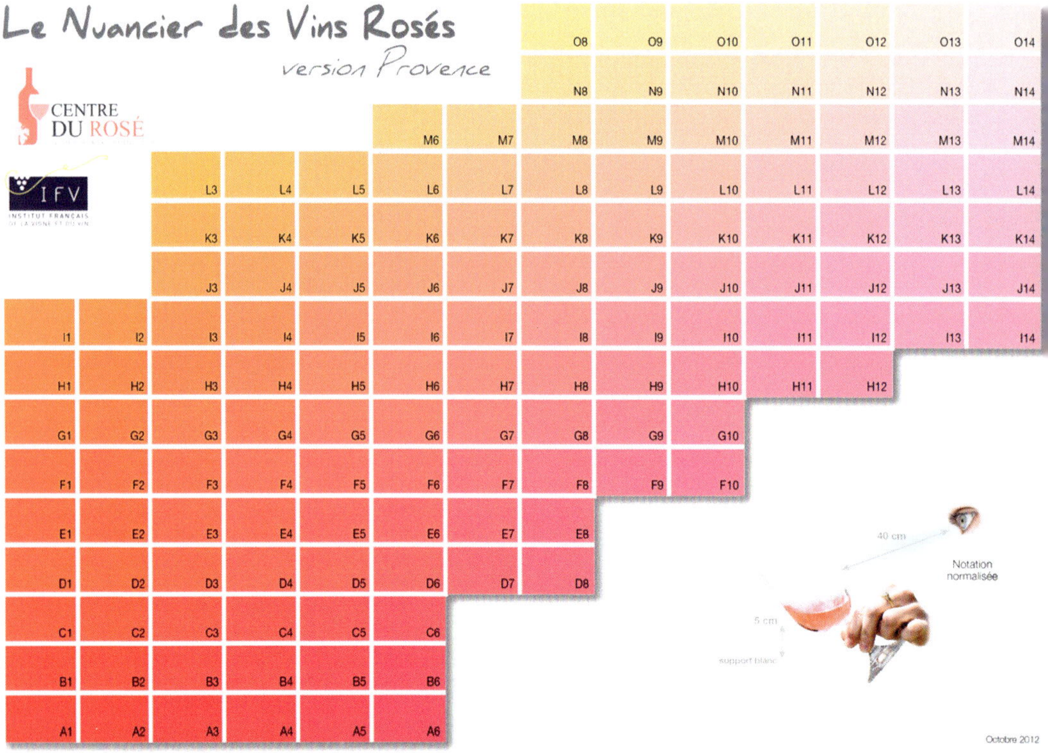

Chile

There has been a steadily increasing demand for Chilean rosé since 2007, speeding up dramatically since 2012. Although present in most producers' portfolios, it is usually part of the second, non-premium range. Production quadrupled between 2002 and 2014.

Until a few years ago, Chilean rosés were mainly produced with Cabernet Sauvignon, with Pinot Noir and Syrah regarded as unusual varieties. Today, it is possible to find rosé made from almost any variety, although they are most commonly made with Bordeaux varieties, Syrah and Pinot Noir, sometimes with a touch of the local variety País. In cool areas, the red varieties are more likely to be Pinot Noir and Syrah, in warmer areas Cabernet Sauvignon and Merlot. Some Carménère is used, of which Chile has the world's largest plantings after phylloxera wiped it out in Bordeaux. There are also blends. Despite these climate-dependent variations, Fernando Almeda, winemaker at Miguel Torres, believes it is still difficult to define regional styles, as every estate follows its own preferences.

Almeda feels that 'to produce a pale popular style rosé I think we have an opportunity with the País grape and Cinsault, mainly in the Maule and Itata Valleys, because of its thin skins, neutral aromatic profile, low cost of grape production, availability and sense of origin.' **De Martino Gallardia** (www.demartino.cl) makes a pale Cinsault rosé with fresh, raspberry fruit and floral notes from a cool-climate vineyard in the Itata Valley, using naturally low-yielding old vines.

According to Almeda, Chilean rosé is already becoming much lighter and drier. 'We have passed from high colour (Colour Intensity – CI – higher than 1.0), high residual sugar (15/20 g/l), high alcohol (14.5 per cent [abv]) and low total acidity (2.5/3.5 g/l) to lighter colour (less than 0.7 CI), lower residual sugar (less than 10 g/l to dryness), lower alcohol 13 per cent and higher total acidity (4 to 5 g/l).'

Many rosés are still a slightly darker pink, with lots of jammy, ripe, red and black (blackcurrant) fruit with fresh, herbaceous, leafy-green acidity, such as **Casas del Bosque** (www.casasdelbosque.cl) Reserva, Leyda, which is 100 per cent Syrah. This fresh, leafy-green character is typical, especially with Bordeaux varieties, although not always with as much of the black fruit usually associated with early harvesting. Monos Locos, Maule Valley, has made a rosé with this style, by using Sauvignon

Blanc tinted pink with Carignan, which fully emphasizes the vibrant, green character.

Other Chilean rosés are more like a *clairet*. **Domaine Barons de Rothschild Los Vascos** (www.lafite.com/en/the-domaines/vina-los-vascos) Colchagua produces a 100 per cent Cabernet Sauvignon, which makes a good alternative to a light red for summer drinking. Some producers are making rosés from Carménère, including **Apaltagua** (www.apaltagua.com) in the Maule Valley (they make a rosé that is 85 per cent Carménère, 15 per cent Syrah) and **Santa Carolina** (www.santacarolina.cl) in the Rapel Valley (100 per cent Carménère).

As always, there are a few sparkling rosés, such as **Cono Sur**'s (www.conosur.com) from the Bío Bío Valley, the cool-climate of which produces inviting aromas of strawberry and rose for a tangy and refreshing wine. **Miguel Torres** (www.migueltorres.cl/en) has made a uniquely Chilean, shell-pink, traditional fermentation sparkler, using País. The wine has herby aromas with hints of sugared fennel seeds, soft honeyed fruit and yeasty notes.

Argentina

In 2003, of the 100,000 hectares of vines in Agentina planted for fine wine, 48 per cent were for white wine, 43 per cent for red and 9 per cent for rosé. Today there is a wide range of styles based on vinification, grape variety, and terroir. Plantations of red varietals have continued to grow; by 2008 there were twice as many red vines as white, with white varieties decreasing by 21 per cent, although Chardonnay has become increasingly popular. Malbec is the most planted with 25 per cent of red vines, Cabernet Sauvignon at 18 per cent and Syrah 13 per cent. Small amounts of Gewurztraminer are sometimes used for blending in rosé wine.

There are still some producers who make the old-fashioned, sweet style, but on the whole, Argentine rosés are dry and crisp. The most popular variety is Malbec, produced mainly in Mendoza, but there is also Syrah, notably in San Juan province, as well as Cabernet Sauvignon and a small amount of Pinot Noir. Some rosés are darker in colour and more like a conventional red wine. Others are lighter, more floral, and similar to an aromatic white wine.

Until a few years ago, rosé wine was unfashionable in Argentina and was typically made by simply blending white and red grape juice, with distinctly indifferent results. Today rosé is one of the fastest-growing segments of the premium wine market, with techniques moving to *saignée* off the red wines, or earlier harvesting, and short maceration for a fresher style.

Lighter rosés include **Zolo** (www.vinodelsol.com) Signature Rosé, (Luján de Cuyo, Mendoza), launched in 2017, which is a blend of 60 per cent Syrah, 35 per cent Bonarda, and 5 per cent Cabernet Franc grown at 1,000 metres. It is light and fresh with cherry and plum fruit. **Finca Wölffer** (www.wolffer.com/finca-wolffer) Rosé (Agrelo-Lujan de Cuyo), was launched in 2015, and aimed at the premium rosé market in the Hamptons (where Wölffer also has a winery making rosé, see p.123). It is in the paler, fresher style with a blend of lighter-pigmented reds and white varieties in the blend (52 per cent Malbec, 11 per cent Pinot Noir, 11 per cent Pinot Gris, 10 per cent Bonarda, 8 per cent Torrontés and 8 per cent Cabernet Sauvignon). The wine is made at the nearby Dominio del Plata winery, owned by Susanna Balbo.

Darker, full bodied rosés tend to have a higher proportion of Malbec. **Kaiken** (kaikenwines.com), Mendoza, founded by Aurelio Montes in 2000, makes a Malbec Reserva Rosé (first made in 2008) from fruit grown at 950 metres that is full of juicily sweet strawberry fruit backed by a crisp, dry finish. Colomé Amalaya Rosado was first released in 2012 from the Californian Donald Hess's **Amalaya Winery** (www.amalaya.com), Cafayate, Salta. The vines are planted at 1,800 metres for freshness and there is intense Malbec cherry, strawberry fruit and floral notes from the blending in of 5 to 10 per cent Torrontés. **Bodega Weinert's** (www.bodegaweinert.com) Montfleury (Luján de Cuyo) is a fruity blend of 48.5 per cent Cabernet Sauvignon, 48.5 per cent Malbec, 2 per cent Cabernet Franc and 1 per cent Gamay. **Hernando de Domingo Molina** (www.domingomolina.com.ar) Malbec (Hermanos Valle Calchaquies, Salta) has very dry, structured, red fruit with a savoury, mineral finish. Despite lots of fruit, this is not a fruit bomb, but a well-structured wine.

François Lurton was the first to plant Pinot Grigio in Argentina and uses it to make a Rosado, as does Bodega Piedra Negra Alta (Uco Valley, Mendoza), whose Pinot Grigio is pale pink with peachy apricot fruit and creamy, soft acidity.

Sparkling pink wines are also produced, some by the 'traditional method'. Classic-style sparkling rosés, made with Pinot Noir and/or Chardonnay.

- **Cruzat Larrain** (bodegacruzat.com) Sparkling Rosé NV is a 'traditional method' wine made from Pinot Noir with a touch of Chardonnay. Ageing on the lees for two years gives it a creamy, toasty character. There are delicate cherry fruit notes with elegant, persistent, creamy bubbles.
- **Moët & Chandon** (www.chandon.com.ar) established their vineyard in 1959. Chandon Rosé NV is from Pinot Noir fruit from several vineyards of varying altitude, to contribute fresh acidity. Aged for 18 months on the lees gives the wine a toasty character and ripe Pinot (cherry) fruit, fresh acidity and creamy texture.

Using Malbec gives an Argentinian character, often in a full-bodied, fresh, strawberry fruit style, as seen in the following two sparkling pink wines.

- Malbec Rosé Bubbles Brut, **Bodegas Gouguenheim** (gouguenheim.com.ar), Mendoza. Patricio Gouguenheim uses some of his best Malbec from the the Tupungato region to make a fine, dry wine.
- **Reginato** Rosé of Malbec NV. A medium-bodied rosé made using the Charmat method. With a deeper colour and pronounced fruit, there is also a hint of tannin structure and floral spice.

8

PINK SPARKLING WINE

ROSÉ CHAMPAGNE, FRANCE

Having discussed the history of pink champagne in Chapter 3, here I am focusing on the style and vinification differences of pink champagne. For decades, rosé champagne was fashionably unfashionable and its share of the French champagne export market hovered around the 2–3 per cent mark.

Bollinger created its rosé champagne in 1976. Veuve Clicquot created its in 1977, Bollinger in 1976, and Krug in 1983. Richard Bampfield MW noted that 'ten or fifteen years ago the best wines still didn't go into most houses' rosés; they were often just an afterthought, but now more houses are growing clones of Pinot Noir on the best sites, specifically to make rosé.' Market leaders Laurent-Perrier and Billecart-Salmon, have done much to raise the profile of rosé champagne. As quality has improved, so has its popularity.

Within the rosé champagne market, there are different styles. Some producers are making light and delicate pink wines, whilst others are addressing the challenge of making champagnes with pronounced red fruit character that still retain the essence of champagne.

Champagne has for years been admired for its lightness and neutrality of fruit. Producers have worked hard to use black grapes without imparting colour or strong red-fruit flavours. Today, as Essi Avellan MW, author of *Champagne* notes, rosé champagne can be 'a more masculine, more vinous and more powerful style of champagne.' Dom Perignon's oenologist, Vincent Chaperon, admitted that the company is still developing its rosé house style, saying, 'The rosé must push the Pinot Noir expression to the limit. The 2005 has a lot of that; it's a serious rosé. People who like burgundy will find some bridges with it.' Guy Seddon, Corney & Barrow's fine wine buyer, believes 'there is definitely a move towards a more Burgundian/vinous style that's drier and more terroir-based,' and 'it's the grower champagnes that have helped to push rosé in a more serious direction.' Many of these rosé champagnes, often made by skin contact rather than blending red and white wines, have a stronger expression of terroir.

Tim Hall, champagne ambassador and owner of champagne specialists Scala Wine, told me that he believes that 'rosé champagne was the big exception to the main methodological tenet that champagne is about suppressing primary fruit with secondary and tertiary flavour i.e. the first duty of rosé is to be pure and fruity instead. But more are coming with serious built-in complexity, clever reserve wines and barrel fermentation – mainly from small single estates ('growers') such as La Villesenière made using *saignée*.'

There are at least three distinct styles of rosé champagne:

1. Delicate, pink wines with a hint of red fruit. Depending on the percentage of Chardonnay, these can also include a fresh, citrusy acidity.
2. Those featuring more structural red fruit character, with greater weight; maybe considered more suitable to accompany food.
3. Rosés where the base wine has had longer ageing on the lees or in wood, where the lees or oak character dominates the red fruit character.

There are two methods for making champagne pink, but it is usually impossible to establish the technique by taste or colour, although many *saignée* wines are considerably darker. While a darker colour might indicate *saignée*, this could also be part of the house style.

Rosé champagne, especially for the prestige cuvées, is often some 20 per cent more expensive than white champagne. This reflects not only its popularity, but also the higher production costs. The production of sufficiently mature, high-quality red wines for rosé is difficult and expensive in Champagne. The additional red-wine vinification, as well as playing with smaller batches, adds to the costs. Avellan believes that climate change has so far been beneficial for the quality of rosés in Champagne, with more chance of picking fully ripe red grapes due to warmer years.

White wine base champagnes blended with red wine

The most common method for creating pink champagne is the blending together of red and white wines. Called *rosé d'assemblage*, this is an exception to the 2009 European Union rule, prohibiting blending red and white wines to make rosé.

This is the easiest method for controlling the final colour. The white wine base can be all Chardonnay, *blanc de blancs* (for a fresh, creamy, citrus base, with long elegant acidity), a blend of Chardonnay and Pinot Noir/Meunier, or a *blanc de noirs* from only black grapes (which can have a more perfumed character, with hints of red or black fruit).

The amount of red wine added varies from around 10–15 per cent (there is no official limit), made from Pinot Noir, a blend of Pinot Noir and Meunier or, less often, only Meunier. The proportion can affect the intensity of colour, the amount of red fruit character and tannins. Those with a small addition of red wine are usually pale pink with barely any red fruit character.

Red wine with good structure, even if only 10 or 15 per cent of the final product, can contribute greater weight and structure. **Champagne de Telmont** (www.champagne-de-telmont.com) in Damery adds 15 per cent red wine made from old-vine Pinot Noir and Meunier. The old-vine fruit gives more structure, red berry fruit and roundness to the red wine, and enough weight to contribute a subtle hint of dryness on the finish. **Ployez Jacquemart** (www.ployez-jacquemart.fr) uses a base wine of 50 per cent Chardonnay and *blanc de noirs* from 25 per cent Pinot Noir and 25 per cent Meunier, *premier* and *grand cru*. Ten per cent red wine of Pinot Noir from a *premier cru* with riper fruit is added. This extra weight and ripeness is further emphasized by ageing the base wine for one year in oak.

Fruit and floral characters can be contributed by younger vines or by using Meunier. **Benoît Cocteaux** (www.champagnebenoitcocteaux.com) uses 15 per cent Pinot Noir red wine, but from young vines, giving pronounced fresh, red fruit character. **Beaumont des Crayères** (www.champagne-beaumont.com) Grand Rosé NV uses a smaller amount of red wine (10 per cent), uniquely from Meunier, giving a distinctive floral character to the very delicate red fruit.

Champagnes from pink base wine

Alternatively, the base wine can be made pink by bleeding the juice off after the desired amount of maceration (*saignée*). Cold maceration is preferred, to obtain colour without tannins. This is less common than *rosé d'assemblage*. The term *saignée* is often featured on the label of wines made in this way. Tim Hall comments that 'as a style, [this is] more and more varied, although *saignée* is not so new. There was a rash of *saignée* made ten years ago in a traditional way.' Some have commented that the *saignée* method makes a heavier style. Alice Lascelles (*How to Spend It* 2017) commented that 'Whether the *saignée* method actually makes a better rosé than blending is a moot point (there are plenty prepared to argue it makes no difference) … it has become something of a badge of honour among growers.' Laurent-Perrier is one of few Grande Marque houses using the maceration technique to make their rosé. There appears to be no limit to the number of hours of skin contact.

Champagne Guy Charbaut (www.champagne-guy-charbaut.com), Ay, is made with a base rosé wine from Pinot Noir with relatively long maceration of 12–15 hours to extract fruit flavour. Sometimes 10 per cent Chardonnay is added for elegance, if necessary, which can also tone down the colour. This wine has very attractive crisp, fresh, red fruit character. **Larmandier Bernier** (www.larmandier.fr), *premier cru* Vertus, is almost all Pinot Noir, macerated for 24–48 hours, depending on the vintage, with the addition of some Pinot Gris to lighten the intensity.

Vollereaux (www.champagne-vollereaux.fr), Pierry (neighbouring Epernay) makes pink champagne from 100 per cent Pinot Noir, with a long maceration of 36 hours, similar to that of *clairet* wine, at a low temperature (which emphasizes the fruit and diminish the tannins) and then bled off the skins. **Charles Legend**'s (charleslegend.com) brut rosé, Côtes de Bar, has even longer maceration with 46 hours skin contact, resulting in intense, wild berry fruit balanced by fresh acidity.

Champagne Gratiot (www.champagne-gratiot.com) Almanach No. 3, Marne, uses both methods. The base wine includes 26 per cent *saignee* rosé made with Pinot Noir and Meunier for extra red fruit, plus 10 per cent addition of a red wine from Pinot Noir and Meunier. The wine undergoes malolactic fermentation for extra creaminess.

Pierre Brocard's (www.champagnebrocardpierre.fr) 2011 vintage is 100 per cent Pinot Noir; a rosé base wine made with 52 hours of maceration (in effect a red champagne). He has found that ageing the wine for five years on the lees softens the tannins. His son Thibaud's recent winemaking background in Burgundy made him think of linking the two regions of Burgundy and Champagne, something which he felt global warming encouraged.

Maxime Blin (champagne-maxime-blin.com) in northern Champagne makes two rosé champagnes using both styles. One has a base wine made from Pinot Noir, of which 85 per cent *blanc de noirs* and 15 per cent is a red wine. The resulting wine is pale pink with a very delicate red fruit character. The *saignée* champagne has a more structural character and is arguably better for gastronomy.

As for many champagne houses, rosé is a recent style, it is not always evident how these wines will age. Avellan wrote that 'mature rosé champagnes develop beautiful winey qualities, such as a velvety texture with spicy and complex gamey notes, which combine brilliantly with aged champagne's toasty or biscuity layers. They are great gastronomic companions.' They also often take on more floral potpourri characters, and with slightly longer ageing can take on more of a burgundy character. She continues, 'The rosé versions of prestige cuvées are the *crème de la crème* of champagne: Cristal Rosé, Dom Pérignon Rosé, Laurent-Perrier Alexandra Rosé, Dom Ruinart Rosé and Pommery Cuvée Louise Rosé are fabulous examples of the ageing potential, depth and complexity of rosé champagne. They are also true rarities. Due to minuscule production, many producers do not even mention the rosé on their website. The rosé version often costs two to three times more.'

Moët & Chandon was the first to launch a sparkling wine, in 1976, in California. Taittinger created Domaine Carneros, also in California, in 1987. Other champagne houses have followed, making sparkling wine, including sparkling rosé, in North and South America, Australia and New Zealand. None of these champagne-owned estates are aiming at making imitation champagne. Their wines are quality sparkling wines with regional character.

Champagne houses have also invested in producing still rosés, especially in Provence. Champagne Bruno Paillard owns Domaine Sarrins while Champagne Vranken-Pommery owns Chateau La Gordonne in Provence and Listel, making them a major producer of rosé wine.

ENGLISH PINK SPARKLING WINE

In the early 1950s a British wine (as opposed to English wine, made with English-grown grapes), Rosayne, was launched, produced by Anglo-Mediterranean Wines of Shepton Mallet. An 'exhilarating pink wine with the champagne sparkle', according to the advertisement, it was made with 'Mediterranean grapes and its pink sparkle comes from them alone.' According to an announcement in *The Straits Times* in 1954, it was being promoted in the 'colonies' to sell the wine in time for Christmas, with sales people visiting Malaya, Hong Kong, Egypt, Sudan, East Africa, Aden, Southern and North Rhodesia, Belgian Congo and West Africa. A 'Novelty of the new wine is that one bottle holds exactly one champagne glass.' A rival product, made at the same time, and in the same village was Babycham (a sparkling perry, from pears) also in glass-sized bottles.

Things have moved on, with true English sparkling wines now produced in high quantities. The production of bottle-fermented sparkling wines is one of the major growth areas today in UK wineries. In the mid-1980s vineyards such as Carr Taylor and Lamberhurst proved that British grapes could be used for producing good examples of this type of wine. Pink sparkling wines, produced either from single varieties or a blend of traditional and non-traditional varieties, are achieving a sound success. **Bolney** (www.bolneywineestate.com) in West Sussex, makes a sparkling rosé from 100 per cent Rondo (a cross of Zarya Severa and Saint Laurent), an early-ripening variety with big fruit flavour. This wine is bubbling over with ripe red fruit and good acidity, for a very distinctive style. Their vision was to make a uniquely English wine, full of freshness and vitality, and not for ageing. **Denbies** (www.denbies.co.uk) in Surrey makes a sparkling pink with a blend of Seyval Blanc and Rondo which is full of juicy blackberry fruit and cream.

Vineyards across southern England, such as Nyetimber (see below), in West Sussex and **Ridgeview Wine Estate** (www.ridgeview.co.uk), in East Sussex, **Chapel Down** (www.chapeldown.com), **Gusbourne** (www.gusbourne.com) and **Hush Heath** (hushheath.com) in Kent, **Exton Park** (www.extonparkvineyard.com) and **Hambledon** (www.thehambledon.com) in Hampshire and **Sixteen Ridges** (www.

sixteenridges.co.uk) in Worcestershire, have been planted solely with champagne varieties (Chardonnay, Pinot Noir and Meunier) for the production of classic bottle-fermented sparkling wines, including rosés. As a blend, these grapes make an elegant style of wine with good intensity and ageing potential. Exton Park makes a rare 100 per cent Meunier, which is dry (6g/l residual sugar) with a smooth, creamy texture and juicy black fruit.

Nyetimber
Gay Street, West Chiltington, West Sussex, RH20 2HH
Tel.: 01798 813989
nyetimber.com

Winemaker Brad Greatrix, along with his wife Cherie, discussed with me elements he felt important for English sparkling rosé. Most important are the moderate maritime climate and the long growing season. This allows harvest to creep in late, around mid-October with grapes at full phenolic ripeness, alcohol around 10.5% abv and high acidity. This usually means that, even if the rosé is slightly darker, it will always be light and fresh. Sometimes this lighter style does not seem able to carry heavy oak ageing.

Greatrix explained how this worked in his favour when making a sparkling pink wine. To start with, great care is taken in the selection of the red grapes for use in the red wine in the assemblage. These must be the ripest, to avoid any notes of greenness in the wine. A second run through the vines harvests grapes for the base wine. The trial blends with full sight of colour, but then a comparative tasting of the rosé base blend is held in black glasses with other base blends of the year (*classic cuvée, blanc de blancs*, etc). Greatrix says, 'The point is to be sure we can recognize the rosé by aromas and flavour profile without seeing the colour.' A rosé is not defined by its colour alone. but by red fruit aromas and taste. This can mean that sometimes Nyetimber's rosé will be darker. Originally (2007–9), they made single vintage wines, but then decided that the desired style could be better achieved through blending different vintages. Lees ageing to give weight and complexity, and contribute to the wine's ability to age, is important, because after the first flush of youth and vibrant fruit, the wine can take on richer notes, 'like raspberry crumble' according to Greatrix.

A number of high quality wines are emerging, showing the characteristic English lightness with pronounced red and/or black fruit character. With a growing number of vintages behind them, producers have been able to do more blending and to create non-vintage house styles such as Exton Park NV (70 per cent Pinot Noir, 30 per cent Meunier) which has creamy, fresh red fruit.

Vintage sparkling rosés are using extended lees ageing to give extra weight to the wines. Chapel Down Rosé Brut (100 per cent Pinot Noir) with 18 months ageing on lees and 85g/l residual sugar aims at fresh, creamy red fruit and fresh acidity. Ridgeview Rosé de Noirs (86 per cent Pinot Noir, 14 per cent Meunier) is a very pale pink, with lots of ripe black fruit. The Gusbourne Rosé (50 per cent Pinot Noir, 35 per cent Chardonnay, 15 per cent Meunier) spent 24 months ageing on lees and aims at a fresh, fruity style balanced by good weight and toasty character coming from the long lees ageing. Hush Heath's Balfour (48 per cent Chardonnay, 44 per cent Pinot Noir, 8 per cent Meunier) is very pale pink and dry (9g/l residual sugar) with crisp red fruit and creamy texture from long ageing on the lees for four years. Sixteen Ridge (100 per cent Pinot Noir) uses first press juice to make a rosé base wine giving ripe, creamy cherry fruit with balancing acidity.

FRANCIACORTA, ITALY

According to Tom Stevenson, writer and champagne and sparkling wine authority, the Franciacorta region is 'the only compact wine area producing world class sparkling wine in Italy.' When it was granted DOC status in 1967 there were eleven producers of sparkling franciacorta, although Berlucchi represented more than 80 per cent of the production. Franciacorta was granted DOCG status in 1995, covering just over 2,000 hectares of vines in the district of Brescia in Lombardy, central northern Italy.

Franciacorta currently exports only 15 per cent of its annual production of 17.5 million bottles but wants to increase that to 30–40 per cent. The UK, USA and Japan are the major export markets, with the UK on-trade seen as a key place to target. 'We think the British restaurants, wine bars and clubs are exactly where Franciacorta can be increasingly popular,' says Vittorio Moretti, president of the Consorzio Franciacorta, the region's trade association.

Pinot Noir and Chardonnay are used, with some Pinot Blanc to adjust acidity. The rosé must have at least 25 per cent Pinot Noir in the base wine and can contain 100 per cent.

Franciacorta is produced using the 'traditional method', the same as for champagne. The grapes are manually harvested. Once in the cellar they undergo gentle whole-bunch pressing and the juice is fermented. After this initial fermentation the wines are blended by variety, vineyard and year, before adding the sugar and yeast for the second fermentation in bottle. Franciacorta rosé must spend a minimum of twenty-four months on the lees, vintage rosé a minimum of thirty months on the lees and *rosé riserva* a minimum of sixty months on the lees.

Not all producers make a rosé version, and percentages of varieties can vary. Ca'del Bosco, **Bosio** (www.bosiofranciacorta.it) vintage rosé and the *rosé riserva* from **Barone Pizzini** (www.baronepizzini.it) are made with 80 per cent Pinot Noir and 20 per cent Chardonnay. **Majolini**'s (www.majolini.it) brut rosé is 100 per cent Pinot Noir, their demi-sec, 50 per cent Pinot Noir and 50 per cent Chardonnay. Cavalleri's vintage rosé, also 80 per cent Pinot Noir, 20 per cent Chardonnay, first made in 1979, has 10 per cent of the wine aged in big old barrels.

CAVA, SPAIN

In 1872, in Catalonia, Josep Raventós produced his first bottle of sparkling wine using the champagne method (as he was still permitted to call it then), to produce a quality sparkling wine for the Spanish market. It was called Catalonian 'Xampany' (sounding like 'champagne'). Raventòs was not concerned with the varieties or terroir. The most important part was to say it was made in the same way as champagne. By 1959 the name 'cava' (cellar) was given to the wine, in reference to the long ageing period (at least nine months) during which the bottles undergo their second fermentation in the cellars. The term 'cava' became official in 1972 when Spain agreed with the French authorities to ban the commercial names of the time, Champán and Xampany. The appellation was granted in 1986, when Spain joined the European Union.

Throughout the 1970s, work continued to improve viticulture and vinification, and by the late 1970s cava was ready to be launched as a very competitive product (cheap but good quality) in the international market. Today, two-thirds of the cava produced, more than 150 million bottles, is exported each year all over the world. But 85 per cent of exports are basic, commercial wines. Cava's ultimate path to success came from embracing its point of difference and from renouncing the original focus of imitating champagne. Premium cava would aim not to be a cheap champagne, but a wine with its own personality.

Trepat and Pinot Noir were permitted during 1998, due to the high demand for rosé. Previously the only options were Garnacha (Grenache) and Monastrell (Mourvèdre). Monastrell plantings within the Cava DO have decreased dramatically over the years, despite being one of the original varieties, and now account for a mere 0.1 per cent. Currently Garnacha has the highest percentage of planting, with Trepat and Pinot Noir not far behind. Trepat can currently only be used for rosé production, but I believe there is a desire to change this. A lot of producers like it for its elegant, strawberry-scented profile. In the right environment (at higher altitudes) it can give very fresh and elegant rosés. Most Trepat is grown in Conca de Barbera, though some producers grow it in the Penedès, for instance, Augusti Torello Mata grows some on slate soils in the high Penedès.

Expression of terroir started to be achieved by the late 1990s. A few producers undertook the pioneering work that paved the way for the whole region. **Recaredo** (www.recaredo.com/en) is arguably the first hero producer of terroir in Penedès. Initially there was widespread market reluctance to pay more for a cava than for a champagne, but this dwindled as people tasted the difference between mass-produced and terroir-driven cavas. The revolution in the cava region is taking place in the vineyard, and today's top wines are just the nascent results. The Cava DO has the highest proportion of organic and biodynamic vineyards in Spain. A young generation of cava producers, insistent on good quality, has revived ancient vines, and wants to change the image of mass-produced cava.

The challenge for the future is to change the perception of cava among consumers. Though there will always be a market for cheap and cheerful sparkling wines, there is also room for more exciting, premium pink cavas.

In 2016, almost 9 per cent of the 245 million bottles produced were pink, representing an increase of 2.7 per cent of rosé cavas since 2015. Producers believe that pink cava consumption is increasing.

Rimarts (www.rimarts.net) cava rosado is made from Pinot Noir and Garnacha, aged for 9–15 months with 2g/l residual sugar while their Rosae is made with 100 per cent Pinot Noir, aged for a minimum of 22 months and has 22g/l residual sugar.

> **Maria Rigol Ordi**
> C/Fullerachs, 9, Sant Sadurní d'Anoia
> Tel.: 938 910 194
> www.mariarigolordi.com
> The Rosat Reserva Brut Naturex is a good example of a wine from an old estate revitalized by the younger generation. The family of Anaïs Manobens Mora's grandmother always had their own cava on the table, and when her father stopped producing it, she revived the cava production. They make only around 100,000 bottles, but have rapidly become well-known. They buy in strictly-controlled organic grapes. As few Trepat vineyards are organic, they changed to Pinot Noir for their rosé cavas. This is grown in the foothills of the Serra de Font-Rubí hills, at 395 metres. The wine is aged for a minimum of 15 months and is dry with 11.5% abv. There are Pinot flavours of cherries and roses, with some yeasty notes and elegant, vibrant acidity. Only 3,700 bottles are made. (They also make a Trepat varietal rosé cava.)

Recaredo's (www.recaredo.com) rosé is also *brut nature*, from 71 per cent Monastrell (Mourvèdre), 23 per cent Pinot, 6 per cent Grenache. I am not convinced about using Mourvèdre for sparkling wine as it can make for a heavier style; this is a more gastronomic style. The owners of the biodynamic **Raventos i Blanc de Nit** (www.raventos.com) are descendants of the first cava-maker called Raventós (who worked with Codorniú). Their wine has 50 per cent Macabeu, 25 per cent Xarel-lo, 20 per cent Parellada and 5 per cent Monastrell, aged in bottle for at least fifteen months and released with a vintage. Technically, this is not a cava, as they left the Cava DO to create a more rigorous, terroir-based appellation called Conca del Riu Anoia.

There are no rosé Parajes (the new highest quality level for *gran reservas* from a single region), largely because, contrary to Parajes requirements, many rosés are blends of varieties from various terroirs.

Lenka Sedlackova MW, whose research paper focused on cava, thinks that many producers do not take rosé seriously. Xarel-lo (for white cava) is the variety with the biggest potential for high quality. There is a move back towards indigenous varieties and producers like Recaredo have been grubbing up their Pinot Noir.

Rosé styles are changing, becoming paler, but change will always be slower in sparkling pinks, because of the time on lees. Styles are getting drier too, especially for the domestic market. Brut styles dominate exports but Brut nature is very popular in Spain. A good example is **Gramona**'s (www.gramona.com) Argent Rose, a brut nature which is 100 per cent Pinot, aged for 30 months on lees. It is also pale in style. Both **Vilarnau**'s (www.vilarnau.es) Brut Reserva Rose (Trepat and Pinot Noir) and the **Augusti Torello Mata** (www.agustitorellomata.com) Rosé Reserva, made with Trepat (and 6g/l *dosage*) are good.

ROSÉ DE LIMOUX

Travelling north from the region of Catalonia, to the northern flanks of the Pyrenees, in France, one arrives in the region of Limoux, where the white Blanquette and Crémant wines are made. Blanquette de Limoux claims to be the world's oldest sparkling wine. In 1531, the Benedictine nuns from the Saint Hilaire Abbey next to Limoux discovered the secret of bubbles, using the *méthode ancestrale* (see below). A century later, the secret had moved through France and was used by champagne monks.

The first plantings of Pinot Noir in the appellation were in the mid-1980s, for both red and rosé wines. By the late 1980s, **Sieur d'Arques** (www.sieurdarques.com) had tried to make their first sparkling wine from a rosé base wine using a blend of Chardonnay, Chenin Blanc and Pinot Noir. In 1990, the appellation for Crémant de Limoux (white) was granted for sparkling wines using international varieties and sparkling wines made in the traditional method, as with champagne, with a second fermentation in the bottle and one year ageing on the lees. That same year, producers lodged a request for an appellation for Crémant de Limoux Rosé. This was granted in 2004.

Altitude is used to retain freshness and acidity. The northern vineyards can be planted at between 100 and 250 metres while those in the warmer southerly regions, with steeper slopes are planted between

330 and 500 metres. A blend of grapes from warmer Mediterranean-influenced sites and cooler sites with an Atlantic influence, contributes to the complexity.

Further crisp acidity is obtained high acidity varieties such as Chardonnay (the principal variety), Chenin Blanc and Mauzac in the blend. Pinot Noir can be added as *blanc de noirs* or as a rosé for colour and darker fruit character. The grapes must be manually harvested and gently pressed.

> ### Méthode ancestrale
>
> *Méthode ancestrale* (ancestral method) is the oldest method for making sparkling wine. The primary fermentation is stopped before completing, and a secondary fermentation occurs in the bottle, ending when the yeast cells use up the residual sugar. There is no *dosage* (sugar addition), to kick-start the secondary fermentation, and the wine is not disgorged to remove sediment or lees remaining afterwards. The alcoholic fermentation is arrested by cold, with a controlled rise in temperature. The half-fermented wine is then bottled and capped. Fermentation is resuscitated with a controlled rise in temperature.
>
> There is currently a dispute by the Cerdon producers against Clairette de Die being allowed to use an appellation for rosé *méthode ancestrale* which is feared will open the floodgates for other regions, such as Beaujolais, to do the same. *Pétillant naturels* (pét-nats) are made this way.

BUGEY-CERDON

Cerdon lies west of Geneva, in the foothills of the southern Jura mountains. Bugey (with Cerdon as a named *cru*) was elevated to AOC in 2009, having previously been VDQS since 1958. Sparkling Bugey rosé follows the same rules as still Bugey rosé (see page 101), but sparkling rosé Bugey-Cerdon, must be made either from 100 per cent Gamay or a blend of Gamay and Poulsard.

Until late 2016, Cerdon was the only rosé AOC *méthode ancestrale* (see box). It is the largest *cru* in Bugey but produces fewer than 2 million bottles annually.

CLAIRETTE DE DIE

Clairette de Die's vineyards are in the foothills of the Vercors mountains, east of Valence and the Rhône Valley. Like Bugéy-Cerdon, the vineyards are at relatively high altitudes, up to about 500 metres, ideal for growing grapes for sparkling wines.

Clairette de Die may have been one of the first appellations to use *méthode ancestrale*, gaining its AOC in 1942. The semi-sweet white Clairette de Die *méthode ancestrale* sparkling wine is made from a minimum of 75 per cent Muscat à Petit Grains, with up to 25 per cent from the Clairette grape. The new appellation rules for rosé Clairette de Die require the same mix, but with a minimum of 5 per cent red grapes, the naturally-occurring red version of Muscat à Petit Grains and Gamay. The latter must make up no more than 10 per cent of the blend. Gamay is grown traditionally in only part of the area, where red and rosé still wines are made under the Châtillion-en-Diois AOC. Clairette de Die currently produces about 12 million bottles of white *méthode ancestrale* sparkling wine and estimates that in future it may produce an additional 10 per cent as rosé.

BEAUJOLAIS

In the last few years a new pink sparkling wine style has evolved in Beaujolais and is growing in popularity. It is generally, but not always, produced according to the *methode ancestrale*. There is currently no appellation for this style.

Jean-Paul Brun at Domaine des Terres Dorées, Charnay, makes a sparkling pink called FRV100 Rosé NV. The name FRV100 is a play on the word effervescent. Made using the *méthode ancestrale* technique, the wine has a delicate 7.5–8% abv and some residual sugar. The vintage will never appear on the label, as there is no allowance for sparkling Gamay in Beaujolais, though the wine is always single-vintage.

PINK CIDER

Jake Grove reported in the *Independent Mail* in 2017 that rosé has reached into the cider world. 'Rosé cider ... has taken hold among those who still want to enjoy a more beer-like beverage, but with that slightly sweet–dry balance from being a rosé.' Rosé cider is contributing markedly to the current dynamism of this sector, which is seeing strong growth in a French market where it already represents 5 per cent (in volume terms) of total cider production (a million hectolitres per year). Its colour is linked to the presence of anthocyanins that in most cases are supplied by the inclusion of red-fleshed apple varieties in the manufacturing process.

9
SPANISH AND PORTUGUESE ROSÉ

SPAIN

The sheer scale of wine production in Spain, from the cooler north eastern regions on the Atlantic coast, through the northern foothills of the Pyrenees and the eastern Mediterranean coast to the sunny vineyards of the south, near North Africa, makes it impossible to generalize about the style of *rosado* produced. While bulk production dominates the market, there are producers looking to make distinctive regional styles from local and international varieties.

As with elsewhere in Europe, a darker *clairet* (*clarete*) has a long historic tradition. The most famed *clarete* is that from Cigales, detailed in Chapter 3 (see page 45). Viticulture in northern Spain prospered during the Middle Ages, partly due to the demand from the pilgrims following the Camino de Santiago to the Galician town of Compostela, and the red wines, probably lighter *claretes*, were highly regarded. Valdepeñas also has a long history of producing a distinct wine known as *aloque* (also a type of *clarete*). Hemingway noted in 1960 that the *rosados* of Valdepeñas were a rustic version of Tavel. Jeffs (1971) wrote, 'the musts separately pressed from red and white wine grapes may be mixed before fermentation, as is done in Valdepeñas.'

Towards the end of the eighteenth century, viticulture was the region's main activity. In 1855 the vineyards were hit by oidium, but survived until most were devastated in 1892 by phylloxera. They were replanted by grafting onto American rootstocks. During the nineteenth and twentieth centuries, dark pink *clarete* became the everyday wine of the workers.

In Ribera del Duero, most people had a small vineyard and underground cellar for producing their household wines. Today a tradition remains for producing wine in private cellars, usually the deep pink wine *ojo de gallo* (eye of the chicken), which is kept in barrel until bottled.

Until the middle of the twentieth century, wine cooperatives continued to make *clarete* wines. They increased production by exporting large quantities of *rosado* in bulk. During the 1980s private wineries and cooperatives began bottling and labelling quality wine. The Denominación de Origen (DO) for Navarre, first approved in 1933, has been updated to reflect the shift from bulk to quality production. In 1989, Joanna Simon wrote, 'Spain – Rioja, Navarra and Penedès – is up and coming. Note the experience of The Fulham Road Wine Centre among a range of interesting pinks, its 1988 Viña Vermella (Penedès) is one of the most popular – once, that is, the savants with a Portuguese induced prejudice against pink have been persuaded to try some. So, why not you?'

A high proportion (62 per cent) of Spanish *rosado* production is shipped in bulk, in tankers to 'elsewhere', making up a quarter of all rosé wine shipped internationally. It achieves notoriety, not through its quality but when the tankers are opened and contents spilled on the ground by irate Languedoc producers, complaining about low prices. Spain is the world's second biggest producer of rosé, but has yet to achieve critical acclaim for much of it. The cheap and cheerful *rosados* have been popular amongst consumers, but largely failed to achieve success amongst the critics. But success in volume sales also led to a profusion of average-quality wines; until recently, many *rosados* were merely bright pink with strawberry candy fruit and a sharp bitter acidity. These were cheap, best drunk young and ice-cold on a hot day. Even recent tastings have included wines with notes such as 'Ripe red berry fruit. Soft, sickly fruit. Red boiled sweets, good acidity, but hollow, weak.' Or 'Ripe rosehip fruit. Sweet, fruity weak.'

Eric Asimov in the *New York Times* (2011) had interesting conclusions from a blind tasting of twenty Spanish *rosados* available in the US. The 'rosados were as inconsistent as any group of wines I've recently come across, maybe even more so … We reflexively expect rosés to be

> **Unión Campesina Iniestense**
> Calle San Ildefonso,1, C.P:16235 - Iniesta, Cuenca
> Tel.: 967 490 120
> cooperativauci.com
> This cooperative in south-eastern Spain was founded just after the Second World War. With 7,000 hectares, it is a big producer and exporter. Two of its rosés are made with the local variety Bobal, which has naturally high acidity, allowing it to age quite well. Gardino is pale pink with dry, red fruit, and fresh, but without the vibrant acidity of wines from further north. I tried the display bottle, a year older – which I was assured would not have aged well – but it had mellowed to a soft peach and cream character, which was quite pretty. Señoro de Iniesta 2016 had a fraction more residual sugar, and was a touch darker in a more traditional style, but similar on the palate.

light, dry and fresh, not inconsequential but lithe and agile enough for lunchtime drinking. Instead, we found too many wines that were chunky, with powerful fruit flavors, residual sugar, or high alcohol; that lacked energy.' On the plus side 'there were a fair number of zesty, tangy wines that may not conform to the Provençal ideal but are fascinating enough to deserve recalibrating one's expectations.'

Against this backdrop of industrialized winemaking, a growing number of exciting *rosados* shine. Today, not only fresh, fruity summer *rosados* of good quality can be found, but also *rosados* which have embraced modern techniques whilst retaining some Spanish traditions. Using local Spanish varieties, judicious use of *saignée* (*sangrado* in Spanish), American oak and other techniques, a modern, high quality and distinctive style of Spanish *rosado* is fast emerging. *Rosado* has not been a big sector of the Spanish domestic market, although it has become increasingly fashionable in recent years. In traditional rosé areas like Cigales and Tierra de León, *rosado* is the drink of choice. In Madrid, red and white wine are still the most popular. Bodegas Muga produces 2.5 million bottles of which only 400,000 are *rosado*.

The real surge in quality came not only from new vinification techniques but also from using varieties other than Garnacha and Tempranillo. There is now a broad range of styles. Although Garnacha certainly continues as a favourite, it often is combined with other grapes for a more complex result. Merlot, Cabernet Sauvignon, Pinot Noir and Petit Verdot are also playing their part in the Spanish *rosado* boom. Most wine produced in northern Spain is red.

Tasting in 2017, I came to similar conclusions to Asimov. Quality and styles varied enormously, but an exciting number of interesting *rosados* are worth looking out for.

At the 2017 *Drinks Business* Rosé Masters, the publication's editor, Patrick Schmitt MW, summed up the results. 'The judges were highly impressed with the quality achieved for a wine costing a little over £10, which came from Rioja, and that was the Izadi Larrosa, hence its Gold-medal winning score. Indeed, Rioja proved itself a first-rate source of good-value rosé based on Grenache and Tempranillo, with the region's Ontañon Clarete also gaining a Gold. (Rioja can also create brilliant top-end rosé – with the region's Marqués de Murrieta the only winery to get a Gold in the £30–£50 price band, aside from Château d'Esclans.)'

Spanish styles seem to fall into three groups: traditional, modern, and international pale pink. Some wines straddle two categories. Some producers have two or three different *rosados*, one in each style.

Sadly, I think, the number of darker *rosados* produced is falling fast, as more are made in the international paler style which vineyards have discovered sell better on the international market. As elsewhere, the darker, more traditional style appeals to a niche market.

Traditional style

Typically, this is a blend of white and red varieties (a minimum of 50 per cent of red varieties), first pressed and with varying amounts of maceration. Some traditional *clarete* wines, fermented with the skins or part of them, are made in this style. These wines are typically lighter on the palate and a little more savoury, with red fruits, flowers, herbaceous and stone fruit notes.

In Tierra de León, Prieto Picudo, a small dark grape, was traditionally used to make *rosado* wines using an unusual technique called *madreo* (mother). This involves filling the tank with a combination of direct-pressed juice, juice bled off after longer maceration, and unpressed bunches, which make up 5–10 per cent of the volume, contributing the flavours of whole-bunch fermentation. The method is not dissimilar to that for Rosé des Riceys. The **Dominio Dostares** winery (www.dominiodostares.com) restored this tradition with their Tombú Rosado.

Bodegas Lopez de Heredia
Avda. de Vizcaya, 3, 26200 Haro, La Rioja
Tel.: 941 310 244
www.lopezdeheredia.com

Possibly the most famous traditional *rosado* is Viña Tondonia (www.lopezdeheredia.com) from this winery in Rioja. Made from 30 per cent Tempranillo, 60 per cent Garnacha (Grenache) and 10 per cent Viura, it is aged in barrels for four and half years. In 2017 the vintage available was the Gran Reserva 2000. It was evidently no longer pink, but had an onion skin to tawny colour and was smooth and fresh, with body and complexity due to barrel ageing. Wine writer Anthony Rose described it in *The Drinks Business* list of Top Ten Serious Rosés in 2014 as 'unique, savoury, with aromatics of rose and cloves and superb berry fruit … one of the most deliciously distinctive Rioja rosés you'll ever come across.'

Muga
Barrio de la Estación s/n, 26200 Haro, La Rioja
Tel.: 941 31 18 25
www.bodegasmuga.com

Also in Rioja, this winery made its first *claretes* in 1932. Current owner Juan Muga explained that they still use the same methods and the same combination of grapes (60 per cent Garnacha, 30 per cent white Viura and 10 per cent Tempranillo) as in the 1930s. The grapes are blended together and macerated for 12 hours, then barrel-fermented for twenty-five days, giving extra richness and complexity, with notes of toast and rich apricots. A difference from the original style, which leads this wine to straddle the two categories of traditional and modern, is that the wine is fresher because the Garnacha is now sourced from north-facing vineyards at 600 metres. This gives the wine very fresh acidity and contributes to the long, mineral structure. The red berry fruit has cool-climate austerity. The oak does not dominate, but gives weight and a hint of dry tannins on the finish. There is good complexity from well-handled oak, and fresh fruit. In 2017 Muga launched an international pale rosé – see p.185.

Bodegas Gordonzello
Alto de Santa Marina, s/n, 24294 Gordoncillo (León) Castilla y León
Tel.: 987 758 030
www.gordonzello.com

Miranda Sira Burón has increased plantings of Prieto Picudo, using *selection massale*, from 35 hectares to 100, with half their production being *rosado*. Their top *cuvée*, Gurdos, is made using the *madreo* method. A darker colour with lovely intense fruit and savoury complexity, it sells well locally, in the US and South America. The paler, more international style (to my mind less interesting) is made for sale in Asia and Europe.

Dominio del Aguila
c/ Los Lagares nº 42, 09370 La Aguilera (Burgos)
Tel.: 638 899 236
www.dominiodelaguila.com

Jorge Monzón, who has worked at Romanée-Conti, Vega Sicilia and Bodegas Arzuaga-Navarro, has worked full time at Dominio del Aguila in the Ribera del Duero since 2013. The estate uses the traditional underground cellars of the region to provide cool ambient temperatures. The 2012 Pícaro del Águila Clarete, made with old-vine Tempranillo, Blanca del País (Albilla), Grenache, and other varieties has beautiful elegance. Albillo is a local white grape with neutral flavours, a light perfume aroma and high glycerol content, which gives smoothness to the wines and is sometimes added for added aromatics. The whole-bunch grapes were foot-trodden and macerated to extract colour and fruit. It is fermented, including malolactic fermentation, and aged for twelve months in French oak, to create a niche product with only 1,212 bottles and 128 magnums. While the oak is still evident on both nose and palate, it is well integrated with the ripe raspberry and sour cherry fruit, salty mineral notes, long mouth-watering acidity and soft, silky tannin finish. This wine, at five years old, still has several years to go.

Modern style

From the 1950s Spanish wineries (particularly from Navarra and Catalonia) started to emulate French rosés and use the *saignée* method to bleed the juice off the skins before fermentation. **Bodegas Las Campañas** (www.verema.com) (now Domecq Wines) adopted *saignée* techniques, together with fermentation at below 16°C. Many others followed its example, meeting a huge demand for *rosados* in the 1970s and 80s. The wines were not barrel-aged and had a bright, attractive colour, clear fruity aromas and a light, refreshing taste. These can be robust *rosados* with bright, raspberry-pink colour, red berry aromas, and fresh fruit on the palate. Today some also use barrels.

International consultants, such as Denis Dubourdieu and Michel Rolland, played roles, giving a modern international interpretation to traditional wines. Rolland, who traditionally makes more overt fruit-driven styles, often with oak character has worked with the Lurton Brothers in Toro since the early 2000s and, since 2007, for the Abbad family at Bodegas Olvena in Somontano, where they produce a Merlot *rosado*.

Bodegas Tobia
C/ Senda Rutia S/N, 26214 Cuzcurrita de Río Tirón, La Rioja
Tel.: 941 301 789
bodegastobia.com

When Oscar Tobia returned to his family vineyards in Rioja in 1994, and set up Bodegas Tobia, he also set about modernizing the winemaking. One of his first steps was to make his *rosado* by destemming the bunches, for improved purity of fruit character, and another was introducing new oak barrels. He created the Fermentado en Barrica (fermented in barrel) *rosado* in 1996, a revolution in the world of rosé wines, ten years before Lichine released his oak-fermented Garrus in Provence. Initially, Tobia was, initially, not allowed to sell the wine with the appellation, because the technique was not included in the regulations for Rioja, but he persisted, won the support of other winemakers, and finally succeeded in changing the rules. Today Fermentado en Barrica is one of the most recognized rosés in Spain. It is made from a blend of Tempranillo (55 per cent, old vine, north-facing, Atlantic influence, 480 metres, on clay and gravel), Graciano (35 per cent, 345 metres, on stony limestone soil, more Mediterranean climate) and Merlot (10 per cent, Atlantic influence, 590 metres). The must was filtered after thirty-six hours of maceration, then separately vinified and aged for five months with *battonage* in Allier barrels. The three wines are blended at the end of the ageing period. Production is limited to thirty-four barrels. It is a powerful rosé with firm structure and ripe red fruit.

J Chivite Family Estates
NA-132 Km. 3,1, 31132 Villatuerta, Navarra
Tel.: 948 811 000
www.chivite.com

The old family estate of the Chivite family, in Navarra, just to the north of Rioja, was one of the first to modernize winemaking, including *rosado*. Julián Chivite senior brought in Denis Dubourdieu as a consultant. Chivite senior died in 1996 and the four siblings: Julián, Carlos, Mercedes and Fernando took over the business, with Fernando as chief winemaker. In 1997 Frank Prial, wine columnist for the *New York Times* from 1972–2004, wrote that 'Navarra wines have been eclipsed by Rioja's, but that's changing because of Chivite, the province's largest wine exporter.' He went on to note that 'one of the best [*rosado*] is the 100 per cent Grenache called Gran Fuedo, from Bodegas Julián Chivite.' The business suffered when first Carlos and then Mercedes died of cancer, in 2005 and 2006, then in 2010 Julián and Fernando went their separate ways. Fernando launched his own Navarra rosé, called Arbayun, while Julián created J Chivite Family Estates.

Julián has kept the Gran Feudo Edición Rosado *sobre lías* (aged on the lees). Merlot and Cabernet Sauvignon form the basis of this wine, which is then blended with Grenache aged in French oak, on the lees, to make a gastronomic-style *rosado*. Their Las Fincas, a pale rosé made in collaboration with Juan-Mari Arzak (of the eponymous San Sebastián restaurant), which was launched in 2015, has a more regional style with a blend of Grenache and Tempranillo, good weight and structure, ripe, strawberry fruit, mouth-watering acidity and a firm, dry finish.

The J Chivite Colección 125 Rosado is a barrel-fermented blend of Tempranillo designed for ageing in bottle. It uses low-temperature maceration and fermentation in French oak barrels, followed by ageing on the lees for at least for six months, and is bottled more than twelve months after the harvest. Production is limited to 1,837 bottles. The new oak is evident on the nose and palate when young, balanced by ripe, sweet, red cherry fruit. The oak gives heavier weight and structure than Las Fincas, with a creamy roundness, and hints of savoury spice and umami.

Marques de Murrieta

N232/ LO-20 Logroño-Zaragoza (Exit 0), 26006 - Logroño, La Rioja
Tel.: 941 271 374
www.marquesdemurrieta.com

This winery is located in the Rioja, in the north-western sub-region of Rioja Alta. Its higher altitude vineyards have a long ripening season and produce fresher fruit. Mazuelo (Carignan) is often used to contribute acidity to Rioja red wines. Murrieta's Primer *rosado,* in a pretty fluted bottle, is 100 per cent Mazuelo, manually harvested when fully ripe in late September. The grapes are destemmed and gently pressed, before cold fermentation in tank, avoiding malolactic fermentation. After fermentation, the wine is left in contact with its lees for forty days, adding density. Carignan can be difficult to use for rosé, ranging from ripe strawberry fruit to quite severe, and this wine comes out on the more severe end of the spectrum. Very dry, with wild red berry fruit and tannic finish on the end, it is more of a gastronomic wine than one for aperitifs.

Bodegas Félix Callejo

Avda. del Cid, Km. 16,400, E-09441, Sotillo de la Ribera (Burgos)
Tel.: (34) 947 532 312
www.bodegasfelixcallejo.com

Further south lies the region of Ribiero del Duero, better known for its red wine production, its most famous wines being Pesquera de Duero and Vega Sicilia. The Viña Pilar 2016 from Bodegas Félix Callejo is around 100 per cent Tempranillo, made with cold, 24-hour skin contact, fermentation in tank and short (two months) barrel ageing. The resulting wine has an intense, raspberry-pink colour with a high intensity nose of red fruit, sour cherries, floral notes and caramel. The cherry compote character continues on the palate with a round, soft finish.

Tamaral (www.tamaral.com) Rosado DO Ribera del Duero, from 100-year-old Tempranillo vines grown at 900 metres in Pesquera de Duero, is made using *saignée,* bleeding off early. It has fresh, vibrant raspberry fruit, given an extra sweetness from 14% abv. The silky structure reveals a salty mineral core.

Bodegas Arrocal

09443, Eras de Santa María s/n Gumiel de Mercado, Burgos
Tel.: 947 561 290 / 606 292 102
www.arrocal.com

This winery in Ribera del Duero was founded in 2001, and produced its first vintage in 2005. The *rosado*, La Rosa de Arrocal is a modern take on the traditional *clarete* with a blend of 50 per cent Tempranillo and 50 per cent Albillo (white), harvested manually as late as early October. The Tempranillo is macerated for 72 to 96 hours at a low temperature to extract maximum fruit. The intensity of colour is reduced by blending with white grapes. The resulting wine is amazingly fresh and vibrant, with raspberry fruit with an almost jam-like richness, fresh, zesty, leafy acidity and a dry finish. Only 4,500 bottles a year are made.

Pago del Vicario

Carretera Porzuna, Km.16, 13196 Las Casas
Tel.: 902 09 29 26
www.pagodelvicario.com

A completely different modern *rosado* is the Petit Verdot of Pago del Vicario in Castille, south of Madrid. This appears to be the only Spanish *rosado* made solely from Petit Verdot, a variety more commonly associated with the cooler regions of Bordeaux. For Pago del Vicario, it seems to have thrived in the hot plains of central Spain, from vineyards at 600 metres, to produce a very dark pink *rosado*, made to be drunk young. It has intense, rich, creamy black cherry and mulberry fruit with hints of jam and bitter almonds. Although there is a mineral core with firm tannins, it is, overall, soft and supple, making it a joyful and exuberant wine.

Bodegas Pittacum

C/. La Iglesia, 11, Arganza del Bierzo – 24546, León
Tel.: 987 548 054
www.terrasgauda.com

Bodegas Pittacum was founded by six friends in 1999, and bought by Terras Gauda, a dynamic business with several other vineyards, in 2002. The winery is located in the DO Bierzo region, in the north east, near Tierra de León, which benefits from an Atlantic maritime influence moderated by warmer influences from the south. The *rosados* in this DO must have a minimum of 50 per cent Mencia, a pale-coloured, fragrant variety, and may include white varieties. Bodegas Pittacum's Petit Pittacum Rosado, is made with old-vine Mencia and Godello, grown on north-facing, cool, clay hillsides. With minimal maceration for a light colour, the wine is smooth and silky with floral notes, strawberries and raspberries.

Bodegas Bilbaínas
c/ Estación, 3, 26200 Haro, La Rioja
Tel.: 610 486 999
www.bodegasbilbainas.com

In 2015 they produced their first vintage of Viña Pomal, DO Rioja, made with a blend of 70 per cent Grenache and 30 per cent Viura. The grapes had 12 hours of skin contact. The wine has a pale, salmon colour and ripe, berry-fruit aromas. More structural than fruity, it has lovely long acidity and a dry tannic finish.

Bodegas Alodia
Ctra. A, 1229, km. 11,3, 22147 Adahuesca (Huesca)
Tel: 974 318 265
www.alodia.es

In Somontano, the Parraleta variety was traditional, but lost out to international varieties and had almost died out before being rediscovered by Bodegas Alodia. They now make a Parraleta *rosado* (14% abv) from the last surviving stocks of this vine. Harvested mechanically at night, the grapes are destalked and cool macerated for three days to achieve colour and fruit. The fermentation lasts for 25 days before ageing in American oak barrels for 14 months, with *battonage*. The wine is further aged for a short time in bottle to get the roundness and final bouquet.

Pale international style

In recent years, trendy lighter rosé wines have appeared, made with very little maceration, in the Provence style (pale in colour and dry).

In April 2017, Muga (see page 179) launched a rosé called Flore de Muga, which is 100 per cent Garnacha. The wine has creamy red fruit, lovely long acidity and mineral backbone. It is paler in colour than their other rosés, with a more international modern style.

The eastern, Mediterranean, coastline, produces lighter rosés than the *claretes* of northern Spain, often with a high percentage of Grenache.

> **Heretat MontRubí**
> L'Avellà 08736 Font-Rubí, Alt Penedès (Barcelona)
> Tel.: 938 979 066
> www.montrubi.com
> Gaintus One Night's Rosé DO Penedés is from a select harvest of Sumoll grapes grown specifically for this wine. Skins are allowed a cold maceration for one night only to obtain the soft colour and then pressed the next morning at low pressure. Fermentation takes place in 700-litre concrete eggs with regular *batonnage* over three months.

Catalonia has two native varieties which produce excellent *rosados*: Sumoll and Trepat. The Sumoll was almost completely abandoned, and is still not included in the Penedés DO's list of authorized varieties.

The climate for the DO Conca de Barberá is temperate Mediterranean, with hot summers and cold winters, and cooler temperatures at higher altitudes. Mountain ranges protect the area from the wind. Humidity is slightly higher than in neighbouring DOs. The local grape is Trepat, considered an interesting alternative to the usual Merlot and Pinot Noir in the production of *rosado* wines, both still and sparkling (see cava, pages 167–70). Rosés can be made as traditional wines in oak, more modern, fresh, fruity style wines, or delicate, pink, dry wines. Trepat's natural light colour makes it easy to extract fruit while keeping the colour pale.

According to Catalonia based wine-writer Miquel Hudin, the Catalan variety Lledoner Roig, related to the French clone Grenache Gris (Garnatxa Grisa), has seen a dramatic decline in numbers, both in Roussillon and over the border in Catalonia. Today there are a mere 61 hectares of Lledoner Roig recorded, plus vines interspersed with old Carignan vines. New plantings are of Grenache Gris. Although most choose to make a white wine from this pink grape (*roig* means reddish in Catalan), there are some *gris*-style rosés.

Cabernet Sauvignon is used in the succulent and vivacious Enate Rosado by Viñedos y Crianzas del Alto Aragón at **Bodegas Enate** (www.enate.es). It is harvested at optimum maturity and undergoes short maceration and tank fermentation at 16°C.

DO Utiel Requena

Halfway down the eastern coast of Spain, is the DO Utiel Requena, located between the Mediterranean coast and the high plateau of La Mancha in the centre of the country. The area slopes down slightly from north-west to south-east. The vineyards of Utiel–Requena escaped the devastating effects of the phylloxera virus because they were planted with the Bobal grape variety, which is more resistant than others. This gave producers time to replace vines by grafting varietals onto American rootstocks. Bobal makes up over 75 per cent of the plantings. The soil has a high limestone content, the summers are long, hot (up to 40°C) and dry, and the winters cold (down to -10°C), often with frosts and hail. The moderating influence of the Mediterranean is important. In this DO, **Bodegas Coviñas** (www.covinas.com) makes rosés with Bobal, with fresh strawberry and cherry fruit, and good acidity.

CANARY ISLANDS

A unique wine of the island of La Palma is *vino de tea*. *Tea* is the local name for the Canary Island pine (*Pinus canariensis*). These wines, which may be white, red or rosé are matured in pine casks for up to six months, giving them a resin flavour. The launching of the Regulatory Council of the La Palma DO in 1993 has played an important role in the regulation for this type of wine.

Only three producers appear to make *vino de tea*, from vineyards perched on terraces of volcanic soil. Sadly, all three estates have recently stopped producing their *rosado vino de tea*, and now just produce a standard *rosado*. Hopefully, they will make this wine again. I tasted the red Taedium of **Bodegas Noroeste de la Palma** (vinosveganorte.com), made principally with Negramoll, with some Muñeco and Listán Prieto to try and understand the flavours gained by ageing in pine barrels. The wine had pronounced resinous, earthy notes with hints of Christmas spice. On the palate one could discern dry red fruit, with a tannic edge and pine and earthy flavours. It is a style that needs adjusting to, and not for those searching for a simple pink rosé. Drunk with food, the wine takes on black chocolate and menthol-pine flavours backed by very gentle, supple, dry tannins. They taste similar to the Retsina rosé made by Kechris in Greece (see pages 275–6). I would love these producers to make the *rosado* again!

On the island of Tenerife, Viñatigo make a *rosado* that is 100 per cent Listán Negro. The rosé is complex, with strawberry and herbaceous aromas, raspberry leaf, and saline notes, showing the distinctive saline, mineral quality of these volcanic, sea-windswept islands. A sweet Brumas de Ayosa Malvasía Rosado Dulce by Bodegas Comarcal del Valle de Güimar, is the only wine on the market featuring the rare Malvasía Rosada.

PORTUGAL

Portuguese wine is strongly associated with Mateus Rosé, once the biggest selling rosé in the world. Created to have mass-market appeal, it brought attention to Portugal's table wine – and income – and has remained for many the face of Portugal's rosés.

When the American GIs came to Europe during the Second World War, many were used to the off-dry, pink, jug wines from California, and looked for similar European wines. In southern Italy they drank Five Roses. In Portugal, producers responded by making medium-sweet *frizzante* rosés.

Mateus Rosé (www.sograpevinhos.com), launched in 1942 by Fernando van Zeller Guedes, whose family owned vineyards in Vinho Verde, was based on locally made lightly sparkling red and white wines. After the war, it continued to appeal to the rapidly developing North American and northern European markets, where rosé was increasingly fashionable. Production grew rapidly in the 1950s and 1960s. By the late 1980s, supplemented by a white version, it accounted for over 40 per cent of Portugal's table wine exports.

In 1944, Lancers, a medium-sweet, lightly sparkling rosé wine was launched by J. M. da Fonseca at Azeitao near Setubal in Portugal. The brand was created when Henry Behar of Vintage Wines of New York saw that veterans of the war were returning home from Europe with a taste for wine. Lancers, initially sold in a stone crock, continues to be moderately successful in the US, while Mateus is better known in Europe.

In 1951, Sacheverell Sitwell wrote in *The Sunday Times* that Mateus Rosé was '... the most delicious vin rosé that I have ever tasted ... Mateus is delicious beyond words; and since I am told that it will travel and is exported to Brazil, it is a pity that one cannot buy it here in England.' The bottles took on collectible status, with many remembering, from the 60s and 70s, the essential Mateus bottle to hold candles (with wax dripping down) or for displaying pampas grass. Although I recall the bottle from my student days in the late 1970s I cannot remember the wine. Ruth Ellen Church wrote in 1968 that, 'Popular favorites from Portugal are those two pretty pinks which come in pottery jugs, Lancer's [sic] and Mateus. Whether they are admired more for flavour or for the container I wouldn't know, but both are a little sweet and easy to like. There is a Mateus still rosé, also. Lagosta and Pombal are still Portuguese pink wines which are pleasing and refreshing. The former is known as "the lobster wine." In its home country it is served with lobster.'

While Lancers rosé is often described as being one style, Jan Read (1982) made tasting notes at the Fonseca cellars, and described the styles made for different markets. The Faisca Rosé was, 'Very pale pink. Fresh rosé nose and taste. Fruity and fairly dry. Contains less sugar than most. Agreeable,' while Lancers Rosé had 'Darker colour. Fruity nose. Fresh, slightly sweet, but with a dryish aftertaste. Pleasant.' The Lancers Rosé (American style) was described as 'Sweet and much aerated'.

The Grocer (1988) noted that popularity for rosé peaked in the 1970s, when massive advertising for Portugal's Mateus Rosé boosted sales, and more than four million cases were sold annually to the US alone! As soon as this ceased, however, sales slipped, and by 1988 had not recovered. Mateus fell from grace for several reasons. Owner Sogrape made a bad situation worse in 1983, when it sued its US distributor, Schenley, to try to regain distribution rights, and lost. So, Mateus was not only not selling well, but a resentful distributor had total control.

Mateus Rosé is more floral than fruity, with dried raspberry notes, and made from some ten different red grape varieties. Most come from the Beiras region. Even though Sogrape owns 1,500 hectares of grapes, it buys in most grapes for Mateus. Sogrape now makes less than two million cases of Mateus, so it can be more selective which grapes it buys, rather than being desperate to buy everything to fulfil orders.

In 2014, Portuguese expert and wine writer Sarah Ahmed commented that, 'Though Mateus Rosé continues to outperform the market in this category, Californian brands such as Blossom Hill, Gallo and Echo Falls have been by far the biggest beneficiaries of the rosé phenomenon,' and 'in the main, Portugal's entry-level rosés have failed miserably to build on the success of Mateus Rosé thanks to clumsy use of residual sugar and a lack of freshness.' At this time Mateus went upmarket with the launch of a new top tier range, Mateus Expressions.

The article from 1988 in *The Grocer* went on to say, quite significantly that 'today, like white wines, rosés tend to have crisper acidity, lower alcohol and lighter body when grown in cooler places, which means places with maritime influence or high altitude. There's not really a particular geographical place in Portugal that is famous for making rosés, although as far as drinking is concerned, rosé is predominantly a seaside wine, also much exported. Every imaginable red grape, Portuguese and foreign, is made into rosé.' It is this lack of regional definition which has plagued so many regions.

Pedro Canedo (formerly at Mateus now with Quinta Nova) commented on the excellent and consistent quality of the Mateus wine, but felt it was a shame that the wine was non-vintage and that it was a generic Portuguese product without any sense of terroir. Mateus' move from dark to clear glass bottles has had a positive impact on sales, which were up 10 per cent in 2016. Clear glass does mean problems of light strike (see pages 28–30) but the increased sales make it worthwhile. Rosé is growing fast in Portugal, especially wines priced at €6.50 (US$7.75) and more, and is building on the back of growth for premium white wines.

Vinho Verde

Vinho Verde is the biggest DOC (Denominação de Origem Controlada) in Portugal. It is located in the cool, rainy north-western province of Minho, in one of the greenest and wettest parts of Portugal. The land is largely an elevated granite plateau traversed by rivers, including the River Minho (or Miño, in Spanish) which divides the region from Rías Baixas in Spain. Vinho Verde was first demarcated as a wine region in 1908 and became a DOC in 1984. Forty per cent of Vinho Verde production is rosé and red, which is unremarkable considering this was the original base for Mateus rosé. The rosés, usually made from Espadeiro and Padeiro grapes, have fresh red fruit with a bracing minerality and slight leafiness that adds a nice complexity. Many have residual sugar around 15g/l, and although they have good acidity, this is not enough to counter this level of sugar. The best examples have around 8g/l residual sugar, giving emphasis to the ripe fruit, and better balance to the acidity. The drier wines are refreshing and easy to drink, with alcohol around 11% abv.

Tejo

In another, northern region, the Tejo, it is interesting to see how producers are evolving the rosé market. Located north of Lisbon and the Alantejo region, along the River Tejo, Tejo produces a diverse range of wines, including red, white, rosé and 'traditional method' sparkling wines. Tejo region used to be known for high-volume, good value, generic wines. However, over the past 15 years, producers have ripped out a third of its vineyards from high fertile soils, and instead focused on lower production from more premium sites.

Today the Tejo is the fifth-largest wine producing region in Portugal, and in 2017 was in the middle of a three-year marketing push to reposition itself as a premium wine region. Its native red grapes include Touriga Nacional (for flavour in the mouth and long ageing potential), Trincadeira and Castelão, as well as Alicante Bouschet, some of which are old vines. Styles of wine vary dramatically depending on the end market, making it less easy to define a Tejo style.

Quinta da Badula
Rua do Casal – Arrouquelas, Rio Maior, Santarém
Tel.: 966 915 722
www.quintadabadula.com

A small family estate started in 2007. They made their first rosé in 2015 from 50 per cent Touriga Nacional and 50 per cent Syrah, and decided to make the 2016 a little drier, creating a wine with a dry, tannic finish and fine, austere fruit, making it more of a gastronomic wine This is definitely not in the style of the easy, commercial rosés.

Quinto do Casal Monteiro
Estrada Municipal 1, 2080-201 Almeirim
Tel.: 243 592 414
www.casalmonteiro.pt

Here, they make their rosé with 40 per cent Touriga Nacional, 30 per cent Syrah and 30 per cent Tinto Roriz. They use free-run juice, as they found it difficult to create a rosé with finesse from these varieties if there was any maceration. The wine has a peach Melba character, or peaches and redcurrants with a little touch of confectionary sugar on the finish. It has good acidity with a slightly tannic dryness on the finish. As 90 per cent of sales are for export, they chose to make this a pale Provence-style rosé, but admitted the pale colour was not so popular in Portugal.

Quinta da Requeixada
Travessa do Vareta, n°11, 2080 - 184 Almeirim
Tel.: 243 597 491
www.fiuzabrighteng.com/quinta-da-requeixada.html

At this winery owned by the Fiuza family for over fifty years, they make a rosé from Cabernet Sauvignon and Touriga Nacional. Touriga Nacional is harvested slightly earlier than for the red wine to ensure freshness. Cabernet Sauvignon has been included to appeal to an international market. Grapes are macerated for 24 hours, resulting in a pale pink wine with fresh, red berry fruit character that is further emphasized by 5g/l residual sugar and balanced by crisp acidity.

Quinta Casal Branca
Estrada Nacional 118 Km 69, 2080-187 Almeirim
Tel.: 243 592 412
www.casalbranco.com

This winery make rosé as a very small part of production under its Terra de Lobos label, and is learning how to develop the style. They used to make a weightier rosé from a blend of Touriga Nacional and Aragonez (Tempranillo), grown on limestone, using the *saignée* method, off the red wine. The wine was a dark pink, with firm fruit structure, dry and fresh. But while this weightier style appealed more to the local market, it proved less successful on the international market, where pale rosés were considered the benchmark. They have moved from *saignée* to night harvesting and direct press to ensure freshness and, with successive years have steadily reduced the duration of skin contact. The 2014 vintage still had longer skin contact and was a deeper colour. The 2015 had four hours of skin contact before fermentation at 16–18°C. The resulting wine showed good Tempranillo with fresh fruit and a hint of tannic dryness on the finish. However, market demands wanted less structure and more fruit, and for the latest vintage Tempranillo was replaced with Syrah to give crisper red fruit, juicy acidity and good dryness. As the style has adapted to market demands and the export market has grown, the rosé has become paler. The Cruz Sobraal family feel the new style is pleasant, but the old style was far more exciting, and I have to say I agree.

The Douro

The region is best known for making port and red table wines. However, some port houses are making pink port and dry table wines of high quality. There are even pink ports being made. **Croft** (www.croftpink.com) made the first pink port in 2008, capturing the fruit flavours without the tannins.

Niepoort
Rua Cândido dos Reis, 598, 4400-071 Vila Nova de Gaia
Tel.: 223 777 777
www.niepoort-vinhos.com

Redoma is made primarily from the local grapes Tinta Amarela and Touriga Franca, from old vines grown at 200–400 metres altitude, fermented in new French oak barrels, followed by malolactic fermentation, and aged for six months in stainless steel. The well-integrated oak gives hints of nuts, toast and ripe creamy weight, apricot and peach fruit and an orange peel savoury finish.

Quinta Nova
5085-222 Covas do Douro
Tel.: 254 730 420
www.quintanova.com

This has been a port house since 1726 and is currently owned by Amorim, who bought the estate in 1999. Quinta Nova was its single estate port with 35 hectares. From 2002–05 Armorim started replanting red varieties, analysing the exposure, soils and alignment, at sites between 80 and 300 metres. Having established their premium reds and whites, Armorim realized that the market for premium whites also liked premium rosé. As noted earlier, statistics indicate that in Portugal there is a decline in cheaper rosé and an increase in premium rosé. In 2015, they experimented and created two rosés, one with partial oak fermentation and one fully oaked and aged in cask. The 1,500 bottles of each created to test the market sold out within one month of release. In 2016, they made 6,000 bottles of the partially oaked wine and 4,500 of the fully oaked *reserva*. This is new territory; the demand is there but the market does not seem to want to pay as much for rosé as for red wine. The oaked reserve is a gastronomic rosé, which would go well with a gutsy local *bacalhau* (salt cod stew).

Grapes are sourced from parcels having less sun exposure. The parcels are all different, with grapes reaching ripeness at different times, leading to up to fifty different harvest dates. Each parcel is fermented separately in small tanks. Tinta Francisca is used for its lighter colour, fruit aromas and flavours. Tinta Roriz provides structure and has an outstanding affinity with oak, ensuring that the *reserva* blend benefits well from the oak treatment. Touriga Franca provides freshness and acidity A key feature is the pressing, using the *blanc de noirs* technique, in which the grapes are pressed whole, very gently.

Rosé 2016, Quinta Nova de Nossa Señhora do Carmo was made with Touriga Franca and Tinta Roriz grapes, harvested earlier than for the red wines. Grapes were gently pressed, with minimal skin contact, followed by a long (six week) fermentation with ambient yeasts to extract maximum flavours. The wine was partially oaked for a few months. The oak is dominant when young with a rich, creamy character and a slight hint of pineapple, but is also beautifully integrated, balancing the pronounced wild red berry fruit. A powerful but elegant rosé, it handles its alcohol of 13.5% abv well. The wine has potential for age, and is indeed a wine I look forward to tasting as it ages.

AZORES

The islands of the Azores were first colonized in the fifteenth century, with vineyards planted by the Franciscans. Verdelho was commonly planted and the wines shipped around Europe. After the fall of Imperial Russia, bottles of Verdelho do Pico were found in the tsars' cellars. Originally all nine islands were used for viticulture, but after phylloxera, vines remained only on the islands of Pico, Terceira and Graciosa. The most productive island is Pico. The islands are volcanic and windswept, with almost no diurnal range. The climate is hyper-maritime with a moderate range throughout the year and temperatures ranging between 4 and 30°C. Pico's snow-capped mountains do impart some extra coolness, but not much. The vineyards are protected by a network of dry stone walls of volcanic rock, with each plot (*curral*) around nine by twelve metres. Sarah Ahmed describes the island as the Santorini of Portugal. Ninety-five percent of the grapes are Arinto do

Açores, with the remaining grapes Verdelho and Terrantez do Pico. Other islands grow mainly Verdelho.

Azores Wine Company
Rua dos Biscoitos, nº3 São Mateus, 9950-542 Madalena – Pico
Tel.: 292 098 070
azoreswinecompany.com

Rosé Vulcânico is a *rosado* which proved challenging and divisive at tasting. Provence winemakers were lost when they tasted it. I found it intriguing, and kept coming back for more. From its salty, mineral aromas, to its salty, tight red fruit and umami complexity, this wine had a mysterious character, which made Stefanie Köhler of *Cuvée* magazine, declare it the Chablis of rosé. The small production of just 6,500 bottles was made with Saborinho (also known as Negramoll), Agronómica, Aragonez (Tempranillo), Touriga Nacional, Merlot and Syrah, some from vines that were over 100 years old.

Antonio Rizzo

Rizzo, a graduate from England's Plumpton College, experimented for the 2016 vintage with small quantities of two pink wines on Pico. His Terras de Lavas rosé is a blend of Syrah and Merlot that is more orange than pink. Whole-bunch pressing in a wooden press, because it is relatively slow, allows for extra skin contact. After pressing, the juice is removed from the skins. The volcanic soils and maritime winds have a clear impact on the wine, which has a strong mineral, saline character with red fruit and fresh acidity. His second wine is a pink *pet nat*. Using the same varieties as for the still wine, and the same press, the wine is fermented first in tank, with second fermentation in bottle. A similar saline character is evident, backed by red fruit, and slightly tannic, with an interesting olive-brine character. The wine is unusual, and the savoury character takes some getting used to, but one could imagine drinking it as an aperitif, with olives.

10
ITALIAN ROSÉ

Italy was the biggest wine producer in the world in 2016, producing 48.8 million hectolitres compared to France's 41.9 million hectolitres, according to the International Organization of Vine and Wine (OIV).

The dramatic archaeological discovery, in 2017, of evidence of winemaking in large pottery jars in a cave in Monte Kronio, Agrigento, south-west Sicily, has pushed back the history of winemaking in Italy by 3,000 years, to the Copper Age, around 4000 BC. Winemaking was well established by the time of the Greek colonization around 800 BC. Grapes were so easily cultivated, they named the country 'Oenotria', meaning 'the land of wine'. The Etruscans, followed by the Romans, took a great interest in winemaking skills. Large-scale, slave-run plantations sprang up in many coastal areas and spread so much that, in 92 AD, emperor Domitian had to destroy a great number of vineyards to free up fertile land for food production.

Following the fall of the Roman Empire, winemaking continued until the late nineteenth century when, along with elsewhere in Europe, phylloxera took hold and destroyed many of Italy's vineyards. The replanted vineyards were often designed for maximum quantity, not quality, and Italy became a global source of inexpensive table wines. During the 1960s, moves began towards making wines of quality; in 1963, Italy launched its first official system of classification of wines.

At the tenth annual Italia in Rosa conference held in Valtènesi in 2016, Tiziana Sarnari, market analyst for wine at the Istituto di Servizi per il Mercato Agricolo Alimentare (ISMEA) discussed the lack of statistics available, which make it difficult to assess the true nature of the Italian rosé market, or the regional division between red and rosé.

The institute is now setting up a mechanism to collect data, to help producers plan a cohesive strategy to promote Italian rosés.

Rosés are made throughout Italy, from over fifty indigenous varieties, plus international ones. Unless a wine is classified as DOC or IGT, the variety cannot be indicated on the label. Italy has many denominations (appellations) for wine, many of which include one or more types of rosé: including 334 DOC, 74 DOCG and 118 IGT. Given the wide number of grape varieties, analysis is complicated. As Italy is a long country, it has different climates, from that of the Alps in the north to that of Sicily in the south, near North Africa. Most vineyards are in coastal regions and/or located at altitude, which helps to moderate the heat.

The majority of Italian red and rosé wines come from the south, and Puglia in particular, followed by Emilia Romagna, Tuscany, Veneto and Sicilia.

As in other countries, there are two main styles, *chiaretto*, the equivalent of *clairet*, and *rosato*, the equivalent of rosé.[5] The name *chiaretto* derives from the Italian term *chiaro*, meaning 'light' or 'pale' (red). Whereas in other countries, *clairet* wines are darker than rosé, in Italy, the colour is not the defining element of the style, so that some *chiaretti* are lighter than some *rosati* – which can be very confusing. *Chiaretto* generally, but not always, has longer skin contact than *rosato*.

Chiaretto evidently has the older lineage. It is mentioned briefly as a wine style in the book *Monferrato in the Corografia fisica, storica e statistica dell'Italia e delle sue isole* (1838); in the medical journal *Giornale delle scienze mediche* (1848) *chiaretto* is mentioned in both Monferrato and the Valle d'Aosta and in the trade catalogue for an exhibition in Vienna, *Relazioni dei Giurati Italiani sulla Esposizione universale di Vienna del 1873* several *chiaretti* are listed, from Monferrato, Castel Ceriolo and elsewhere in Piedmont, from Sicily and Liguria, and are variously described as being white, red and sweet.

Every region produces *rosato* wines, often with regional variations, and colours range from pale to dark. Many of the best are closer to red than pink. According to Giovanna Pradini of Perla del Garda di Morenica in Lombardy, interest has grown in developing regional styles of rosati, with wines reflecting both varieties and regions. *Rosato* is a

---

5 In this chapter, I use the term rosé to include both Italian *rosato* (plural *rosati*) and *chiaretto* (plural *chiaretti*).

traditional style in Puglia. Some places, such as Abruzzo and Sicily, have a *rosato* style called *cerasuolo*. The sheer range and variety of pink wines available, and the many regional appellations, make it impossible to list them all. Below are examples to illustrate the diversity of styles.

The classic methods of direct press and *saignée* are used, as well as varying lengths of maceration. Shorter macerations (roughly 6–12 hours) are called *vino di una notte* (wine of one night). Longer macerations (roughly 24–48 hours) lead to what are referred to as *vino di un giorno* (wine of one day).

THE *CHIARETTI* OF LAKE GARDA

In Italy, *chiaretto* wines are mainly (but not exclusively) made in the north, around Lake Garda, where Lombardy and Veneto meet. This lake, the largest in Italy, runs from mountains in the north to the plains of Lombardy, acting as a moderating influence on the climate, allowing for Mediterranean vegetation. The mild climate and fertile lands on the southern shores made it a wealthy area, home to aristocrats and landowners.

In 1885, Pompeo Gherardo Molmenti married a noblewoman from Moniga del Garda, Amalia Brunati, who brought in her dowry 15 hectares of land by Lake Garda. Molmenti was interested in agriculture and during visits to France, including Bordeaux, he came across the *clairet* produced there. Molmenti appears to have been inspired by these lighter red wines and, on returning home, studied making red wines with a shorter maceration using a method called *alzata di cappello* (removing the mass of grape skins that surface during fermentation). In 1896, he made his first *chiaretto*, with the first labelled bottle in 1904.

Chiaretto received official status, under the DOC rules, during the 1960s. The key types are Valtènesi *chiaretto* and Bardolino *chiaretto*, made in different styles, with different blends.

Valtènesi *chiaretto*

Valtènesi, on the south-western shore of the lake, in Lombardy, has a distinct microclimate influenced by proximity to the mountains and lake. The Valtènesi DOC was created in 2011 when a number of producers who grew mainly Gropello wanted their own identitiy and not to be one of the many styles of the existing Garda DOC. Valtènesi *chiaretto* is a blend of at least 50 per cent Groppello (Groppello Gentile or Groppello di Mocasina), and can be 100 per cent, with smaller amounts of Marzemino, Barbera, Sangiovese and Rebo (a cross between Merlot and Teroldego). Valtènesi *chiaretto* must be produced 'by short maceration on the skins' and cannot be released before 14 February following the vintage. A sparkling *chiaretto* is also allowed.

Alessandro Luzzago, president of the Valtènesi Consortium – the local wine producers board – and owner of **Le Chiusure** (www.lechiusure.net) in San Felice del Benaco says he 'is well aware that the local *chiaretto* needs a clear definition of its identity, and that despite its history and traditions, production of modern rosé needs innovation in both field and cellar'. To help them achieve this, the Consortium and the Valtènese producers started to work, in 2013 with the Centre de Recherche et d'Expérimentation sur le Vin Rosé [CREVR] which, according to the Valtènesi Consortium, 'tastes and analyses *chiaretto* samples each year with the aim of better expressing the distinctive features of our wines and our territory, and forming a language to communicate these to consumers'.

Luzzago sees that Valtènesi and Bardolino are bound by 'a common destiny, dedicated to the production of Italian rosé, as Provence is for France.' However, Lake Garda both separates them – leading to 'completely different grapes in very close territories: Corvino in Bardolino and Groppello in Valtenesi' – and binds them in a united geographical region.

Colours of Valtènesi *chiaretti* are increasingly pale, in an attempt to obtain more delicate and elegant wines, retaining a distinct character based on Groppello. Harvest dates are moving earlier, maceration times becoming shorter and, most importantly, oxygen protection is improving.

Luzzato sees these results paying off. 'At Le Chiusure our production of *chiaretto* has more than doubled over the last five years. In 2017 at Le Chiusure we are looking at producing two or perhaps even three pink products, to help us grow our knowledge and have more stories for our customers.'

The *chiaretto* of **Azienda Agricola Pratello** (www.pratello.com), Sant'Emiliano, is a blend of Groppello, Marzemino, Barbera and Sangiovese grown at 180 metres above Lake Garda. The grapes undergo eight hours of cold maceration. The wine has ripe redcurrants, with raspberry and strawberry fruit, balanced by a firm weight and very fresh acidity.

At the southern end of Lake Garda, Giovanna Prandini, owner and winemaker of **Perla del Garda di Morenica** (www.perladelgarda.it), makes her *chiaretto* with 100 per cent Rebo, as she feels Groppello is not suited to her hotter vineyards. This cannot be sold as DOC, but she feels the sacrifice is worthwhile. Prandini sought a young fresh style to go with food. Her wine has fresh, dry red fruit with a firm mineral character. For many years she has sold her wines in a bottle of her own design.

Bardolino Chiaretto

Bardolino Chiaretto in the Veneto, granted DOC status in 1968, is made on the south-eastern shore of Lake Garda. The soil is composed of Dolomite rocks which came down in the glacial age, and contains a high percentage of magnesium, giving salty freshness to the wine, especially in vineyards higher up from the shores of the lake, where it typically gives a mineral palate with salty, fresh acidity and long, clean, red berry fruit. **Benazzoli** (www.benazzoli.com), which lies further south, between Bardolino and Valpolicella, nearer the better sites for red wine production, has a different profile, with fresh red fruit, firmer structure and tannins reflecting the terroir.

The main grapes are Corvina (35–80 per cent), Rondinella (10–40 per cent), Molinara (maximum 15 per cent), with up to 15 per cent of Rossignola or Garganega (one or both, maximum 15 per cent).

Traditionally the *chiaretti* were relatively light red wines, generally fresh and fruity, popular locally, but little exported. The catalogue for the 'Italian Wine Exhibit' at the 1934 Chicago World's Fair describes Bardolino as 'Identified with a bright ruby color, a characteristic pleasing bouquet, lightness of body, an enticing tastiness and neatness of taste … an easy favorite with discriminating patrons. Its alcoholic strength ranges to about 12 per cent by vol. … Served through the intermediate course of the dinner.'

During the 1960s and 1970s when the region experienced popularity and sales soared, quality started to suffer due to overproduction. During the 1980s, big reds were considered to be a sign of quality, and producers tried to emulate the neighbouring wines of Valpolicella, but the terroir and varieties struggled to achieve these wines and today red Bardolino

Superiore DOCG amounts to less than 1 per cent of Bardolino's total production.

With declining sales, Bardolino producers needed to reassess their wines. Recognizing that they no longer had the charm and lightness for which they were best known, they decided to have another look at their *chiaretto* and to return to their roots. This involved shifting grapes from production of red Bardolino to their *chiaretto* – the sales of which, in five years, have increased from 4 to 11 million bottles a year.

Le Fraghe
Loc. Colombare 3 37010 Cavaion Veronese (VR)
Tel.: 0457 236 832
www.fraghe.it

Owned by Matilde Poggi, this winery is named after the strawberries that used to grow in this area, before the era of mass production. Since her return to organic farming in 2009, the wild strawberries have started to return. Until 1980, the vineyards were co-planted with a mixture of varieties, but have since been replanted with a single variety per plot. Poggi particularly likes the variety Corvina, because of its low concentration of colour, and it now makes up 80 per cent of her vines.

Unusually, Poggi still makes her *chiaretto*, Rodòn, in the traditional style using *saignée* from her red Bardolino Le Fraghe wine, which she feels is more ecological (as the juice would otherwise go unused). Making a good rosé this way is, she explained, difficult. Selecting the harvest date for the different parcels, from south-facing plots at 190 metres, means keeping in mind the two styles of wine. When macerating the grapes, choosing the correct time to bleed off the juice for the *chiaretto* is critical. Poggi admitted that it can mean being on hand, sometimes throughout the night, to bleed off the juice at exactly the right moment to avoid excessive colour, fruit or tannins. She generally macerates for no more than six or seven hours. The *chiaretto* is fermented with ambient yeast: her Rodòn *Chiaretto* 2015 had fragrant floral and intense strawberry fruit balanced by salty minerality and long fresh acidity. The *saignée* method gives a spicy note from skin contact. After bleeding off the juice, Poggi goes on to blend this with juice from grapes harvested later to make her red Bardolino, which has hints of strawberry and berry fruit, fresh acidity and the mineral austerity typical of its terroir.

Since the 2014 harvest, *Chiaretto*'s winemakers have been working together on a Chiaretto Revolution (chiaretto.pink) marketing campaign. With the fashion for pale pink rosé, the emphasis has been on making light pink *chiaretti* with aromatic and floral notes. Originally made as darker wines, bled off the red Bardolino wines, the new paler *chiaretti* have, on the whole, been harvested earlier, with a shorter pressing. Some of these new commercial versions may seem less interesting, but are clearly tapping into market demand. In 2017, a separate DOC Chiaretto di Bardolino was created. For me, the most exciting examples of Bardolino *chiaretto* style are not too pale and show good expression of both fruit and terroir.

LAGREIN KRETZER OF ALTO ADIGE

The traditional Lagrein Kretzer, is a *rosato* made from the local Lagrein variety usually used in red wines. The name suggests origins in the Lagarina valley of Trentino. The variety was mentioned as early as the seventeenth century, in the records of the Muri Abbey near Bolzano. Kretzer is derived from the term *kretze*, a woven basket formerly used to sieve the must and separate it from the skins.

At the 1934 Chicago World's Fair, it was described thus: 'Lagrein of Gries near Bolzano, including two types: One lighter (Lagrein Kreitzer [sic]), sprightly and fruity, with from 11.5 to 12 of alcohol by vol. per cent; the other, Lagrein Scuro is 'dark', a red wine'.

Some 10 per cent of the **Muri Abbey** (ww.muri-gries.com) cellar's Lagrein production is today made into Kretzer. The monastery's version is matured in stainless steel tanks to produce a gently sparkling, fruity, fresh and youthful wine, ready to drink just months after the harvest. **Josef Weger**'s (www.wegerhof.it) version has a tangy raspberry sweetness. Heinrich Mayr's **Nusserhof** (www.fws.it/it/nusserhof) makes a Lagrein Kretzer which was described by Italian expert Ian d'Agata as 'Creamy, with fresh strawberry fruit flavours, fine-grained tannins and a lovely freshness.' Longer skin contact results in a pale red colour. The wine has soft, but firm, tannins, rich cherry, strawberry and dried redcurrant fruit, and long, fresh acidity.

MOSCATO ROSAS OF THE NORTH-EAST

These sweet, dark pink Muscats are made with the red-skinned, red-juice grape called Moscato Rosa in Italian and Rosenmuskateller in the Alto Adige and Austria. With an intense aroma of red roses, the wine is a distinctive pink. The Moscato Rosa vine shares similarities with the Croatian Muškat Ruža Porečki (also a rose Muscat). D'Agata notes that the variety is good for air-drying because of its thin skin, although best results seem to come from late harvesting to maintain the freshness and aromatics. A good example will have roses, ripe, rich cherries, strawberries and raspberries with sweet spice notes.

These wines can be found in the northern region of Trentino–Alto-Adige and Friuli Venezia Giulia as well as in Austria, Germany and Croatia.

VENETIAN *RAMATO*

Ramato (meaning copper) is a traditional style of wine from Friuli Venezia Giulia, that is sometimes pink, sometimes copper-tinged. It is made with Pinot Grigio, a white variety with pink-tinted skin. *Ramato* is currently receiving attention as it combines two fashions: orange wine and rosé.

To maximize the wines' aromatic potential, they have a longer skin contact. According to David Gleave MW, pink Pinot Grigio 'was first bottled in the 1950s, but didn't really start to become popular until the 1980s, by which time technology had improved and the fashion was for very clear, light white wines. Many producers fined any tinges of pink (and flavour) out of the wine. As a result, the *ramato* style fell out of fashion, even though a few producers (Specogna, La Fattoria, Livio Felluga) stuck with it.'

Modern Pinot Grigio *rosato* is a pale pink rosé, light, delicately fruity, for easy drinking. Grapes are generally pressed immediately after harvest and skin contact is minimized. Temperature of fermentation impacts the level of colour extraction, though arguably it has a greater impact on the aromatic profile of the wine. It is not always the case that reds are always fermented at higher temperatures than whites. An example is Gossip, IGT Venezia Giulia from **Di Lenardo** (www.dilenardo.it). Because the grapes are harvested at full ripeness, when they have taken on a pink tint, they are lower in acidity than a standard rosé grape, so the gentle tannic structure from the first twelve hours of fermentation on the skins at a cold temperature is essential. The wine has a pretty, golden-salmon-pink colour with ripe, peach fruit and fresh acidity, with tannins barely noticeable. Apart from the colour, this wine tastes more like a white wine, and was until recently being sold, moderately well, as such. The 2016 vintage was bottled in clear glass and, as a rosé, sales have risen considerably.

ROSATI OF THE GREAT RED WINE REGIONS OF PIEDMONT AND TUSCANY

Making a rosé profitably here is a challenge, as local reds are so highly valued. When some producers made small quantities of rosé as a teaser to introduce new customers to their wines, many were taken by surprise by the high level of interest, so much so that they are now looking at making premium rosés, many with distinctive red-wine character, with greater fruit and structure to accompany their reds.

Piedmont

In Piedmont, *chiaretti* were historically made from a blend of red and white grapes reflecting the ripeness of the vintage when its delicacy was valued. In the nineteenth century, *chiaretto* was made as a by-product of red wine, and *chiaretti* became the weak wines of the workers. Chilled for a few hours in the local *ghiacciaia* (ice-houses), *chiaretto* could be a refreshing summer drink. The name and style has been revived to answer the market demand for rosé. Several *chiaretti* are made, from a wide range of varieties, and range in style from pale rosé to a darker wine, with the style depending on the region, the local red wine (as the region has many varieties and DOCs) and house preference. The DOC for Monferrato *Chiaretto* accepts all styles and colours, and can include Barbera, Bonarda, Cabernet Franc, Cabernet Sauvignon, Dolcetto, Freisa, Grignolino, Pinot Noir or Nebbiolo, making it impossible to define one single style.

> **Pescaja**
> Frazione San Matteo, Via Cima 59, 14010 Cisterna D'Asti (AT), Piedmont
> Tel.: 0141 979711
> www.pescaja.com
> Giuseppe Guido says that in 2014 he was approached by a client in Luxembourg who wanted to add some rosé (which he did not make) to his order. In 2015, Guido harvested fruit from his young Nebbiolo and Barbera vines to make his rosé. His Fléury 2015, a dark pink with ripe peach and blackberry fruit, mineral acidity and a tannic finish, was a success. His main concern now is for the future. What will he do when his vines are mature enough to produce good red wine? Is this demand for rosé a temporary trend or will rosé become a permanent part of his portfolio to the extent that he needs to think of planting vines specifically for rosé production?

Majoli *Rosato*, Coste della Sesia DOC, from **Tenute Sella** (www.tenutesella.it), is made from a blend of *saignée* and direct-press Nebbiolo grapes from Bramaterra. Originally this wine was made from juice bled off from the red wine but is now made from earlier harvested grapes, direct press juice and short skin maceration.

Some producers are making more traditional *chiaretto*. **Villa Giada**'s (www.andreafaccio.it) Monerrato Chiaretto is a *vino di una notte* made from Barbera and Nebbiolo. It has a darker colour because Andrea the winemaker 'is fighting the temptation to become a total victim of fashion – a tough call in the world of rosé.'

Some sparkling pink wines are made with local varieties such as Barbera, Nebbiolo and Neretti San Giorgio in the *metodo classico* (with the second fermentation in bottle). Made with a rosé base wine, they have pronounced red fruit character.

Tuscany

Local rosé, *rosato di Toscana,* has grown steadily over the past five to seven years. A boom in sales for red chianti had led to new vineyards being planted. While the vines were too young to make good chianti, producers used the grapes to produce *rosati*. By the time the vines were old enough to produce chianti, the boom for reds was slowing down, but *rosato* sales kept increasing. Producers, even those not making *rosato* with their young vines, started to think of adding it to their portfolio. So, from around 2011, a flurry of *rosati* started to appear. With little local white wine, these *rosati* had commercial appeal.

As eighty per cent of Tuscan wine is red, red grapes predominate. Sangiovese is Tuscany's most prominent grape, with many different clonal varieties, as many towns have their own local version. Cabernet Sauvignon has been planted here for over 250 years, but has only recently become associated with the rise of the Super Tuscans. Other international red varieties in Tuscany include Cabernet Franc, Merlot, Pinot Noir and Syrah. The most widely planted local red varieties are Canaiolo, Colorino, Malvasia Nera and Mammolo.

Rosati di Toscana are crisp, and the taste of the Sangiovese grapes comes through strongly. They can also be made with a blend of Bordeaux varieties, but other varieties can be present depending on the local red wine DOCs. In the north of the region, bordering Liguria, varieties such as Ciliegiolo are used.

Different styles and stories illustrate the variety amongst the *rosati* of Tuscany, but all link back to their red wine roots.

Tenuta di Biserno
Palazzo Gardini, Piazza Gramsci, 9, 57020 Bibbona (LI)
Tel.: 0586 671099
biserno.it

One of the more recent *rosato* producers, this is run by Lodovico Antinori, who worked with the Ott family in Provence to create his first *rosato* in 2015. Dedicated to his daughter Sofia, Sof comes in an elegant frosted glass bottle. It is made from Cabernet Franc and Syrah grown on a parcel also used for their Insoglio red, where Sangiovese never thrived. The wine is fresh, with vibrant red fruit and a lively, crisp acidity for drinking young.

Villa Pillo's (www.villapillo.com) *rosato* is also new. An equal blend of Sangiovese and Merlot makes for a fruitier style, with juicy, red fruit balanced by creamy smoothness and long acidity to make a lovely rosé wine. Another recent *rosato*, under IGT Toscana, comes from Marco Ricasoli of

Rocca di Montegrossi (www.roccadimontegrossi.it), in Chianti. Made from Sangiovese, with five months ageing on the lees, it has pronounced cherry fruit, and vibrant, mouth-watering acidity with typical Sangiovese character.

Salcheto
Via di Villa Bianca, 15, 53045 Montepulciano (SI)
Tel.: 0578 799031
www.salcheto.it

'Natural' winemaking for rosé is always interesting in pushing the boundaries and exploring the potential for varieties and terroir. Salcheto's Obvius *Rosato*, first made in 2013, is a field blend of 90 per cent Sangiovese with Canaiolo, Mammolo, Merlot, Cabernet Franc and Petit Verdot. Made with ambient yeast, and without sulphur or malolactic fermentation, it is aged in Acacia barrels for three months. The wine is a dark orange-pink colour; the Acacia barrel emphazises the beautiful round, ripe, red fruit, while the ambient yeast gives a firm, savoury structure. The wine has fresh, balanced acidity. Not a delicate wine but full of complex and interesting character.

Sesti
Castello di Argiano, 53024 Montalcino SI
Tel.: 0577 843921

Their *rosato* is the first to be produced in Montalcino, and was originally created for the estate's own summer drinking. The Sangiovese grapes (a Brunello clone), are picked earlier than their Brunello di Montalcino counterparts destined for red wines. Selected from higher-yielding vines to avoid high alcohol, the fruit is destemmed without crushing, rested in tank for up to 12 hours, and then delicately pressed. Fermentation proceeds with ambient yeasts in stainless steel. Malolactic fermentation occurs depending on the vintage.

Bolgheri DOC

Some Tuscan *rosati* have higher appellation status than IGT Toscana. The modern history of the Bolgheri *denominazione* began at the end of the Second World War when Marchese Mario Incisa planted Cabernet Sauvignon grapes on his Tenuta San Guido estate, in an area known only for rustic Sangiovese and Trebbiano wines. Liking the results, he planted his **Sassicaia** (www.tenutasanguido.com) vineyard with Cabernet in the early 1960s. Teaming up with his brother-in-law Nicolò Antinori and winemaker Giacomo Tachis, Incisa improved his Sassicaia wines during the 1970s, gaining them international fame. This put Bolgheri on the map, and in 1983 it was established as a DOC (Sassicaia has had its own DOC since 2013). The *rosato* and red wines can contain up to 100 per cent Cabernet Franc, Cabernet Sauvignon, or Merlot, alone or in combination, along with up to 50 per cent Sangiovese and/or Syrah.

Carmignano

Carmignano has two DOCs for *rosato*. Barco Reale di Carmignano Rosato, sometimes called Rosato di Carmignano, is made from Sangiovese (at least 50 per cent), Canaiolo Nero (20 per cent), Cabernet Franc and Cabernet Sauvignon (10–20 per cent, alone or together), and allowing the white grapes Trebbiano Toscano, Canaiolo Bianco and Malvasia Bianca (up to 10 per cent in total).

The sweet Vin Santo di Carmignano DOC allows for a pink version, called *occhio di pernice* (eye of the partridge). This must contain at least 50 per cent Sangiovese. At the end of the nineteenth century, *occhio de pernice* was exported widely by the winery of Marquis Niccolini.

Ciù Ciù

Località S. Maria in Carro, Contrada Ciafone, 106 - Offida (AP)
Tel.: 0736 810001
www.ciuciuvini.it

This is a family-run estate on the east coast, founded in 1970 and planted from the outset with local varieties for reds, such as Montepulciano and Sangiovese. When the estate began to create its concentrated red wine, Bacchus, Piceno DOP, the Bartolomei family decided to make a *rosato* in combination with it, which falls under the Marche IGP rules. The grapes are harvested when ripe for their red wine, Sangiovese first, then the Montepulciano one to two weeks later. The blend is fifty–fifty, Montepulciano for fruit flavours and colour, Sangiovese for acidity. After eighteen hours of maceration, the juice is bled off for the rosé into stainless steel, for cool temperature fermentation for twenty-five days. The varieties are fermented separately. Ciù Ciù is not looking to make a pale 'Provence-style' rosé but instead aims for depth of colour and complexity. This *rosato* is dark pink with a lovely ripeness of red fruit with a subdued, tannic core.

CERASUOLO

Cerasuolo means 'cherry' in Italian, and until the early 1970s was a term used loosely to describe the colour of darker *rosati* around Italy. Cerasuolo di Vittoria in Sicily is, however, a red wine.

Cerasuolo d'Abruzzo

This is the newest DOC of the central Italian region of Abruzzo, created in 2010. The title covers the cherry-red, brightly flavoured wines formerly labelled as Montepulciano d'Abruzzo Cerasuolo. Cerasuolo d'Abruzzo wines must contain at least 85 per cent of the Montepulciano variety, with the remainder made up of 'other red-skinned, non-aromatic varieties allowed in the Abruzzo region'. Varieties include Aglianico, Nebbiolo and Sangiovese.

The rules for Cerasuolo d'Abruzzo DOC include communes in all four provinces in Abruzzo and restrict land to below 500 metres, or exceptionally, 600 metres when south-facing.

Some good examples are **Giuliano Pettinella**'s Tauma from old vine Montepulciano grown in two small vineyards, together making up less than 0.5 hectares; under 2,000 bottles are made, making it something of a cult wine. First made in 2011, the wine is fermented with ambient yeast in small, old wood barrels, with no temperature control and ageing on the lees. The wine has intense colour with rich fruit and savoury, saline complexity. **Cantina Terzini**'s (www.cantinaterzini.it) is 100 per cent Montepulciano, a dark, ruby pink (*cerasa*), with full-bodied, fresh, red berry fruit, a hint of minerality and a firm structure. At the first Pink Rosé Festival in Cannes (2017), sommelier Franck Thomas awarded this wine a prize as an all-round rosé suitable for matching with food. **Valle Reale**'s (vallereale.it), also 100 per cent Montepulciano, has vibrant cherry and wild red berry fruit aromas and while on the palate there is powerful fruit structure of ripe cherries, with hints of fresh herbs and spice.

PUGLIA

Puglia, the 'heel' of Italy, has the strongest tradition, in terms of history and size, of producing *rosati*. In medieval times, the Counts of Provence ruled the kingdom of Naples, of which this area was part, so maybe there were cultural exchanges on winemaking! However, until recently, Puglia was known for its high production of bulk red wine. In the nineteenth century, buyers from Piedmont would come to buy the local wine for making Vermouth.

Puglian *rosati* barely received a mention until the Second World War, when the American general, Charles Poletti, previously governor of New York (the first Italian-American to serve as governor), was appointed US Army Civil Affairs Officer in Italy, for his knowledge of Italian language and local culture. He landed in Salento and approached local producer Piero **Leone de Castris** (www.leonedecastris.com), who was also President of the Farmers' Union of Lecce and Mayor of Salice Salento, for wine supplies for the troops. De Castris gave Poletti a bottle of *rosato*, which the general loved. As the war drew to a close, the general investigated how to ship the wine back to America. As bottles were scarce at the time, and shipping these from industrial northern Italy was out of the question, the general and the winemaker put their heads together. They decided that the empty beer bottles left around by American soldiers would serve their purpose. The wine was called Cinque Rose (Five Roses), and became the first Italian *rosato* to be bottled and exported, arriving in America in mismatched beer bottles. Today it is made with Negroamaro and a small percentage of Malvasia Nera di Lecce.

In the early 2000s, Puglian producers began looking into raising the quality of their red wines. Modern *rosati* from this region are quite new, and to the outsider, the range of styles, the multitude of small appellations with varying terroir and varieties can be confusing. The creation of the association of Puglia in Rosé, uniting fifty-two wineries throughout Puglia to promote the wines of the region has helped change their image and the marketing strategy of producers. According to Lucia Nettis, founder and director of the association, the large area with diverse styles needed an umbrella organization to coordinate their promotions and marketing.

Due to the shape of the 'heel', the Puglia region has the longest coastline in Italy, with maritime influences from both the Ionian and Adriatic seas moderating the heat and contributing freshness to the wines. Complex geology and different varieties lead to a range of different styles.

The Salento Peninsula occupies the southern half of the region. Almost flat, it has a strong connection to its Greco-Roman past. The southern-most tip is Salento, where Negroamaro is the main variety, with Primitivo di Manuria, Sussumaniello, Montepulciano and Malvasia also grown. Just to the north lies the Itria Valley, where Primitivo (Zinfandel), Negroamaro and Aglianico dominate. Moving further north, around the city of Bari, almond and olive groves vie with vineyards. Bombino Nero, Uva de Troia and Primitivo are typical.

Northern Puglia, in the Daunia region, is slightly hillier and more connected to the customs and winemaking practices of central Italy. Northern Puglia was known as the granary of Italy, with fields of durum wheat, for making pasta. Here, Sangiovese and Montepulciano are more popular, alongside the traditional Puglian varieties of Negroamaro, Nero di Troia and Bombino Nero. A late ripener, with high phenolics and anthocyanins, Bombino Nero needs very short maceration time to produce colour, making it popular for rosé production because good colour can be achieved with low tannins.

Other varieties include Ottavianello (the local name for Cinsault), and Malvasia Nera di Lecce (a cross of Malvasia Bianca Lunga and Negroamaro), another late ripener with high sugar and low acidity but bringing perfume to a blend.

Garofano
Località Tenuta Monaci, 73043 Copertino (LE)
Tel.: 0832 947512
vinigarofano.it

Stefano Garofano's 100 per cent Negroamaro *rosato* (Girofle, IGP Salento) has 40 per cent direct press and minimal skin contact and the remainder undergoing twenty hours of maceration. After fermentation, this is aged in concrete tanks for a few months. The dark pink (described by the producer as 'coral') wine is weighty, with fresh, red berry fruit and mouth-watering, chewy acidity.

Pietraventosa

Str. Vic.le Latta Latta s.n., 70023, Gioia del Colle, Bari
Tel.: 335 573 0274
www.pietraventosa.it

Marianna Anninio has vineyards at 400 metres altitude on limestone hills. Her *rosato*, Est Rosa, IGT Murgia, 100 per cent Primitivo, is bright pink, despite only five hours maceration – due to Primtivo's high colour pigmentation – followed by long, slow, cold (13°C) fermentation to keep the freshness. The resulting wine has surprisingly vibrant fresh acidity, with firm, mineral structure (from the limestone), able to support the full-bodied red berry fruit and 5g/l residual sugar. Different clones of Primitivo have developed, and the Primitivo *rosati* from the region of Mandaria, on the western side of the 'heel', tend to be richer.

CALABRIA AND SICILY

Calabria, in the toe of Italy's boot also makes delightful *rosati* wines. Gaglioppo is a traditional variety.

Fattoria San Francesco di Iuzzolini

Località Quattromani, 88813 Cirò (KR)
Tel.: 0962 32228
www.fattoriasanfrancesco.it

This winery makes two *rosati* with Gaglioppo, IGT Calabria. Donna Rosa, a pure Gaglioppo aged in oak, has a bright, cherry/red-pink colour. On the palate sour and sweet black cherries mingle, backed by a firm mineral core and carried by vibrant acidity. This is a truly delicious wine with lovely balance. Slightly less exciting (for me) was the Lumare, also aged in oak, but with the addition of Cabernet Sauvignon. A little heavier and less fresh it still has ripe fruit and a touch of tannic structure – a good rosé for lovers of red wine.

Tenuta delle Terre Nere

Contrada Calderara, sn, 95036 Randazzo (CT), Sicily
Tel.: 095 924002
www.tenutaterrenere.com

Sicilian *rosati* include those from vineyards on the slopes of Mount Etna, the volcanic soils of which give a special mineral character to the wines.

Marco de Grazia made his first *rosato* in 2007, with Nerello Mascalese (a variety indigenous to Sicily) and Nerello Cappuccio from largely north facing slopes some up to 900 metres. The wine is fresh and mineral-laden. De Grazia explains what he was aiming for thus: 'The Platonic ideal, as I see it, would be the rosé that has the body of a white and the soul of a red'.

11
ROSÉS FROM NORTHERN AND CENTRAL EUROPEAN VARIETIES

Global warming combined with advances in viticulture has resulted in the spread of vineyards northwards. Rosé production is well suited to cooler climates, when red grapes may fail to ripen sufficiently for red wine production. Production quantities and vintages are subject to greater variation. This chapter includes cooler-climate rosés from the northern regions of Europe as well as some from warmer Central Europe, where a number of common varieties are found.[6]

ENGLAND AND WALES

The development of English winemaking has involved both historic research and experimentation. In 1938, George Ordish researched the history to ascertain good locations for vines to flourish. In 1947–8 Edward Hyams planted vines at his home in Molash, Kent, and set about researching old vines around the country. During the 1950s Ray Barrington Brock established a research station at Oxted in Surrey, where he trialled some 600 different grape varieties and built a winery, in which he experimented with methods of winemaking to suit those grape varieties that were growing well.

---

6 As of 2010, newly established Belgian, Luxembourgish and Polish vineyards have also started to plant Zweigelt and are beginning to make rosé. Rondo and Regent are particularly popular in Poland where they make vibrant, fruity, high acid rosés that range from dry to off-dry.

In 1951, the first modern commercial vineyard was planted in England, at Hambledon in Hampshire, by Major-General Sir Guy Salisbury-Jones. Merrydown Wine Company at Horam in East Sussex, was next, planted in 1955 with German white varieties, followed by the Gore-Brownes planting a vineyard in Beaulieu, Hampshire from 1957–60. From the early to mid-1960s, vineyards spread across the country, with new sites, new training and pruning systems and above all, new grape varieties introduced.

The real expansion of the vineyard area and the establishment of both sizeable vineyards and wineries started in earnest in the late 1960s and early 1970s, with a large number planted between 1976 and 1995, including some very large estates. The area decreased in size for ten years, but since 2004 has again grown dramatically, to over 1,956 hectares in 2015, from 133 wineries, with 500 vineyards. A sign of maturity is that, although the number of vineyards and wineries has grown only slightly, the average size of vineyard has doubled since 1989.

The last 20 years has seen a marked change in wine styles and types sold in the UK. In the late 1960s and 1970s, when English wines started to appear on the market, they were influenced by the hugely popular light, fruity German white wines, with a hint of residual sugar. By the 1980s English and Welsh wines had changed to reflect market preferences, removing the names of the varieties (many of which were associated with early wine styles) from the labels and starting to give the wines more creative names.

The last twenty years has seen a marked change in British wines. As consumption patterns have changed, so has production, and rosé is an increasingly popular style. In the 2004 *English and Welsh Wine of the Year Competition* the rosé category proved to be the most popular. There is a much greater understanding of which varieties perform well in the UK (Rondo, Dornfelder and Pinot Noir are the current favourites). This is a promising, and growing, category.

Sixteen Ridges (www.sixteenridges.co.uk) Pinot Noir rosé from Herefordshire, is made from a combination of free-run and direct-pressed juice, with 6 to 12 hours skin contact. As temperatures are usually quite cold by the time of harvest towards the end of October, temperature control is not used. The wine has pronounced cherry fruit with a fresh, leafy acidity.

Bolney's (www.bolneywineestate.com) Bolney Rosé from West Sussex uses Meunier and a small amount of Rondo, and is made to be a 'crowd-pleaser'. The two varieties give full, ripe redcurrant and raspberry fruit (emphasized by 7g/l residual sugar) and long, fresh acidity.

Hush Heath's (hushheath.com) Nanette rosé, from Kent, is made with Pinot Noir, Pinot Meunier and Chardonnay, with a touch of oak ageing to give extra weight. There is full, weighty cherry and red berry fruit with good acidity.

Yorkshire Heart (www.yorkshireheart.com), one of the most northerly wineries in England, makes a rosé from Rondo, bled off the red wine. The rosé is very light and delicate with subtle raspberry and rhubarb fruit and fresh acidity.

GERMANY

In 2015, Germany was the third largest rosé market in the world, behind France and the USA. Ten per cent of the wine sold in Germany was rosé, although only half of the wine consumed was German-produced. Eleven per cent (815,000 hectolitres) of total German wine production is rosé. The top four states contribute the bulk of this (9.5 per cent of the total 11 per cent of production): Pfalz (3.3 per cent of total production), Rheinhessen (2.5 per cent), Baden (1.9 per cent) and Württemberg (1.8 per cent – rosé is 15 per cent of Württemberg's production) with the other regions producing less than 0.5 per cent of total production.

Much German rosé is produced from high-yielding Portugieser, with 15–30g/l residual sugar, bottled by the litre, and consumed with a splash of sparkling mineral water in half-litre glasses. The result is a little like white Zinfandel. The semi-sweet style is aimed at the younger consumer for easy summer drinking, while older consumers prefer drier rosés. Rosé of substance is generally not very sought-after, and higher priced wines tend to gather dust. I went looking for good German rosé in a large wine emporium in Germany, and the manager was only able to recommend a single wine.

Felicity Carter, Editor-in-Chief of *Meininger's Wine Business International*, enthusiastically declared that 'Pfalz rosés rock!' explaining her enthusiasm with the more serious comment that they were exceptionally good value for money. Belgian sommelier and wine writer Peter Kupers said he is 'increasingly charmed by Baden rosé, where geological complexity and Pinot Noir make a great combination. Going further north, the Ahr is also "interesting" for older tourists quaffing off-dry rosé. A few producers make more age-worthy efforts such as Meyer-Nakel. Deutzerhof makes some exciting wines.'

The labelling can be confusing.

Weissherbst (Weißherbst) must be QbA or *Prädikatswein* (the highest quality level, made from 100 per cent of one named variety – for non-*Prädikatswein* the figure is 85 per cent of the named variety), and labelled with the varietal name. Most common are Spätburgunder Weissherbst, Portugieser Weissherbst and Schwarzriesling Weissherbst (Meunier), but other varieties are allowed. There are no restrictions as to the colour of the wines, so they range from pale gold to deep pink. They can also range from dry to sweet, such as rosé *Eiswein* from Spätburgunder.

Rosé can be used to denote a *cuvée* of one or more red wine varieties such as Pinot Noir, but no white varieties can be included. **Weingut Knipser** (www.weingut-knipser.de) in the Pfalz, calls its rosé Clairette in a nod to the traditional wine of Bordeaux. It is made with Cabernet Sauvignon, Cabernet Franc and Merlot, in a darker salmon with very crisp, green, zesty, lime acidity. Lovely fresh, red fruit with a hint of spritz with some riper apricot notes reflects the 6g/l residual sugar.

Two 2016 vintage Pinot Noir wines from the Nahe show very different styles. **Rosé de Diel** (www.diel.eu) Nahe Schlossgut, is a fresh, fruity style with ripe, blackberry fruit and a hint of residual sugar, balanced by a stony acidity and a hint of spice on the finish. **Zwölberich**'s (www.zwoelberich.de) Spätburgunder, is more complex. Fermented in tank with ten days in new oak to achieve a 'strawberry and cream' flavour, this rosé is a very dry, serious wine with ripe, strawberry fruit, mouth-watering acidity and great structure.

Germany has some traditional, light red coloured wines, their paleness depending on the amount of white grapes in the blend. They are produced using the historic method of co-planting red and white varieties, called *gemischter Satz*, and using the mix of white and red grapes to make the wine.

Rotling has its origins in Saxony, where it was called *Schieler*, a phonetic variant of *Schiller* (see page 47). The fruit for a Saxon Schieler has to come from Weinbauregion Sachsen. A *Rotling* must be a pale or clear red. It is common in Franconia, Weinbaugebieten Regensburg and Bayerischer Bodensee. In Württemberg, it is known as *Schillerwein*, where it may only be used with QbA or QmP wines. All over Germany the term *Rotling* can be used for pale red wines produced from a mixture of red and white grapes which are pressed and vinified together. Sparkling wine can be made from any base wine that qualifies as *Rotling*. *Schaumwein* and *Perlwein* quality levels are allowed. *Rotling* wines tend to be darker pink. In Baden, they are known as *Badisch Rotgold* and made with a minimum 51 per cent Pinot Gris and a maximum of 49 per cent Pinot Noir, with the varieties indicated on the label. The grapes are crushed and fermented together. The must weight of the base material must be at least the quality of QbA. *Badisch Rotgold* sparkling wines may be produced in *Schaumwein* or *Perlwein* quality levels.

Feinherb typically comes from lower-yielding vineyards used for red wine with fully ripe fruit. The wines generally have high acidity, but are rarely tart. Many German rosés balance their acidity with an intentional bit of residual sugar and are sometimes marked *Feinherb* to denote a slight off-dry style. For wines in this style the Germans tend to look to Spätburgunder, which can produce some of the most nuanced and complex pink wines. It is usually made from direct-pressed grapes rather than *saignée*. This is an unregulated category, and is usually sweeter than *halbtrocken* which has a maximum of 12–18g/l residual sugar, depending on the acidity. Good examples will balance the sugar and acidity to emphasize the fruit. **Jakob Schneider** (www.schneider-wein.de), Feinherb, Nahe Spätburgunder Rosé has well balanced sugar and acidity emphasizing the ripe cherry compote character with hints of cinnamon and rich dark spice.

One of the most northerly vineyards in Germany is **Weingut Montigny** (montigny.de) in Schleswig Holstein, 100 kilometres north of Hamburg. Here, they make a rosé called So Mookt Wi Dat ('This is how we do it' in local dialect), from a blend of varieties. The climate is mild and the ripening season is long. Made with 10.5% abv and 15.2g/l residual sugar, the wine has lively acidity.

AUSTRIA

Until recently, rosé in Austria was looked down on as merely a by-product of red wine making, cheaper and of lesser quality. Today, rosé wine is produced in all of Austria's wine-growing regions and in a variety of styles: young wine, like Primus Pannonicus from Burgenland, Zweigelt and St Laurent wines from Niederösterreich (Lower Austria), or Schilcher from Weststeiermark (West Styria). It is popular throughout the summer months and is often drunk as a spritzer with soda water.

Vintage variation, which has a big impact on the making of red and sweet wines, is less significant for rosé wines. Cooler vintages will be crisper, with wild berry fruit, while warmer vintages will be more luscious and fuller. Andreas Wickhoff MW of **Weingut Bründlmayer** (www.bruendlmayer.at) notes that, 'With the rise of biodynamics and the "slow wine" movement, you might see also rosés with a touch more colour, extract, tannin structure, low/no SO_2 levels, with lots of character, mostly for the good. Although these wines still have a minority share in Austria. I wouldn't say that rosé is an exciting *new* style in Austria, but, what is true, is that the offer has become larger, also thanks to the continuous consumption growth this category has seen.' Weingut Bründlmayer has seen it with its sparkling brut rosé. 'It's by far our best *Sekt* [sparkling] seller.' Weszeli's Davis Weszeli feels the rosé market is steady, with only a marginal increase. His best sales are in the tourist centres in the Alps of western Austria and at lakeside resorts, with almost all the sales occuring between April and September.

Zweigelt (a cross of St Laurent and Blaufränkisch) is a popular variety for rosé (it is the most widely grown red variety in Austria), either on its own or in a blend. It has dark juice, so direct press with short skin contact works well. The wine can be quite savoury. Styles range from simple, easy drinking summer wines to richer styles, both sparkling and sweet.

Etz (www.etzwine.at) from Kamptal and **Fritsch** (www.fritsch.cc) from Wagram make vibrant cherry and raspberry fruit rosés with crisp acidity for easy summer drinking. **Huber** (www.weingut-huber.at) in Traisental makes a slightly richer version with opulent cherry fruit and a hint of sugar to exaggerate the fruit, fresh acidity with typical Zweigelt spice, minerality and a touch of tannin structure. **Jordan** (www.weingut-jordan.at) in Pulkau makes a Zweigelt *blanc de noirs* which after four hours gentle pressing, makes a dark pink wine with red fruit aromas, that tastes like a white wine.

> **Artisan Wines**
>
> DI Franz Schneider, Erzherzog-Friedrichstrasse 19, 7131 Halbturn
> Tel.: 699 108 149 30
> www.artisanwines.at
>
> Here in Bürgenland, Franz Schneider makes a range of wines named Pure, which aim to have fresh, vibrant fruit character. His sparkling Zweigelt is full of strawberries and white cherries with a touch of residual sugar, while his still Zweigelt is drier with red cherries and a touch of minerality. Gently pressed without maceration on the skins, the wines are fermented under controlled temperature in tanks with short maturation on the fine lees and no malolactic fermentation. Excited by the potential of producing high quality rosé, Schneider is now experimenting with an oaked Merlot rosé.

Hesperia from **Weingut Felsner** (www.weingut-felsner.at) in Kremstal, is an interesting ice wine made from Zweigelt. With 12g/l residual sugar, it has luscious, raspberry and cherry fruit, fresh acidity and a dry mineral finish.

Zweigelt is often blended with a softer variety such as Spätburgunder, the spicy St Laurent grape and Dornfelder. **Schloss Gobelsburg** in Kamptal (www.gobelsburg.at) makes Cistercien Rosé, a blend of Zweigelt and St Laurent for a rosé with juicy, strawberry fruit, a hint of spice, fresh, vibrant acidity and a mineral, saline core. The rosé from **Loimer** in Kamptal (loimer.at/en) has a small percentage of Spätburgunder for a plusher, black fruit character, to balance the mineral herbal character, and a hint of tannic structure on the finish. Terrassen Rosé from **Walter Buchegger**, Kremstal (www.buchegger.at) uses half Spätburgunder, with a mix of Zweigelt and Merlot making up the rest. The wine is ripe and sweet, with plum and black cherry fruit and the Zweigelt spice and mineral backbone. **Retzer Vineyard** in Weinviertel makes its Helenthal rosé with 50 per cent Zweigelt, 40 per cent Merlot and 10 per cent Pinot Noir. The Zweigelt gives crisp red fruit and chewy structure, while the Merlot and Pinot Noir fills out the rest, with creamy summer fruit and a fresh, leafy mineral acidity. **Weingut Weszeli** (www.weszeli.at) makes a Zweigelt and Cabernet Franc rosé called Terrafactum, which is quite different. Very pale in colour, it has floral, peach aromas and on the palate is full of redcurrants, cranberries and peach fruit, emphasized by 7g/l residual sugar balanced by long, zesty, green apple acidity and a chalky texture. At 11% abv, it has appealing, easy, fresh fruit.

Josef Umathum (en.umathum.at) in Bürgenland is best known for the reds produced from the vineyards near Lake Neusiedl, farmed biodynamically since 2005. Umathum's aim is to make a serious rosé wine which can age for 3–4 years. He green harvests (i.e. thins the crop) in July to reduce yields and then harvests the remaining grapes when fully ripe. Rosa is a blend of one third each of Zweigelt, Blaufränkisch, and St Laurent, using the *saignée* method with 1–3 days' skin contact creating a dry, structural wine with a light tannin finish. Birgit **Braunstein**'s (www.weingut-braunstein.at) biodynamic vineyard in Burgenland makes a blend of 80 per cent Zweigelt with 20 per cent Blaufränkisch which has long, fresh acidity, red fruit and hints of orange peel and herbs on the finish.

In the south-east, in Weststeiermark (West Styria), lies the smallest viticultural area, with only 500 hectares. Zweigelt rosé is made, but also *Schilcher,* with the traditional variety Blauer Wildbacher (see page 48).

A bizarre rosé, rarely seen, is *Uhudler* from southern Bürgenland, made from a blend of crossings between the European *Vitis vinifera* and native North American *Vitis labrusca* and *Vitis riparia* brought over in the late nineteenth century to counter phylloxera. These hybrids were encouraged in the 1930s because they produced intense, strawberry fruit flavours, even in cool vintages, as well as a foxy flavour which some (me included) find unpleasant.

After the Second World War, controls over European winemaking increased and these American hybrids were banned. However, their fruitiness made them very appealing, and in many places they are fiercely defended and planted. Rumours were circulated that the vines contained dangerous levels of methanol which would make drinkers go mad! By the 1970s *Uhudler* was permitted for private consumption only, and this bootleg quality only served to make it more attractive.

Under Austrian Wine Law, *Uhudler* can be sold in parts of Bürgenland, made only with Concord, Delaware, Elvira und Ripatella. In 2003, it became illegal to plant these vines until 2030, so it will remain a niche product.

SWITZERLAND

Switzerland could equally well be listed as having French or Italian influence. Of the 14,890 hectares, 11,150 are in the western, French region, 1,000 in the Italian region of Ticino, and the remaining 2,620 scattered in the eastern Swiss-German half. Fifty-eight per cent of production is red wine, which includes rosé. Most producers are small, with only 7 per cent owning more than 50 hectares. Less than 2 per cent of Swiss wine is exported, making it a rare find outside the country.

Quality has improved dramatically over the last thirty years with the introduction of stricter appellation rules. With 253 varieties being cultivated, and wide variations in altitude, climate and the individual styles of small producers, the diversity is enormous, but rosé rarely uses the more interesting and indigenous varieties. Fresh acidity and a purity of fruit are hallmarks of these rosés.

The regional varieties Gamaret and Garanoir, both crossings of Gamay and Reichensteiner, ripen early, and have similarities to Gamay. Gamay and Pinot Noir are largely used in both the French and German regions. Around the Valais town of Dôle, along the upper reaches of the Rhône, they produce Dôle Blanche, a pale *vin gris* made from Pinot Noir and Gamay, with short skin contact. In the Ticino, 90 per cent of the plantings are Merlot, used for their big red wines, but some is also used to make Merlot Bianchi *blanc de noirs* and rosé. (See also *oeil de perdrix*, page 60 and *Schiller*, page 48).

SLOVAKIA

Slovakian wines are light, lively and fruity, thanks to unique climatic and geological conditions. Having steadily invested in its winemaking industry for the past twenty years, by adding modern equipment, cultivating carefully and improving techniques, recent years have seen a young generation of winemakers increasingly experimenting with natural and biodynamic wines. Over the last fifteen years, the fastest growing category of wine in Slovakia is rosé, although it still accounts for only 5 per cent of production.

With a total vineyard area of almost 17,600 hectares, the vineyard regions are still small. Forty-eight are permitted, comprizing thirty-one white and seventeen red. There was a surge in popularity in the early years of the twenty-first century, and since 2010, a slow and steady increase in both production and consumption.

The most popular red varieties are Frankovka Modrá (Blaufränkisch/Kékfrankos – 9 per cent); Svätovavrinecké (St Laurent – 7 per cent) and Cabernet Sauvignon (3 per cent). Red varieties are planted on 4,371 hectares, a quarter of total plantings.

There is a wide range of styles from dry to sweet, pale to dark, still and sparkling. Some are light, fruity and floral, some more structural and mineral. Several winemakers are experimenting with oak, field blends, or harvesting at different stages of grape maturity.

The majority of wine production is situated in the warmest, southeastern corner of the country bordering Austria and Hungary. With only around 400 producers, many with only a few hectares, some wines are only produced in small quantities. Tasting a selection of rosés made from Modrý Portugal (Blauer Portugieser), Frankovka Modra and Cabernet Sauvignon in both dry and off-dry styles revealed a common character of vibrant red fruit (strawberries, raspberries, rhubarb, redcurrants and cherries) and fresh leafy acidity in a summer-pudding-style opulence. Alcohol tends to be moderate, between 11.5 per cent and 12.5% abv. Some also had a touch of residual sugar emphasizing the fruitiness.

Three rosés with regional varieties showed luscious fruit character. **Terra Parna**'s (www.terraparna.sk) Rosé Modrý Portugal is dry with sweet, ripe cherry fruit on the palate, fresh redcurrant and sour cherry acidity with mineral notes and a hint of spritz. **Karpatská Perla**'s (www.karpatskaperla.sk) Frankovka Modra is a vibrant, fruity wine with notes of redcurrant and rhubarb, and crisp, cherry fruit with good acidity. **Repa** (www.repawinery.sk) Svätovavrinecké has ripe, vibrant strawberry fruit emphasized by a hint of residual sugar and a hint of leafy, fresh acidity.

The Cabernet Sauvignon rosés had opulent fruit emphasized by a touch of residual sugar. Some were not dissimilar to the more fruity and leafy Chilean rosés. **Berta**'s Cabernet Sauvignon has luscious cherry compote fruit, soft red berries, rosehip syrup and perfumed, fragrant rosewater. It was dry, with a hint of residual sugar. **Rariga** (www.vinorariga.sk) Cabernet Sauvignon is fresh and perfumed with an almost elderflower and leafy character, with rhubarb and redcurrant fruit (and a touch of residual sugar), and a hint of spice on the finish. **Velkeer** (www.velkeer.sk) Tri Ruze Cabernet Sauvignon is rich with ripe, jammy raspberry fruit as well as fresh, herbaceous and green fruit and lively leafy acidity, which really stood out when matched with beetroot and fresh goats' cheese at dinner! **Pinka** (www.rosepinka.com) Cabernet Sauvignon has what appears to be a typical Slovakian character of ripe fruit and leafy acidity, but is less opulent and more restrained with a weightier structure with ripe redcurrant and rhubarb fruit, balanced by good weight, ripeness and leafy acidity. The fruit is less overt from the use of ambient yeasts. With only 1,399 bottles produced, this is a beautifully hand-crafted wine. A sparkling brut rosé from Modra, Modragne made by **Fedor Malik** (www.fedormalik.sk) has red fruit with a firm, mineral acidity, making it a serious pink fizz.

Although harder to sell, a few natural rosés are also made. For me, they illustrate the challenging nature of wine; they are not wines to feel comfortable with, but they challenge preconceptions and push boundaries. It was particularly interesting to be able to try these copper coloured natural rosés. **Pivinkca Brhlovce** (pivnicabrhlovce.sk) Rustikal Pink has saline, mineral aromas. On the palate are redcurrants and strawberries with a dry, mineral, saline and bitter orange core and long acidity. Rozália from **Strekov** (www.strekov1075.eu), an unfiltered and fizzing *pet nat*, is yeasty and leesy with bitter orange and red berry fruit aromas. On the palate, there was long, fresh acidity, with a savoury, mineral core and riper notes of toffee and yeast.

HUNGARY

Rosés first started to appear in Hungary in the early 1990s. Today, large quantities are made and rosé is one of the fastest growing sectors of the Hungarian market, especially amongst young people. Wine writer Robert Smyth, based in Hungary, commented in the *Budapest Business Journal* that, 'More and more beer drinkers are beginning to shed certain prejudices toward rosé as a girl's drink and are coming to realize that a good pink glass of wine is highly potable.' *Fröccs* (frothy) is a traditional way of serving white wine with sparkling water as a spritzer, which is now being used to serve rosé wine during the summer.

> **Dúzsi Tamás**
> Szekszárd, Kossuth Lajos u. 8, 7100 Magyarország
> Tel.: 30 541 6764
> www.duzsitamas.hu
> Tamas Dúzsi senior lives in Szekszárd, where he has become known as the 'rosé king'. Tamás started his rosé career by accident in 1996, when he had a 20-hectolitre overflow tank of single vineyard Sióagárd Lányvár Kékfrankos red wine fermenting in the back garden behind the cellar. The tank was too full, and during the ferment the must bubbled over, leaving just the juice fermenting on its own. A neighbour noticed, and called to ask if everything was all right, but it was too late to salvage the tank of red wine and a tank of dark pink wine was left. Dúszi allowed the ferment to finish, and tried the wine out on friends and customers. Everyone loved it! So it was bottled and sold, and the next year, under more controlled conditions, the same wine was made.
> Seventy per cent of the production at Dúszi Tamás is now rosé, and the repertoire has been expanded to include a range of single varietal rosés. In 2008, Dúszi decided to make all of the single varietal rosés (except Kékfrankos) from single vineyards.

According to winemaker László Romsics (formerly at sparkling wine giant Törley, now at the Villány producer Csányi), 'The majority of Hungarian rosés are very fresh and fruity. They are light in body, have balanced, fresh acidity and [are] very ready to drink.' Winemakers focus on intensity of aromas and high acidity, preferring a refreshing, relatively low alcohol (around 12–12.5% abv) to a more weighty, structured style.

On the whole, rosés are drunk young, although Dúzsi noticed that at the May Budapest Rosalia Festival in 2016, their aged rosés were the biggest sellers – many of their rosés age well, especially Kadarka and Pinot Noir rosés. With a couple of years of age, his Pinot Noir takes on a richer character with notes of mango, apricot and peach, and hints of marmalade, while still retaining good acidity.

There is also a growing trend amongst winemakers to make a premium (sometimes oaked) rosé with greater weight and complexity. **Pastor** in

Szekszárd (www.pastor.hu) noted that his customers expect weightier, full-bodied rosés to be more expensive, and, from his experience, this is the style preferred in restaurants. **Péter Vida**, Szekszárd (www.vidaborbirtok.hu) feels there is a market for more gastronomic rosés, but not necessarily for higher quality wines at higher prices. International varieties are often used to further emphasize their seriousness in the (international) premium market.

St Andrea
Egerszalók, Ady Endre út 88, 3394 Hungary
Tel.: +36 36 474 018
standrea.com/en

Here, they made their first oaked rosé, Rózaa, in 2015. Made with a blend of Merlot, aged in new oak, and Pinot Noir and Kékfrankos in old oak, the final blend has vibrant fruit, red cherries, raspberries, redcurrants and strawberry fruit with powerful, fresh, chewy acidity. The oak gives a hint of tannic structure. I expect it will develop with age, revealing more complex flavours.

Csaba Malatinszky
H-7773 Villány, Batthyány L. u.27
Tel.: 72 49 30 42
www.malatinszky.hu

Malatinszky used to make his oaked rosé from Merlot, which he found produced too soft a rosé, especially if malolactic fermentation occurred, making a flat wine. For the 2015 vintage he changed to Cabernet Franc. Fermented in new Zemplén (Hungarian) oak (milder than French oak) and aged in tank, the wine is made from the free-run juice of grapes picked later than for standard rosé but earlier than for reds; the wine is a darker pink. There are powerful, red fruit aromas with generous, ripe, red fruit and strawberries, with lovely creamy acidity and gentle tannins with a dry finish. The oak is not evident other than in giving the wine greater structure. Because of the darker red–pink colour, Malatinszky commented that even though Hungarian rosés are darker than many from other parts of the world, this is closer to a pale red and was hard to position in the marketplace. Only 1,200 bottles were made.

Szent Gaál
Zomba, 7173 Hungary
Tel.: +36 74 431 256
vorosfeher.hu

Winemaker Joco Rappay, at this Szekszárd winery, makes two rosés. The single vineyard Cabernet Sauvignon, harvested late at the end of October is made with a blend of whole-bunch direct-press and first and second press, and with 70 per cent of the juice barrel fermented (and aged in new, second- and third-fill barrels). The cask sample was oaky on the nose and creamy on the palate. The oak was well-integrated into the round, ripe, red berry fruit and the lovely fresh acidity.

The second rosé appears to be a standard blend of 25 per cent Blauer Portugieser, 50 per cent Zweigelt and 25 per cent Kadarka, but Rappay is bold in his winemaking. After site-selecting the best grapes, the Zweigelt and Kadarka are cofermented at a warm temperature in tank and then blended with the traditionally vinified Blauerportugeiser. The wine has intense red berry and cherry fruit with vibrant acidity, with enough weight to make it a serious rosé.

Regional rosé styles are still not emphasized, but one distinguishing feature of the rosés from the northern regions of Mátra and Eger might be that they have a lighter, crisper acidity, sometimes from Pinot Noir, while those from the southern regions of Villány and Szekszárd seem fuller-bodied and riper, with more Kékfrankos, Cabernet Sauvignon, Cabernet Franc and Merlot. A Pinot Gris rosé from **Losonci** (www.losonci.hu), Mátra, is fermented on skins to create an orange wine from a white variety; its dark pink colour allows it to appeal to the rosé market. However, these are loose generalizations; the main aim is still to make a fresh, fruity style rather than a regional style. Around Lake Balaton, most varieties can be found. The volcanic soils of the north shore and Somló give an extra minerality. No varieties are specific to any one region.

Kékfrankos has proved to be particularly good for rosé throughout Hungary. As a red wine, it often reminds me of Cabernet Franc, with crisp, red fruit and leafy acidity, which translates well for rosé. When Tamás Dúzsi junior drove to Provence to bring a sample container of Kékfrankos grape juice to the CREVR in Vidauban for experimental vinification, they too were impressed with its potential. Its crisp red fruit and fresh acidity is perfect for rosé. It is used both as a single variety rosé and blended with other varieties.

Kadarka can have more Pinot Noir floral and cherry fruit character with excellent acidity. With its tendency for uneven ripening, it is sometimes made with some grapes fully ripe and others still green, giving a natural blend of fruit and acidity. Néro, created in 1956 and named for its deep colour, is currently proving a particularly popular variety for rosé. Brief skin contact results in a pretty pink with a light, fresh style. Zweigelt, as seen in Austria, can produce a savoury, spicy rosé which blends well with softer varieties. **Frittmann** (frittmann.hu/en) makes a very pale pink Zweigelt and Pinot Noir rosé which is very fruity, juicy and perfumed with gentle acidity. Pinot Noir seems to be rarely made into a rosé on its own, probably because it is of higher value as a red wine. Smaller percentages are blended with other varieties. Kakas from **Vylyan** in Villány (www.vylyan.hu/en) is a blend of Pinot Noir, Kadarka and Merlot. It has fragrant, fresh, leafy acidity, raspberry and rhubarb fruit and perfumed roses and cream weight.

Bordeaux varieties are also popular. **Mólnar** (www.molnarpincevillany.hu) estate in Villány said that they noticed that restaurants preferred Cabernet rosés, but were unsure whether this was from a greater weight to go with food, or the appeal of the international Cabernet name. **Simigh** (www.simigh.hu/en) in Tolna specialize in rosé production. The Cabernet Sauvignon, harvested late and given a warm ferment, has good intensity of ripe fruit, red berries, redcurrants and raspberries, and very fresh, leafy acidity. With nice weight, it is fresh and charming.

Sparkling rosé is a fast-growing sector. **Sauska** (sauska.hu/en) started off in 2009 with 20,000 bottles and now produces 40,000 bottles. A vintage sparkling rosé is set for launch in 2018.

12

FRENCH-INFLUENCED MEDITERRANEAN ROSÉ

Broadly speaking, the wines in this section are united by common grape varieties and a Mediterranean climate, as well as a French connection. While there are many similarities, there are also clear regional differences. Regions around the Mediterranean are often described sweepingly as having the same climate, but the harvest dates around the coastline can vary by almost two months! Altitude and proximity to the sea contribute huge diversity. The area is home to a mix of appellations, regulations, and winemaking methods, with few common rules.

This section includes wines from the South of France – both Languedoc-Rousillon and Provence wines not included in the main appellations – Corsica, North Africa, Malta and the Levant.

LANGUEDOC AND THE SOUTH OF FRANCE

I am frequently asked, 'What is the difference between Languedoc and Provence rosés?' The assumption seeming to be, that as both regions are in 'the South of France' and have similar grapes, they are indeed similar.

'Languedoc-Roussillon' covers a wine region stretching from the Rhône Valley to the Pyrenees, along the Mediterranean coastline, linked historically by the *via Domitia*, which stretched from Italy to Spain. The area has around 2,800 square kilometres under vine and is the single biggest wine-producing region in the world, responsible for more than a third of France's total wine production. Rosés are made under a wide variety of appellations and indications geographique protégée (IGP) denominations, as well as vin de France, which can appear confusing. Compared to Provence, fewer rosés are made as appellation wines, but many more as IGP.

This scale of IGP Pays d'Oc production in Languedoc-Roussillon lends itself to enormous diversity which, coupled with fluid regulations, makes it very difficult to summarize. Tasting many rosés, both IGP and appellation d'origine protégée (AOP), has shown that far from a pattern emerging, there are always exceptions: unexpected varieties, quality and style. When I mentioned the production of Languedoc rosé to Louise Hurren, marketing and communications specialist for the Languedoc Outsiders (languedoc-outsiders.com) winemakers' group she noted, 'I think you put your finger on it when you wrote "so many permutations". That is exactly why one cannot get the essence – this diversity makes it impossible to define Languedoc wine (including rosé) except to say that it can be very different, depending on the producer/variety/method/terroir …'.

In marketing terms, Hurren has learned to work with this diversity, and to appeal to consumers and buyers by emphasizing it. 'We like to say that Languedoc-Roussillon is where creativity meets diversity, because the region is a total patchwork of terroirs, which means we can grow a wide range of grapes very successfully, creating endless styles. I used to be pretty unexcited about rosé but since living here and being exposed to such wildly different styles, I feel like there's always potential, but it's a bit of a lucky dip!'

The 'lucky dip' element is significant, because while there are many exciting red and white wines in the region, exciting rosés are less easy to find. A reputation for making cheap and quaffable wine has not inspired producers to explore further.

Makers of appellation wines in Europe pay fees to fund promotion of the appellation. This has more value for wines sold at good prices, but less if the customer wants only cheap rosés over the summer. If the producer feels the benefits are not worth the cost and effort, he can make the wine as an ordinary vin de France. This becomes a vicious circle, with vin de France wines not always able to command higher prices, and producers less interested in making superior wines. In many cases, the wine stays no more than a simple rosé. Katie Jones of **Domaine Jones** (domainejones.com) ruefully commented that she has 'tasted a lot of boring rosé, probably made from Grenache. And we still find undrinkable rosés on the market.'

This is where the creativity described by Hurren appears. Jones makes a mere 3,000 bottles of vin de France rosé. This was made originally for its 'colour and fruit more than the origin … so we could drink it during the summer!' After reviewing the varieties she had available to make a rosé, Jones created hers from Carignan for its refreshing acidity, and 10 per cent Muscat to give fruit and charm, but not enough to give Muscat character. 'We have a style and we like it!'

In many respects, the rosé scene here reminds me of rosé production in California, where producers are experimenting with varieties and methods to make interesting rosés. This Californian connection should come as no surprise. In 1964, the Skalli family moved from Algeria to Corsica and then to Languedoc. When Robert Skalli took over the family business in the late 1970s, he studied winemaking in California, purchasing the St Supéry Estate in the Napa Valley. Robert Skalli became convinced that the climate in California was similar to that of the Languedoc, and that the region could also produce quality monocépage wines. From 1981, Skalli, with Jacques Gravegeal and other enthusiastic producers, worked towards the creation of the vin de pays d'Oc appellation, which would allow, and even encourage making wines with a single variety. Skalli's **Fortant de France** (fortant.com) is a major producer of varietal wines. Many producers are taking advantage of lighter regulations by making an IGP wine, or for even greater freedom, by making a vin de France, to experiment with different varieties and vinification techniques to make their rosé a little special.

The key to appreciating the rosés of the Languedoc, is often in the choice of variety and combination of varieties. The Pays d'Oc designation was created in 1987. Today it includes fifty-eight different varieties and, as seen with the addition of Nielluccio (below), is open to new ones. The five biggest selling rosés in 2015 from the Pays d'Oc IGP were single variety Grenache Noir, Cinsault and Syrah, a rosé blend, and fifth, a single variety Merlot. These five wines have proved to be popular in the UK, due to clear labelling, varietal indication and price.

While classic international varieties such as Syrah, Cabernet Sauvignon and Merlot are frequently found, there are some other varieties found throughout the region which give a distinctive character to the wines. Some have a historic tradition, others are new introductions or vine crossings bred to adapt to the local climate.

Muscat rosés

The black Muscat Hamburg, where the skin contact tints the wine pink, and white-skinned Muscat à Petits Grains, can be found either as varietals or as part of a blend in fragrant rosés, from the Black Sea, around the Mediterranean, and as far afield as Uruguay and Australia. The wines are made dry, often with a fresh mineral acidity with floral aromas and fruit of varying intensity. Muscat grapes, as with Moschofilero in Greece (see p.272), usually undergo a gentle winemaking process, in order to extract a pale pink colour and keep the aromatics, but avoid strong phenolics.

According to tradition, in the fifteenth century King René of Provence introduced Moscato di Amburgo (Muscat Hamburg) from Tuscany to the Ventoux region. There are records of it growing around Forcalquier in the early seventeenth century, where it was used as a table grape. The fruity rosés of Manosque, from the region of Pierrevert, originated, according to Rosemary George's *The Wines of Southern France* (2003), when the market for these black table grapes disappeared in the 1970s and producers brought the grapes to the local cooperative. Unsure of what else to do, cooperatives made the grapes into a sweet, fruity wine, tinged pink by the dark skins. However, because the grapes were grown as table grapes, the wine had no appellation status.

To keep the style, some producers started to plant Muscat à Petits Grains in the early 2000s and make a rosé through blending with traditional rosé varieties. These wines can be labelled IGP, and are generally dry with floral, fragrant aromas. Wines made with Muscat Hamburg can only be labelled as vin de France. These wines can have pronounced Muscat character with floral aromas and are pretty and often dry. Some producers also use this variety for gently sweet, sparkling pink wines.

Gris varieties

A *gris de gris* is a white or rosé wine, particularly in the region running from the Rhone, across Languedoc-Roussillon down to Catalonia (see p.46) made exclusively with grapes of a variety defined as '*gris*', such as Grenache Gris, Aramon Gris, Piquepoul Gris, Sauvignon Gris, and Terret Gris.

The big advantage of these *gris* varieties, in a market where pale is fashionable, is that their pale colour allows for greater extraction without the wines taking on a darker colour. Grenache Gris is a pinkish-grey mutation of the red Grenache grape and is not permitted in Provence. Little research has been conducted into the history of Grenache Gris, so it remains in relative obscurity. It tends to appear in vineyards only among other Grenache bush vines, and is often blended indiscriminately. Like its family members Grenache Noir and Grenache Blanc, Grenache Gris is vigorous, resistant to drought and prefers warm, dry environments.

Les Vignobles Foncalieu
Domaine de Corneille, 11290 Arzens
Tel.: 04 68 76 21 68
www.foncalieu.com

Here, they have made a Griset Gris de Gris, IGP Pays d'Oc, from old vine Sauvignon Gris, which Languedoc expert Matthew Stubbs MW noted 'smells and tastes very much like a Sauvignon Blanc wine but is in fact a very pale rosé.' Foncalieu also make a Piquepoul rosé, IGP Coteaux d'Ensérune Piquepoul Noir (not a *vin gris*). According to Stubbs 'the Piquepoul Noir is a much rarer and distant cousin of the more widely planted Piquepoul Blanc. There are only around 100 hectares of the Piquepoul Noir planted. This wine is slightly darker than the Griset, not as aromatic but with a really nice taut structure, excellent acidity and a garrigue note on the finish.'

Domaine Gayda
Chemin de Moscou, 11300 Brugairolles
Tel.: 04 68 31 64 14
www.gaydavineyards.com

La Minuette is a blend of Mourvèdre and Sauvignon Gris, which I found intriguing. The blend of a structural black grape with a delicate *gris* grape actually works surprisingly well. Pale, almost *gris* in colour, the wine has a subtle blend of wild, red berry fruit and creamy peach with a long, fine, stony, mineral elegance. They are also making a Grenache Gris in amphora.

Calmel and Joseph
chemin de la Madone, 11800 Montirat
Tel.: 04 68 72 09 88
www.calmel-joseph.com

A good example featuring Grenache Gris is Calmel and Joseph's Grenache Rosé 2016, from 70 per cent Grenache Gris and 30 per cent Grenache Noir. The grapes are macerated separately for 4 to 5 hours to extract colour and fruit, followed by cool temperature fermentation and three months on the lees with *battonage* for greater extraction. The wine is full of redcurrant and raspberry fruit (from the Grenache Noir), fresh, creamy acidity, and a mineral core (from the Grenache Gris) with a dry finish.

Francois Lurton
Domaine de Poumeyrade, 33870 Vayres
Tel.: 05 57 55 12 12
www.francoislurton.com

Rosé Sans Soufre from the Mas Janeil estate in Rousillon, has kept to a classic blend of Grenache Gris, Grenache Noir, Syrah and Mourvèdre, but the use of ambient yeast and no application of sulphur has led to a less overtly fruity wine (delicately perfumed peach and floral notes) with hints of almonds and rich texture. Grenache Gris, with its very pale colour, makes it possible to have longer skin contact for greater texture without affecting the colour.

Nielluccio

Following trials in Italy and Languedoc, a Nielluccio clone was identified that had higher acidity, juicier fruit, lower tannin and a paler colour than Merlot and Syrah, whilst resisting drought better than Cinsault. It produced a rosé with intense aromatics, vibrant acidity and red fruit character. Forty hectares were planted in the Languedoc in 2011, and Nielluccio is now beginning to appear in blends as a minor or major contributor. Its use is largely in red wines but a few rosés also incorporate it, including Terrasses de Gabrielle's Summer of Love (100 per cent Nielluccio), where it creates acidity like a Loire white, with the spice of a Syrah, and Saramon, a vin de France from **Mas Sibert** (www.massibert.fr), which is 70 per cent Nielluccio and 30 per cent Syrah.

Carignan

Until recently Carignan was regarded as the mean and nasty workhorse, planted extensively after phylloxera ravaged the vineyards of the south, and volumes of quaffable wine were needed. In the 1980s, large amounts were uprooted and replaced with 'noble' varieties such as Cabernet Sauvignon, Merlot and Chardonnay. Where old plots of Carignan have survived, they are found to produce red wines of great character, encouraging new plantations. Carignan Renaissance (www.carignans.com), is 'a movement to raise the grape's public recognition to a level equal to its importance as one of the world's top ten wine grapes by volume.'

A few 100 per cent Carignan rosés are produced in Languedoc, in a very fresh style with lively acidity and fresh, strawberry fruit. These include those from the **Foncalieu** cooperative (www.foncalieu.com) – Le Notaire Carignan Rosé and La Rareté Carignan Rosé – and La Loupe Carignan rosé from **Maurel Vedeau** (www.bonfilswines.com). Domaine Jones, as mentioned above, adds a touch of Muscat.

Domaine Revelette
chemin de Revelette, 13490 Jouques
Tel.: 04 42 63 75 43
revelette.fr

Peter Fischer at this winery in Coteaux d'Aix makes biodynamic wines with ambient yeast and long fermentation over several months in cement tanks. His 100 per cent Carignan Pur rosé is bled off the Carignan red wine. The wine has crisp, red fruit, crunchy acidity and gentle tannins when young, becoming mellower with a few years of ageing, taking on gamey, savoury aromas and Christmas spice vaguely reminiscent of Pinot Noir, with fresh, red fruit.

Domaine Vaquer
1 Rue des Écoles, 66300 Tresserre
Tel.: 04 68 38 89 53
www.domaine-vaquer.com

Frédérique Vaquer is from Burgundy, and likes darker rosé; he makes L'Ephemére from old Carignan, Grenache and Syrah vines. The wine goes through 12 hours of maceration and ambient yeast is used, achieving attractive complexity of red and black berry fruit, hints of tannic structure and a very dry finish.

Grenache Noir

Grenache forms the foundation for many Mediterranean rosés. Its relatively pale skins, fresh red fruit and high sugar levels make it ideal for pale rosés looking for fruit and weight, even if harvested early. The Grenache Association (www.grenache-association.com) was founded in 2010 to support winemakers, educate consumers and the wine trade and promote wines made with Grenache (see also page 83).

Château Maris
chemin de Parignoles, 34210 La Livinière
Tel.: 04 68 91 42 63
www.chateaumaris.com

Not all Grenache rosés are fruity. The Rose de Nymphe Emue from the biodynamic Chateau Maris, run by Robert Eden and Kevin Parker in the Minervois, is aged for six months in concrete tanks. The wine has a complex balance of fine salty, savoury notes, with wild berry fruit, lifted by good acidity.

Mas Delmas
29 Avenue du Stade, 66600 Rivesaltes
Tel.: 04 68 51 88 10
www.masdelmas.com

The vin de France, Ceci n'est pas, produced here uses Grenache grapes from different parcels at different altitudes, grown on a mix of clay, chalk and schist, in a deliberate move to blend the different terroirs. Grenache is poured through the lees (sometimes from a different vintage) and fermented on it, then aged in barrel for a year. The wine has good weight and concentration and is dry but not fruity. Only 1,500 bottles are made.

Rare varieties

While many Mediterranean-style rosés concentrate on the obvious varieties of Grenache, Cinsault and Mourvèdre, amongst others, a wealth of other varieties have became increasingly rare following phylloxera and the standardization of wine styles. But many of the old varieties are well adapted to the local climate and have their own unique character.

Wine Mosaic (www.winemoasaic.org) was set up to preserve this biodiversity. This non-profit project champions varietal diversity by 'protecting and promoting original grape varieties of the Mediterranean.' The project believes that standardization of grape varieties poses a threat to this diversity, since a mere 30 grape varieties are responsible for around 70 per cent of the world's wine production.

Through Wine Mosaic, I was introduced to the varieties Aubun and Mollard.

Aubun

Aubun is a red grape grown primarily in the Rhône valley, with similar characteristics to Carignan, in that it tends to give high yields, and produce wines that have some weight balanced by a slightly bitter flavour. Auban vines showed some resistance to phylloxera early in the nineteenth century epidemic, as well as to downy and powdery mildew. The vines tend to bud late and not be affected by spring frost. In 2000, there were 1,400 hectares of Aubun in France. Aubun is easily confused with Counoise; they were also grown mixed as a field blend in some older vineyards.

Eléonore de Sabran-Pontéves of **Domaine de Lansac** (www.vin-domaine-lansac-tarascon.fr) makes a rosé, Les Quatre Reines, IGP Alpilles, from ungrafted Auban, planted in the 1960s, between the Rhône and the Alpilles. The vines are planted in sandy soil, but for further protection against phylloxera, she floods the vineyards for 40 days every winter. This dry rosé has crisp, red fruit with a firm, mineral finish.

Mollard

Mollard is a variety indigenous to the Hautes Alpes region in northern Provence, which nearly died out during the twentieth century. **Domaine Allemand** (www.domaine-allemand.com) has been very active in restoring the fortunes of this variety. Their vineyards lie on alluvial soils with chalk at 600 metres, in the Durance valley, surrounded by mountains. The relatively cooler climate contributes freshness. Their Goût des Vacances is made with Mollard, blended with Cabernet Franc, harvested manually. The wine is a pale pink, dry, fresh rosé. Varietal character adds floral and sweet almond aromas with ripe, wild berry and cherry red fruit, bitter almond tannins and long, fresh acidity.

Crossings

Caladoc

Caladoc is a red French grape variety, planted primarily in southern wine regions such as Languedoc. A crossing of Grenache and Malbec, it was created by Paul Truel in 1958 at the Institut National de la Recherche Agronomique (INRA), when he was developing a vine for southern France that was less prone to *coulure* (rot) than either of its parents.

While the grape is used in several *vins de pays* in Languedoc and Provence, it is not permitted in any appellation d'origine contrôlée (AOC) wines. Although some producers make a wine with 100 per cent Caladoc, its appears to be best in a blend. L'Angèle from **Domaine de l'Angèle** (domainedelangele.fr) in Vaucluse, includes 35 per cent Caladoc in its classic rosé blend along with Grenache (45 per cent), Syrah (10 per cent) and Cinsault (10 per cent), to give freshness to the red fruit and mineral acidity.

Château Thuerry
Château Thuerry, 83690 Villecroze
Tel.: 04 94 70 63 02
www.chateauthuerry.com

This winery in Provence makes two Coteaux du Verdon IGP rosés with Caladoc. L'Exception, from 73 per cent Merlot and 27 per cent Caladoc, has cold maceration for four hours before fermentation, then ageing in new French and American oak for seven months with *battonage*. The wine is dark red-pink with a pronounced sweet, raw oak character. At 14% abv it is a powerful wine, with ripe fruit and long, fresh acidity. Almost sweet and luscious, it is bone dry. L'Exception 2 is also made with Merlot and Caladoc, and has a whopping 14.5% abv. After the same cool maceration, this wine was fermented and aged for five months in amphora with lees stirring. The same ripe fruit is evident, but instead of being emphasized by sweet oak, the fruit is used to balance the tight minerality and almost stony character of a wine developed in amphora. While the sweet American oak makes the first wine approachable young, the amphora wine still seems tannic and closed.

Outside France, Caladoc has limited plantings in Lebanon, Bulgaria, Russia, South America, Portugal and Israel.

Marselan
This black variety was created by INRA in 1961 by crossing Cabernet Sauvignon and Grenache Noir. It was introduced to vineyards in the Languedoc, Rhone Valley, northern Spain, California, Switzerland and Israel, but is rarely used as the sole variety in rosé. Two examples of single varietals are those from Les Caves Richemer, a cooperative based in

Marseillan on the Languedoc coast, and (not in this region) Domaine de Tariquet, which is an IGP Côtes de Gascogne.

Styles

Apart from the range of varieties, there are a few different wine styles common in the region.

Famille Fabre

Château de Luc, 11200 Luc-sur-Orbieu
Tel.: 04 68 27 10 80
www.famillefabre.com

The family created quite a buzz at Vinisud 2017 with their new oak-aged Rosine 2015 – a classic blend of 40 per cent Cinsault, 40 per cent Grenache and 20 per cent Mourvèdre. The decision to age in oak (which appears to be a rarer style in Languedoc) came from discussions with local chefs who wanted a rosé with more weight and complexity to go with food. Louis Fabre added Mourvèdre to give the weight to handle oak ageing, and harvested the fruit riper than usual. The wine has good ripe fruit and well-integrated, not overly dominant oak.

Gérard Bertrand

Route de Narbonne Plage, 11100 Narbonne
Tel.: 04 68 45 28 50
www.gerard-bertrand.com

A major producer in the Languedoc with numerous properties, Bertrand has received considerable acclaim at a number of competitions for his Château La Sauvageonne Rosé La Villa, made from Vermentino, Viognier, Grenache, and Mourvèdre from vineyards at 150–350 metres. Direct-press and free-run juice were used, and the first three varieties were cofermented. The wine is aged in barrel.

Domaine Montrose

34120 Tourbes
Tel.: 04 67 98 63 33
www.chateau-montrose.com

While many Languedoc rosés have more fruit than their Provence counterparts, some emulate the Provence style. Domaine Montrose, with vineyards on largely volcanic soils, works with winemaker Michel Legoaec, who used to work in Provence, and imbues his wines with a taste of Provence. His Château rosé has a mineral, slightly salty edge, with light red fruit and grapefruit acidity. The Prestige, which has had some time in oak has ripe, silky peach fruit, which is smooth and well-balanced and integrated with a firm dry, salty, mineral core.

Domaine Ventenac
4 rue des Jardins, 11610 Ventenac Cabardes
Tél. : 04 68 24 93 42
www.maisonventenac.fr

This domaine from the Cabardès AOP, just outside Carcassonne, reflects the unique mix of Atlantic (Bordeaux) and Mediterranean varieties found in parts of Languedoc. The appellation rules stipulate a minimum of 40 per cent Bordeaux varieties and 40 per cent Mediterranean. This wine has 30 per cent Cabernet Sauvignon, 20 per cent Cabernet Franc, 20 per cent Grenache, 20 per cent Syrah and 10 per cent Malbec (exact percentages dependent on the vintage.) Winemaker and owner Oliver Ramé is a great advocate for the purity of fruit found on the domaine's limestone soils and his rosés have a vibrant, fruity freshness. The Cuvée Diane has a beautiful crystallized-violet floral aroma, complemented by soft, ripe raspberry and peach fruit body, balanced acidity and a slightly dry finish.

Domaine Virgile Joly
22 Rue Portail, 34725 Saint-Saturnin-de-Lucian
Tel.: 04 67 44 52 21
www.domainevirgilejoly.com

Colour is still an important issue, however good the rosé. Winemaker Virgile Joly explained that the appellation of St Saturnin traditionally made darker pink rosés, but as these were difficult to sell, producers were making paler and lighter styles. He was changing slowly, but his 2015 – a powerful wine with ripe, red fruit, long, delicate, tannic structure, and more like a *clairet* or *Schiller* – proved almost impossible to sell. His 2016 will be a pale colour, seen as more commercial.

The Saint Saturnin area is also home to a traditional fortified *vin de liqueur*, called *Carthagène*. This is a *mistelle*, where the grape juice is fermented to 2–3% abv, then fermentation is stopped with *eau de vie*, bringing it up to 16.5% abv. The base wine is the same as the rosé, made with Grenache, Cinsault and Syrah. It is dark rose pink with aromas of roses and red fruits. Some vintages have almost a lychee and perfumed exotic fruit character. Although few make this wine now, those that do are making it fresher, with better acidity.

While there are a number of pink sparkling wines around, one in particular has stood out. Rosé Frizant from **Mas de Daumas Gassac** (www.daumas-gassac.com) is made from white varieties and juice bled off their red wine. With 70 per cent Cabernet Sauvignon and 30 per cent a blend of Mourvèdre, Pinot Noir, Sauvignon Blanc, Petit Manseng and Muscat, the wine is delightfully exuberant with strawberry fruit and fresh acidity.

As the appellations have subtle differences, and many more wines are made outside the appellations, and due to its size and diversity, it is hard to generalize about the rosés of Languedoc-Rousillon. Many of the rosés appear to have fractionally greater weight, structure or fruit than Provence rosés, while using a similar blend of varieties.

CORSICA

Located 90 kilometres west of Italy, 170 kilometres south-east of France and 11 kilometres north of the island of Sardinia, Corsica is the most mountainous island in the Mediterranean. The climate is warmer and drier than in mainland France. The sea moderates the heat, creating a consistent temperature and sharply reduces the diurnal temperature variation. Throughout the mountainous terrain are several meso-climates created by the differing degrees of altitude, latitude and maritime influences. Several different soil types are found in the wine growing regions of Corsica.

In the thirteenth century, Corsica fell under the rule of the Republic of Genoa. Over the next 500 years, the Genoese established strict laws governing the harvest and winemaking practices the island. They also banned exports of Corsican wines to ports outside Genoa. The most sought-after wines from Corsica were those in the 'Greek style' from the Cap Corse region. In 1769, a year after the Genoese ceded control to the French, Scottish writer James Boswell praised the diversity and quality of Corsican wines, comparing them favourably to the wines of Malaga and Frontignan, suggesting they were sweet. Under Napoleon's rule, Corsica was allowed to export wine and tobacco duty-free across the French Empire.

In the nineteenth century, the Corsican government tried to improve the island's economy by promoting its wine industry. Efforts included widespread planting of the indigenous Sciacarello grape and construction of a large wine cellar near the city of Vizzavona. The phylloxera epidemic of the late nineteenth century dealt a crippling blow, and was followed by a period of mass depopulation as Corsicans migrated to other countries. According to Rosemary George, 'rosé was not made in Corsica until the mid-1960s. Previously the choice was red or white, but then the tourist demand came and now [2001] a substantial part of the island's production is rosé.'

Following the independence of Algeria from French rule, many Algerian *pieds-noirs* migrated to Corsica and began planting vineyards. For instance, **Domaine de Vaccelli** (www.uva-corse.com/domaine/domaine-de-vaccelli) was created in 1962 by Roger Courrèges, originally from near Béarn, who came to Corsica from Algeria. Between 1960 and 1976 the vineyard area in Corsica increased fourfold. Many of Corsica's oldest established wineries were founded then on the eastern plains. Vineyards were mechanized and started to overproduce, reaching peak production in 1976.

In the 1980s, the European Union introduced subsidies to encourage the uprooting of vines, to reduce production and improve quality. By 2003, these programmes had contributed to the loss of 7,000 hectares, as well as the introduction of modern winemaking techniques and equipment such as temperature-controlled fermentation tanks.

Some 80 per cent of Corsican wines are sold locally, with a heavy dependence on the tourist trade. Corsica is beginning to develop export markets and efforts are paying off. A much greater range of Corsican wine is available in the UK and US than before, though the wines tend to be expensive, as production costs are high and yields low. Marcel Orford-Williams, buyer for The Wine Society notes 'the sheer quality of the wines now being produced here. The rosés in particular are world class and fast making inroads onto the wine lists of top restaurants everywhere.'

In 1968, Patrimonio was established as Corsica's first AOC. Today, Corsica has nine AOC regions, including the island-wide designation Vin de Corse AOC, which accounts for around 45 per cent of AOC wines produced in Corsica. Most of the wine exported from Corsica is sold under the IGP designation l'Île de Beauté or IGP Mediterranée.

The leading red grape varieties of the region are Sciacarello (3,000 hectares) and Nielluccio (700 hectares), largely planted following the grubbing up of the high-producing vineyards. Vins de Corse rosé wines must include at least a 50 per cent composition of Nielluccio, Sciacarello and Grenache, and no more than 50 per cent of combined blend of Barbarossa, Carignan, Cinsault, Mourvèdre, Syrah, and Vermentino. Carignan and Vermentino are further relegated to comprising no more than 20 per cent of the entire blend.

Sciacarello (or Sciaccarello) is an Italian red grape variety, grown primarily in Corsica and believed to be a parent vine of the Ligurian-Tuscan variety Pollera Nera. Its naturally high acidity means that it can be harvested at full maturity, creating soft and spicy, full-bodied rosés. It is often blended with Nielluccio or Grenache, rarely into a varietal wine. It is most noted for wines from Ajaccio, which tend to be highly perfumed.

Nielluccio is thought to be related to Sangiovese. There is confusion about its origins, with some experts describing it as indigenous while others say it is of Italian origins, possibly genetically identical to Sangiovese, which came to Corsica from Genoa during the thirteenth century. As in Languedoc, several clones have been studied and different ones are used, depending on whether for rosé, light red or heavier red wine. The German *Vitis International Variety Catalogue* database of known grape cultivars does not give Nielluccio a separate entry, but includes it as a synonym of Sangiovese. Some list the grape as a separate entry but note its close similarities to Sangiovese. The name translates in Corsican dialect as 'the grape that bursts under the teeth', due to its tough skin, with plenty of juice. Early budding, Nielluccio produces lightly-coloured wines with high alcohol levels. It is commonly used for rosé.

In Patrimonio, on the northern coast, Nielluccio is the main variety. In 2002, the region changed its AOC regulations to require at least 75 per cent Nielluccio in rosés, with Grenache, Sciacarello and Vermentino permitted to round out the rest. For leading grower, Antoine Arena (Patrimonio), 'This is where Nielluccio is at its most characteristic, on limestone slopes.' Eric Poli from **Clos Alivu** (www.uva-corse.com/domaine/clos-alivu) makes a Nielluccio-dominant rosé with red berry and floral aromatics and crisp saline finish.

The Ajaccio wine region, surrounding the capital, Ajaccio, on the south-west coast, produces rosés made primarily from Sciacarello.

Jean-Charles **Abbatucci** (domaine-abbatucci.com) makes fresh rosés with a savoury herbal touch, such as his cuvée Faustine, a blend of Vermentino, Sciacarello and Nielluccio.

In spring 2017, a group of Corsican producers jointly launched a new brand, Île de Rosé, aimed at supermarkets, hoping to exploit the market for Provence-style wines. Four cooperatives (Uvib, Uval Vignerons Corsicans, Aghione and Saint-Antoine) are participating with private domaine **Clos Alivu** (whose owner, Eric Poli, is president of the local wine board). The wine is made from grapes harvested around Corsica, comprising 60–70 per cent Sciaccarello, 10 per cent Nielluccio, 10 per cent Grenache, 10 per cent Cinsault, in a special bottle with a relief map of Corsica, with plans to use Corsican-grown corks. Made in a Provence style with direct-press and cool tank fermentation, the wine has good acidity with a clean, crisp, mineral core and ripe, red berry fruit. It is very fresh and vibrant, with fresh, red fruit and a serious herby, salty side.

MALTA

Malta was not a region I had considered for rosé, but when judging at the International Rosé Championship in Krakow fellow panellist George Meekers, head of sales at **Delicata Winery** (delicata.com), who lives in Malta, gave me this introduction. Malta's best rosés are nearly always surprisingly delicate and well-balanced, and never strongly alcoholic. This is remarkable from an archipelago located south of Sicily and much closer to hot Tunisia than to Provence (Tunis is 400 kilometres to the west, Marseille 1,100 kilometres to the north-west). One of the most suitably adapted grape varieties grown in Malta since the mid-1990s is Grenache Noir, with 25 hectares. Delicata's Medina is made from Grenache with a hint of Cabernet Franc. Their Gozitan Victoria Heights Shiraz from Gozo is picked early and has direct cold-pressing.

Ġellewża Frizzante is a popular semi-sparkling style, to many drinkers synonymous with Maltese rosé, created by the Delicata Winery. Ġellewża is a native red-skinned *Vitis vinifera* variety. Delicata's Lifestyle *frizzante* is made from vines found sprawling across 100 hectares of vineyards, the last surviving stocks of old and often ungrafted vines of indeterminate age, largely dry-farmed in tiny rubble-walled blocks, on poor soils, and trained in the sprawling bush method.

NORTH AFRICA

Algeria

Filipo Pananti, an Italian poet, wrote detailed descriptions of his time in Algeria, after he was captured off Sardinia in 1813 and held captive by Barbary pirates. 'The wine, which is made by Christian slaves, is quite as good as that of Rosés in Spain: but it loses a great deal of its flavour, after a visit from the locusts.' A few years later, in 1830, Algeria came under French rule and more vineyards were planted to provide wine for the colonists. Algerian wine exports to France filled the void left by phylloxera. An influx of winemakers from the German wine region of Baden brought with them more modern winemaking techniques and helped to increase the quality of Algeria wine. Even after France resumed normal levels of wine production, Algerian wine was still widely used in regions like Languedoc as a blending component to add colour and strength to the wines. By the late 1930s, Algeria was the world's biggest exporter of wine and by the 1950s, together with Tunisia and Morocco, Algerian wine accounted for nearly two-thirds of the wine that was internationally traded. This continued until Algerian Independence in 1962.

Algerian rosés are produced in a range of colours varying from very pale grey-pink (Gris d'Aboukir) to the deepest rose pink. Algerian wines are characterized by overripe fruit, high alcohol and low acidity. The grapes often go through a short fermentation process and are bottled after little to no oak ageing.

Tunisia

When Tunisia became a French protectorate in 1881, a sluggish wine trade experienced a revival with the influx of colonists. Success was short lived, as phylloxera arrived in 1936, swiftly followed by the Second World War. After the war, a short revival occurred, with the establishment in 1948 of Les Vignerons de Carthage, a union of Cap Bon wine collectives and the arrival of French vintners and viticulturists who launched a major replanting programme in the 1950s. Production increased and improved for the next few years, until Tunisian independence in 1956. Although the wine trade did not completely fade away, the local winegrowers' lack of expertise in modern-day winemaking and wine logistics led to a slow decrease in output, which persisted for almost thirty years. In the late 1980s, local winemaking experienced a small resurgence. Interest in viticulture was slowly renewed; and within ten years, the wine trade saw growth in both local and international markets. In response to demand, the Union Central des Coopératives Viticoles (UCCV), which accounts for 70 per cent of wine production, emphasized the importance of modernizing vine growth and winemaking methods.

Requiring large capital investment, many of Tunisia's more successful vineyards have partnered with foreign investors, who import technology and know-how. A marked increase in wine exports has helped bring in more foreign investors looking to work with local wineries and wine companies. **Domaine Neferis** (www.mdewines.com) in Grombolia, Cap Bon works with Sicilian partners Calatrasi, using Australian winemaker consultants, producing a 100 per cent Grenache rosé called Château Defleur. Most wine sales are through tourism.

In the early 2000s, wine production in Tunisia consisted of 60–70 per cent rosé and *vin gris*, 25–30 per cent red and less than 10 per cent white. Tunisia shares most of its grape varieties with southern France. Common varieties include Carignan, Mourvèdre, Cinsault, Alicante Bouschet, Grenache, Syrah and Merlot. Pinot Noir, Syrah, Merlot and Cabernet Sauvignon were introduced in the early 1990s.

Most wine production is in Cap Bon and the surrounding area, which is cooled by maritime breezes, and vineyards planted at altitude. Tunisia has an appellation d'origine contrôlée system with the following AOCs: Grand Cru Mornag (principally rosé), Mornag (principally rosé), Coteaux de Tébourba (principally rosé), Tébourba (known for its *vin gris* made with Grenache and Cinsault), Sidi Salem, Kélibia, Thibar and Coteaux d'Utique. Because of Tunisia's warm weather, grapes mature earlier than in Europe.

Most rosés are made by direct press, although 15–20 per cent use *saignée*. Locally there is a preference for darker Carignan-dominant rosés which resemble a *clairet* style. Malolactic fermentation is blocked to preserve as much acidity as possible and the wines are made to be drunk young and fresh.

According to *Rayon Boissons*, the French drinks magazine for large retailers, in 2014 the top two best-selling foreign domaines were Groupe Castel's range of branded wines from Tunisia Boulaouane and Sidi Brahim. The wines are made in Sloughia, at the eastern edge of the Atlas Mountains, then blended in France, and bottled or filled into bag-in-boxes, primarily as inexpensive wines for the French market. Around three million bottles are produced annually. The grape composition and range has varied over the years. In 2010 the rosé was 40 per cent Cinsault and 60 per cent Grenache Gris; now a Grenache Syrah is sold, described as 'round and fruity'.

Morocco

Morocco's first Arab dynasty, in the ninth century, gave a dispensation to the Berber tribes around Meknes to make wine. As a French protectorate in the first half of the twentieth century, wine production boomed in Morocco, especially on the sunny plateau around Meknes. At its peak of production in the 1950s the country produced three million hectolitres of strong red wine known as *vin médicin,* used to fortify weaker French wines. After Morocco's independence in 1956, the wine industry collapsed, as the country lost most of its winemakers, its consumers and its main export market. When the European Union banned blending foreign with European wines, Morocco turned to creating its own labels.

In the 1990s, wine production started to improve, due to foreign (primarily French) investment and know-how. This was achieved by offering foreign wine companies long-term leases of vineyards from the state agricultural company SODEA. Several large Bordeaux-based wine companies, including Groupe Castel, William Pitters and Taillan, entered into such partnerships, which have been quite successful in reviving the Moroccan wine industry. Castel's brand, Moroccan Gris de Boulaouane (www.groupe-castel.com) was the best-selling foreign wine in France as of 2005, and the vineyard area expanded to 50,000 hectares in the early 2000s. Some smaller investors, more oriented towards higher quality wines than the high-volume market, have followed.

Morocco is one of the biggest wine producers in the Muslim world. Even though production has fallen to almost a tenth of output during its heyday of the 1950s, it still produces around 35 million bottles each year. Red wine dominates, with over 75 per cent of production; rosé and *vin gris* account for almost 20 per cent, and white for the remaining 5 per cent. Most is everyday *vin de table,* but producers are experimenting and the quality has risen enormously.

Economic and political stability in Morocco has resulted in more tourists visiting the country, which has benefited wine consumption.

Les Celliers de Meknès (www.lescelliersdemeknes.net) had the largest volume share in 2015 with 32 per cent, with red, rosé and white wines.

Vin gris is particularly popular, sometimes slightly darker than French versions, with an orangey-pink hue. It is made mainly from varieties such as Cinsault and Grenache, but also from Cabernet Sauvignon. Moroccan vineyards, such as at Meknès, at relatively high altitudes have good diurnal temperature variation and a very dry climate. The acidity can be on the low side, but often with good fruit and structure. **Les Trois Domaines**, part of the Celliers de Meknès, Guerrouane Gris Cinsault is a fresh, fruity, easy-to-drink, dry rosé.

Muscat, reminiscent of the fruity rosés of southern France, is evident in rosé such as **Val d'Argan**'s (www.valdargan.com) Rosé, made with Syrah (*saignée*) and Muscat Hamburg (direct press), fermented in tank.

Domaine de la Zouina

Commune d'Aït Bourzouine, Province d'El Hajeb, Meknès 51000
Tel.: 212 5354 33034
www.domainezouina.com

The vineyard lies at 800 metres, the cooler climate providing freshness and acidity. It was taken over by two Bordelais, Gérard Gribelin (from Château de Fieuzal) and Philippe Gervoson (director of Château Larrivet Haut-Brion) in 2002 and makes some rosés. Volubilia Rosé, made with Syrah and Tempranillo, has a deep pink colour, while Volubilia Gris, from Caladoc, Marselan, Mourvèdre and Cabernet Sauvignon, is pale shell-pink.

THE LEVANT

Lebanon

Over 4,000 years ago, the Phoenicians sold Lebanese wine throughout the Mediterranean region. Barrels of wine were shipped out from the thriving ports of Tyre, Sidon, and Byblos to many destinations, including pharaonic Egypt. The grapes of the Phoenician era, such as Marami and Baytamouni, no longer exist, but Château Musar (see p.252) does use old local varieties Obaideh and Merwah in its rosé. The Phoenicians seem to have protected their wine from oxidation with a layer of olive oil, followed by a seal of pinewood and resin.

In 1517, the region was absorbed into the Ottoman Empire. Winemaking was forbidden, except for religious purposes by the Christians, who were mainly Maronites, or Greek and Armenian Orthodox. The Christians also developed Arak, an ouzo-like spirit flavoured with aniseed. As the French expanded their influence eastwards, winemaking increased. **Château Joseph Spath** (Chbat) was founded in 1847, followed by **Château Ksara** (www.chateauksara.com) in 1857, when Jesuits planted Cinsault vines taken from cuttings in Algeria. In 1868 a French engineer, Eugène François Brun, set up **Domaine des Tourelles** (www.domainedestourelles.com). In 1918, after the First World War, the French civil and military administration created unprecedented demand for wine. The French influence between the world wars promoted a culture of wine drinking, as did Beirut's sophisticated Mediterranean culture.

After the Second World War and Lebanese independence, the region became a cosmopolitan financial hub, creating further opportunities for wine. **Château Kâfraya** (www.chateaukefraya.com) was founded in 1946 by Michel de Bustros, planting vineyards at 1,000 metres on the foothills of Mount Barouk.

From 1975–92, the Lebanese civil war slowed the development of the wine trade. The end of the conflict brought a new momentum to viticulture, with the creation of new vineyards. Since then, wine estates have increased from five to forty, although not all are operated commercially. Viticulture is concentrated within the small Bekaa valley at altitudes of between 900 and 1,500 metres, where elevation allows cool nights to balance the warm days. There are three regions: the northern Baalbeck is very dry, the central Zahlé is more temperate, and the south, near the Litani River Dam, is more humid.

Ksara is the largest producer, supplying 70 per cent of Lebanese output, using grapes from 300 hectares, of which 20 are owned outright. In the last ten years, wine production in Lebanon has more than doubled. Dry rosés make up 15 per cent of Ksara's production, an important domestic category, which it dominates. Habib Karam of **Karam Wines** (www.karamwines.com) commented, 'You have to look at the culture of drinking where rosé is produced. In Lebanon rosés are for beach drinking, consumers expect, light, refreshing styles with low alcohol. In Lebanon, rosé is drunk in the summer, red in winter.'

Traditionally, the Lebanese home market was fond of darker, dry, Tavel-like rosé. Many local rosés have a traditional Provence taste, with dry herby notes and a dry finish, with a Lebanese twist of red berries, strawberries and a sweet–sour acid fruit character described as pomegranate. *Saignée* is used, often resulting in slightly darker wines. Some rosés are also being made in a more modern style.

Cinsault is particularly popular for rosé, with other varieties including Cabernet Franc, Cabernet Sauvignon, Caladoc, Carignan, Clairette, Grenache, Marselan, Merlot, Mourvèdre, Syrah and Tempranillo, and white varieties Sauvignon Blanc, Ugni Blanc, Obaideh and Merweh.

Château Musar
Ghazir – Keserwan
Tel.: 09 925 056
www.chateaumusar.com

Winemaker Tariq Sahre told me that for their pale pink Jeune Rosé they allowed the market to direct the style, which meant creating a paler rosé. Everyone is 'knowledgeable and believes pale is better quality, while darker rosé appeals to a niche market'. He harvests grapes for rosé with a potential alcohol of 13%, with phenolic maturity. Due to the heat of the Bekaa Valley, if harvested earlier the grapes are unbalanced and green. The big diurnal temperature variation gives good acidity and fruit character.

The Jeune Rosé 2015 had 20 per cent Mourvèdre and 80 per cent Cinsault planted at over 1,000 metres. The direct-press method is used and the wine is tank fermented for freshness. The Jeune 2016 had 5 per cent more Cinsault, for a lighter colour. The wine is made to be a delicate, dry and fresh wine, with good weight and structure from ripe fruit.

Château Musar Rosé is made primarily with indigenous grapes Obaideh and Merwah, and some Cinsault on their own rootstocks, from low-yielding old vines planted at around 1,400 metres, with 15 to 18 hectolitres per hectare. The direct-press method was again used and the wine fermented and barrel-aged for six to nine months in French (Nevers) oak. The wine is bottled a year later and aged for a further two years before sale. The oak ageing contributes to a firm structure with a dry, salty finish, hints of orange peel and mature rosé character.

Some producers, such as Château Ksara, also make a *vin gris* style. The Gris de Gris 2016, from 60 per cent Grenache (gris or noir, unspecified), upwards of 20 per cent Cinsault, and some Sauvignon Blanc is made using direct press and cool fermentation. This pale rosé has garrigue aromas, round, ripe, red berry fruit, a ripe, fat body and good acidity.

Habib Karam of Karam Wines says that good rosé is the most difficult wine to make. 'They must have the aroma of fruit on the nose and on the palate, and to capture both in the right balance, is a challenge. I achieve the fruit and freshness in my rosé Arc-En-Ciel using Syrah, Cabernet Sauvignon and from this new vintage added Pinot Noir to the blend. Our rosé goes through a long vinification process using indigenous yeast. I ferment at a low temperature (12°C.)'

Frederic Cacchia, winemaker of **Adyar Wines** (www.adyar.org.lb) believes the rosé market is becoming increasingly important, due to a growing number of female drinkers. These consumers like pale, fresh, easy-to-drink wines, preferring rosé and white wines with floral and fruit character. These are generally the more technical styles, not the traditional wines. Whether this trend will last remains to be seen.

Israel

Israel has a very dynamic wine industry. It shares an ancient winemaking history with Lebanon, with details in the Bible of the importance of making wine. Like in Lebanon, Ottoman occupation halted winemaking apart from that for religious purposes. In the nineteenth century, Baron Rothschild from Bordeaux planted Bordeaux and southern French varieties, resulting in modern wines often having a French influence.

The most successful regions for high quality wines are those with higher elevations (from 500 to 1,200 metres) like the Upper Galilee, Golan Heights and Judaean Hills.

The four main vineyards, Carmel, Barkan, Golan Heights and Teperberg, control 70 per cent of the local market and wine exports. About fifty commercial wineries make over 500 hectolitres a year.

Today, the majority of rosés are lighter in colour and structure than the heavier traditional style. A wide range of varieties is used, including Barbera, Cabernet Franc, Carignan, Cinsault, Grenache, Malbec, Marselan, Merlot, Mourvèdre, Pinot Gris, Pinot Noir, Sangiovese, Syrah, Viognier and Zinfandel.

Adam Montefiore, who used to work for Carmel, and chronicled the history of Israeli wine, explains that 'Rosé in Israel has a checkered history. In the 1970s and 1980s, Grenache rosé was a big brand. The wine was deep-coloured, semi-dry, verging on semi-sweet, but it was very popular.' By the 1990s, with the start of the boutique winery boom, tastes began to change, and winemaking improved. Victor Schoenfeld, a Davis graduate, arrived at the Golan Heights Winery in 1991 and helped pioneer a winemaking revolution in Israel. Rosés such as Yarden White Harvest and Gamla Rosé Sparkling wine were influenced by his Napa background. But rosé remained little-considered by wine connoisseurs. It was not until around 2007 that rosé started to be taken seriously.

> **Château Golan**
> Eliad, 12927
> Tel.: 04 660 0026
> www.chateaugolan.com
> One of my favourite rosés is made here by Uri Hetz. The Geshem rosé is a blend of 90 per cent Grenache and 10 per cent Syrah (and sometimes a touch of Barbera). The grapes spend a few hours on the skins before pressing and the juice is then transferred to old barrels, where the wine undergoes spontaneous fermentation. After three months on the lees, the wine is blended in tank. The result is beautifully balanced and elegant.

Recanati Winery (www.recanati-winery.com) began producing Gris de Marselan in 2014 as its second rosé. The wine is pale in colour with ripe, red berry fruit and cool, crisp, clean acidity. Assaf Paz at **Vitkin** (www.vitkin-winery.co.il) has continued to lighten up his Israeli Journey rosé with more Grenache and less Carignan and only direct press juice, resulting in a fresh elegant wine. **Golan Heights'** (www.golanwines.co.il) Yarden Rosé Brut, made with Chardonnay and Pinot Noir, shows great elegance and reflects both its high altitude (over 1,000 metres) and volcanic soil origins.

Domaine du Castel
Shvil Israel, 9089500
Tel.: 02 535 8555
www.castel.co.il

Rosé du Castel from Domaine du Castel in the Jerusalem Hills uses a blend of 60 per cent Merlot, 20 per cent Cabernet Franc and 20 per cent Malbec, the same as for their red wines, but picked earlier – this wine is not bled-off the red (although Castel's first rosés were made this way). The wine has fresh white flowers, with peach and herb notes, finishing with ripe, strawberry fruit and fresh acidity. Eli Benzakein, the owner of Castel, is also working on an oak-aged rosé.

Jezreel Valley Winery
Hanaton
Tel.: 04 870 8701
www.jezreelwinery.com

As with other non-European rosés, the blends are moving away from the traditional European combinations. Here, Yehuda Nahar makes a dry rosé from 37 per cent Syrah, 38 per cent Carignan, 15 per cent Argaman (a crossing between the Portuguese Souzão and Carignan) and 10 per cent Sauvignon Blanc. With a darker colour, red fruit, roses and redcurrants, fresh, leafy acidity and a dry tannic finish, it is a light-red rosé.

As production increases, some winemakers are looking at more complex styles, with a few ageing in oak, including Nahar, above. The styles are extremely diverse, as each producer makes rosé in his own style, searching for the best rosé to suit terroir and varieties.

Dalton Winery
Dalton, 13810
Tel.: 04 698 7683
www.dalton-winery.com

This winery in the Upper Galilee, under winemaker Guy Eshel, doubled its rosé production in 2016 to meet growing demand. Eshel aims to make a rosé in a modern Provence style with no *saignée*, in an Israeli environment. His unoaked rosé is made from a blend of 65 per cent Syrah, 25 per cent Grenache and a small amount of Barbera and Zinfandel, hand harvested.

It has a creamy, silky texture with ripe raspberry and peach fruit and extra lusciousness from the 5g/l residual sugar, balanced with fresh acidity.

Eshel is also experimenting with a more complex style. Dalton's Alma Coral is half rosé, half *ramato/vin gris*. Made from 50 per cent Pinot Gris, with 25-hour skin contact it is stainless-steel fermented. The other half is Grenache noir with a short (4-hour) skin contact and is oak barrel-fermented. Ambient yeast is used for both halves. The oak is still powerful and competes a little with the phenolics from long maceration, but is balanced by ripe, creamy peach fruit and fresh acidity. An intellectually challenging rosé, its individual character threw many tasters, but its complexity and weight made it a good gastronomic style.

When talking to winemakers about the style of Israeli rosé, they say that sites, soils, varieties, blends and methods are still being studied. Their consensus was that Israeli rosé is still evolving.

13

THE BALKANS, THE ADRIATIC AND THE EASTERN MEDITERRANEAN

UNIQUE VARIETIES

After the expansion of the Ottoman Empire in the sixteenth century, the wine-producing regions of the eastern Mediterranean were much reduced, often just producing sacramental wine for small communities. Many areas remained untouched by outside influences and continued to use local varieties, with many islands spared phylloxera.

Production of rosé, though not big is growing. These areas are of particular interest because of their diversity, and their potential to offer varieties, especially in the hotter areas, adapted to global warming. The number of unique varieties and small regions makes it difficult to give an overview of general styles in this chapter.

THE ADRIATIC

Slovenia

The most dynamic wine-producing regions of Slovenia are along the borders with its neighbours, Italy, Croatia, Austria and Hungary. Winemaking traditions have developed following a mix of culture, topography, microclimates and specific traditions. The vineyards cover 16,000 hectares, divided

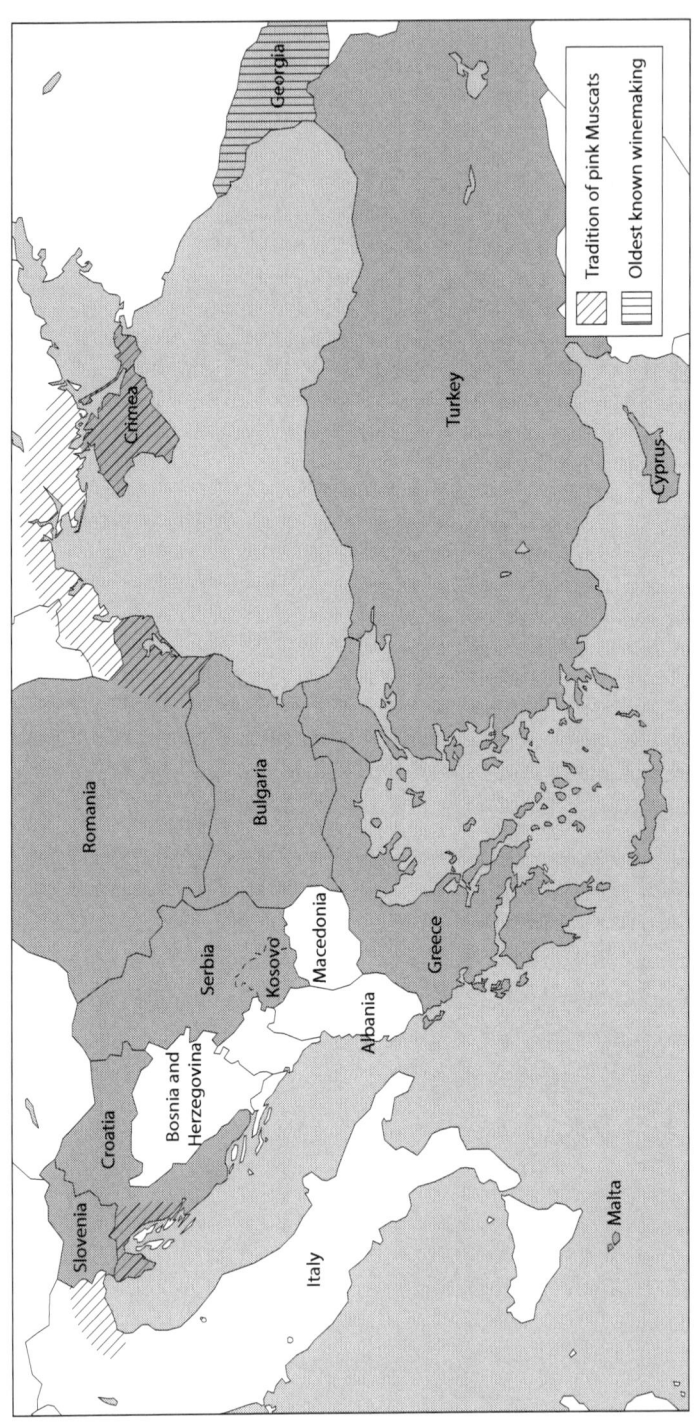

Rosé-producing countries of the Balkans, the Adriatic and the eastern Mediterranean, illustrating the wealth of indigenous varieties used in rosé wines.

into three regions: Podravje, Posavje and Primorska. The diversity of its wines is disproportionate to its size and population.

The largest region is Podravje (9,650 hectares) in the north-east, bordering Croatia, Hungary and the southern Austrian region of Styria. Ninety-seven per cent of the production is white wine, including sparkling and dessert wines.

Posavje, in the south-east, is the smallest region with 4,400 hectares. Within this region is the Dolenjska sub-region where Cviček, a fresh, light and slightly sour, pale red wine is produced.

The most developed of the three wine regions, with an annual output of over 250,000 hectolitres, is Primorska, in the north-west, bordering the Italian region of Friuli. The Kras Plateau (Carso in Italy) near the coast, has iron rich Terra Rosa limestone that produces briny and deeply mineral reds and whites. Further north along the Italian border, in the Vipava Valley and Goriska Brda, sedimentary soils converge with the flysch rock that makes up the foothills of the Alps. The wines from these regions, both white and red, are the most structured in Slovenia.

The majority of production is white, a third is red and a small amount is rosé, the market share and popularity of which has been growing over the last five years. Of the red varieties, Refosco d'Istria (Refosk Teran is related) is the most common, followed by Žametovka (Koelner Blauer), Merlot, Modra Frankinja (Blaufränkisch), the Cabernets and Pinot Noir. Any of these can be used, but choice will depend on the producer and local traditions.

Rosés come in different colours, from pale ruby to pale salmon colour with the trend going towards lighter shades. In the past rosés were darker. Styles can be dry to off-dry, with herbal to (more often) red fruit flavours of cherries, raspberries and strawberries. The wines are generally light.

Two examples come from the Primorska region. The first is **Batič** (www.batic.si) Rosé (Vipava Valley) made with spontaneously-fermented Cabernet Sauvignon, which has ripe, wild red fruit, herbal notes and a touch of residual sugar balanced by fresh acidity. The second, **Štoka Teran** (www.stoka.si) Rosé, from Kras, made with Teran, Cabernet Sauvignon and Merlot, using the direct-press method, is vinified in tank at cool temperatures to make a light and fresh rosé.

Croatia

Located in the northern part of the Adriatic, east of Slovenia, Croatia has three regions: Eastern Continental Croatia, Western Continental Croatia and Coastal Croatia. These, in turn, are divided into over 300 geographical wine regions, each with a strict classification system to ensure quality and origin. The majority of Croatian wine is white (67 per cent), with most of the remainder being red (32 per cent), and only a small percentage rosé.

Opolo, meaning half-and-half, is the old name for rosé wine in the southern coastal region of Dalmatia, where red wine diluted with water when served was regarded as the wine for the poor. The name is still used for some rosés.

Rosés in the hotter south tend to be more powerful, while rosés from Istria (northern coastal region) tend to be paler and more delicate.

Many traditional grape varieties survive alongside international varieties. The most popular varieties for rosé are Pinot Noir, Cabernet Sauvignon, and Plavac Mali (Zinfandel/Primitivo). Some also use Borgonja, Babić, Plavina, and Teran (related to Refosco). **Veralda** (www.veralda.hr) makes a cheerful Refosco with bright cherry and raspberry fruit and a dry finish.

Opolo from **Vinarija Rak** (www.vina-rak.hr/en) in Sibenik, Dalmatia is made from 100 per cent Babić. Babić is allegedly widely planted and often blended with other grapes, but few producers choose to make a wine labelled as Babić, because the market sees it as less prestigious than Plavac Mali. Extended maceration for ten to fifteen hours gives pronounced strawberry fruit with blood-orange freshness and leafy acidity, finishing on a saline note.

Che Non Che from **Bruno Trapan** (trapan.hr) in Istria is a 100 per cent Teran sparkling wine which its maker Charine Tan describes as 'wild berries and leafy. High acidity and not overly yeasty. Fruit-forward yet with a hint of earthy character. Compelling (though a tad strange and unfamiliar) flavours.' She adds that the wine needs a year or two of age.

Dingač IGP was the first Croatian appellation, recognized 1961. Here, the indigenous Plavac Mali has been producing the best wines for centuries. Dingač has its own path, carved into the mountain by the winegrowers, linking the vineyards to the port of Trstenik from where the wines were shipped around Europe. As the area is very steep, all work in the vineyard is done by hand. Despite very sunny weather, with the sun reflected by the quartz soils and the sea, these vines manage to keep balanced acidity and develop layered aromas.

St Heels from **Saint Hills**, Dingač (saintshills.com) is a Plavac Mali rosé with 13.5% abv that is floral and fruity with mineral notes. It is lighter and less savoury than most Plavac Mali rosés. Markus by **Daniel Szabo** (Dalmatia) is made from old vine Cabernet Sauvignon, Merlot and Babić grapes harvested from the higher parts of Dingač. There is strawberry and raspberry fruit with lime juice, and orange zest, for a refreshing, mouth-puckering finish. It is fresh, lean and structured.

Dalmatian Islands

The islands are extensions of mountain ridges on the mainland running east–west. Hot Mediterranean summers plus a karst landscape in which the water sinks down into sink holes and caverns leave little surface water. Agriculture has developed with steep terraces, dry stone walls and methods to preserve water.

Opolo, **Senjanović**, Vis (www.vina-senjanovic.hr), is made from Plavac Mali using direct press with minimal skin contact and free-run juice. There is ripe, red plum and cherry fruit with notes of violets and fresh green herbs finishing with a note of spice typical of the variety. Tannin hits the mid palate and persists till the end. Residual sugar and acidity level balance out the wine well.

Jo Ahearne MW, having made award-winning wine in Provence, has set up **Ahearne Winery** (ahearnevino.com) on the southern Dalmatian island Hvar where she makes her rosé wine, Rosina, from the variety Darnekuša. This wine is full of cherry and black fruit and vibrant acidity. This is the only rosé made from this variety. 'I chose Darnekuša because of its acidity,' says Ahearne:

> I wanted to make a rosé with a spine that could last more than the six months a lot of them do. It doesn't have much colour or alcohol so the freshness will always be there. And since it is light in colour you don't have to be fining the colour out like they do in Provence if you have a bit of skin contact for the flavour. I didn't want a big alcoholic rosé. The idea of rosé in Croatia is now moving on from the more traditional opolo which could be more light-red than rosé and there are some nice light and fruity wines. The concept of 'serious rosé' is a

little slower in taking hold but there are a few examples which I'm sure will grow in number over the next few years.'

THE BALKANS AND WEST OF THE BLACK SEA

Serbia

The only non-maritime region in this chapter spreads north-to-south, with its wine-growing areas following the valleys of major rivers such as the Danube and the Morava.

Grape varieties in Serbia range from those common in Central Europe (Frankovka – Blaufränkisch/Kékfrankos, Portugieser, Kadarka and Pinot Noir) which are typical in North Serbia (the Pannonian Plain), to those which require more Mediterranean sunshine, such as Vranac, Prokupac and Marselan, commonly grown in the hills and mountains of Central and South Serbia. This diversity gives consumers a large selection of rosé wines.

Quality has improved in the last ten years with investment in vineyards and technology. Some 25,000 hectares of vineyards are used for commercial production with another 9,000 hectares of old, neglected vineyards and plots used for family needs.

Historically, a darker coloured rosé wine called *'ružica'* was made, resembling *clairet*. During the communist period, large industrial wineries produced a *ružica* that was little more than a spritzer wine. The best modern *ružica* comes from Central and Southern Serbia and is made from at least 50 per cent Prokupac, blended with both local and international varieties. The Tre Morave region is the largest wine producing region in Serbia.

Primarily producing red and rosé wine with Prokupac as the main variety, the vineyards are generally located at slightly higher altitudes, with sunny hillside terraces, giving a long, slow ripening seasons. Rujno from the **Spasić Winery** (www.vinarijaspasic.com) is a 100 per cent Prokupac *ružica* which shows off the variety's character of dark cherry, redcurrants and spice, with leafy freshness and mild tannins. Petite Rose 2015 from **Ivanović Winery** accentuates the dark fruit character by adding in 30 per cent Cabernet Sauvignon and 10 per cent Merlot, to create a more full-bodied, intense and fruity wine with raspberry, strawberry and morello cherry fruit. Another traditional, darker style rosé is the šiler, described on page 50.

The black-skinned Muscat Hamburg was popular for making rosé in the nineteenth and twentieth centuries. The style is still made, usually with some residual sugar. The best examples are from cooler regions, where a better balance of acidity can be achieved. These wines can have delicate floral aromas, with rose petals on the nose paired with strawberry, redcurrant and blood orange notes, and some residual sugar, perfectly balanced with vibrant acidity.

Contemporary rosé styles have gained momentum since 2000. There are two dominant styles: off-dry rosé with accentuated fruitiness and bone-dry, pale pink wine. Modern Serbian rosés tend to be pale and dry in the international Provence style. Some wineries make both styles.

Off-dry rosés vary in colour from ruby-pink to pale pink. The wineries are switching more and more to the pale pink style, to address consumers' preference for pale-coloured wine. The wines are often made with international varieties such as Cabernet Sauvignon, Merlot, Syrah and Frankovka (Blaufränkisch). Zvonko Bogdan Rosé 2015 from **Zvonko Bogdan Winery** (www.vinarijazvonkobogdan.com/en/winery) is made with 50 per cent Merlot, 30 per cent Cabernet Franc and 20 per cent Frankovka, to produce a semi-sweet wine that has significantly contributed to the rise in popularity of rosé wine in Serbia. Sweetness is balanced with fine acidity. Spicy notes of Cabernet Franc and Frankovka add complexity to an otherwise lush, fruity wine.

Bulgaria

Since the fall of communism, Bulgaria has been reinvesting in its viticulture and cellars. Rosé is growing in popularity, with different styles appearing. Caroline Gilby MW suspects part of their growth could be due to the shortage of good white wines, with market demand for a lighter, more refreshing wine, besides the big reds. Descriptions of rosés focus on variety and fruit. Gilby notes that there seems to be a trend to make rosé as pale as possible using direct pressing and very clean must. A typical example can be found at **Terra Tangra** (www.terratangra.com), in the Sakar Mountain, where they make a light-coloured Mavrud with minimal skin contact, that has very light floral and citrus notes. Mavrud, a small-berry, late-ripening variety is popular for these pale rosés since its dark colour tints the wine with only short skin contact. Another good example is Korten rosé from **Domaine Boyar** (www.domaineboyar.com), made from the early ripening and juicy Early Melnik.

International variety pale rosés include **Karabunar Winery**'s (bulgarian-heritage.com) Castellum Pinot Noir Rosé, a pale wine with white cherry and peach fruit, **Domaine Peshtera**'s (www.domainepeshtera.com) Pixels Rosé from Grenache, and **Bononia**'s (bononiaestate.com) Ooh La La from Cabernets Franc and Sauvignon.

Darker styles made with local varieties are appearing too. **Logodaj** (www.logodajwinery.com) makes the fruity Nobile rosé with the Broadleafed Melnik variety which is more successful than some of the tough reds made from this variety. **Borovitza** (baiw.org/en/winery-borovitza) makes a slightly darker rosé with Gamza (Kadarka).

Some wineries use *saignée* to concentrate the reds and use the run-off to make rosé. **Black Sea Gold**'s (www.bsgold.bg) Pentagram Syrah is made this way, as is Peshtera's **Villa Yambol** (villayambol.com) Rosé (Cabernet Sauvignon with 13.5% abv and 5g/l residual sugar), the biggest selling rosé in Bulgaria. Some wineries that were set up only to make reds, **Bessa Valley** (www.bessavalley.com) for instance, are now making rosé too; their Enira, from Merlot, Syrah and Cabernet Sauvignon came about due to market demand.

Some of the new small wineries are clearly doing different things to experiment and to make a statement, such as **Zagreus** (zagreus.org) Hand Made Rosé from Mavrud, which is fermented in acacia barrels, and **Alexandra Estate**'s (www.alexandraestate.com) Malbec Rosé.

There is the occasional Sauvignon Blanc-based pink with small percentage of red wine, such as the new winery **Stratsin** (www.stratsinwinery.bg), along with a range called Classic, which is darker and sweeter.

Romania

During the communist era, centuries of viticultural traditions were destroyed. Lands were confiscated, hillside vines uprooted and industrial-scale vineyards planted on the plains. After the revolution, everything was privatized. Quality wine only started to reappear around 2000.

In 2016, 63 per cent of production was white wine and 37 per cent red and rosé combined, with rosé probably being a minor part. In 2016 the rosé production in the highest Romanian denomination (DOC, *denumire de origine controlata*) was 1.2 per cent of the total but rosé is also produced under the three other denominations: *indicație geografică* (geographical indication), *vin varietal* (not DOC, not IG but allowed to write the grape variety on the label) and Romanian wine (without DOC, IG or variety on the label).

In 2016, one of Romania's largest wine producers, **Vincon Romania** (www.vincon.ro), forecast that their mainstream and premium rosé sales would increase by 35 per cent that year. They then relaunched their Rosé Verite, an off-dry Cabernet Sauvignon rosé, in a new, trendy bottle shape. The speed in growth of rosé production meant that in 2016 Gianina Rusu, Vincon's financial director, was already estimating that the rosé production would be 'double that of 2015' which was already up 51 per cent on 2014, despite rosé production only starting in 2008. According to a Nielsen study, the Romanian rosé market in 2015 reached 2 million litres by volume and US$13 million. Maria Gavrilescu, Vincon's marketing director, believes that rosé consumption is dependent on many factors but also, most obviously, that 'because of the colour, the general perception is that rosé is a wine for women, especially when off-dry and during [romantic] dates'. She did however clarify that price point significantly impacted this perception, with premium, super-premium and dry rosés most likely to find acceptance among a male audience.

In 2017 the leading Romanian business newspaper *ZF English* (www.zfenglish.com), estimated, based on market data analysis, that rosé has reached some 15 per cent of wine consumption in Romania. This would make Romania the second biggest consumer of rosé in Europe (in terms of market share, not quantity, and excluding consumption of Italian sparkling rosé). The average Romanian drinks 4.5 litres of rosé per year, just under a third of the level consumed in France.

It is hard to define a Romanian style, but the more developed the region, and the better the producer, the more a regional character emerges. Following a 2017 tasting held by Zoltán Szövérdfi-Szép of sixty-eight Romanian rosés to try and establish the regional trends, the general conclusion was that Romanian rosé production is still in its infancy. Even though some top producers are trying Provence-style rosés, amongst their top six rosés there were some very dark styles.

According to Caroline Gilby MW, Romanian Pinot Noir gives the most elegant rosés, while Fetească Neagră gives 'sour cherry and violets'.

North East Romania

Moldova, the biggest producing region, is in the east-northeast (confusingly) on the border with the Republic of Moldova. The northern part of the region has high altitude vineyards and a cooler climate. The south is lower, warmer and drier. In the far south, there can be a problem with acidity, and a tendency towards a slightly higher level of residual sugar. Two good examples are **Crama Gîrboiu**'s (www.cramagirboiu.ro) Cabernet Sauvignon, Merlot and Fetească Neagră blend, which is 20 per cent barrel-aged for two months, producing a weighty wine, with some tannins, dominated by sweet red fruits, with a long finish. **Gramma Winery**'s (www.crameromania.ro) Fetească Neagră and Merlot blend, is dominated by flowers and fruit with high acidity, and is exceptionally elegant.

Two local varieties have become fashionable for rosé. Băbească Neagră (black old lady), the same grape Moldovans (from the Republic of Moldova) call Rara Neagră. Its high acidity, light body and smooth tannins make it good for rosé and it has been compared to Pinot Noir. It is currently used in rosé blends with Busuioaca and Feteasca Neagră by **Averesti** (vindeaveresti.ro). Busuioacă de Bohotin, an aromatic pink-skinned Muscat variety, produces a dark pink wine, with notes of honeysuckle and ripe juicy peaches, and sometimes a barely perceptible aroma of bitter almonds. At full ripeness, it can achieve 250–270 potential grams per litre of sugar, with natural high acidity.

Both dry and off-dry versions of Busuioacă from **Casa de Vinuri Cotnari** (www.vinuricotnari.ro) are made. The dry Colocviu la Paris reflects the naturally high sugar content of the ripe grapes, with 14% abv, but still retains fresh and well-defined acidity. The aromatic fruit has hints of peach, ginger, pepper and orange peel. The off-dry Iris has lower alcohol at 12% abv, with residual sugar emphasizing the rose-petal and peach aromas, and a softer, creamier character with grapey Muscat fruit, hints of tangerine peel and fresh acidity.

South to south-east: Oltenia

Drăgășani vineyards lie on hills rising up to between 300 and 400 metres above the Olt river (the country's largest after the Danube). The wines from this region are typically slightly more elegant. The 100 per cent Cabernet Sauvignon **Stirbey** 2015 (www.stirbey.com) made by German winemaker Oliver Bauer (who has his own estate – see below) has red fruit, an elegant nose, crisp acidity and a long finish. **Avincis** (www.avincis.ro) 2015 is a Cabernet Sauvignon and Merlot blend, with white and tropical fruits, vine peach, red fruit and fresh cranberry with herbs and spice on the finish (made by French winemaker Ghislain Moritz). **Bauer**'s (www.cramabauer.com) 2016 from Negru de Drăgășani 100 per cent is fruity and elegant, and Bauer has discovered it ages well (I am holding him to his promise to taste some older vintages with me). Negru de Drăgășani is a 1993 cross between Negru Vartos and Băbească, producing grapes with juicy black cherry and berry fruit.

> ### Domeniul Coroanei Segarcea
> 4A Unirii Street, Segarcea, 205400 Dolj
> Tel.: 251 210 516
> www.domeniulcoroanei.com
>
> Oltenia also has many quality rosé producers including Domeniul Coroanei Segarcea. Domeniul Coroanei has, since 2005, been working with Ghislaine Guiraud from Montpellier University, who wanted to do something completely different and to experiment, making Romania's (possibly) first oaked rosé, Hope, in 2011. Guiraud, retiring in 2017, has been training a former student, Ombeline Pages, to take on her portfolio.
>
> Minima Moralia Hope is only made in exceptional years. The 2014 vintage was aged for between one and three months in old barrels. The Pinot Noir (40 per cent) and Cabernet Sauvignon (30 per cent), both had 4-6 hours of maceration, while the Pinot Gris (30 per cent) was given 12 hours of maceration. The Cabernet was aged for four months in new French barrels. The Pinot Noir and the Pinot Gris were aged in stainless steel tank with *battonage* for over a month. Oak flavours are barely noticeable, but the oak does give weight to the smooth, creamy structure. Vibrant Pinot cherry fruit and Cabernet berry fruit are present, with powerful, mouth-watering acidity. The Elite Rosé (100 per cent Pinot Noir) is dry, with almost sweet, ripe cherry fruit, good weight and structure and mouth-watering acidity.

Before 1938 Tămâioasă Roză was called Muscat de Frontignan; it is a pink Muscat. It is a only grown around the small town of Segarcea in the west of the region. Three thousand old vines, planted between 1906 and 1920, were found while clearing the old communist vineyards. From cuttings sent to France for grafting, they now have 14 hectares. **Domeniul Coroanei** (www.domeniulcoroanei.com) harvests them in late September, resulting in enough sugar to obtain both good alcohol levels (12.5% abv) and 27g/l residual sugar. Good acidity levels balance the sugar, creating a wine with beautiful, floral, red fruit and delicate sweetness.

Dealu Mare, Dealurile Munteniei (Hills of Muntenia)

Due to the clay layer above the limestone in these hills in south-central Romania, the soils remain humid even in drought and provide good drainage during heavy rains. Temperatures are cooler higher up near the mountains. The Carpathians also protect the vineyards east of Tohani from the icy Russian wind (*krivatz*).

Muntenia, including the Dealu Mare appellation, produces elegant rosés with a higher level of complexity compared to other regions. In terms of elegance, SERVE is the leading winery. Aurel Rotărescu, the charming winemaker, has been making wine here since communist times, giving him a great depth of knowledge of the region and varieties. His first dry rosé was in 1996. His Sissi rosé 2016 (Pinot Noir, 12.5% abv) is elegant with crisp acidity, a fruity, elegant nose with a complex blend of sweet raspberry, sour cherry and tropical fruits, with long citrus and red fruit berry acidity on the finish. Julia Scavo noted 'redcurrant, sour cherry and raspberry. Long refreshing finish, perfect balance, intensity, with a delicate body,' and enthused that this was 'all we want from a rosé!' Their medium-bodied Terra Romana 2016, made of 51 per cent Fetească Neagră and 49 per cent Merlot is full of strawberry and red fruits, with high acidity and a long, crisp finish with sugared grapefruit notes.

Davino (www.davino.ro), Aurelia Vișinescu at **Domeniile Sahateni** (aureliavisinescu.com) and the Antinori-owned **Vitis Metamorfosis** (www.vitis-metamorfosis.com) make dry rosés worth trying.

Crama Basilescu (cramabasilescu.ro) Busuioaca de Bohotin 2012, tasted with four years of age, had taken on an orange-pink colour with marmalade, barley sugar, quince and hints of dill aromas. There are fresh red fruits, redcurrants and raspberry jam. Good acidity balances the high sugar levels (120g/l residual sugar). A younger vintage tasted with two years of age was evidently fresher but with similar fruit character that showed candied orange peel, marmalade, peach jam and honey with herbal notes, orange peel, ginger, spices and raisins, and a long aromatic finish.

West: Banat, Crișana, Maramureș

Banat and Crișana are in the west-north-west, on the Hungarian border. This area is generally affected by the climate of the Hungarian Pannonian plains. Vineyards closer to the West Carpathians may rise to 500 metres, but most lie between 80 and 200 metres. Temperatures are moderate with low frost risk and ample rain.

On the whole, the Banat wines are easy-drinking and popular. **Recas Sole** (cramelerecas.ro/en), made with 100 per cent Merlot, is worth noting. In Crișana, further north, they have more body. **Elite Wine** (elitewine.ro) in Miniș has an elegant 70 per cent Pinot Noir, 30 per cent Fetească Neagră blend with crisp acidity, and lovely natural fruits. 'Carassia', the traditional sparkling wine of **Carastelec Winery** (www.carastelecwinery.com) and Bendis, the *charmat* sparkling wine from **Petro Vaselo** (petrovaselo.com) winery, both made of Pinot Noir, are attractive sparkling rosés.

Many Romanian rosés, especially at the entry level, are off-dry or sweeter. The best have a good balance of sweetness and acidity, are completely dry or very sweet. The – perhaps surprising – conclusion I came to when tasting Romanian rosés was just how much they had to offer in their own right, not merely as imitations of international styles.

NORTH OF THE BLACK SEA

Winemaking has a long tradition in Ukraine dating back to the fourth century BC, beginning in the southern Crimea and later furthered by Orthodox monks around Kiev and Chernihiv. The first large winery in modern times (near Yalta) was established during the rule of Catherine II (the Great), making primarily fortified, dessert and a little red wine. Pink Muscats are traditional in the southern part of the Crimea.

Massandra
Vynoroba Yehorova St. 9, Yalta, Crimea
www.massandra.co.uk

Massandra South Coast Rosé Muscat wine is a medium-dry rosé dessert wine with grapey, floral fruit. The grapes, grown on southern plots of land with slate soil, are typically harvested when natural sugar reaches 26 per cent. Some old wines are still available, with searches on the internet showing auction houses and specialist wine merchants selling wines such as the 1929 Livadia, 1939 Gurzuf and the 1947 Massandra Collection Pink Muscat for Sotheby's. Massandra is still an active winery. The Dessert Rosé Muscat, produced since 1945, and the Massandra Rosé Muscat, made since 1955 are both aged in oak casks for two years. Aromas of Muscat and tea roses are noticeable on both wines, which have high alcohol and sugar (16% abv and 20g/l residual sugar for the Massandra Rosé).

The Magarach Institute
Kirova St. 21, Yalta, Crimea

Part of the Ukranian Academy of Agricultural Sciences, this was founded by Tsar Nicholas I in 1828 to be a model of winemaking and winemaking research. The 1836 Muscat Pink from the Institute's Magarach collection, is listed in the *Guinness World Records* book as the oldest existing Russian wine. The Institute still functions as the scientific research station for the local wine industry. Their Muscat Pink Magarach is made with technology developed at the end of the nineteenth century.

The **Inkerman Winery** (inkerman.ru/wine) makes a pink dessert Muscat from Chersonesus.

EASTERN MEDITERRANEAN

Greece

A tenth of Greek wine production is rosé, but this is slowly growing, driven by its popularity amongst women drinkers and tourists. The pink trend in Greece appears to have initially been driven by female drinkers, with ouzo preferred by men. Until six or seven years ago, most rosés were a pronounced pink-red colour with vibrant fruit but, with the fashionable trend for very pale rosés, over half the production is now pale.

In 2010 Konstantinos Lazarakis MW wrote on Elloinos (www.elloinos.com):

Once widely ignored, rosés today are some of the most appealing and versatile wines that can accompany food. Almost every wine-producing region in Greece produces a wine of this kind from local grape varieties and, therefore, Greek rosés come in a wide range of styles and can be suited to any taste. However, whatever grape variety is used ... they share some common characteristics in order to appeal to the Greek palate. They all display a great fruit character, freshness and are extremely pleasing, inviting one to enjoy a glass or two.

While there are also excellent rosés made with international varieties, I have concentrated here on the indigenous varieties of Greece and its islands, which are unique.

Xinomavro

This variety is largely used for red wines, but a few rosés are made, especially in the north of Greece, near Thessaloniki, where the cooler climate accentuates the fresh, tart cherry fruit and minerality of the variety. Examples include **Chatzivaritis Estate**'s (chatzivaritis.gr) Chloe, while Nikos Karatzas at **Oenops Wines** (www.facebook.com/pg/oenopswines) makes his Apala with 60 per cent Xinomavro and 40 per cent Cabernet Sauvignon; the wine was described by Yiannis Karasakis MW as having unique notes of 'cherries, laurel, tomato undertones and sweet spices. Ripe and fresh. Mint and basil on the palate with bright acidity, low tannins and fruit purity.' Amyndeon, where the vines benefit from cool summers, has its own rosé appellation. **Kir Yianni** (kiryianni.gr) makes the 100 per cent Xinomavro Akakies, in both still (dry) and sparkling (semi-dry) versions. **Karanikas** (www.karanika.com) also makes a sparkling brut rosé, as does **Thymiopoulos** (www.thymiopoulosvineyards.gr) from Naoussa. For Yiannis Karakasis MW, 'the rosés from Amyndeon are excellent because you get the freshness, the precision and the elegance all together ... It is a pity that not too many produce wines from this region.'

Agiorgitiko

Further south in central Greece, Agiorgitiko can be found in a range of rosés. With naturally low acidity, this variety benefits from the additional acidity obtained at high altitude. Given a short maceration, this variety can produce rosés with bright, ruby red pink tones and vibrant, ripe cherry fruit. A good example is Rousala by **Bizios** (www.biziosestate.gr) in the Asprokambos Valley (800–850 metres altitude). The wine has 12–15 hours cold maceration and cold fermentation to give a fresh, cherry fruit rosé. **Gaia** (www.gaia-wines.gr) with vines at 800 metres, long, cold maceration for 14–18 hours and cold fermentation, makes a fresh cherry fruit rosé with hints of fresh green herbaceous notes. Agiorgitiko is sometimes blended with other grapes, such as Syrah, for greater weight and black fruit, as in the case of **Semeli**'s (www.semeliwines.gr) Oreinos Helios, made with Agiorgitiko grown at 600 metres. It is also occasionally made in a Provence style, such as **La Tour Melas** (latourmelas.com) Idylle (33 per cent Agiorgitiko, 33 per cent Grenache, 33 per cent Syrah), made by French winemaker Elsa Picard, which has good, vibrant acidity, but less fruit than the darker versions. An interesting *vin gris* is made with 15 per cent Agiorgitiko and 85 per cent Cabernet Sauvignon by **Angelos Noulas** (www.noulaswines.gr) from Atalanti in Attica. It is given short, cold prefermentation maceration and fermented dry. Released with a few years of age, the vintage available in 2017 was 2013, proving a rosé can age and have depth and complexity.

Moschofilero

Skouras (www.skouras.gr) make a Cuvée Prestige (70 per cent Agiorgitiko grown at 850 metres, 30 per cent Moschofilero 750 metres), with the Moschofilero giving extra perfume to the fresh red fruit. A few producers make rosés purely with Moschofilero, yielding rich, floral aromatics, although care must be taken not to over macerate to obtain a pink colour since that can result in an overly phenolic character. Good examples are **Gentilini**'s (www.gentilini.gr) Notes from the island of Kefalonia, which has three days of cold extraction, for a bright pink rosé with lots of floral aromas (although only 6,000 bottles are made) and **Palivos**'s (palivos.gr) La Vie en Rose, PDO Mantineia in Arkadia. Tomi rosé from **Troupis Winery** (www.troupiswinery.gr) from vineyards at 700 metres, is pale pink with a rich floral nose and perfumed fruit.

The pale pink Iereia from the **Bosinakis Winery** (www.bosinakis.gr) has fragrant roses and *loukum* (Turkish Delight) aromas. **Panikos Lantides** (www.lantides.gr) Nemea, makes a pale Moschofilero rosé which, he noted was a style preferred by tourists coming to Greece. He also makes a darker, more complex rosé which is sold to Greek restaurants in Germany, Austria and Belgium.

Limniona

This red variety from Thessaly has recently been revived. It has rich, black fruit, good acidity and silky tannins. **Theopetra Estate** (www.tsililis.gr) and **Domaine Zafeirakis** (domainezafeirakis.gr) use Limniona with Syrah in their rosés. Theopetra's is more structured and Zafeirakis's more delicate.

Mavrotragano and Avgoustiatis

Toinos (www.toinos.com) Mavrosé, from the Cycladean island of Tinos, with vines on granite soils at 450 metres, is a blend of 50 per cent Mavrotragano and 50 per cent Avgoustiatis which has fresh strawberry and cherry fruit with fresh acidity and mineral length. Further south, on the island of Santorini, **Sigalas**'s (www.sigalas-wine.com) EAN is also made with Mavrotragano.

Kotsifali

In Crete, **Silva**'s (www.silvawines.gr) Psithiros blends local variety Kotsifali with Grenache for a ripe fruit flavour with garrigue-type aromas. **Diamantakis**'s (www.diamantakiswines.gr) Prinos uses 70 per cent Syrah with 30 per cent Mandalaria. Grapes are harvested from small plots at 450 metres altitude, with minimal skin contact during the making of the wine. A traditional dark pink rose with lots of wild berry fruit, fresh acidity and a firm tannic finish.

Across all varieties, Karakasis noted changing styles 'from the sweet rosé of the past to lighter more Provence-style with impressive packaging. Xinomavro, Agiorgitiko and Moschofilero based wines show more character but there is also excitement from blends between indigenous and international varieties. Greek rosé is a work in progress.'

Cyprus

Cyprus' geographical isolation protected it when phylloxera struck elsewhere and the island was untouched. Today the island is still phylloxera-free, with older vines on their own rootstocks. Traditionally the rosés are dark in colour here. In 1965 Allan Sichel commented on the *kokineli* style of rosé: 'The term "rosé" is comparative, the wines being lighter in colour than most Cyprus wines, but often scarcely light enough to merit this description in comparison with other rosés.'

Today traditional Cypriot rosés can be bright pomegranate pink, dark enough to almost be pale red wines with pronounced ripe fruit, fresh acidity and a delicate hint of tannin. Pale Provence-style wines are also made for the export and tourist markets.

Eighty-five per cent of production is IGP, with new appellations launched in 2007, encouraging the quality wines of the higher altitude vineyards above 600–750 metres. Solar exposure and poor soils at the higher altitudes produce grapes high in flavour, aroma concentration, and of great intensity. Producers returning to old vineyards up in those hills, have also rediscovered the island's indigenous varieties, all on their own rootstocks. Two are of particular interest for rosés: Maratheftiko and Lefkada, both of which confer a uniqueness not found in Cypriot international-variety rosés.

Maratheftiko

This variety was rediscovered around twenty-five years ago. A low-yielding variety, it represents 3 per cent of Cypriot plantings. It requires co-planting with other varieties for fertilization and fruit development. Maratheftiko produces wines with deep, bright red colour, soft tannins, high acidity and dark berry and floral aromas. A good example is Pampela from **Vouni Panayia** (www.vounipanayiawinery.com), IGP Paphos, made from Maratheftiko and Mavro (13% abv). The vineyards are planted at between 800 and 1,150 metres on calcareous soils amongst the pine forests of the Troodos mountains, with original roots. Unusually for a rosé wine, the fruit is a blend of blue-black fruit with floral hints leading to ripe red fruits and luscious strawberry fruit. Delicate mineral tannins and fresh, leafy acidity give the wine a *clairet* style finish. The **Vasilikon** (vasilikon.com) Einalia 2015, IGP Paphos from Syrah and Maratheftiko has fresh red fruit aromas with hints of toasty lees. This wine is weightier, with powerful, ripe red fruit, strawberry cordial and hints of dry tannins, and seems much more of a red wine. There is wild bramble fruit and fresh acidity with quite a structural, savoury character.

Lefkada (aka Verzami)

Brought to Cyprus by the Byzantines, this variety is mostly found in the Paphos area. It requires a full maturation to avoid astringency, with intense colour and fruity aromas, such as **Zambartas** (www.zambartaswineries.com) 2015 from Lefkada and Cabernet Franc. Ripe, sweet strawberries and raspberries provide a jammy lusciousness but the wine is not sweet and has firm, mineral structure with crisp, leafy, mineral acidity. **Nicolaides** Aphrodino Rosé (Cabernet Sauvignon and Lefkada) has a dark red hue with flavours of sweet, ripe raspberry and earthy notes, with integrated, chewy acidity and a tannin finish (14% abv, 12g/l residual sugar). A good example of high residual sugar in a serious wine: the sugar, when balanced by acidity and complemented by tannin, contributes positively to the body.

Retsina

Retsina developed in ancient times from the habit of coating the inside of amphora, and later, barrels, with Aleppo pine (*Pinus halepensis*) resin to protect and preserve the wines during storage and transport. The name retsina as a protected designation of origin and traditional appellation for Greece and parts of the southern regions of Cyprus.

Retsina was an everyday drink in the 1960s when it was first bottled. The Kechris family had produced Kechribari retsina since 1939. Until the 1950s it was drunk draught from the barrel (as the resin is said to protect the wine from oxidation) or in bulk. By the 1970s, the quality of retsina had started to go downhill. The yields grew, fermentation moved to giant tanks, and less careful winemaking led to a decline in quality. Greater quantities of resin were added to cover the faults and the bad reputation for retsina settled in. International winemakers arrived in the 1980s and improvements in red and white wines started but, similarly to rosé, retsina was left behind as a rustic folk wine.

> **Kechris**
> 33, Olympou St. 57 009 Kalochori, Thessaloniki
> Tel.: 23107 51283
> www.kechri.gr
>
> In 1984, Stelios Kechris took over the family domaine, determined to restore their retsina to its former glory. Modern retsina is made with a lump of resin placed in the fermentation tank, which seems simple enough, but as Kechris and his oenoligist daughter Eleni explained, they are continuously working to improve their wines. The balance of ripe fruit and high acidity is important to balance the resin. This is harvested from different locations, and the taste will vary according to location and vintage. Some resins can be very bitter. This is still a new study and regional styles are still being identified. The choice of the resin will depend on the vintage and wine potential.
>
> Their first rosé retsina was made in 2010. Made with Xinomavro, the wine undergoes cold temperature maceration for 24 to 36 hours before fermentation in barrel. A piece of resin is placed in the barrel and the wine fermented at a temperature which brings out the fruit flavour, while restraining the resin character, yielding a bright, ruby-pink colour. The wine has vibrant cherry fruit with long, fresh acidity and a touch of the mineral eucalyptus resin character. The oak is not evident on aromas and flavours, but contributes extra weight and depth.

Turkey

Turkey is not the most obvious place to go seeking intriguing rosés. Despite an ancient winemaking history, modern commercial wineries only began in the 1920s, under Atatürk. When, in 1927, alcohol production was nationalized, wineries were spared, and eventually supported by the government.

By 1946 there were 28 small-sized wineries across the country. During the 1950s, French grape varieties were brought in, leading to a decline in quality and volume. The arrival of wine-drinking tourists by the late 1980s was the impetus for wineries to invest in technology and quality, and today over 600,000 hectares are planted under vine (the fourth largest area in the world), although most are table grapes. According to the International Organization of Vine and Wine (OIV), total wine production in 2005 was 287,000 hectolitres, of which about 1 per cent was rosé, although the precise amount is uncertain.

Ampelographers estimate that Turkey is home to between 600 and 1,200 indigenous varieties of *Vitis vinifera*, though fewer than sixty of these are grown commercially. Some of the native Turkish varieties include Yapıncak and Papazkarası, grown in Thrace; the Sultaniye of the Aegean coast; the Öküzgözü (Turkish for 'ox eye', named after the size of its grey-blue fruits) and Boğazkere (used to make Buzbağ) of Eastern Anatolia; the Çalkarası of the Denizli Province in Western Anatolia, and the Kalecik Karası, Narince and Emir of Central Anatolia.

A couple of regions stand out. In Thrace, **Gülor** winery (www.gulorwine.com) was established in 1993 by Güler Sabancı. Their Rosé 2015 (80 per cent Öküzgözü, 20 per cent Sangiovese) was made with direct press, four-hour skin contact and tank fermentation at 17°C. Its firm, mineral and savoury-fruit structure, makes it more of a serious dining rosé than an aperitif wine.

The Aegean coast, mostly near İzmir, accounts for 20 per cent of Turkey's wine production. Its more pronounced Mediterranean climate becomes harsher at altitude, where mild winters and warm summers give way to temperatures as high as 40°C in summer and as low as -10°C in winter. Soils range from clay loam in the lower elevations to calcareous chalks at 1,100 metres.

Rosés here are often made with the Çalkarası grape, which is typically characterized by fresh, red fruit and floral notes. Some notable examples include Leyla 2016 from **Kavakidere Saraplari** (www.kavaklidere.com) Aegean, 100 per cent Çalkarası. Pale in colour, typical of fresher international styles, the wine is dry with fresh acidity but with complex notes, zesty umami and orange flavours, reminiscent of a more aged rosé. The complex flavours of this wine just keep growing. **Paşaeli**'s (www.pasaeli.com) Blush, also 100 per cent Çalkarası, comes from vines at 850 metres where the warm days and cool nights preserve acidity. Minimal skin contact – under two hours – gives a pale colour which is successful in export markets. Fermented in tank, it is aged on lees for three months. The wine has good structure and weight, and mouth-watering acidity but it is not an overtly fruity wine. Paşaeli makes another wine from 100 per cent Çalkarası, with fourteen hours' skin contact to give the wine a darker colour and full-bodied red fruit with some tannic structure, almost like a light *clairet*, and with the same mouth-watering acidity.

Eski Üzüm, which means 'old grape', is a barely known variety. It is farmed by few growers in the north Aegean and Paşaeli is the only rosé producer of this variety. Owner Seyit Karagozoğlu is 'very, very excited about this variety. I know we have "rediscovered" an old variety that was on its way to being extinct. Now we must work to preserve it! It is a red grape, not black, so the wine is more gris than noir.' Paşaeli's Eski Üzüm has a pale colour after only four hours of skin contact. The wine is very delicate with good crisp acidity.

The remaining portion of Turkey's wine production takes place in scattered pockets throughout the Eastern and Central Anatolia regions. The region of Central Anatolia is the most climatically difficult region in which to produce wine, with most vineyards located at altitudes close to 1,250 metres. Winter frost is a serious viticultural hazard, with winter temperatures often dropping as low as -25°C. In the summer, grapes of this region can receive up to 12 hours of sunshine a day. The vineyards of Eastern Anatolia around Elazığ, Malatya and Diyarbakır are located in the Euphrates valley.

Gordias' Nana Gordias 2014 is 95 per cent Kalecik Karasi and 5 per cent Muscat Hamburg. Grapes were grown at 1,150 metres and processed with short skin contact and cool fermentation in tank. Ripe and jammy with intense black fruit and near-sweet ripeness, the wine is almost voluptuous, with fresh acidity carrying the fruit.

14
THE BUSINESS OF ROSÉ

THE GROWTH OF ROSÉ

Rosé wine was once a wine just like red wine or white. Straightforward, simple. Starting maybe thirty years ago, rosé started its climb to fashion. Its share of worldwide wine consumption has been growing, from 7.8 per cent in 2002 to 9.7 per cent in 2016, growth of almost a quarter, at the expense of other wines, over a period with largely static world wine consumption.

Demand for rosé wine is growing strongly, especially in the US, and having a big effect round the world. In common with other wines, the share of rosé crossing borders has increased in recent years, as wine becomes more international. Although rosé is increasingly traded internationally – in 2002, 22 per cent of worldwide rosé production was exported, rising to 38 per cent in 2017 – the majority is still consumed in the country which produced it. Domestic markets, with their local traditions, are therefore important.

The first book on rosé wine was published in 2007 by rosé winemaker Jeff Morgan, *Rosé, A Guide to the World's Most Versatile Wine*, but has long been out of print. A sign of rosé's rise is the publication of four recent books, starting in 2016 with *Rosévin – Historien, vinerna & maten därtill* (*Rosé Wine – the Story, Wines & Matching Foods*) in Swedish, because, according to the author, Anders Mellden, 'there were no books, and the small information in wine literature was normally not up to date'. Three more followed in the US, in the first half of 2017, all consumer-oriented: *Rosé All Day: The Essential Guide to Your New*

Favorite Wine by Katherine Cole, *Rosé Wine: The Guide to Drinking Pink* by Jennifer Simonetti-Bryan MW, and *Drink Pink, A Celebration of Rosé* by Victoria James.

Two technical books have been written. In 2009 *Le Vin Rosé*, edited by Claude Flanzy, Gilles Masson and François Millo, and in 2013 Jan Stávek's *Rosé: veselý i vážný vícebarevný svět vína* (*Rosé: the multicoloured world of wine*, in Czech), based on his doctoral thesis on rosé winemaking.

SELLING THE PINK COLOUR

The most basic definition of rosé wines is that they are pinker than white wines and lighter than red wines. Most importantly, within the range of pinks, the shade or intensity is important.

The colour pink

Articles and postings on social media regularly tell us how fashionable pink is. It is 'in'. The message has become that pink wine is beautiful too, as witnessed by recent press headlines: 'Think pink! How rosé became the booze of choice for millennials' (*Guardian*, UK, July 2017), 'Rosé, really? The story of pink wine's path from tacky to chic' (*Washington Post*, US, June 2017), 'Rosé Is Seeing Explosive Growth as Its Summer Rival, Beer, Goes Flat' (*Bloomberg*, USA, August 2017), 'Le rosé, une manne pour les vignerons' ('Rosé, manna for winemakers', *Le Monde*, France, July 2017), 'We're drinking pink – the rise of rose' (*Newsroom*, New Zealand, March 2017).

In addition to the still, sparkling and fortified wines covered in this book, other alcoholic drinks have been released in pink, reddish or 'rosé' versions, to capitalize on the fashion for things pink and harness the promotional power of social media. Some, like rosé cider, are made from coloured fruit juice (from pink-fleshed apples). For others, coloured juices and flavourings, often to give fruity notes, are added to a conventional base product, such as beer (Hoegaarden Rosée, Kronenbourg 1664 Rosé) and pastis (Pastis 51 Rosé from Pernod). Hamptons-based vineyard Wölffer Estate (see page 122) have gone a step further than the pink gin widely drunk in late nineteenth century Britain (made by mixing gin and Angosutra bitters), by making a rosé gin from a rosé wine base and adding a small amount of grape-skin extract.

Some rosé-related items have a more lighthearted side, tapping into the buzz around rosé, such as gummy bears made from rosé wine. Melissa Kravitz describes an unexpected novelty in her article 'New Ways To Drink Rosé All Day If You're Already Sick Of Pink Wine' (2016) on Forbes.com, 'Beach toys got a booze-friendly transformation this summer, thanks to Wine Awesomeness, which engineered a DIY rosé water gun to help you squirt a boring bottle of pink wine to new levels of exciting.' Its inventor Birk O'Halloran, of Iconic Wine, told me the idea received 'a ton of shares and comments through Facebook, many by wine professionals.'

Frosé – frozen rosé – hit the social media in 2016. It is a slushy cocktail of half-frozen rosé, lemon juice and sugar or fruit, whose proportions depend on the recipe.

The perfect shade

As discussed elsewhere in this book, rosé wines come in many shades, depending on the grapes used, local traditions, and the intended market. Even in 1975, Vandyke Price noted that the colour was often determined by what 'the winemaker thinks will most appeal.'

The growing fashion for Provence rosé has been accompanied by a powerful message that a pale rosé is 'good', that paler is 'better', an indication of quality. This has led many consumers to seek paler rosés and sometimes reject those they see as too dark.

Imogen Blake of the *Daily Mail*, reviewing the UK market (2017), said, 'Paler rosés are becoming more and more popular with customers, with Sainsbury's reporting that sales of their paler Bordeaux and Provence wines have grown by 24 per cent in the last year, before increasing by 58 per cent in the last month. Wine experts have tipped 2017 to be a particularly big year for rosé, as Brits choose lighter and drier styles from the south of France over darker and sweeter varieties such as Zinfandel.'

Many producers – around the world – have told me they feel pressure to make their wines paler. In response, many have lightened the shade of their wines – some just a little, others a lot. Producers usually emphasize that the pressure is to match the *colour* of Provence rosés, not necessarily the *taste*; they are happy to retain their traditional taste. Nonetheless, changing the colour entails at least some change to the taste.

Areas with traditionally dark rosé, such as Tavel and Italy, face a dilemma. Should they respond to the market pressure they experience, and make their rosés paler? Or is the colour part of their brand identity? One response is to retain their traditional wines and add new ones to their range. These new wines can then reach a new customer base, without devaluing the traditional brand. Some have bowed to market pressures and replaced their traditional style with the new, paler rosé; others have chosen instead to work to reinforce their brand and extend their existing market.

In summer 2017 *Decanter*'s Ask Decanter page addressed the question, 'Is pale rosé better?' Ellie Douglas's response was: 'It's a common misconception that the paler the rosé, the better the quality. Paler styles are commonly found in the popular rosé region of Provence, other regions can often have a deeper hue.' She then quotes Nicolas Bronzo from **La Bastide Blanche** winery in Bandol (bastide-blanche.fr), who sees the trend towards pale rosés influencing the winemaking techniques for some: 'You don't want it too dark – a commercial problem exists. We do this by regulating the skin contact.'

Export manager Arianna Zanatta of **Vigneti Villabella** (www.vignetivillabella.com) says they used to make a darker traditional-style *chiaretto* Bardolino. This was harvested at full ripeness and macerated for several hours, to create a full-bodied, darker rosé sold as a gastronomic wine. Villabella abandoned this for a modern-style rosé, harvested slightly under-ripe with much shorter maceration, which is pale, creamy white with a hint of pink, sold as an aperitif wine. Sales tripled with this new international blush style. But is it *chiaretto*?

Bodegas Gordonzello (see p.180), Tierra de Léon, Spain, found that their traditional wines, of dark ruby colour, sold successfully in North and South America, but their colour was less well accepted in Asia and Europe. They felt they had to adapt to their customers, so in 2016 prepared a trial run of 5,000 bottles of a pale international version made with Prieto Picudo. They tested the European market with it in 2017. The paler colour was particularly successful in Switzerland, and least successful in the Netherlands and Denmark.

In response to the trend towards paler rosés, Christian Holthausen in the *Guardian* (2014) was prompted to remind us that colour is only one attribute of a rosé: 'the colour ... actually tells you very little about a rosé's intrinsic value, so it's best to avoid oversimplification. A rosé from Provence is not going to taste like rosé from South Africa, so there's no way to reify a hierarchy of shades of pink. Much depends on style, region, quality and type. Although some rosés are designed to be sweet while others aren't, our individual emotional connections to a particular colour can make us taste "sweetness" that isn't there.'

Just for the girls?

Jason Wilson of the *Philadelphia Enquirer* highlights the struggle against the common perception of rosé as a woman's drink (2012):

> *'What are you, a girl? Is this Girls' Night Out?'*
> *That's what a friend, an investment banker, said on a recent evening as the waiter delivered my glass of rosé wine to the table.*
> *I considered my manly friend, from his pink tailored shirt to the insipid Coors Light he was drinking. 'At this stage of my life,' I said, 'I'm comfortable enough in my manhood to drink pink wine.'*
> *Yeah, that's right. I'm man enough to profess my fondness for rosé wines, especially on a steamy summer evening, before dinner as the sun begins to set. Maybe while poring over the sports page, too, if you need to.*

For whatever reason, pink is seen as girly, to the extent that articles on rosé regularly feel the need to affirm the presence of men as rosé drinkers, as if they – men – need to justify their drinking of pink wine. Thomas Pastuszak, Sommelier & Wine Director of The NoMad Hotel in Manhattan is widely quoted as saying, 'Real men drink pink'. Brian Freedman wrote in *Forbes* in 2016 of the rapid growth of rosé sales in the US: 'Much of this growth is being attributed to men, who make up an increasingly important segment of the market for rosé. In fact, the term "brosé" has been successfully used to refer to the kind of dry pink wine that men can drink with confidence.'

In France, rosé has less of an image problem amongst men. Research paper 'Drink pink: a cross-cultural examination of the perceived image of rosé' in *Wine and Viticulture Journal* (July/August 2016) suggests that:

> *French consumers are very opposed to the idea that rosé is a feminine drink and especially prone to think that it is particularly appropriate*

for a summer's day. Thus, the results of the current study confirm that in France rosé seems to have a reputation of being an inexpensive, light, summer drink, enjoyable and acceptable for all. This image is tied into a ritualistic form of drinking, specifically for holidays, with outside eating, which is much less formal than a typical French meal, but appropriate to particular foods. Yet this viewpoint, whilst it does not see rosés as great wines, nevertheless, considers that they are acceptable for all people in the right circumstances. In France, rosé is seen as a lifestyle accessory rather than a serious wine and a key symbolic marker of relaxation and family time.

THE WINE

The main segments of the market for rosé wine are the still, sparkling and fortified rosés described in detail within this book. Three newer categories are also relevant.

Rosé wines designed for summer, perhaps poolside, drinking with ice, were introduced in 2004 by the cooperative **Vinovalie** (www.vinovalie.com) in Gaillac, France, after director, Jacques Tranier, noticed the trend for putting ice in rosé. Their Rosé Piscine (trademarked, meaning 'Swimming-pool Rosé') has a slightly higher sugar level and a blend of grape varieties to give a stronger flavour suited to dilution. It has been very successful, now selling over 1.3 million bottles in France. In 2014 it was launched in Brazil, and in 2017 in the US.

Flavoured rosé wines have become very popular, largely as inexpensive, everyday summer drinks. 'Any consumer looking for a lower alcohol or rosé wine in a French supermarket will probably end up staring at a bottle of Rosé Pamplemousse [Grapefruit rosé],' wrote Jean-Philippe Perrouty for *Wine Intelligence* (2014). In an article entitled 'Grapefruit Wine Is France's Latest Obsession', Emily Monaco of *Eater* wrote: 'In 2011, a homemade cocktail from Southern France took the rest of the country by storm. In this land of wine, it must have seemed a daring decision: just in time for summer, Maison Castel, a world-renowned Bordelais wine producer, took a risk and released Very Pamp, a bottled cocktail of rosé wine mixed with grapefruit juice. And though they could never have known it at the time, this simple regional specialty would go on to become a national favorite.' Sales figures are impressive. In 2013, 35 million bottles were sold in France, a six-fold increase since 2011.

Lower alcohol rosé wines have been introduced. These 'have been well received, primarily in the rosé wines category, so we will continue to launch in this category in the summer of 2016', wrote Anna Rosenberg, Category Manager at Sweden's Systembolaget. In 2016 FoodBev Media in the UK reported that 'Alcohol-free wine brand Eisberg has added a sparkling white and rosé to its range, as it continues to broaden the non-alcoholic options available to consumers this Christmas.'

Sweet or dry?

The degree of sweetness of rosé wine is as much a personal preference – and subject for debate – as its degree of paleness. Preferred levels vary by country and by market segment.

Sweden's alcohol monopoly Systembolaget highlights (in its *2016 Launch Plan*) the segmentation of rosé wine in Sweden – which is also typical of the USA – and the need to help consumers choose: 'We have also introduced flavour types for rosé in order to make it easier for customers to choose the right drink. This is particularly important now that we are seeing two dominant and, to some extent, opposing flavour trends, namely rosé wines with a clear sweetness, and very dry, Provençale-style [sic] rosé wines.'

After Sutter Home introduced it in 1976, off-dry to sweet white Zinfandel became massively popular in the US. According to USA Trade Tasting (2016), 'While some people refer to White Zinfandel as the "gateway wine" for many Americans, it is also accused of damaging rosé's reputation in the minds of the masses. For a period of time, White Zin was synonymous with sugar-bomb sweetness, the kind that makes your mouth hurt after just half a glass.'

Sweet wines are also popular in South Africa, where in 2016 Distell stated that its sweet rosé 4th Street 'is now the biggest wine brand', and now states it is the world's fastest growing wine brand. South African Wine Industry Information Systems (SAWIS) gives more details in *Liquor Consumption Patterns in South Africa 2015*. Carina Gous, Marketing Director, Wines, for Distell, said that extensive market research indicated an opportunity in the market for sweeter style wines. In 2009, Distell launched 4th Street, a 'sweet rosé, targeting females 20 to 40 years old who aspired to a sophisticated urban life style.' These women 'did not want to drink spirits or beer'. When launched in a 750 millilitre and 1.5 litre pack, growth was slow, but volumes exploded when 3 litre and 5 litre boxes were added. Rising to half of the sweet red and rosé market in the medium price wine sector in 2014, 4th Street grew faster than its competitors, to take 66 per cent of that market in 2015, driven largely by female consumers, in urban areas.

At the opposite end of the sweetness scale come the dry (and pale) Provence-style rosés. This style has become increasingly fashionable, featuring in a constant stream of articles in contemporary general media and wine press. In Europe, rosé wines have tended to be dry, with a few exceptions, such as Rosé d'Anjou from the Loire. Just as pink is 'in' when it comes to rosé, so is dry. In the US, the growth of premium rosés, in an otherwise static market, is in dry and pale rosé.

Rosé d'Anjou and Cabernet d'Anjou have not shared the success of Provence. Producers say that the fashion for Provence rosé – dry and pale – has lured away part of their market. This presents them with an interesting marketing challenge, though perhaps not impossible, given the success of sweet rosé and other sweet wines in some parts of the world and market segments.

Despite the success of dry rosés, sweeter rosés have a good future according to IWSR (International Wine & Spirit Research) analyst Giles Gough. Quoted in the *IWSR Vinexpo Report 2017*, he says, 'Emerging wine markets will be a key driver – especially South Africa – where "natural sweet" rosé has captured the imagination of emerging middle-class drinkers … Even in developed markets, the sweeter rosé style has an important role to play in talking to younger drinkers, who otherwise may defer entry to the category, or not at all.'

The *Wine and Viticulture Journal* research study found two sides to the story in the US. Younger (often female) drinkers, new to the market, tend to prefer 'blush' style wines, which are also sweeter and less expensive. Those who consider themselves more educated drinkers, on the other hand, prefer dry-style wines and consider rosé unacceptable in any context. This may help explain the recent growth in sales of dry rosés in the US.

SEASONALITY

Summer is the popular time for drinking rosé wine. In the northern hemisphere, the peak season is June to August, with interest starting in April and May, and sales tailing-off in September.

Rosé has long been viewed as a summer drink. Nan Ickeringill wrote back in July 1963 in the *New York Times*, 'Summer and roses [sic] go together. When the weather is too hot for a red wine and the food too flavorful for a white wine, a well-chilled rose is the usual compromise. Such a wine is not only light and easy on the palate, but also relatively inexpensive and, at least on the surface, safe to serve with almost anything.'

The market has grown up around the image of drinking cool, refreshing rosé wine in summer. Although many producers would prefer year-round sales, the seasonality has some benefits. Most northern hemisphere rosés are not ready for drinking before spring, so it is very convenient to sell out by the end of the summer. This way payment is received well before autumn and the next harvest.

Over the years, there has been much talk about extending rosé sales beyond the summer season – if this does not reduce summer sales. A Beverage Media Group report on rosé sales by Ed McCarthy quotes Lorena Ascencios, head buyer of Astor Wines and Spirits in New York City as saying, 'Rosés are absolutely selling all year-round. Two years ago I bought a huge number of rosés, and was a bit worried that I'd be stuck with them. In December, customers were still asking for rosés. We sold them all.' Nonetheless, winter sales remain relatively small.

We have particularly clear details of seasonality for Sweden, from the state alcohol monopoly Systembolaget. In 2015:

> *The market share for rosé ... varied from 2.3 per cent in December to 15.8 per cent in July. Rosé wine sales are tracking a globally increasing sales trend, but the summer of 2015 posed challenges in the form of poor weather, which left a clear mark on sales. A completely unscientific comparison between two weeks of bad and good weather*

showed a massive increase in sales of 70 per cent when the sun came out. Rosé is, in other words, very heavily weather-dependent, and shares consumption opportunities with, first and foremost, red wine. The combined red and rosé sales over the summer season is, in principle, constant, and the weather determines which category the customers prefer.

Emelie Westrup, Systembolaget's Category Manager for rosé described how they plan to deal with the seasonality.

It doesn't matter how strong the rosé wine trend is – it will continue to be a seasonal product. We have been wanting to seasonally adjust the range of rosé wines for many years now, and the new evaluation periods from June to August will give us new potential to do precisely that. We're going to be looking at the potential for evaluating the rosé wine category during the peak season alone, and varying the size of the range during the rest of the year, to ensure that the range is constantly adjusted in line with customer demand … This summer, we'll be trialling an expansion of the rosé wines range in a few stores and then cutting it back during the off season. Our hope is that by next year, we'll be able to seasonally adjust the rosé wine range in all of our stores.

In winter 2010, **les Maîtres Vignerons de Saint-Tropez** (www.vignerons-saint-tropez.com) introduced a rosé specially tailored for winter drinking, Grain de Glace. Some is sold to restaurants in ski resorts. Côtes de Provence appellation rules allow release of rosé for sales to consumers on 1 December, leaving just enough time for Christmas sales. The 80,000 bottles produced, though, are a tiny proportion of their sales, hardly reducing overall seasonality.

Christian Holthausen in the *Guardian* (2014) approved the popularity of rosé but misses it outside the summer, 'It is wonderful that rosé is now being appreciated in the absolute sense, but it's still considered to be an exclusively "summer wine" by far too many of us. With the exception of Valentine's Day, it's a tall order to procure a glass of rosé in restaurants between September and May.'

It might be thought that producers from one hemisphere would have an advantage, being able to reach the summer market of the other hemisphere only a few months after production. Felix Riley, of Australian importer Felixir, disabuses us of this:

It's a major challenge for importers reconciling the release of northern hemisphere wines with the local market [Australia]; indeed, this was an early answer to why no other importers were making much of a go of rosé before me. Some French producers bottle very early (December) – this was the first year I managed to land new vintage wines for January, mid the rosé high season; unless ultra-organized it's typically an 8-week turnaround between ordering with a producer and getting the wines landed into warehouse here.

With many producers not bottling until February, even organized importers aren't landing the new vintage until April as the rosé drinking season dwindles here. Sure, some of the jewel domaines (Tempier et al.) may get some interest with their new vintage landing, but I suspect this is a lot of noise with not honestly a huge number of bottles sold. Indeed, the challenge is that the ideal time to ship rosé is August/September – though this is greatly marred by the French August holidays, followed swiftly by vignerons in vintage which stretches the resources of smaller domaines and can render export orders on the back burner!

SHOULD ROSÉ BE DRUNK FRESH – OR AGED?

To prepare for summer sales, major northern hemisphere trade buyers look to place orders from January to March. At this point most rosés can only be tasted *en primeur*, and are not yet ready for drinking, nor showing their best. Buyers take a calculated risk on how these will evolve for the summer season.

As rosé's freshness has been a key selling feature, consumers seek the latest vintage, often rejecting even the preceding vintage if a newer one is present on the shop shelf. This encourages retailers to clear the previous year's stocks before the new vintage hits the shelves for summer. This makes for little interest in older vintages. Rosé is rarely seen as a *vin de garde*, apart from exceptions like Bandol and Tavel. Tastings of old vintages of the latter, led by a sommelier, have been held at the five annual *Couleur Tavel* fairs, celebrating aged Tavel wines, since 2013.

Interest is stirring in aged rosé from other areas, though aged rosé is still a niche product. In 'Discovering *rosé de garde*', in *le Figaro Vin*, 2014, Aymone Vigière d'Anval reported the introduction by the Provence Wine Board (the CIVP) of a new section for aged rosés (*vins rosés de garde*) to its annual *Concours des Vins de Provence* competition. This was open to vintages from 2010 and earlier; the vintage cut-off is raised each year. Despite the free publicity to medal winners, the number of entries is small.

Consumers – and producers – need to be educated about good aged rosés and what to expect from these. On asking rosé producers for 'old vintages' to taste, they have often expressed surprise at my interest. Many keep no bottles of previous vintages; even those that do, rarely try them. When a producer shares an old bottle of rosé with me, he is usually very pleasantly surprised by the character of the wine. *Vins de garde* can be an attractive sales niche, a way to stand out from the crowd and enhance a vineyard's reputation, but at the moment they are not a significant part of the market. Interestingly, my highest ever score when judging a rosé was for an aged rosé, the Cuvée Margoton 2010 by Olivier Leflaive in Burgundy. Tasted in 2016 its complex fruit character and beautiful Pinot Noir fruit was outstanding.

ENTRY-LEVEL VERSUS EXPERIENCED DRINKERS

The age of consumers affects their interest in rosé. The 2015 Gallo Consumer Wine Trends Survey found that Millennials are almost twice as likely to purchase rosé as Baby Boomers, and four times more likely to select a bottle of wine based on its label. This latter may explain the non-traditional names given to some new brands – to make them appeal to Millennials. Much of the promotional activity for rosé is oriented towards Millennials, who seem to be the main participants, for example, of the festivals Pinknic and La Nuit en Rosé.

In South Africa, many drinkers stick with the sweet rosé which is popular as an introduction to wine. Katlego Mkhwanazi, in her article 'Rosé in the pink on local wine market' for South African newspaper *Mail & Guardian*, wrote that 'Marilyn Cooper, former chief executive of the Cape Wine Academy and cofounder of the Soweto Wine and Lifestyle Festival, says rosé is perfect for people who've just started drinking wine. Sweet rosé is often people's first introduction to wine before they move on to sweet whites, dry whites, soft reds and, lastly, heavier reds. But many often fail to explore a range of wines beyond the pink drink.' As mentioned earlier South Africa's leading rosé brand, Distell's 4th Street, is sweet and aimed at young, urban women.

As mentioned above (Sweet or dry?, p.285), the experience of US drinkers may affect their preference for sweet or dry rosé.

PACKAGING

Bottle design

Wine is usually supplied in bottles typical to the region of production. Although producers often follow the same pattern for their rosé wines as for their whites and reds, they sometimes use different bottles, sometimes to distinguish one range from another.

Provence wines are unusual for using innovative bottle shapes, not standard Bordeaux or Burgundy bottles, often to make their wines stand out. During the 1930s, local producers of quality wines started to think of bottling their wine – as opposed to relying on a *négociant* or shipper – and decided to design their own bottles. During the 1980s, it was not uncommon to visit a Provençal domaine which used an individual bottle shape, to be told that it had been designed by the grandmother. Competition must have been intense, as families vied to design the most elegant and distinctive bottle. Many used classical amphorae or medieval jars as their inspiration. Some are versions of the skittle bottle or *flûte à corset*. Domaine Ott still uses bottles designed in 1930 by René Ott, with the long sloping shoulders resembling that of the Rhone bottle: bulging middle and narrow base with a small flared rim. Aimed at the restaurant market, the new bottle was instantly recognizable as from Domaine Ott.

Baron Louis Rasque de Laval of Château Sainte Roseline told me (in 1989) how, in 1949, the *Lampe de Meduse* (Torch of Medusa) shaped bottle, based on an ancient lantern with wide base and long tapering neck, was created by his family, and named after the *Ordre Illustre des Chevaliers de Méduse*, a seventeenth-century fraternity which guaranteed wine to returning sailors in Marseille. As with Ott, the bottle (still used) is instantly recognizable as from Sainte Roseline.

By 1962, the growers Syndicat de Côtes de Provence were encouraging a uniform bottle style and chose the *flûte à corset*, usually known in English as the 'skittle' bottle because of its shape. This is widely recognized, though sometimes with mixed reactions. Although widely adopted at first, use has fallen as Provence's market has grown. It is often appreciated in the US, where it is seen as embodying the attractive image of Provence. In France it tends to be viewed as old-fashioned, and associated with pre-1990s rosés, seen as less interesting than the current wines (see illustration of bottle shapes).

Dr Jamie Goode described for *Meininger's Wine Business International* a good example of using bottle shape as a selling tool (2015). 'Château de Berne [in Provence] are now widely known for their distinctive square bottle. Thomas Lagarde, wine director at Vignobles de Berne, explains that four years ago he had problems selling a Viognier wine, until he put it in a square 50 cl bottle, and then it sold out. So he started using this bottle across the range, giving customers a choice between the new bottle and the standard one. "Eighty per cent were buying the square bottle, so we shifted," he says'. As sixty per cent of de Berne's production uses this shape, the price premium on the bottles – which cost twice the standard price of €0.30 – is presumably worthwhile.

Personally, I have a love-hate relationship with the fancy bottle designs. Some of these fantasy bottles are very beautiful and creative, attracting attention on the shop shelf and on a restaurant table. However, the purist in me would prefer a sober bottle where the quality of the wine and reputation of the producer is a sufficient attraction. I even find myself ignoring the fancy bottles as a gimmick, trying to show off.

THE BUSINESS OF ROSÉ 293

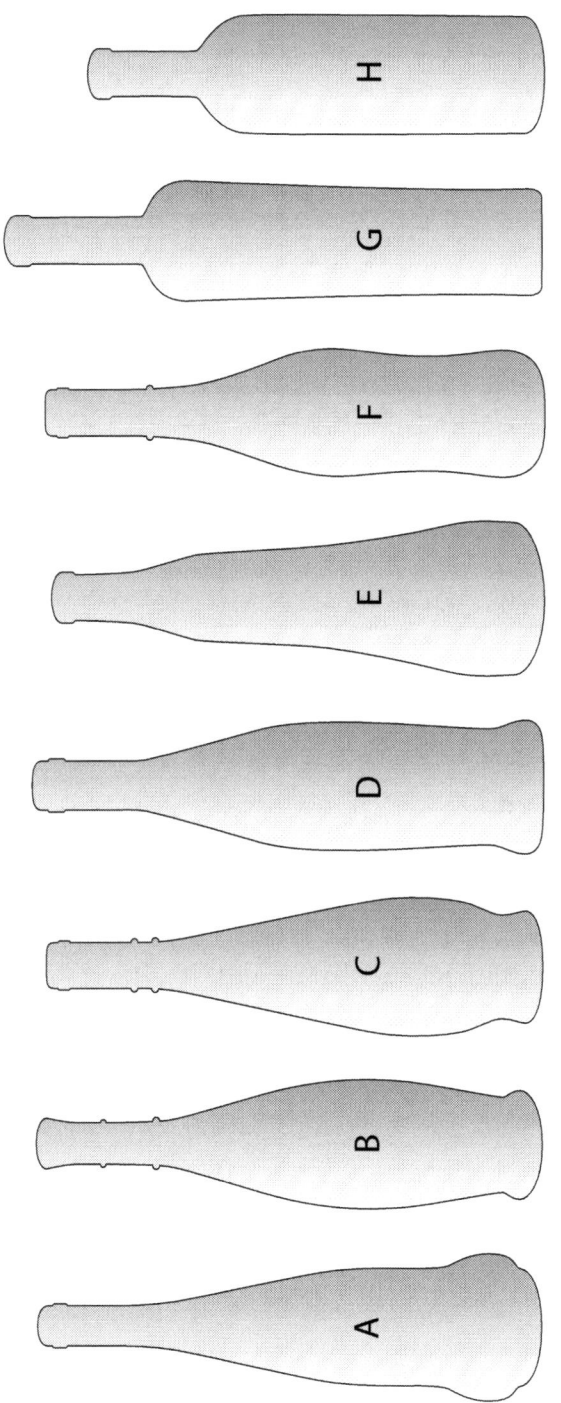

The evolution of rosé wine bottle shapes. A, Lampe de Meduse, Ste Roseline; B, Domaine Ott; C and D, Château l'Aumerade; E, Provence (originally the négociant bottle) F, Provence flûte à corset; G, Château de Berne; H, classic Bordeaux bottle.

Bottle colour

Most rosé is sold in colourless glass bottles, with the colour of the wine easily visible. As Elke Wolff, marketing specialist at packaging supplier M.A. Silva, California confirms, 'It's all about color. Although clear glass is not good for rosé wine because the UV light breaks down the color and the wines turn brown, the winemaker wants to show the beautiful rose color.' And consumers want to see the beautiful colour too.

From its inception in the 1940s, Mateus Rosé was sold in a signature, flask-shaped green bottle, which became widely recognized. In 2015 this was changed to clear glass. Writes Neil Bake in *The Drinks Business*, 'Designed to show off its pink colour and fresh style, the new clear glass Mateus bottle is intended to attract modern UK rosé drinkers who, according to research carried out by the brand owners Sogrape Vinhos in January this year, have a preference for purchasing Rosé wine in clear glass.' Sogrape UK's Managing Director Matt Douglass noted that consumers wanted to see the colour of the wine, 'Along with taste, we recognize that modern wine consumers are interested in the colour of their preferred rosé and we want to give them what they want.' Market tests were promising with Sogrape reporting a 15 per cent increase in sales on average in countries where the new colour was tested.

The occasional rosé wine is sold in coloured bottles. Some producers use coloured glass to improve the keeping-qualities of the wine, seeing this as more important than showing the colour of the wine. Frank Petit of Clos Beylesse exports his Domaine de l'Abbaye Côtes de Provence wine in cobalt blue bottles, after his Caribbean shipper some 20 years ago asked for dark bottles to protect against the sun. Many producers of sparkling pink wine use a dark glass bottle to protect against light strike (see pages 28–30). In 2016, Château de Crémat in Bellet changed to dark glass and Clos Cibonne (a cult rosé in the US) sells in a dark bottle.

It is not unknown for an unexpectedly deep-coloured rosé to be sold in dark bottles. With the belief that pale rose is 'good', producers may fear the reaction of consumers to the dark colour, so make it less obvious. The reaction of consumers upon finally seeing the colour of the wine can be imagined.

Bottle sizes and alternative packaging

Sold, like other wines, mostly in standard-sized bottles (750 ml/75cl), rosé wines are also particularly popular in a wide range of other packaging. Bag-in-box (BiB) containers are popular, with about 40 per cent of rosé wine sold in BiBs, according to Michel Couderc of the CIVP. BiBs are often used for entry-level wines, and are good for parties, as many people can be served quickly. Some restaurants prefer them, even for better wines, as the wine stays fresh for some weeks. For IGP Pays d'Oc some 69 per cent is supplied in BiB, compared to 23 per cent for Provence AOP wine. For Provence, the proportion sold as BiBs is declining, as producers head upmarket. Of Bordeaux rosé sold through mass retailers in France, 37 per cent is supplied in BiBs. Magnums are growing in popularity, excellent for making an impression, perhaps at a party, or as a gift, and more attractive than BiBs, which represent good value and convenience. Even so, they remain a niche market, making up under 1 per cent of sales. Rather than representing economy of scale, magnums are a premium product, typically more than twice the price of a standard bottle.

Alex Beggs gave an example in *Vanity Fair* of the increasing popularity of magnums, quoting Jeremy Seysses, owner of Provence's **Domaine de Triennes** (www.triennes.com), 'Magnums and double magnums are far more fun, though the latter don't fit in a fridge door.' A few years ago, Triennes shipped 30 magnums to the US, increasing to 2,400 in 2015, plus 274 double magnums, together representing 1.2 per cent of its US sales.

Novel packaging has been introduced for smaller packages of rosé, as with other wines: cans, beer bottles, even single-serve plastic goblets. Largely aimed at Millennials, they are convenient to carry, easy to open, and suit casual drinking. Although wine does not age as well in these as in larger, glass bottles, this is not an issue as they are drunk soon after purchase. Curiously, half-size (37.5 centilitre) wine bottles have not caught on.

Barokes Wines pioneered supplying wine in cans in 2007. Irene Stokes, sales and marketing director, told me: 'Initially, Barokes produced both sparkling and still rosés in a can. However, we dropped the still rosé a few years back as the sparkling rosé was far more popular. We only produce sparkling rosé now to meet consumer demand.' Japan was their first market and is the largest; Stokes says 'the Japanese do not have preconceived ideas re the can packaging'.

In November 2016, Aldi UK launched a range of wines in 50 centilitre beer bottles, including a sparkling rosé. These were 'seasonal products, available for a limited time only'. Rosé in single-serve plastic goblets is supplied by Intrepid Fox, alongside red and white. The concept was given a boost when Marks and Spencer invested in a range for their stores. The goblets are sold through retailers, and in the hospitality sector where their ease of serving is a benefit.

GENERATING THE BUZZ

Advertising and social media

The launch, by Sacha Lichine's Château d'Esclans, of Garrus in 2007 as 'the most expensive rosé in the world' – at €80–100 (US$95–120) a bottle – achieved great media attention for rosé, and showed that rosé is a serious wine, like reds and whites. Lichine told Roger Voss of *Wine Enthusiast* in 2014 that he targeted his marketing at the Riviera crowd and the luxury hotels of Antibes and Cap Ferrat. 'I knew we had arrived when I got a call from one of the top yacht builders saying, "Could you please send me the dimensions of your three-liter double magnums?" He wanted to make sure he built a fridge on a yacht that was big enough.'

From 2008, the promotional efforts of EU producers of rosé wine were boosted by the introduction of subsidies of up to half the cost of promoting EU wine outside the EU, such as to the US or China. According to a European Court of Auditors report, these reforms were 'aimed essentially at improving the competitiveness of EU wine producers and balancing supply and demand, this in the context of a long persisting structural surplus of supply over demand.' Producers round the EU were quick to take up these subsidies. Provence's CIVP boosted promotional activity in the US, helping the recent increase in sales of Provence rosé there. As explained by Valerie Lelong, Head of Export Marketing and Communications at the CIVP, 'Promotions have only been subsidised outside Europe (countries like the US, China). This is why, for some years promotion has evolved, sometimes even reoriented, towards other countries. All wines are affected, and – for us in Provence – particularly rosé.'

In France, featuring drinkers in advertisements for alcohol is prohibited under the *Loi Evin* law. As a result, advertisers may require different images in France from elsewhere. The CIVP, for example adapts its Provence rosé advertising campaigns in France, by removing the people.

Sarah Abbott MW sees glamourous photos shared on Instagram in the US as a key factor in the growth of the American market for rosé. She told a masterclass at Vinisud 2017 that many of the 60 million Instagram users in the US share photos of rosé in glamourous situations: bottles of rosé by the sea, with meals, and being drunk by Millennials having fun in the sun. To her, this helps French wine because on social media people are tagging 'rosé' not 'rosado'. She sees the word 'rosé' becoming synonymous for the style, in the 'same way that champagne became known as sparkling.'

Stephen Cronk, who launched Mirabeau Wine in Provence in 2009, believes passionately in the use of social media, which he sees as giving small brands a voice. He says that he seeks to build relationships with consumers, as 'our success depends on how much our brand pulls customers towards it', making his brand more attractive to supermarkets. This worked for him when UK supermarket Waitrose listed Mirabeau's rosé in 2011; he says sales have grown 80 per cent a year for five years. He has made a big sales feature of his family and their story of leaving suburban London to make great wine in Provence. 'Consumers want to see the face behind the brand,' he says. Cronk knows he is succeeding when 'people come into our shop after buying our wine back home, for example in Dan Murphys [a leading Australian chain of liquor stores], to spend time talking with us.'

Local wine marketing boards often set up a showroom for their wines, to increase market visibility, create buzz, and bring in incremental business. The Syndicat des Côtes de Provence launched their showroom, the *Maison des Vins*, in 1994, by the main RN7 road in les Arcs sur Argens. After recent, major refurbishment, 60,000 visitors a year are expected, half from outside the Provence-Alpes-Côte d'Azur region. A selection of sixteen appellation wines from its members is always available for tasting, and is changed weekly. Eight hundred wines are available for purchase, at cellar-door prices, with annual sales of €800,000 (US$950,000).

Rosé festivals and events

The growing number of events dedicated to rosé wine illustrate its growing importance. These have arisen as opportunities for people to get together, drink rosé and have fun. All but one are aimed at consumers. A key element is the photos shared on social media of the groups of people – largely women – at these events with a glass of rosé, always looking happy.

Annual days for rosé wine have been created: International Rosé Day (since 2005, not to be confused with International Rose Day) on 14 August (midway between one Valentine's Day and the next) and, in the US, National Rosé Day on the second Saturday in June (since 2014). An early festival, Pink Out, was held in 2007 by the Rosé Avengers and Producers, 'an international group of winemakers and wine drinkers dedicated to righting the wrongs done to dry rosé'. Group founder Jeff Morgan felt that drinking rosé wine was becoming, at the very least, acceptable: 'I think we've turned a corner. At least in the major metropolitan areas of America, it's no longer uncool to be seen sipping a glass of pink wine. This was not always the case. Six or eight years ago, such an action in some circles (not mine) was a clear admission that you knew nothing about wine. Or worse, that you had lousy taste in wine.'

The Italia in Rosa wine festival was also started in 2007. It is held annually at Moniga del Garda, by Lake Garda, near where Valtènesi rosé is made. Rosé producers from Italy have a big presence, as do those from Provence. Festivals have been launched around the globe in the last ten years. Eddie McDougall has organized an annual Rosé Revolution in Hong Kong and other Asian cities since 2010. Lucy Jenkins in *The Drinks Business* quotes McDougall, 'The Rosé Revolution has built a reputation ... as an opportunity for beginners, day drinkers, wine lovers and experts alike to mix and mingle whilst enjoying an awesome day out.' The wines presented are largely from international brands. In Zagreb, Croatia, Women On Wine has organized an annual Pink Day festival, since 2013. Sanja Muzaferija launched it 'to promote moderate drinking of ever more popular rosé wine, but also to celebrate optimism, the beginning of spring, femininity.' Seventy producers from Croatia and elsewhere show their wines to the public. New York's annual La Nuit en Rosé was founded in 2014 by Pierrick Bouquet, who went on to launch Pinknic, a 'Giant Rosé Picnic and Music Festival' first held in 2016 on Governors Island in New York City. The annual Pink Rosé Festival, launched by Laurent Fiore in Cannes in 2017, is 'the first professional festival celebrating rosé wines'. It is trade-only, with producers and buyers from France and overseas. A key feature is the targeted appointments between buyers and sellers.

Wine competitions

Wine competitions are useful for publicizing wines from a region or appellation, or of a special style. The first rosé-only competition, Le Mondial du Rosé, was started in 2004 by the Union des Œnologues de France 'to give to the rosé wines of the world a special attention'. The US's first rosé competition, Rosé Today, was launched in California in 2013, by Bob Ecker, who started it because, 'As a wine judge participating in numerous competitions, [he] noticed that rosé wines were still not getting the recognition they deserved.' In 2015 Rosé Rocks was launched as a competition for 'Any wine that is rose [sic] in colour that has been fermented in South Africa.'

The International Rosé Championship – of which I am president – was launched in 2017 in Kraków, Poland, by Michał Bardel, editor-in-chief of Polish wine magazine *Czas Wina*. Bardel, who had wanted a truly international competition, said that 'at the first edition of IRC we had wines from more than 20 countries and we expect much more next year.' He wanted a new approach, not based solely on scores, but 'leaving more time for discussion between judges.' Wines were grouped, taking into consideration 'factors like grape variety, RS level, vintage, oak ageing, bubbles. Our judges were aware of all these factors, but – of course – unaware of the country of origin, producer or the name of the wine.' The time given for discussion was something I was particularly keen on encouraging. With judges coming from different backgrounds and countries, we needed to be able to discuss the key elements for quality. This certainly stretched our knowledge of unusual varieties and regional styles and challenged our preconceptions of what makes a good rosé. Interestingly enough, my panel's top wine was a dark pink, fruity Gaglioppo from Calabria, while another panel chose a dark, full-bodied Portuguese rosé.

VINEYARD ECONOMICS (COSTS, CAPITAL, PRODUCTION)

To make more rosé wine, a producer can use juice otherwise destined for red wine (hence making less red wine), plant more vines, increase his yields, or buy in juice or grapes.

Making rosé instead of red can have cash-flow benefits for producers who age their reds, as Ophélie Neiman describes in *Le Monde* (2017):

A red wine, whose grapes are harvested in autumn 2017, vinified with, say two years of élevage, will not be placed on sale until autumn 2019. By the time the vigneron touches the first receipts, at least thirty months will have passed. And he must wait longer before he gets any profits from it. Let us now consider rosé; it is made with the same grapes, but, as it needs very little time for élevage, it is put on sale from the following spring. Perhaps even from January. In one year, the producer has almost recovered his funds.

(Her example is based on two years of maturation for the red; when less, the example should be correspondingly adjusted.) Cash comes in quicker; space and equipment are released; business risk is reduced.

At Artisan Wines in Austria, Franz Schneider told me that by doubling his rosé production over the past three years and reducing the amount of red, he could tap into the increased Austrian demand for rosé and improve cash flow. Instead of ageing his red for 14–15 months in barrel, his rosé sold out by the end of the summer.

Neiman points out the challenges and risks. Significant investment is required: 'Including the refrigerated tanks to ensure gentle fermentation, inert atmosphere to protect the juice from oxygen, and the various equipment, [a producer] needs typically 200,000 euros worth of equipment for 10 hectares of vine.'

She quotes Franck Crouzet, director of communications of the Castel Group, who outlines the challenge: '[rosé] is a very fragile wine, which requires investment in advanced equipment, and labour. When we are told that producers have an interest in making rosé for the cash-flow benefits, I laugh.' Producers run the risk of being left with unsaleable stocks; she quotes Marine Chauvier, winemaker in Roquebrune-sur-Argens, Provence: 'If you don't sell your rosé, it quickly deteriorates. Its quality is best for a year and a half. If you still have stock past this date, you're in trouble'.

If a grower plants new vines, he must wait – typically four years or longer – before using them to make appellation wine. This is expensive, as the land needs to be prepared, then planted, then cared for, before the grapes can be used.

Increasing the yield may seem an obvious option, but the quality of the grapes may fall. Where appellation rules apply, higher yields may not be possible without going to a lower level of geographical indication. For example, a rosé producer in the Côtes de Provence appellation region in France who is in the Var department, can produce wine as AOP Côtes de Provence or IGP Var. Made as the former, his maximum permitted yield is 55 hectolitres per hectare, as the latter 120 hectolitres per hectare. But moving to a less-restrictive geographical indication is rarely commercially attractive, as appellation wine sells for significantly higher prices, and the total value will likely fall.

If a winemaker buys in grapes or juice, even wines in various states of completion, then sells the resulting wine under his own name, he is what in French is called a *négociant*. There are many in France and elsewhere; many are large businesses.

In 2000 when many of pink wine pioneer Jeff Morgan's winemaker friends in California were simply throwing away the bled-off juice from their red wines, he launched Solorosa rosé using their juice (for Morgan's story, see page 117).

Smaller growers, lacking resources and equipment, may group together in cooperatives, to make and market their wine more effectively. For Côtes de Provence, fifteen hectares is said to be the minimum economic size for a vineyard, so by joining a cooperative, growers with less land have an effective outlet for their grapes. In Provence 60 per cent of rosé wine is made by cooperatives. These tend to be the largest producers and can be very dynamic businesses and very responsive to the market. Estandon Vignerons in Provence, with 500 members, supplies 10 per cent of Provence's production.

PRICE

The biggest factor affecting the price of rosé is the appellation or geographical indication. In France, AOC appellation wines are more valued than IGP, which in turn are more valued than vin de France. Popular appellations are more expensive than others. Within Provence rosés, for instance, Côtes de Provence has, in mass retailers, a 15 per cent price premium compared with Coteaux d'Aix and Coteaux Varois. Producers of Côtes de Provence who have *cru classé* status believe they have a further advantage.

The image of the producer or brand is also very important. Hence their marketing efforts, described in this chapter.

Rosé champagne has been marketed as a superior product to standard champagne, achieving a 15–20 per cent price premium. Despite (or perhaps because of) this premium, rosé has steadily increased its share of champagne, from 5 per cent in 2004 to 12 per cent now.

Provence's *Observatoire de l'économie mondiale du vin rosé* (Rosé Wine Economic Observatory) sees three categories of wine traded internationally:

1. Entry level, shipped in bulk tanks, for making branded wine, aromatized wine, varietal blends (€30 per hectolitre). Largely from Spain and South Africa, with some from Italy.
2. Mid-range, often shipped in bulk, bag-in-box varietals. Often used for IGP Pays d'Oc or US blush brands (€90–100 per hectolitre).
3. Quality, shipped largely in bottles, typically appellation and quality wines. The CIVP reported that the average price of Côtes de Provence AOP wine in 2016 was €209 per hectolitre in bulk and €4.40 per bottle FOB for export (€587 per hectolitre).

Whereas red and white wines range in price from the inexpensive to those costing hundreds of pounds or more, for rosé wines the price range is much more limited. A challenge facing producers of rosé, says Michel Couderc, head of economics of the CIVP, is to develop a broader range of products at higher price points, together with a market for these, so that consumers have a wider choice of options, as for bordeaux, burgundy and champagne.

DISTRIBUTION CHANNELS FOR ROSÉ

Distribution channels for rosé wine include:

- Importers and distributors. These are effective for developing sales quickly, by tapping into existing sales teams. Exports can be attractive, though they come with higher shipping costs. As wine is typically made to suit local and domestic tastes, sometimes the product will need to be adapted to suit overseas tastes.

- Mass retailers and hard discounters. Good for clearing volume, but pay low prices and have little brand loyalty.
- Wine shops, restaurants and bars. These can be attractive but a concerted sales effort is required to convince the buyer to stock the item if going direct rather than via importers and distributors. Franco's Restaurant in St James, London, whose director, Jason Phillips, is 'the most rosé-obsessed man in London', according to Daisy Meager of *Munchies*, is an ideal buyer, making a feature of listing a large number of rosés, largely Italian.
- Cellar-door. This typically has the highest profit. Smaller wineries often have a higher proportion of sales via the cellar-door. This was borne out by a study of Australian winemakers, which found cellar-door sales growing strongly. In Provence, cellar-door sales are important to many wineries, and linked to tourism. Cellar-door is good for slightly unusual products, such as oaked or darker wines and those using less familiar varieties (see p.116).
- Internet, directly to the drinker. A growing channel.

Figures from the CIVP indicate sales in 2016 for Provence were split thus: 40 per cent large retailers, 26 per cent export, 15 per cent wine shops, restaurants and bars, 15 per cent cellar-door, 4 per cent other.

PRODUCTION, CONSUMPTION AND TRADE WORLDWIDE

As stated at the start of this chapter, rosé makes up almost 10 per cent of wine sales worldwide. Four countries dominate world rosé production, supplying 84 per cent of the total: France, Spain, USA and Italy. South Africa trails in fifth place with 4 per cent, other countries make less. Over 43 per cent of exports are supplied as bulk wine, 25 per cent by Spain alone.

France dominates rosé consumption, consuming just over a third (34 per cent) of world production. Other key consumers are the USA, Germany, UK, Italy and Spain. Together these take 70 per cent of world consumption.

Popularity of rosé varies by country. Over half the wine consumed in Tunisia is rosé, with 35 per cent in Uruguay. In France, 30 per cent of wine consumed is rosé. Other countries where rosé is a large share of the wine drunk are Belgium (20 per cent), Netherlands (12 per cent), USA, United Kingdom and South Africa (each 11 per cent), Germany, Switzerland and Spain (each 10 per cent) and Italy (6 per cent).[7]

Because wine consumption per person in France is high and 30 per cent of this is rosé, the French drink far more rosé than in other countries, at 15.6 litres per person per year. This is just more than in the next highest, Uruguay (12.4), three times that of the next highest, Belgium (4.9) and over ten times that of the US (1.3 litres per person per year).

Data is not easily available. 'Economic information for rosé wines is relatively difficult to obtain or to reconstruct,' says the International Organisation of Vine and Wine's (OIV) 2015 report *The Rosé Wine Market*. It adds, 'rosé and red wines are not always separated in economic data derived from reporting obligations. The distinction is very rarely made on an international level, and occasionally on a national scale, but is made fairly frequently at the local level, where product production specifications exist (Geographical Indications or brands).' Wine Australia's *Production, Sales and Inventory Report 2016*, for example, groups figures for 'red and rosé' together. This means that data must be gathered from multiple sources, sometimes estimated, and then cross-checked. Sources include official organizations, consumer or distributor panels, and consumer surveys.

Recognizing the need for comprehensive data on rosé wine worldwide, the CIVP (Provence Wine Board) established its *Observatoire de l'économie mondiale du vin rosé* (Rosé Wine Economic Observatory) 'for the collection, analysis, and publication of economic data related to the global rosé market'. Collecting data from around the world, it publishes regular statistics of rosé production, consumption and market trends.

Figures separating sweet rosé wine (or blush) from dry rosé are also difficult to find. As *Vins de Provence*, the US marketing arm of the CIVP, said in 2014, 'Traditionally, the U.S. wine industry has grouped dry rosé wines together with sweet blush wines. This method of categorization perpetuates the misperception that rosé is the same as blush.' This is changing: the US Trade Tasting said, in 2016, that 'the marketing group Vins de Provence reported earlier this year that the US wine industry no longer groups dry rosé wines together with sweet blush wines, a distinction made necessary as dry rosé wines grow in popularity.'

---

[7] Source: OIV/CIVP

Volumes of organic rosé wines are especially hard to obtain. Sweden's Systembolaget provides one of the few sets of hard figures: 'Sales of organic rosé wines increased by 100 per cent, year-on-year, and accounted for 13 per cent of rosé wine sales in 2015. This trend will probably continue, with rosé catching up with white wine in terms of share of sales.'

The table on page 306 includes production, export, import and consumption volumes for the key countries involved, along with the value of exports, compiled from a variety of sources. Data for the key countries is included, with that for smaller players combined under 'other countries'.

Australia

Exports of red and white dwarf those of rosé, which makes up less than 2 per cent of exports. Though from 2013–17 the value fell by a third, this masks important changes in the make-up of the wine exported. The very large proportion of exports of bulk wine have been declining in recent years (though still 77 per cent) – with exports of rosé in bottles at last increasing dramatically – by 30 per cent – in 2016–17. This reflects the success among Australian producers in making and exporting quality rosé.

The UK takes 30 per cent of bulk rosé and 30 per cent of the bottles, with the Netherlands and New Zealand each taking 13 per cent of the bottled wines.

Canada

Imported rosé has grown significantly in recent years, as shown by the precise figures available from Ontario's Liquor Control Board of Ontario, a quasi-monopoly and one of the world's largest suppliers of alcoholic beverages. Sales of imported rosé table wine grew much faster – 116 per cent growth (by volume) from 2012–16 – than those of Canadian producers – which grew just 9 per cent over the same period. The share of imports increased from 47 per cent to 64 per cent, while that of Canadian rosés fell from 53 per cent to 36 per cent. In Ontario in 2016, despite the growth, rosé table wine made up just 2.5 per cent of wine sales, 10.2 million litres, though that represented a significant increase from the 1.9 per cent (6.4 million litres) in 2012.

Country	Production (1,000 hectolitres)	Proportion of world production of rosé (%)	Proportion of world rosé exports by volume (%)	Proportion of world rosé imports by volume (%)	Consumption (1,000 hectolitres)	Proportion of world consumption of rosé (%)	Estimated price of rosé exported (FOB at customs) €/0.75 litre	Estimated value of rosé exports (million € FOB at customs)	Estimated proportion of world exports of rosé by value	Proportion of the country's exports shipped in bulk (%)	Bulk exports as a proportion of world rosé exports (%)
France	7,313	31	16	21	7,990	34	2.60	495	31	18	3
Spain	4,664	20	41	-	940	4	0.50	244	16	63	26
USA	3,640	15	11	6	3,290	14	2.00	262	17	44	5
Italy	2,197	9	16	3	940	4	1.80	343	22	29	5
S. Africa	899	4	5	-	470	2	0.90	54	3	62	3
Germany	610	3	-	16	1,880	8	-	-	-	-	-
Chile	422	2	-	-	-	-	0.80	-	-	44	-
Argentina	380	2	-	-	-	-	-	-	-	-	-
Portugal	361	1	-	-	-	-	1.50	-	-	28	-
Uruguay	266	1	-	-	235	1	-	-	-	-	-
UK	-	-	-	13	1,410	6	-	-	-	-	-
Belgium	-	-	-	5	705	3	-	-	-	-	-
Netherlands	-	-	-	4	470	2	-	-	-	-	-
Canada	-	-	-	2	268	1	-	-	-	-	-
Sweden	-	-	-	2	148	1	-	-	-	-	-
Australia	-	-	1.5	-	-	-	1.00	18	1	84	1
China	82	-	-	-	-	-	-	-	-	-	-
Other countries	2,666	12	9.5	28	4,700	20	1.40	158	10	-	-
TOTAL	23,500	100	100	100	23,500	100		1,574	100	not applicable	not known
Volume (1,000 hectolitres)		23,500	8,930	8,930		23,500					

World production, consumption and trade of rosé wine in 2015. All figures are for 2015.

Source: CIVP, OIV, France Agrimer, Abso Conseil

China

China is viewed as a major growth opportunity, as wine consumption, though currently low, is increasing fast. Rosé consumption is very small – 1 per cent of the market – as the market is dominated by red wine, whose colour is viewed as lucky. Nonetheless, volume doubled between 2010 and 2014, and the market share of rosé increased, suggesting good potential. Recent research from Mintel found that the higher earners have the highest consumption of rosé wine, making them presumably the most promising market for rosé.

France

France dominates world statistics for rosé. It is the largest producer, the largest exporter by value, the largest importer by volume and the largest consumer by volume! And exports of quality Provence rosé are increasing strongly, especially to the US.

South Africa

Most rosé sold domestically is South African as very little wine is imported; wine imports are under 2 per cent of consumption, at the top-end of the price range. As described above, in recent years growth in the domestic wine market has been mainly due to new entrants into the sweet red and rosé sector, driven by female consumers in urban areas. Around 80 per cent of this is sold in wine boxes.

As South African wine expert Cathy van Zyl MW says, the dry rosé category took off around 2007 with the growth in rosé's popularity worldwide.

Spain

Spain is the world's second largest producer of rosé, and by far the biggest exporter by quantity with 41 per cent of world exports. Even so, Spanish rosé has little consumer recognition, as almost two-thirds of exported rosé is low-price entry-level wine, shipped in bulk overseas. Spanish bulk wine alone makes up a quarter of the world's rosé crossing borders. This means the major challenge for Spanish producers is to move their wines upmarket.

Sweden

Sweden's national alcohol monopoly, Systembolaget, provides an excellent view of national wine sales. Their *2017 Launch Plan* reviews the state of the market and their plans for it. After fifteen years of consistent growth, the volume of rosé fell for the first time, probably due to bad weather. 'Sales of rosé wine fell by 4.4 per cent to 14.8 million litres in 2015, while the retail value of sales increased slightly by 0.4 per cent to SEK 1.2 billion. The clearest trend in the category is that wines costing in excess of SEK 100 account for the biggest growth, and with over 600,000 litres sold, it is also clear that rosé wine is now acceptable in smarter settings. The market share for rosé in the wine category group is 7.5 per cent.' Curiously, among sparkling wines, 'both sweet and rosé sparkling wines are showing the weakest growth.'

United Kingdom

The growing importance of rosé wine in the UK was confirmed in 2009 when the Office of National Statistics wrote about the Basket of Goods and Services for the UK Consumer Prices Index that '[b]ottled rose [sic] wine is also included for the first time reflecting the increased popularity and growing shelf-space devoted to rose [sic]', replacing 'wine boxes'.

USA

The market for dry Provence-style rosés is distinct from that for sweeter blush wines. The Wine Institute of California's rosé sales figures state that, 'For 52 weeks ending June 17, 2017, pink wines accounted for 9.3 per cent of the volume sold in large volume food stores and other large volume outlets in the U.S., according to Nielsen figures', adding that these accounted for 6.1 per cent by value. With the recent growth in imports of Provence dry rosés, it is no surprise that 'From a smaller base, dry rosés gained over 26 per cent volume share of the blush category last year'.

Shane English describes recent growth in the US of rosés from Provence, and Château d'Esclans in particular, in *Shanken Daily News*.

> *Imports of Provence rosé increased tenfold between 2010 and 2016, rising from 123,000 nine-liter cases to nearly 1.3 million cases, according to Impact Databank, as consumers have flocked to the category, especially in the on-premise. The U.S. accounted for 43 per*

cent of Provence's exports by volume in 2016, according to the Vins de Provence trade group, and 2017 is shaping up to be another banner year. Château d'Esclans and its Whispering Angel brand—handled by Shaw-Ross International Importers—has been a major growth driver within the Provence rosé category. Last year, Shaw-Ross sold 200,000 cases of d'Esclans wines in the U.S., and is projecting 300,000 cases for 2017, with Whispering Angel ($20–25 a 750-ml.) accounting for about 80 per cent of the total.

He continues with other major Provence brands for 2016: 'Chateau Miraval ($20–$25), imported by Vineyard Brands, produced 91,000 cases for the American market in 2016' and 'Minuty increased 17 per cent to 28,000 cases in the U.S.' He quotes Chevalier of Shaw-Ross, that, 'Rosés from the Côtes de Provence appellation have been trending at +40 per cent these past four to five years'. Chevalier is confident the trend will continue at least through 2018.

Larissa Zimberoff in *Bloomberg* (2017) tells us that the popularity of rosé has touched the kosher market too: 'Even Kosher drinkers are flocking to rosé. In 2015, Royal Wine Corporation, the leader in Kosher wine and beverages, had nine rosés in its assortment. Today it has 25. Sales have tripled over the past two years in rosé alone, an increase of 89 percent, or 10,000 cases.'

CONCLUSION: THE SWAN EMERGES

In the world of fine wine, rosé has long been regarded as the ugly duckling. A beautiful swan is now emerging!

From the start, I was fascinated by the broad and rich history of rosé traditions from around the world, not just Europe, with unusual varieties, complex methods and different styles: pale, dark, dry, sweet, fortified and sparkling. I have attempted to show that rosé is dynamic. The book's subtitle, 'Understanding the pink wine revolution', is intended to imply this revolution and dynamism. Rosé is such a fast-evolving modern style that new ideas, producers and wines kept pouring in until the very last minute.

For producers I would say, there is no single recipe for commercial success – rosé is not a miracle product, and all kinds of rosé can sell in the right market. For wine merchants, the possibility for a diverse range of wines can potentially expand sales, although consumer education may be required. To consumers I would say be bold. Some of the flavours in serious rosé are unlike any others so take your time and savour their uniqueness.

In summary, my thoughts are as follows:

- Colour may be the biggest issue of all. I am no longer so sure that our division of wine into red, white and pink is appropriate. With some rosé wines almost red in colour and style, and others almost white, the divisions are blurred. Add in rosé made in an orange wine style, and the blurring increases. The obsession with the colour pink should perhaps start to take a back seat.

- With the dominance of an international pale pink style, we are close to losing the originality, creativity and regionality of rosé. Regional diversity has great potential. Look for rare varieties.
- Despite an international style, local markets exist for 'unicorn' microproductions and local styles.
- International winemaking schools are a hotbed of cultural interchange for winemakers. Social media at vintage time reveals a vibrant discussion of techniques.
- The range of winemaking techniques is expanding rapidly, with innovative blends of different styles of maceration, fermentation and ageing mixed in one wine. Old or new wood, big or small barrels, cement tanks or eggs, and terracotta amphorae are all being used.
- Natural winemaking, long perceived as being the enemy of 'fresh and fruity' rosé, is increasingly creating extremely interesting wines.
- There is room to look at rosés older than the very last vintage, to investigate developing a market for aged rosés, and producers who seek to make these.
- Gastronomic rosés are no longer just rosés aged in oak. A growing number of rosés are available (with age or different vinification techniques) which have a complex range of flavours, combining fruit with minerality and salinity, long acidity or creamy broadness. Rosés have moved beyond the summer salads and grilled fish or chicken to more complex food matching.
- Pinot Gris and other *gris* varieties are coming on trend, with wines made in a way which unites white, orange and pink wine styles. Their light colour allows winemakers to play around with more extraction while keeping the colour paler.

Having worked with rosé wine, living in Provence, and having visited many producers over the last thirty years, I thought I knew a lot about rosé. Now, I am amazed at how much there is still to learn. Recent marketing and sales pushes have made us more aware of rosé, but the real pink revolution is only just beginning.

Finally, a big apology to all of those whose wines I was unable to include – there is more good rosé in the world than I will ever be able to taste – but I am doing my best to be ready for book two!

APPENDIX: ROSÉ WINE TERMINOLOGY IN OTHER LANGUAGES

Rosé wine

English: pink wine, rosé wine, blush wine (US usage, usually sweet)
Afrikaans: *roséwyn*
Bulgarian: Розе
Catalan: *rosat*
Chinese: 桃红葡萄酒
Dutch: *roséwijn*
French: *vin rosé, le rosé, rosé tendre* (soft or sweeter rosé)
German: *Roséwein, Feinherb*
Greek: Ροζέ
Hebrew: רוזה (rosé) סמוק (blush)
Hungarian: *roze*
Italian: *rosato, cerasuolo*
Japanese: ロゼワイン
Polish: *vino różowe*
Portuguese: *vinho rosé, rosado*
Romanian: *roze*
Russian: Розовое вино
Spanish: *rosado*
Swedish: *rosévin*

Vin gris
Austria: *Gleichgepresste*
English/American: eye of the partridge, eye of the swan
French: *vin gris, gris de gris, blanc de noirs, oeil de perdrix*
German: *Weissherbst*
Italian: *occhio di pernice*
Spanish: *vino gris, ojo de gallo*
Switzerland: *oeil de perdrix, Süßdruck*

Schiller
Austria: *Schilcher*
German: *Schillerwein, Schiller, Schieler* (Saxony), *Rotling, Rotgold*
Hungarian: *siller, fuxli*
Serbia: *šiler*

Clairet
French: *clairet*
Italian: *chiaretto*
Spain/Portugal: *clarete*

Saignée
English: bled-off, bleeding off
French: *saignée*
German: *Saignée*
Spain: *lagrima*
Italian: *lacrima*
Swedish: *avblödning*

Light strike
French: *goût de lumière*
Italian: *gusto di luce*

False rosé
Red wines made from naturally very pale red-skinned varieties, such as Poulsard in the Jura and Grignolino in Italy, which look like rosés.

BIBLIOGRAPHY

The American Farmer, John D Toy: Baltimore (1826) vol. X.
Amerine, Maynard Andrew, *Wine: An Introduction for Americans*, University of California Press: California (1965).
Ashley, Maureen, 'In the Pink', *Decanter*, June 1986.
Avellan, Essi, *Essi Avellan's Champagne*, AvelVino Media (2017).
Baxevanis, John J, *The Wines of Champagne, Burgundy and eastern and southern France*, Bowman & Littlefield: Torowa, NJ (1987).
Busby, James, *Journal of a Recent Visit to the Principal Vineyards of Spain and France*, C. S. Francis: New York (1835).
Church, Ruth Ellen, 'Eye of the Partridge', *Chicago Tribune* 6 December 1976.
Church, Ruth Ellen, 'Pink wines have many hues', *Chicago Tribune*, March 25 1966.
Couverchel, J-F., *Traité des Fruits, tant indigènes qu'exotiques et dictionnaire carpologique*, Paris: Bouchard-Huzard (1839).
Flanzy, Claude, Masson, Gilles and Millo, François (eds) *Le vin rosé*, Editions Féret: Bordeaux (2009).
'Focus on France: Rosé – a victim of consumer ignorance', *The Grocer* March 26 1988.
de la Framboisière, Nicolas-Abraham, *Les Oeuvres de N. Abraham de La Framboisière*, chez Pierre Bailly (1669), p85.
Fried, Eunice, 'The Wines of Summer', *Black Enterprise*, July 1988.
Fried, Eunice, 'Wine for a Summer Outing', *Black Enterprise*, July 1982.
Garcin, Étienne, *Dictionnaire historique et topographique de la Provence ancienne et moderne*, Chez l'Auteur (1835), Vol 1.
Gayot, André, *Gault et Millau*, GaultMillau SA: France (1996).

George, Rosemary, *The Wines of Southern France*, Mitchell Beazley: London (2003).
Giornale delle scienze mediche, Turin (1848).
Halliday, James, *Australian Wine Companion* (2012).
Hyatt, Thomas Hart, *Hyatt's Handbook of Grape Culture*, A.L. Bancroft & Company: San Francisco (1874).
Jeffs, Julian, *The Wines of Europe*, Faber & Faber: London (1971).
Jeffs, Julian, *The Wines of Spain*, Faber & Faber: London (1999).
Lardier Ricard, J. S., *Essai sur les moyens de régénérer l'agriculture en France et plus particulièrement dans les départements du Midi* (1820).
Lourens, Karien, 'Focus on rosé', *Wineland Magazine* 1 January 2007.
Miller, Philip, *The Gardeners Dictionary*, London (1768) 8th edn., Vol. 2.
Morgan, Jeff, *Rosé, A Guide to the World's Most Versatile Wine*, Chronicle Books: San Francisco (2005).
Muraire, *Mémoire sur les espèces de raisins de Provence qui sont les plus propres à faire les vins de la qualité meilleure*, Chez Esprit David: Aix (1781).
Parker Jr, Robert, *The Wines of the Rhone Valley*, Simon & Schuster: New York (1987).
Read, Jan, *The Wines of Portugal*, Faber & Faber: London (1982).
Redding, Cyrus, *A History and Description of Modern Wines* (1851).
Relazioni dei Giurati Italiani sulla Esposizione universale di Vienna del 1873, Milan (1873).
Revue de Marseille et de Provence, Volume 10 1864.
Sichel, Allan, *The Penguin Book of Wines*, Penguin: London (1965).
Simon, Joanna, 'Think pink in the heat haze', *Sunday Times*, summer 1989.
Smyth, Robert, 'From killer rosés to world-class sparklers', *Budapest Business Journal*, 15 July 2016.
Vandyke Price, Pamela *The Taste of Wine*, Macdonald and Jane's: London (1975).
Zuccagni-Orlandini, Attilio, *Corografia fisica, storica e statistica dell'Italia e delle sue isole*, Florence (1838) vol. 4.
van Zyl, Phillip (ed), *Platter's South African Wine Guide*, John Platter SA Wineguide: Hermanus (1997–2018).

ACKNOWLEDGEMENTS

My initial announcement that I was going to be writing a book on rosé was received with great enthusiasm by some and disbelief by many. Rosé, after all, was not worthy of a serious book!

I appealed for information and help, using contacts and social media. I cannot say I was inundated with information to begin with, but slowly, by word of mouth, people learned I was writing this book; information and wines started to flow in and the wonderful world of rosé began to appear! Many thanks to all those who have responded to my appeals for information through Instagram, Facebook, Twitter and word of mouth.

Jason Letts of Eyrie Vineyards in Oregon was one of the first to respond on Twitter, but the cost of sending a sample was prohibitive. By coincidence I had noticed that fellow writer Wink Lorch was in Oregon and I asked if she was passing near the vineyard and had space in her suitcase. She replied immediately, 'Actually, I have just walked in through the door of the cellars at Eyrie Vineyards!' Three weeks later my bottle arrived via Texsom, London and Savoie. In the end, so many rosés arrived by post, that my postman felt moved to express great concern for my health to my neighbour. Many thanks to everyone who sent in wines and engaged in my on-line conversations!

Many thanks to all the winemakers who have welcomed me to their cellars, vineyards and regions. This has shown me not only the many different styles of rosé, but also the cultural and gastronomic heritage that accompanies these different styles. Polish and Slovakian rosés with beetroot, pink retsina with mezes or robust Portuguese rosé with salt cod – all have opened my eyes to rosé's possibilities.

Apologies if I have misinterpreted any of the details in winemaking, regulations and histories.

In particular I would like to thank Jo Ahearne MW (Croatia and winemaking), Előd Ádám (Romania), Fernando Almeda (Chile), Eric Asimov (*New York Times*), Pedro Ballesteros MW (Spain), Michał Bardel, Ben Bernheim (editing, website), David Bernheim (statistics, marketing, editing and endless support and enthusiasm), Rosalie Bernheim (for cakes when the going got tough), Ernst Büscher (German Wine Institute), David Cartwright, Christy Canterbury MW, Rebecca Clare (my patient editor), Mireille Conrath (Syndicat des Vins de Provence), Michel Couderc (CIVP Wines of Provence), Jeany and Stephen Cronk (Mirabeau), Paul Demeulenaere (Wine Mosaic), Paul Denerley MSc (Plumpton – light strike), Tomi Dúzsi (Hungary), Guy Eshel (winemaking), Sarah Jane Evans MW (Spain), Julian Faulkner (Grand Cros – vintage rosé tasting), Laurent Fiore and his team (Pink!) Chelsea Franchi (Tablas Creek), Caroline Gilby MW (Bulgaria and Moldavia), Italy Gleitman (Israel), Nayan Gowda (vinification), Brad Greatrix, (Nyetimber, English sparkling wine), Peter Handzus (Slovakia), Jason Haas (Tablas Creek). Sarah Hargreaves (IGP d'Oc), Sam Harrop MW (winemaking – with apologies for not including all his comments), Huon Hooke (Australia), Natasha Hughes MW, Barbara Iasiello (OIV International Organisation of Vine and Wine), Kathleen Inman (California), Tomislav Ivanovic (Serbia), Christophe Jammes (CIVL Languedoc Wines), Robin Kick MW, Stefanie Köhler (*Cuvée Magazine*), Bill Kreck (blush, California), Konstantinos Lazarakis MW (Greece), Jason Letts (Eyrie Vineyard, Oregon), Valerie Lelong (CIVP Wines of Provence), Bob Lindo (Camel Winery, English wine), Martin Lopez (Uruguay), Wink Lorch, Alessandro Luzzago (Valtènesi), Dave McIntyre, Meg Houston Maker, Susan Newman Manfull (California), Gilles Masson (CERVR), Bryan Martin (Australia), Fiona McDonald (South Africa), Georges Meekers (Malta), Anders Mellden, Stefan Metzner (Germany), Tony Milanowski (Plumpton College), Mélanie Mora (CIVR Wines of Roussillon), Jeff Morgan (California), José Luis Murcia García (Spain), Sanja Muzaferija (Women On Wine), Wendy Narby (Bordeaux), Serhat Narsap (Turkey), Agnés Nemeth (cava and Hungary), Ivonne E Nill (Rueda del Duero), Lilla O'Connor, Birk O'Halloran (Iconic Wine), Nick Oakley (Portugal), Frank Petit (Clos

Beylesse), Fanny Pothier (Anjou), Andrea Pritzker MW (Australia), Antoine Poupard (Anjou), Gavin Quinney (Château Bauduc), Christina Rasmussen (Westbury Communications – Beaujolais), Philip Reedman MW (Australia), Felix Riley (Australia), Treve Ring (Canada), Radu Rizea (Romania), Michaela Rodeno (California), Mark Rowley (Wine Australia), Christian Scalisi, Bruno and Julia Scavo (Romania), Lenka Sedlackova MW (cava), Mira Šemić (Slovenia), Ruth Sierra de la Gala (Cigales, Spain), Miranda Sira Burón (Tierra de León, Spain), Matt Smith (Intrepid Fox), Dr Andrew Smith (historical references), Madeline Stenwreth MW, Walter Speller (Italy), Irene Stokes (Barokes Wines), Matthew Stubbs MW (Languedoc), Régine Sumeire (Chateau de Barbeyrolles), Kate Sweet (Limm Communications), Joanna Sykes-Darmon (Sopexa), Zoltán Szövérdfi-Szép (Romania), Charine Tan, Exotic Wine Travel (Croatia and Georgia), Clare Tooley, Yvette van der Merwe (S A Wine Industry Information & Systems), Cathy van Zyl MW (*Platters Wine Guide*, South Africa), José Vouillamoz, Fongyee Walker MW (China), Andreas Wickhoff MW (Austria), Stephen Wong MW (New Zealand), Elke Wolff (M.A. Silva), and all the many winemakers who gave up so much of their time to talk to me and answer my endless questions and supported my requests for tasting old, new, cask samples and rare rosés. I hope I have managed to reflect the excitement of some of these discoveries.

A special mention too, to my parents, Albert and Margaret, who first introduced me to wine all those years ago during family holidays, and for all their support over the years.

INDEX

Algeria 247
Alsace 100–101
America *see* USA
Anjou 50–56
  Cabernet d'Anjou 53–6
    chilling, filtration and sulphur use 55
    sugar levels and maceration 53–4
  geology and grape varieties 50–51
  history of wine 31–2
  market competition 286
  Rosé d'Anjou 51–2
  see also Loire
Argentina 156–8
Australia 129–41
  categories of rosé 132–3
  exports 305
  history of rosé 129–30
  marketing 140–41
  sales (2016), and growth 131–2
  styles of rosé 133–5
    aromatic rosé 139–40
    modern Australian/international 136–9
    Provence style 135–6
Austria 220–22
  West Styria 48
authors on wine *see* journalists and authors
Azores 194–5

Bardel, Michał 299
Bauer, Oliver 267
Beaujolais 103–4
  nouveau rosé 104
blush-style wines 109–12
Bonnet, Claude 72
Bordeaux 32–4, 89–96
  Bordeaux Wine Board (CIVB) 92
  changing styles of rosé 94–6, 284

  grand cru classé 95
  grape varieties 33
  harvesting, maceration and pressing 93–4
  rosé and *clairet,* colour 92–3
bottling 28–30, 291–5
Brun, Jean-Paul 172
Bugey 101, 171
Bulgaria 263–4
Burgundy 101–3
Busby, James 67, 129
business of rosé
  advertising and social media 296–7
  competitions 299
  consumers: entry-level versus experienced 290–91
  CREVR and development 9, 27, 30, 72
  distribution channels 302–3
  EU subsidies 296
  festivals and events 297–8
  growth 279–80
  market share 279
  marketing
    and simplistic view of rosé 11
    beyond women's market 283–4
    buyers' fresh or aged question 85, 289–90
    colour and shade 27–8, 29, 280–83, 311–12
    image creation 7–9
    main selling points 284–5
    SOPEXA 70
    sweet or dry tastes 285–7
  packaging
    bottle colour 294
    bottle design 291–3
    bottle size 295
    novel packaging 295–6
  price 301–2

seasonality 287–9
trade worldwide 303–9
   Australia 305
   Canada 305
   China 307
   data availability 304
   dominant producers and key consumers 303–4
   figures: production, consumption, trade 306
   France 307
   South Africa 307
   Spain 307
   Sweden 308
   UK 308
   USA 308–9
vineyard economics 299–301

Canada 125–8
   British Columbia 127
   imports 305
   Ontario 125–6
   sparkling wines 128
Canary Islands 187–8
Canedo, Pedro 190
Carter, Felicity 217
Carteyron, Patrick 93
Centre de Recherche et d'Experimentation sur le Vin Rosé 9, 27, 30, 72
Cerdon 101, 171
champagne *see* pink champagne
Chaperon, Vincent 159–60
Chassevent, Lucie 55
Chile 155–6
China 307
clairet and *clairet* style rosés 6, 31–4, 67, 92, 151
   chiaretto of Lake Garda 198, 199–203
Clouston, Dave 141
colour 6
   clairet and rosé, differences 92–3
   marketing and 26–8, 29, 280–83, 311–12
Cordier, Gerard 98
Corsica 243–6
Côtes de Toul, Lorraine 59–60
Courselle, Marie and Sylvie 33
Craven, Mike 150
Crimea 270
Croatia 260–61, 298
Cronk, Stephen 297
Cyprus 274–5

Dalmatian Islands 261–2
Dokoozlian, Nick K. 113

Ecker, Bob 299
England *see* UK

Fabre, Louis 87
Farnet-Matton family 70
Fayard family 81
France *see* vineyards and winemakers by country *and* individual region names

Germany 217–19
   Prowein trade fair (2017) 131
   Schiller 47–8
Gough, Giles 286
grape varieties
   of Anjou 51
   of Argentina 156
   of Australia 133–5, 138
   of Austria 220–22
   of Bordeaux 33
   of Burgundy 101–2
   of Corsica 245–6
   of Côtes de Toul *vin gris* 60
   of Croatia 260
   of Cyprus
      Lefkada (aka Verzami) 275
      Maratheftiko 274–5
   of England 216–17
   of Germany 217–19
   of Greece
      Agiorgitiko 272
      Kotsifali 273
      Limniona 273
      Mavrotragano and Avgoustiatis 273
      Moschofilero 272–3
      Xinomavro 271
   of Hungary 225–9
   of Israel 253
   of Italy 200, 201, 207
   of Languedoc 234–40
      Aubun 239
      Caladoc 239–40
      Grenache Gris 234–6
      Marselan 240–41
      Mollard 239
      Muscat 234
   of Lebanon 252
   of the Loire 54, 96, 97–9
   of New Zealand 141

pink champagne blends 161, 166, 167
  of Provence
    Cinsault 73, 84
    Grenache 73, 83
    Mourvèdre 82–3
    Muscat 67–8
    Tibouren 73, 84
  of Romania 266
  of Serbia 262
  of Slovakia
  of Slovenia 259
  of South Africa 147, 148
  of Spain 168
  of Switzerland 223
  of Tavel 36, 39–40
  of Tunisia 248
  of Turkey 277, 278
  of Uruguay 152, 153
  of the USA 114
    blends 113, 118
    Grenache 106–8, 112
    Zinfandel 108–9
  see also winemaking
Grazia, Marco de 214
Greatrix, Brad and Cherie 30, 165
Greece 270–73
  Thessaloniki 276
Guiraud, Ghislaine 267

Haas family 118
Hall, Tim 160, 162
history of rosé wine 5–9
  field blends 5–6
  importance of colour 6–7, 31–2
  regional see individual region and country names
  twentieth century 7–9
  wines of Anjou and Arbois 31–2
Hungary (Siller) 49–50
Hurren, Louise 232–3

Inman, Kathleen 119
Institut National de l'Origine et de la Qualité (INAO) 69
Israel 253–6
Italy 197–214
  appellations 198
  history of wine 197
  Istituto di Servizi per il Mercato Agricolo Alimentare 197–8
  regions
    Abruzzo 210
    Calabria and Sicily 213–14
    Piedmont 205–6
    Puglia 211–13
    Tuscany 206–10
  styles of wine 198
  wines
    cerasuolo 210
    chiaretto 198, 205: Bardolino 201–2; Valtènesi 199–203
    Lagrein Kretzer *rosato* 203
    Moscato Rosa 204
    rosati 205–11
    sparkling wines 166–7
    Venetian *Ramato* 204–5

Jamain, Denis 98
Johnstone, Esme 89–91
Jones, Katie 232–3
journalists and authors
  Amerine, Maynard 11, 19, 26, 38, 108
  Asimov, Eric 124, 176–7
  Bake, Neil 294
  Beggs, Alex 295
  Blake, Imogen 281
  Church, Ruth Ellen 107
  Cole, Katherine 280
  Courvechel, M. 67
  de la Framboisière, Nicolas-Abraham 6
  Douglas, Ellie 282
  English, Shane 308
  Freedman, Brian 283
  Good, Dr Jamie 292
  Hemingway, Ernest 37
  Holthausen, Christian 282, 288
  Hooke, Huon 130
  James, Victoria 280
  Jeffs, Julian 7, 56, 58–9, 111, 175
  Jenkins, Lucy 298
  Kupers, Peter 218
  Lourens, Karien 147
  Mellden, Anders 279
  Miller, Philip 67
  Mkhwanazi, Katlego 291
  Morgan, Jeff 117, 279, 298
  Muraire, M. 67
  Neiman, Ophélie 300
  Pananti, Filipo 247
  Redding, Cyrus 6, 32, 57
  Ring, Treve 125
  Simon, Joanna 33, 51–2, 176
  Sitwell, Sacheverell 188–9
  Smyth, Robert 225

Stávek, Jan 280
Stevenson, Tom 166
Vandyke-Price, Pamela 7–8, 26, 281
Voss, Roger 296
Waugh, Auberon 90
Wilson, Jason 283
Zimberoff, Larissa 309
see also Masters of Wine

Karagozoðlu, Seyit 278
Karam, Habib 253
Kechris, Stelios and Eleni 276
Kreck, Bill 109–11
Krejewski, Martin 95–6

Languedoc 231–43
　diversity of wines and marketing 231–2
　Pays d'Oc designation 233
　styles of wine 241–3
　varieties
　　Aubun 239
　　Caladoc 239–40
　　Grenache Gris 234–6
　　Marselan 240–41
　　Mollard 239
　　Muscat 234
　vin gris 63–4
Lebanon 250–53
Lecomte, Olivier 54–5
Leon, Patrick 91
Lhumeau, Jean Louis 97
Lichine, Sacha 74, 91
The Loire 96–100
　Cabernet d'Anjou 53–6
　Coteaux du Vendomois 97–8
　Reuilly 98
　Saint Pourçain 99–100
　Sancerre 98–9
　see also Anjou
Luzzago, Alessandro 200

Malta 246
market share 279
marketing see business of rosé
Masson, Gilles 28, 30, 72
Masters of Wine (MW)
　Abbott, Sarah 297
　Ahearn, Jo 261–2, 318
　Ashley, Maureen 8, 26, 38, 62, 70, 96, 100
　Avellan, Essi 159, 163
　Bampfield, Richard 91, 159
　Coates, Clive 102

George, Rosemary 64, 234, 244
Gilby, Caroline 263, 266
Gleave, David 204
Hughes, Natasha 150–51
Karakasis, Yiannis 271, 273
Lazarakis, Konstantinos 271
Milne, Kym 135
Paris, Nicholas 119
Pritzker, Andrea 129, 131, 132
Reedman, Phil 141
Schmitt, Patrick 73, 178
Sedlackova, Lenka 170
Simonetti-Bryan, Jennifer 280
Stenwreth, Madeline 150
Stubbs, Matthew 235
Twain-Peterson, Morgan 115
van Zyl, Cathy 146, 149–50, 307
Wickhoff, Andreas 220
Wong, Stephen 144
see also journalists and authors; sommeliers
Mau, Jean Christophe 91, 94
Maxwell, Dom 142, 144
Mayock, Robert 107
McDonald, Fiona 149
Mead, Jerry 8, 110
Millo, François 72, 280
Montefiore, Adam 254
Montmollin, Benoit de 61
Morocco 249–50

Nebbe-Mornod, Joelle 61
New Zealand 141–6
　exports 141
　regions
　　Hawke's Bay to Waipara 142–3
　　Nelson and Marlborough 143–4
　　North Canterbury 144–6
　　Waiheke Island to Hawke's Bay 142
　　Waipara 143
　styles of rosé
　　Bordeaux-style 142–3
　　Pinot Noir-dominant 143
North America see Canada; USA

oak 84–5, 94

Parker, Robert 42
Parkinson, Christine 29
Petit, Frank 294
Peynaud, Professor Emile 27, 32
Phelps, Joseph 113
phylloxera 35

pink champagne 159–73
    ageing 163
    blending *(rosé d'assemblage)* 161
    history of 57–9
    marketing 302
    producers 161–3
    saignée 162–3
    styles 160
pink cider 172
Poggi, Matilde 202
Portugal 7, 188–93
    Douro 193–4
    Mateus Rosé and Lancers rosé 188–90
    Tejo 191–2
    Vinho Verde 190–91
Pouchin, Philippe 86
Pradini, Giovanna 198, 201
producers *see* vineyards and winemakers by country
Provence 65–87
    appellations 76–9
    bottle shapes 291–2
    Coteaux d'Aix-en-Provence 78–9
    Coteaux Varois en Provence 79
    Côtes de Provence 78
        Fréjus denomination 80–81
        La Londe denomination 81
        Pierrefeu denomination 81–2
        Saint-Tropez 13, 69, 70, 288
        Sainte-Victoire denomination 80
        Syndicat des Côtes de Provence 292, 297
    exports to the USA 308–9
    geology 38–9
    grape varieties 82–4
    history 65–9
        (1970s–1999) 69–72
        VDQS status 69
    Les Baux-de-Provence 79
    oak 84–5
    wines
        characteristics of style 87
        Garrus wine 74, 81, 91
        négociant wine 75
        pétale de rosé 70–71
        style of rosé 73–4

Quinney, Gavin 34, 92, 93

ramato 21
Rasque de Laval, Baron Louis
Raventós, Josep 167
regions *see* historic regions; vineyards and winemakers
retsina 275–6
Riley, Felix 130, 136, 138–9, 289
Rizzo, Antonio 195
Rodeno, Michaela 114, 116
Rolland, Michel 181
Romania 264–6
    Dealu Mare, Dealurile Munteniei (Hills of Muntenia) 268–9
    north-east Romania (Moldova) 266
    rosé's share of home market 266
    south to south-east: Oltenia 266–8
    Vincon Romania 265
    west: Banat, Crisana, Maramures 269
rosé
    business *see* business of rosé
    descriptors 85–6
    terminology in different languages 313–14
    world production, consumption and trade (2015) 306
rosé champagne *see* pink champagne
Rotărescu, Aurel 268
Ruinart 57

Sahre, Tariq 252
saignée 18–19, 116–18, 134, 162–3
Sarnari, Tiziana 197
Savoie 101
Schiller 47–8
Schneider, Franz 221, 300
Schoenfeld, Victor 254
Schoonmaker, Frank 107
Seddon, Guy 160
Serbia 262–3
Šiler 50
Serres, Olivier de 5–6
Šiler 50
Siller 49–50
Skalli, Robert 233
Slovenia 257–9, 259
sommeliers
    Hillary, Clint 140
    Kupers, Peter 218
    Pastuszak, Thomas 283
    Thomas, Franck 210
    see also Masters of Wine
SOPEXA (1986) 96
South Africa 146–51
    categories of rosé 147–8
    domestic market and imports 285–6, 291, 307
    history of rosé 146–7

Pinot Gris rosé 150–51
sales and changing market 148–9
sparkling wines 151
South America 151–8
Spain 175–87, 307
  Cigales region 45–7
  exports 307
  grape varieties 168
  history of viticulture 175–6
  rosado production 176–8
  sparkling wines 167–70
  styles of wine, and production methods
    modern 180–85
    pale international 185–7
    traditional 178–80
  vineyards and winemakers 169–70, 177, 179–87
sparkling wines 30, 96
  of Argentina 158
  of Canada 128
  of England 164–6
  of France
    Beaujolais 172
    Bugey-Cerdon 171
    Clairette de Die 172
    Limoux 170–71
    see also pink champagne
  of Italy, Franciacorta 166–7
  of Long Island 124
  méthode ancestrale 171, 172
  of New Zealand 144
  of South Africa 151
  of Spain 167–70
Spencer, Stuart 111–12, 114–15
sugar 23–4, 43–4, 53–4, 55, 73
Sullivan, Tom 95
Sumeire, Régine 15, 21, 71–2, 85, 91
Sweden 285, 308
Switzerland, 223
  Schiller 48
Szövérdfi-Szép, Zoltán 265

Tasmania 131
Tavel
  cooperative 37
  history 34–9
  influence 7, 105, 107, 175, 252, 290
  market pressures 39, 282
  viticulture and winemaking 13, 21, 36–7, 290
    geology and climate 40–41
    grape varieties 39–40
    méthode Taveloise 19, 41–2

Taylor, Geoff 29
Tenerife 188
Todd, Steve 131
Trinchero, Bob 108
Tunisia 247–9
Turkey 276–8

UK
  domestic market 296, 308
  England 164–6
    history of wine making 215–16
    rosé varieties 216–17
    sparkling wine 164–6
  USA imports 112
Ukraine 269–70
unions 35–6
Uruguay 151–4
USA
  California 105–25
    diverse rosé styles 116: categories 118–19
    European imports 7
    home market 105
    saignée 116–18
    San Joaquim Valley 113
    white Zinfandel and 'blush' 108–12: Eye of the Partridge wine 109; Mill Creek Vineyards 26, 110–12; sales (2014) 113
  domestic market and imports 285, 308–9
  history of American rosé (1857–1940) and prohibition 106–7
    early producers 7, 107–8, 113–14
  Long Island 122–4
  Pacific north-west 119–21
    Oregon 120
    Washington 121
  Texas 122
  Virginia 121–2

van Zeller Guedes, Fernando 188
varieties *see* grape varieties
vin gris
  of southern France 62–4
    IGP Sable de Camargue 62–3
    rosé de Bessan, the Languedoc 63
    vin vermeil of Cabrières 63–4
  of the north
    oeil de perdrix 60–62
    pink champagne 57–9
  of Tunisia 250
  vinification 56
vineyard economics 299–301
vineyards and winemakers by country

Argentina 156–8, 187
Australia 130, 134–40
Austria 221–2
Bulgaria 263–4
Canada 125–6, 128
Canary Islands 187
Chile 155–6
Corsica 245–6
countries dominating market 303
Crimea 270
Croatia 160–61
Cyprus 274–5
Dalmatian Islands 261
England 164–5, 216–17
France
    Alsace 100–101
    Anjou 52–5
    Aube: Rosé de Riceys 44, 45
    Beaujolais 103–4
    Bordeaux 89–91, 93–6
    Burgundy: Marsannay 101–2
    under IGP Sable de Camargue 62–3
    Horiot Pere & Fils 44
    Jacques Defrance 45
    Languedoc 63–4, 235–8, 240, 241–2
    the Loire 97–9: Chateau Passavent 54–5, 56, 97
    Lorraine: Côtes de Toul 59–60
    Provence 13, 68, 70, 71, 74–5, 84, 86, 87: appellations 76–9; Côtes de Provence 80–82
Germany 218–19
Greece 271–3, 276
Hungary 226–9
Israel 254–6
Italy 167, 200–201, 202, 203, 206, 207–10, 212–14
Lebanon 251–3
New Zealand 142–6
Portugal 191–3
    The Azores 195
Romania 265, 266–8
Serbia 262–3
Slovakia 224–5
South Africa 148–51
Spain 169–70, 177, 179–87
Switzerland (Neuchâtel) 60–62
Tasmania 131
Tunisia 250
Turkey 277–8

USA 26, 118–19
    Long Island 124
    Mill Creek Vineyards 26, 110–11
    Rhone Rangers group 112–15
    Washington 121
    Williamette Valley 120
    see also winemaking
viticulture 11–15
    age of vines 13
    choice of variety 13
    harvesting, date and method 14–15
    marketing and 11–12
    organic 305
    site location 12–13
    yields 14
    see also winemaking

Westrup, Emelie 288
Wilson, Janet 8–9
winemakers *see* vineyards and winemakers by country
winemaking 15–30
    ageing 86, 144
        on lees and malolactic fermentation 24–5
    alcohol 24
    bleeding 18–19
    blending red and white wine 25
    bottling and light strike 28–30
    colour 26–8
    fermentation 20–21
        without maceration 16
    fining and filtration 25
    lees 16
    maceration 17–18
        whole grape maceration 19–20
    polyvinylpolypyrolidone use 25
    pressing 15–16
    sugar 23–4
    sulphite use 20
    temperature control 21
    whole grape maceration (carbonic fermentation) 19–20
    wood 25
    yeast 21–3
    see also grape varieties; vineyards and winemakers by country; viticulture

Zeller Guedes, Fernando van 188
Zinfandel and 'blush' 108–12